Katakana

ア	イ	ウ	エ	オ				
カ	キ	ク	ケ	コ		キャ	キュ	キョ
サ	シ	ス	セ	ソ		シャ	シュ	ショ
タ	チ	ツ	テ	ト		チャ	チュ	チョ
ナ	ニ	ヌ	ネ	ノ		ニャ	ニュ	ニョ
ハ	ヒ	フ	ヘ	ホ		ヒャ	ヒュ	ヒョ
マ	ミ	ム	メ	モ		ミャ	ミュ	ミョ
ヤ	(イ)	ユ	(エ)	ヨ				
ラ	リ	ル	レ	ロ		リャ	リュ	リョ
ワ	(イ)	(ウ)	(エ)	ヲ				
ン								

ガ	ギ	グ	ゲ	ゴ		ギャ	ギュ	ギョ
ザ	ジ	ズ	ゼ	ゾ		ジャ	ジュ	ジョ
ダ	ヂ	ヅ	デ	ド				
バ	ビ	ブ	ベ	ボ		ビャ	ビュ	ビョ
パ	ピ	プ	ペ	ポ		ピャ	ピュ	ピョ

YOOKOSO!

ようこそ

YOOKOSO!

Continuing with Contemporary Japanese

Yasu-Hiko Tohsaku

University of California, San Diego

McGraw-Hill, Inc.

New York St. Louis San Francisco Auckland Bogotá Caracas
Lisbon London Madrid Mexico City Milan Montreal New Delhi
San Juan Singapore Sydney Tokyo Toronto

This is an  book.

Yookoso! Continuing with Contemporary Japanese

Copyright © 1995 by McGraw-Hill, Inc. All rights reserved. Printed in the United States of America. Except as permitted under the United States Copyright Act of 1976, no part of this publication may be reproduced or distributed in any form or by any means, or stored in a data base or retrieval system, without the prior written permission of the publisher.

This book is printed on recycled, acid-free paper.

1 2 3 4 5 6 7 8 9 0   VNH VNH 9 0 9 8 7 6 5

ISBN 0-07-072298-6

This book was set in Garamond and Shinsei Kaisho by GTS Graphics, Inc. and
    Chris de Heer Design
The editors were Thalia Dorwick, Karen Sandness, Richard Lange, Nancy Bell Scott,
    and Chieko Altherr
Text design by Adriane Bosworth
Cover design by Francis Owens
Cover art by Sally Vitsky
Text illustrations by Rick Hackney and Akiko Shurtleff
The production supervisor was Tanya Nigh
The photo researcher was Stephen Forsling
Production and editorial assistance was provided by Pamela Webster and
    Tomoko Gorgon
Von Hoffman Press was printer and binder.

Library of Congress Cataloging-in-Publication Data

Tohsaku, Yasu-Hiko.
    Yookoso!

    Cover title: Yookoso!
    Includes index.
    Contents: [1] An invitation to contemporary Japanese—[2] Continuing with
contemporary Japanese.
    1. Japanese language—Textbooks for foreign speakers—English. 2. College readers.
I. Yookoso! II. Title
PL539.5.E5T64 1993   495.6′82421   93-7948
ISBN 0-07-072291-9 (v. 1 : acid-free paper)
ISBN 0-07-072298-6 (v. 2)

Grateful acknowledgment is made for use of the following:

Photographs: *Page 1* © Andy Sacks/Tony Stone Images; *14* © D. F. Cox/Tony Stone Images; *34* © Fujifotos/The Image Works; *66* © Camera Tokyo Service; *79* © Don Smeizer/Tony Stone Images; *113* © Fujifotos/The Image Works; *139* © Adina Tovy/Photo 20–20; *194* © Charles Gupton/Stock, Boston; *205* © L. Zylberman/Sygma; *206* © Tony Stone Images; *259* © Jon Burbank/The Image Works; *264* © Charles

(Continued on page 478)

Contents

Topics / Vocabulary	Grammar

Culture Notes	Reading and Writing	Skills Practice

Topics / Vocabulary	Grammar

CHAPTER 6: COMMUNICATION AND MEDIA 322

CHAPTER 7: NATURE AND CULTURE 379

REVIEW CHAPTER 2 433

Culture Notes	Reading and Writing	Skills Practice

APPENDICES 447

To the Instructor

Welcome to *Yookoso! Continuing with Contemporary Japanese,* the second part of a complete package of instructional materials for beginning and intermediate Japanese. *Yookoso!* has been developed according to two basic premises: (1) Proficient communication is the goal of foreign language instruction; and (2) language's primary function is to allow people to communicate, interact, and negotiate meaning. These materials provide a starting point for oral and written activities and help students develop proficiency in the four language skills of listening, speaking, reading, and writing, as well as in developing cultural awareness. By promoting free interaction in the classroom, *Yookoso!* also helps students enjoy learning Japanese.

The *Yookoso!* materials and approach have been extensively class-tested with beginning and intermediate students of Japanese. In our experience, students' proficiency in Japanese develops far better and faster with this approach, in which grammar is one of the tools for developing language proficiency, than with materials in which grammar is the focal point. The *Yookoso!* materials do not ignore grammar; rather, they integrate grammar in a different and, we hope, more useful way. Overall, the flexible framework of the *Yookoso!* materials can accommodate various approaches to language teaching and different learning styles.

Objectives of the *Yookoso!* Program

The objectives of these materials are the following:

- to teach the listening skills needed to understand a basic core of topics relevant to everyday life and the students' interests
- to teach the oral skills needed to talk about these topics and to function in basic everyday situations in Japanese
- to teach skimming, scanning, and intensive reading skills

- to teach basic writing skills, including descriptions and some functional writing tasks, such as letter writing
- to provide grammar explanations that help students acquire functional skills more readily
- to provide sociocultural information useful to beginning and intermediate-level Japanese language students

Components

There are two major student components in the *Yookoso!* program: a main text and a combined workbook and laboratory manual. The main text contains a review chapter called Do You Remember? and seven main chapters. All chapters are organized according to topics essential to communication at the beginning and intermediate level, and they include numerous cultural, linguistic, and grammar notes that help put language learning into context.

The workbook/laboratory manual includes listening comprehension activities, **kanji** exercises, and writing activities.

In addition to the main textbook and combined workbook/laboratory manual, the *Yookoso!* package includes an instructor's manual, an audiotape program, and a video program. Using these materials greatly enhances the effectiveness of the textbook.

- The *Instructor's Manual* includes suggestions for using the activities and exercises in the main text, notes on how to incorporate the video program into classroom activities, extra activities and exercises for each chapter, answers to the exercises of both the main text and the workbook/laboratory manual, and tape scripts for the Listening Comprehension sections of both the main text and the workbook/laboratory manual.
- The *Audiocassette Program* includes recorded oral texts from the textbook and the workbook/laboratory manual. (It may be used by students in a language laboratory or purchased by them to use at home.)
- The *Video Program* includes some situations and dialogues presented in the textbook and others related to chapter topics. The majority of segments were shot in Japan and include a variety of interactions in natural settings.

Organization of the Textbook

Do You Remember?

Book 2 of *Yookoso!* begins with a comprehensive review chapter called Do You Remember? We assume that most students will be starting Book 2 after some time away from the study of Japanese, so the activities of this introductory chapter provide an enjoyable but thorough reintroduction to spoken and written Japanese. Some classes, particularly those in intensive or semi-intensive courses, may finish Book 1 in less than a year and begin Book 2 without a significant break, but even for these students, Do You Remember? provides a handy mid-course review going all the way back to the beginning.

Chapters 1–7

Chapters 1 through 7 are organized as follows:

> Opening page, with chapter objectives and a photo
> Vocabulary and oral activities
> Grammar and exercises
> Active vocabulary and **kanji** for the chapter
> Reading and writing activities
> Language functions and situations
> Listening comprehension practice

- The *opening page* of each chapter lists the topics, categories of vocabulary, grammatical structures, language functions, and situations that students will study in the chapter. In addition, it contains a photo related to the theme of the chapter, which can be used as a starting point for oral activities or class discussion.

- The *Vocabulary and Oral Activities* section is intended for vocabulary building and oral communication practice in the classroom. Activities in this section are designed so that students can build up their knowledge of vocabulary and grammar and practice using them in natural communicative situations, in an integrated fashion. Some activities start with 貌 Grammar (number), which provides a cross reference to the relevant sections of Grammar and Exercises.

- The *Grammar and Exercises* section includes concise explanations of grammar with examples and short exercises. This section is closely linked to other parts of the text, including the Vocabulary and Oral Activities section, and the exercises may be done either orally or in writing. In most cases, these series of exercises begin with mechanical drills and proceed through contextualized exercises to creative, free-answer sequences. Answers to the exercises are given in the Instructor's Manual. The separation of Grammar and Exercises from the other sections of the chapter makes it possible to accommodate deductive, inductive, or eclectic approaches to teaching grammar in the classroom.

- The *Active Vocabulary and Kanji* are reference lists of all the new vocabulary and **kanji** that have been introduced for active learning. Students can use these lists for reference and review. The **kanji** in each chapter are selected for their connection to chapter themes and for their high frequency in materials written for adult readers of Japanese. *Yookoso!* includes about 365 characters in Volumes One and Two that are presented as active **kanji,** those which students are required to learn to write.

- The *Reading and Writing Activities* section contains two sets of reading materials and writing assignments. Most of the reading selections are semiauthentic and related to a chapter theme; they are based on a variety of authentic materials, such as magazine articles, personal messages, and advertisements. All reading selections are preceded by activities to facilitate students' comprehension of the content and help them develop good reading strategies. Post-reading activities are mostly comprehension-oriented; in some cases, they encourage students to apply their reading skills to other related materials. Some writing exercises are extensions of the preceding reading activities, in that students write a response to the content of the reading selection or write a similar passage on their own. Other writing exercises encourage students to write about their own lives and ideas by using the vocabulary and grammatical structures they have learned in the chapter.

- In the *Language Functions and Situations* section, students learn how to express themselves in specific real-life situations. Students first study dialogues that illustrate functional language and situations related to chapter themes. Then they practice interacting in role plays enabling them to engage in real communication in meaningful contexts.

- In the *Listening Comprehension Activities* section, students practice comprehending the general content of rather lengthy conversations or narratives related to chapter themes. This section includes training in listening for meaning and tasks to perform based on the listening. It can also serve as the basis for a variety of interactive oral activities in class. A cassette with the listening comprehension selections is part of the Audiocassette Program; a transcript of the selections appears in the Instructor's Manual.

Additional Features

- *Boxed notes* are provided at logical points throughout the text to present helpful information and hints for students. There are four types: Culture Notes, Communication Notes, Grammar Notes, and Linguistic Notes. *Culture Notes* provide information on Japanese culture that is important or pertinent for understanding vocabulary and facilitating oral or written activities. *Communication Notes* provide information useful for communicating smoothly in a variety of real-life situations. *Grammar Notes* present brief information on grammar that is helpful for conducting oral activities or understanding reading materials. *Linguistic Notes* highlight certain characteristics of the Japanese language in a way that benefits beginning-level Japanese language students.

- *Study Hints* provide advice about how to acquire language skills: how to learn vocabulary, **kanji,** verb conjugations, and so forth.

- *Marginal notes* provide brief references to previously presented grammar, offer sociolinguistic information, and so on.

- *Realia, photos,* and *line drawings* make the text more appealing to students so that they will seek out more information on the Japanese people and culture. Some of them may serve as a starting point for oral and written activities, while others are intended to expose students to real culture; others are simply decorative. The authentic realia enrich the learning environment by giving students opportunities to work with real-life materials and develop effective strategies for reading them. Students should be made aware that they need not try to understand everything presented in the realia.

- The *Review* sections follow Chapter 3 and Chapter 7. They include oral activities, interviews, listening activities, roleplay, and cultural readings, along with personal narratives called This Is My Life. These sections combine, recycle, and review vocabulary, grammar, and language functions presented in previous chapters.

The Cast of Characters

The same set of characters appears repeatedly throughout the text. The three main characters are students from North America studying Japanese language and culture at the University of Tokyo. Their classmates, professors, homestay family members, neighbors, and friends interact with them. These people reappear in dialogues, grammar examples, reading materials, and listening comprehension activities. We believe that the use of these characters clarifies the social relationships that are a key factor in determining speech style and the use of honorifics in Japanese. In order to keep the structure of the textbook flexible we have avoided using a "story line" concept.

Orthography

Only authentic Japanese orthography is used in the Japanese-language portions of Book 2. Because students may be starting Book 2 after a vacation and may have forgotten many, if not most, of the **kanji** from Book 1, all the **kanji** in Do You Remember? are marked with **hurigana.** Thereafter, **kanji** newly introduced for active mastery are marked with **hurigana** in the chapter where they are introduced and for the following two chapters. This is a change from Book 1, where new **kanji** were marked with **hurigana** for only one chapter after they were introduced.

Organization of Workbook/Laboratory Manual

The accompanying workbook/laboratory manual consists of three sections:

> Listening Activities (coordinated with audiocassette tapes)
> Kanji Exercises
> Writing Activities

- The *Listening* and *Writing Activities* sections, intended to help students review the grammar, vocabulary, and language functions presented in the main text, are organized along the same line as the Vocabulary and Oral Activities section of the main text. The Listening Activities section is designed to develop listening comprehension abilities through dialogues, interviews, and narratives. The Writing Activities section provides additional vocabulary and grammar practice through a variety of means, from controlled, mechanical exercises to creative, free-response activities. Several activities in these sections are realia-based, and many of them can also be used for speaking practice.

- The *Kanji Exercises* section for each chapter consists of a list of newly introduced **kanji,** including the pronunciations, meanings, examples of use, and stroke order, followed by exercises. This section also includes some interesting and useful notes about **kanji** and the writing systems of Japanese (for example, the radicals, the principles of stroke order). A new feature in Book 2 of the Workbook/Laboratory Manual is *Kanji in Everyday Life,* a set of context-based exercises that teach intelligent guessing and other skills necessary for reading unfamiliar materials.

Methodology

This textbook has been developed based on the results of recent research into second language acquisition and language pedagogy. All activities and exercises have been designed so that students develop proficiency in Japanese rather than simply acquiring grammatical knowledge.

- The main purpose of this text is to teach students how to use language in real-life situations for different communicative purposes. Since activities involving interaction promote communication abilities, the textbook includes a variety of activities that serve as starting points for communicative interaction in the classroom.
- The role of grammar in language learning is less important than previously believed. The study of grammar is neither a sufficient nor a necessary condition for learning to communicate, and it is best learned through self-study outside of class. For this reason, grammar is presented in simple terms and via charts whenever possible. Easily understood explanations and abundant examples make it possible for students to study grammar on their own. Thus, instructors can devote precious class time to more meaningful communicative, interactive activities.
- In each chapter, all activities are related to the main theme, and students can practice listening, speaking, reading, and writing about this theme in an integrated way.
- Topics selected for the textbook are all relevant to college students' lives and interests. Topic-based organization presents meaningful contexts for language learning and raises students' motivation for learning the language.
- For successful language acquisition, learners must be exposed to meaningful input. Activities throughout the text are designed to encourage instructors and students to engage in meaningful interactions.
- The acquisition of vocabulary is of great importance for achieving proficiency, and intermediate students need to expand their vocabularies beyond the comfortable elementary level. For this reason, a large number of vocabulary items is presented throughout the text.

- Language acquisition takes place when learners are trying to comprehend conveyed messages. Also, students must be able to comprehend before they can produce. Thus priority is given to the development of comprehension abilities over production abilities. In order to facilitate students' language acquisition, the activities are sequenced from comprehension activities to simple production activities to creative, personalized production activities.
- Reintroduction of vocabulary, grammar, and language functions at regular intervals facilitates the development of students' proficiency. The cyclical organization of this textbook helps students review materials consistently and repeatedly.
- Group work encourages interaction and communication. For this reason, this textbook includes a variety of pair work, small-group work, and interviews, during which students can practice using language in a stress-free, nonthreatening atmosphere.

Acknowledgments

During the several years this book has been in the works, many people provided me with help, comments, advice, and encouragement. It is impossible to acknowledge everyone, but I would like to thank the following people.

First of all, I would like to express my warm appreciation to those who reviewed an earlier version of *Yookoso!* The appearance of their names in this list does not necessarily constitute their endorsement of the text or its methodology.

Carl Falsgraf (Oregon Japanese Language Project), Michiko Hiramatsu (Foothill College, Foothill, California), Miyoko Iwami (AJALT, Tokyo, Japan), Mitsuyoshi Kaji (AJALT, Tokyo, Japan), Hiroko Kataoka (University of Oregon), Toshiko Kishimoto (Clemson University), Akemi Morioka (University of California, Irvine), Haruko Matsui (AJALT, Tokyo, Japan), Keiji Matsumoto (California State University, Fullerton), Keiko Nishio (AJALT, Tokyo, Japan), Noriko Omae (Simon Fraser University, British Columbia, Canada), Peter Patrikis (Consortium of Language Learning and Teaching), Yoko Pusavat (California State University, Long Beach), John Treat (University of Washington), Eri Yasuhara (California State University, Los Angeles), Toshiko Yokota (University of California, Irvine)

The constructive comments and valuable suggestions of the following colleagues, some of whom helped me class-test earlier versions of this text, were very valuable. My heartfelt thanks go to Sachiko Fuji (formerly at the University of California, Irvine), Mizue Funakoshi-Clark (Indiana State University), Miyoko Hamanaka (Mesa College, San Diego), Hifumi Ito, Noriko Kikuchi, Masato Nishimura, Setsuko Kiyomi, and Yutaka Kunitake (University of California, San Diego), Noriko Kameda (Palomar College), Hiroko Kataoka (University of Oregon), Kyoko Hijirida (University of Hawaii, Manoa), Akemi Morioka, Toshiko Yokota, Toshiyuki Kumashiro, Suzuko Hamasaki, and Yoshiko Takahashi (University of California, Irvine), Yoko Pusavat, Akira Miyazaki, and

Kaoru Ohta (California State University, Long Beach), Tamae Prindle (Colby College), Akiko Kamo (Episcopal School, Baton Rouge, Louisiana), Naoki Takei (Tokyo University of Foreign Studies), Yumiko Shiotani (formerly of the University of Oregon), Mark Blum (Florida Atlantic University), Yoko Collier-Sanuki (University of British Columbia), Etsuko Reiman, Miko Foard, and Kyoko Saegusa (Arizona State University), Tamaye Csyionie (Scottsdale Community College), Akiko Jones (Bowling Green State University), Akiko Kakutani (Earlham College), Ryuko Kubota (Monterey Institute of International Studies), Hiromi Muranaka (Southern Australian University), Mutsuko Motoyama (Illinois Wesleyan University), Paul Krieger (University of the Pacific), Amy Ohta (California State University, Los Angeles), Yuko Yamada (Nebraska Wesleyan University), and Masafumi Honda and Laura Kimoto (University of Hawaii, Hilo). Student feedback played a crucial role in the production of this text. My thanks to all the students who over the years used earlier versions in photocopied form.

I am grateful to many people at McGraw-Hill and their associates for their helpfulness and hard work: Karen Judd, Tanya Nigh, Diane Harmon, Francis Owens, Karen Sandness, Margaret Metz and the superb McGraw-Hill sales staff, Akiko Shurtleff, Stephen Forsling, Anita Wagner, Richard Lange, Christina Dekker, Chris de Heer, Sally Vitzky, Delight Avoke. Special thanks are due Chieko Altherr, Yuko Kubota, and Tomoko Gorgon, who checked the linguistic accuracy and cultural authenticity of the text and provided other editorial assistance.

This text would not have been completed without the generous support, assistance, and encouragement of the following colleagues and friends at the University of California, San Diego: Sheri Brusch, Jane Geddes, Sherman George, Peter Gourevitch, Linda Murphy, Gary Hoffman, Masao Miyoshi, Eric Smith, Linda Williams, Ron Quilan, Jennifer Schroeder, Yuki Kuroda, and Sanford Schane. I also feel that it is important to acknowledge and thank the late Tracy Terrell, whose insights into and ideas on language learning and teaching gave shape to this text.

A word of warmest thanks is due Hiroko Kataoka for her steadfast friendship, patient criticism, helpful advice, and constant encouragement, all of which were indispensable to me at various stages of the development of this text.

Thalia Dorwick deserves my very special thanks and profound admiration. This text could never have been a reality without her vision and courage. I would like to extend my deepest gratitude and appreciation to her for her constant support, her faith in my abilities, her enthusiasm for and commitment to developing an innovative Japanese language text, and her encouragement, thoughtfulness, and care. Her insights, creativity, dedication, wisdom, and expertise have been a constant source of inspiration to me and have been my guiding light throughout the development of this text. It has been a joy working with you, Thalia.

I thank Umechiyo and Takechiyo for their unconditional affection and positive spirit.

A final brief but very sincere appreciation goes to my wife, Carol, for her inspiring love, spirit, understanding, and patience beyond the call of duty. I thank you for giving so much of yourself. This text is dedicated to Carol as well as to my parents, Morio and Ritsuko Tohsaku.

To the Student

Yookoso means *welcome* in Japanese, and we are delighted to welcome you to this program for learning contemporary Japanese. The main objective of this text is to provide you with opportunities to develop four communicative language skills in Japanese: listening, speaking, reading, and writing. You will also learn about Japanese culture in general and about features of Japanese culture that influence the use of the language in daily life.

With the *Yookoso!* approach, you will not only *learn* about the language by reading or hearing explanations of grammar, usage, and culture but also *acquire competence in using* the language through practical experience in communication. *Yookoso!* is designed so that you will have ample opportunities both to *acquire* the Japanese language experientially and *learn about* it consciously.

Yookoso!: Continuing with Contemporary Japanese (the main textbook) and *Yookoso!: Workbook and Laboratory Manual* (the workbook) have different purposes. The main textbook, for use in the classroom, contains many activities that allow you to interact with your instructor and classmates. The workbook allows you to work on listening comprehension skills through practice with tapes and to do written exercises that reinforce the material introduced in class.

Chapters 1 Through 7

The main part of the text consists of seven regular chapters and two review chapters. Each regular chapter contains **Vocabulary and Oral Activities, Grammar and Exercises, Vocabulary, Kanji, Reading and Writing, Language Functions and Situations,** and **Listening Comprehension** sections, all centered on the thematic topic of that chapter.

Vocabulary and Oral Activities

The objective of this section is to provide you with opportunities to hear and speak everyday Japanese. While learning new vocabulary, expressions, and structures, you will practice using them in communicative contexts.

Vocabulary is presented in two ways. Those words presented in the **Vocabulary** boxes are considered essential for you to acquire so that you can survive in everyday situations and carry out daily activities. Words in the **Vocabulary Library** boxes allow you to express yourself more fully during classroom activities, and you need to learn only the ones that are relevant to your personal situation.

Some oral activities are designed so that you will learn how to use grammatical structures in communicative contexts. Those activities are preceded by the symbol ㉘ along with the numbers for relevant **Grammar and Exercises** sections (the kanji in the circle means *study*). Depending on your learning style, you may want to read the grammar explanations and do the grammar exercises before doing the associated oral activities. On the other hand, you may want to plunge right into the oral activities, trying to infer the underlying structures as you practice speaking, and then check your understanding by reading the **Grammar and Exercises** section later. Whichever approach you prefer, the **Vocabulary and Oral Activities** section forms the core of each chapter, giving you opportunities to practice communicating in Japanese.

Grammar and Exercises

This part presents an explanation of the new grammatical structures followed by written exercises. You are not expected to learn all of the rules. Just read the explanations carefully and look at the examples to see how the rules work. Then verify your understanding by doing the written exercises. Be aware, however, that simply learning grammar won't make you a fluent speaker of the language, because when you speak you don't have time to choose and apply grammatical rules in a conscious manner. You will learn how grammatical rules are used in written materials and practice using some grammatical structures in writing in the **Reading and Writing** section.

Vocabulary

This section lists active new vocabulary organized by topics or categories, for your reference and review. Each new word or phrase is presented in **hiragana** or **katakana** (two of the three writing systems used in Japanese) in the first column of the vocabulary box. The **kanji form** (the third writing system), if there is one, appears in the second column. The third column gives the English equivalent of the word or phrase.

Kanji

You will learn how to read and write approximately 25 **kanji** in each chapter. The **Kanji** section in the middle of each chapter lists these active **kanji** simply for reference purposes, while the workbook explains their use and provides practice materials.

Reading and Writing

You and your classmates have come to the study of Japanese with various goals. Some of you may want nothing more than to read signs and menus when traveling in Japan, while others may hope to read Japanese literature in the original someday. You may never write anything more complicated than a brief personal letter, or you may write sophisticated research reports while studying at a Japanese university or working at a Japanese company. Whatever your ambition is, this section will help you build a foundation for developing reading and writing abilities in Japanese.

The reading materials chosen for each **Reading and Writing** section are related to the chapter's theme, and most of them are similar to the actual materials that native speakers of Japanese read in their everyday life. Your objective in most of these reading activities is to understand the overall meaning of the selection or to look for some specific information in it. You are not expected to understand every word and every grammatical structure. You may find some words and structures that you have not studied, but you may skip over them, as long as they are not necessary for understanding the main meaning. The meanings of essential but unfamiliar words are given in side notes, but you do not have to memorize them.

Writing activities are also related to the theme of the chapter. You will practice writing a variety of things by using the vocabulary and grammatical structures that you have been learning. In many cases, the preceding reading selection will serve as a model or a springboard for your own writing.

Language Functions and Situations

This section provides you with opportunities to practice using Japanese in real-life situations through role playing and other creative activities. In addition, you will learn a variety of useful expressions that will help you communicate smoothly with native speakers even with limited vocabulary and structures. You will also find hints for turning your interactions with native speakers into opportunities for extra language learning.

Listening Comprehension

The first step toward the acquisition of a foreign language is to develop a good listening comprehension ability. For this reason, the final section of each chapter is a set of listening activities in which you will check your comprehension of the vocabulary, expressions, and structures you have learned in the chapter. As you develop your ability to understand spoken Japanese, you will find that your ability to produce spoken Japanese also improves.

Review Chapters

When you study a foreign language, it is important for you to review and use previously studied items constantly and repeatedly. The **review chapters,** which appear after Chapter 3 and Chapter 7, give you opportunities to review vocabulary and structures and to synthesize and use them in different contexts. In addition, you will learn more about Japan and the Japanese people through the **Culture Reading** and **This Is My Life** reading selections.

Writing Systems

The best way to learn **kanji** is to have extensive and constant exposure to them. It is important for you to learn **kanji** in actual contexts rather than memorizing them one by one, so most materials in the book are written in standard Japanese style, including **kanji** that have not yet been introduced for active acquisition. The pronunciations of these unfamiliar **kanji** are indicated by **hurigana,** small **hiragana** written above them, so that you can identify them and recall their meanings.

While reading the questions in the grammar exercises, you will have further opportunities to see **kanji** in their natural contexts. When you write the grammar exercises, however, don't force yourself to write the unfamiliar **kanji.** Because **kanji** must be written following a strict stroke order, imitating the printed form without knowing the correct stroke order can lead to bad writing habits, so just write the words represented by nonactive **kanji** in **hiragana,** using the **hurigana** as a guide.

The Characters

Throughout Book 2, you will read and talk about John Kawamura, his classmates and associates, the same set of characters that appeared in Book 1. You will follow them through a variety of school, family, social, travel, and job-related situations.

There are three main characters: two American students, John Kawamura and Linda Brown, and one Canadian student, Heather Gibson. All of them are currently studying at the University of Tokyo. Their academic majors are different, but they know one another through Professor Toshiko Yokoi's Japanese culture class.

John Kawamura   Linda Brown   Heather Gibson   Toshiko Yokoi

Five of their classmates are Masao Hayashi, Hitomi Machida, and Takeshi Mimura, who are Japanese, and Henry Curtis and Mei Lin Chin, who are American and Chinese, respectively.

Masao Hayashi   Henry Curtis   Hitomi Machida   Mei Lin Chin   Takeshi Mimura

John Kawamura lives with his host family, the Yamaguchis. You will meet Kenji Yamaguchi, Yuriko Yamaguchi, Daisuke Yamaguchi, and Satomi Yamaguchi.

Kenji Yamaguchi   Yuriko Yamaguchi   Daisuke Yamaguchi   Satomi Yamaguchi

Linda Brown lives in an apartment in the Nakano area of Tokyo. Her land-lords are Kunio and Yoshiko Sano. Yooichi Takada and Yayoi Murayama are Linda's next-door neighbors. Both Takada and Murayama are company employ-ees living alone. Sayuri Yamamoto works at a coffee shop across the street from Linda's apartment and is a good friend of hers.

Professor Kiyoshi Oono is a professor at the University of Tokyo and John's advisor.

Before Starting Do You Remember?

We know that most of you are coming to Book 2 after a vacation, and that some of you may feel that you have forgotten everything you learned the previous semester or quarter. Even so, recalling and relearning familiar material takes much less time than learning completely new material, so a brief period of review should get you back up to speed in a short time.

That's the purpose of the introductory chapter, **Do You Remember?** Based entirely on vocabulary and structures from *Yookoso!* Book 1, it provides a series of activities and readings that both reintroduce the previous material and allow you to see where you need to do a bit more independent review outside of class. If you happen to need some more practice on a certain point, there are notes telling you where you can find detailed explanations and exercises in Book 1.

If the sight of all those **hiragana, katakana,** and **kanji** is too overwhelming for you at first, start by working through the writing review section in the Workbook/Lab Manual. This will lead you back into the **hiragana, katakana,** and **kanji** through a set of exercises of gradually increasing difficulty. Once you have completed the **hiragana** and **katakana** portions of the review section, you should be able to handle the main text, because all the **kanji** in **Do You Remember?** are marked with **hurigana.** Just seeing those previously learned **kanji** with their **hurigana** may be enough to jog your memory and restore your confidence.

As always, you will learn most efficiently if you listen carefully to your instructor and classmates, use Japanese in class, and find opportunities to practice listening, speaking, reading, and writing outside of class. You may be tempted to "get by" with previously learned material, using the same words and structures over and over, but unless you make the effort to try out the new grammar and vocabulary, you will not learn to communicate effectively in school, social, or business settings. The new patterns, expressions, and words will become yours only when you use them.

Book 2 contains a lot of new material, so if you ever find yourself feeling lost and confused, consult your instructor immediately. He or she can straighten out your misunderstandings, give you study hints, and provide you with a realistic assessment of your progress.

Now, let's see how much you remember.

Do You Remember?

Before going on with Book 2 of *Yookoso!*, let's see how much you remember from Book 1.

アクティビティー　1

ご紹介します。(*I'm going to introduce someone to you.*)

1. Your instructor will briefly describe two students, A and B. Fill in the following table with the information that your instructor gives.

	(A) STUDENT A	(B) STUDENT B	(C) YOUR PARTNER
Name			
Age			
Birthplace			
Nationality			
School			
Grade (year)			
Major			
Courses currently taken			
Residence			
Telephone number			
Other information (hobbies, etc.)			

2. Work in pairs. Do not look at each other's charts, but compare the information you have written down with the information that your partner has written down by asking questions in Japanese.
3. Now ask your partner questions in Japanese and fill in column (c) in the table with his or her answers. (You may fill in the table in English.)
4. If time permits, introduce your partner to the class in Japanese, basing your introduction on the information in column (c).

Refer to pp. 95–96, Book 1.

アクティビティー　2

どこにありますか。(*Where is it?*)

1. Your instructor will describe the locations of nine places on the following street map. Write in the appropriate lot numbers (e.g., "22" for the coffee shop) on the chart on the next page.

Do You Remember?

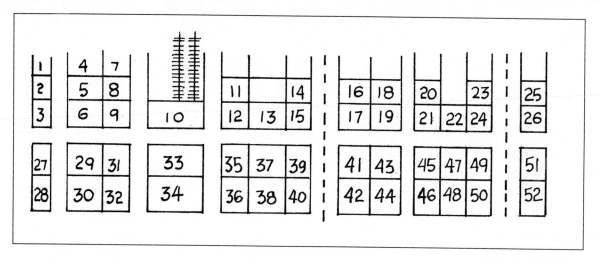

	PLACE	LOCATION
a.	喫茶店（きっさてん）	37
b.	図書館（としょかん）	48
c.	スーパー	51
d.	バス停（てい）	9
e.	駅（えき）	10
f.	デパート	33
g.	映画館（えいがかん）	34
h.	ガソリンスタンド	21　かどう (corner)
i.	ホテル	1

2. Work in pairs. Without looking at each other's maps, check the accuracy of your answers by asking each other how to get from one location to another on the map.

3. At which of the places on the map do you think that you would hear the following comments or questions?

1. 今日（きょう）はバナナが安（やす）いですよ。
2. シングル・ルームはありますか。
3. アイスコーヒーをお願（ねが）いします。
4. タイヤをチェックしてください。
5. 次（つぎ）のバスは駅（えき）まで行きますか。

6. ブラウスは何階ですか。
7. 東京行きの電車は何時ですか。
8. 暗くなりました。始まりますよ。
9. ヘミングウェイの本を読みたいんですが、...

アクティビティー　3

週末の予定 (*Weekend plans*)

1. Working in pairs, practice the following scenario.

STUDENT A	STUDENT B
Invite your partner to see a movie on Friday afternoon or evening.	Politely turn down the invitation by explaining why you cannot come.
Find out if your partner plans to do anything on Saturday or Sunday.	Explain what you will be doing on both days. But tell your partner that you are free on Saturday evening.
Invite your partner to a party at your home on Saturday evening. Tell him or her who is coming to the party.	Accept your partner's invitation. Ask what time everyone is arriving at the party.
Tell your partner what time everyone is coming.	Thank your partner. Tell him or her that you will see each other on Saturday evening.

Reverse roles and practice a conversation in which Student B invites Student A to some other event or activity.

2. You have invited a couple of classmates to dinner at your house. One of them has asked you to write down the directions to your house and leave them in his or her campus mailbox. Write a note that includes the following instructions.

Get off at JR Higashiyama Station. Go out the east exit. There is a bank across from the exit; go straight down the street that runs alongside the bank. Turn right at the second traffic light (about 250 m from the bank to the second traffic light). Turn left at the first light (about 100 m from the previous light). Walk straight for 50 m. My house is on the right hand side next to a coffee shop. It has a red roof and a large gate. If you call me from Higashiyama Station, I can meet you there.

アクティビティー 4

Refer to Chapter 4, Book 1.

世界各地（せかいかくち）のお天気（てんき）(*Weather all over the world*)

The following are transcripts of television weather reports from Japanese language radio programs in London, Honolulu, Tokyo, and Sydney. Read them and fill in the following table.

1. …
朝（あさ）から晴（は）れていて、いいお天気（てんき）ですが、ちょっと寒（さむ）いです。今（いま）、気温（きおん）は
マイナス2度（ど）です。私（わたし）は今（いま）、駅（えき）のホームにいますが、神社（じんじゃ）や、お寺（てら）にお参（まい）りに
行（い）く人（ひと）でいっぱいです。着物（きもの）を着（き）た女性（じょせい）がいますから、ちょっと…

いっぱい *full*

2. …
12月（がつ）に入（はい）っていい天気（てんき）が続（つづ）いていましたが、今日（きょう）はちょっと雨（あめ）が降（ふ）って
います。今日（きょう）の最高気温（さいこうきおん）は25度（ど）で、暖（あたた）かい一日（いちにち）でしょう。私（わたし）のいるところ
からオペラハウスが見（み）えますが、…

最高気温（さいこうきおん） *highest temperature*

3. …
今（いま）の気温（きおん）はマイナス1度（ど）。曇（くも）りです。えー、私（わたし）は今（いま）テムズ川（がわ）のそばにいますが、
霧（きり）が濃（こ）くて、何（なに）も見（み）えません。ヒースロー空港（くうこう）は朝（あさ）から閉（し）まっています。

濃（こ）い *thick, dense*
空港（くうこう） *airport*

4. …
現在（げんざい）、気温（きおん）は30度（ど）で、とても暑（あつ）いです。いい天気（てんき）で雲一（くもひと）つありません。ワイ
キキ・ビーチは、人（ひと）でいっぱいです。

PLACE	WEATHER	TEMPERATURE
London	きりがこくて	マイナス1度
Honolulu	とても暑いです	30ど
Tokyo	朝から晴れていて	マイナス2度です。
Sydney	暖がい あたたがい	25度です。

アクティビティー 5

Refer to Chapter 5, Book 1.

趣味（しゅみ）・余暇（よか）についてインタビューしましょう。(*Let's do an interview about hobbies and free time.*)

Work in pairs. One of you is doing research on how people spend their leisure time. Interview your partner using the following survey sheet. Skip any questions that are not applicable to your partner's situation and go on to the next relevant question. After the interview, report the survey results to the class.

1. 趣味　a. 趣味はありますか。どんな趣味ですか。

b. その趣味はいつから始めましたか。

c. その趣味に一週間に何時間ぐらい、時間を使いますか。

d. その趣味にどれくらいお金を使いますか。

e. それを趣味としているのは、なぜですか。

f. (Add your own question) _____

_____

2. 音楽　a. 音楽は好きですか。

b. どんな音楽が好きですか。

c. どんな歌手や、音楽グループ _guruupu_ が好きですか。

d. どんな音楽が嫌いですか。なぜですか。

e. コンサート _consato_ によく行きますか。

f. 最近、CDや、テープを買いましたか。

g. CDや、テープに一カ月いくらぐらい使いますか。

play instrument h. 何か楽器が演奏できますか。

i. (Add your own question) _____

3. テレビ　a. テレビをよく見ますか。

映画　b. 先週は何時間くらいテレビを見ましたか。

c. どんな番組を見ますか。　_Program_

d. 嫌いな番組はありますか。

e. 映画をよく見ますか。

f. 最近、どんな映画を見ましたか。

g. どんな映画が好きですか。

h. 俳優 (_actor_) は誰が好きですか。

i. (Add your own question) _____

4. 読書　a. 最近、どんな本や雑誌を読みましたか。

b. 先月一カ月で、何冊本を読みましたか。

c. どんな本を読みましたか。

d. どんな本が好きですか。　_dictionary_

e. 好きな作家は誰ですか。

f. 一週間に何時間、読書に時間を使いますか。

g. (Add your own question) _____

After a class discussion on the survey results, write a short paragraph about the overall class results for one section of the survey.

アクティビティー　6

Refer to Chapter 5, Book 1.

いろいろな家庭（かてい）(Many kinds of households)

Each of the following paragraphs describes an individual or family. Match each paragraph with the drawing (on the next page) of the household that it describes.

1. 伊藤武夫さんとひとみさん御夫妻は、結婚してまだ9ヵ月です。子供はまだいませんが、あと3ヵ月で子供が生まれます。武夫さんは男の子をほしがっていますが、ひとみさんは女の子をほしがっています。

2. 吉村利夫君の家族は両親とお兄さんとお姉さんと妹さんと弟さんです。利夫君は弟さんと同じ部屋で寝ていますが、早く自分一人の部屋がほしいと言っています。

   自分一人 one's own

3. 岡崎邦年さんと鈴木まり子さんはまだ結婚していませんが、いっしょに暮らしています。これは日本では「同棲」といいます。岡崎さんは、来年結婚したいと思っていますが、鈴木さんはまだ結婚したくありません。

   同棲(する) unmarried couples living together (to live together)　Cohabitation

4. 竹村里志さんと洋子さんの御夫妻は結婚して10年になります。8歳の息子さんと、6歳と3歳の娘さんがいます。家が小さいので、もう子供は作らないつもりです。

5. 池田荘太郎さんと恵子さんは結婚して42年になります。お孫さんが5人います。時々、お孫さんが遊びに来ます。

6. 花村節子さんは離婚して、お嬢さんの舞さんと二人で住んでいます。前の御主人と会うことはもうありません。

   離婚(する) (to get a) divorce

7. 花村　孝さんは離婚して、一人で暮らしています。お嬢さんは前の奥さんといっしょに住んでいますが、二人に会うことはもうありません。寂しい時はパチンコ屋に行きます。

   寂しい lonely　Pachinko

8. 河原はなさんは今年76歳です。御主人は去年亡くなりました。今は息子さん御夫婦と三人のお孫さんといっしょに住んでいます。

   亡くなる to die

A.

B.

C.

D.

E.

F.

G.

H.

アクティビティー　7

食べ物（た もの）(*Food*)

Refer to Chapter 6, Book 1.

In each of the following groups, one word does not belong to the same category as the others. Identify it and tell why it is different. Then, if you can, add one more word that *does* belong to the category.

1. いか、まぐろ、たこ、魚（さかな）、マトン
2. ぶどう、みかん、りんご、ジュース、メロン、レモン
3. ワイン、水（みず）、コーヒー、紅茶（こうちゃ）、ミルク
4. 皿（さら）、ナイフ、フォーク、コップ、冷蔵庫（れいぞうこ）、スプーン
5. 甘い（あま）、塩（しお）、辛い（から）、まずい、おいしい
6. 味噌（み そ）、すきやき、そば、卵（たまご）、てんぷら
7. 調味料（ちょうみりょう）、醤油（しょうゆ）、砂糖（さ とう）、胡麻（ご ま）、夕食（ゆうしょく）
8. 肉屋（にくや）、八百屋（や お や）、家具屋（か ぐ や）、魚屋（さかなや）、酒屋（さか や）

アクティビティー　8

レストランで (*At a restaurant*)

1. Work in pairs. Practice ordering the items on the following menu by taking turns being the server and the customer.

オードブル・前菜サラダ・スープ
Appetizers/Soups

スモーク名古屋コーチンのオニオンサラダ……	¥ 940
帆立貝のチーズ焼き ………………………	¥ 720
チーズとり合わせ ………………………	¥ 740
季節野菜のマリネ ………………………	¥ 650
ローストビーフサラダ …………………	¥ 850
シーフードサラダ ………………………	¥ 850
シェフサラダ ……………………………	¥ 850
ポタージュ ………………………………	¥ 480

サンドウィッチ
Sandwiches

ミックスサンドウィッチ……………………	¥ 850
クロワッサンサンドウィッチ ……………	¥ 850
コールドローストビーフサンドウィッチ ………	¥ 850
フレンチバケットサンドウィッチ …………	¥ 850

仔牛肉と茄子のスパゲッティ

小海老のトマト風味スパゲッティ

‥ スパゲッティセット　　¥1,310

お好みのスパゲッティ
プティサラダ
コーヒー または 紅茶

ピラフ・カレー・オムライス
Pilaff/Curries/Omelette Rice

ミックスピラフ サラダ添 ………………………	¥ 980
シーフードパエリア サラダ添 ………………	¥ 980
ビーフカレー サラダ添 ………………………	¥ 980
シーフードカレー サラダ添 …………………	¥ 980
オムライス パラドール風 サラダ添 ………	¥ 980

‥ サンドウィッチセット　　　¥1,180
（コーヒー または 紅茶付）

パスタ料理
Pastas

海の幸のスパゲッティ ………………………	¥ 980
仔牛肉と茄子のスパゲッティ ………………	¥ 980
森のきのこスパゲッティ ……………………	¥ 980
小海老のトマト風味スパゲッティ …………	¥ 980
ツナとベーコンのスパゲッティ ……………	¥ 980

Refer to pp. 411–412 of Book 1.

2. As seen in the accompanying illustration, Heather Gibson and Masao Hayashi are talking to a waiter at a restaurant. Complete the following dialogues, giving one line each to Gibson, Hayashi, and the waiter.

[例] A: このスープ、ちょっとぬるいんですが、…
B: どうもすみません。
C: ええ、僕のスープもちょっとぬるいです。

1. A: _____
B: 御注文は。
A: _____
C: _____
2. A: _____
B: _____
C: コーヒーをお願いします。
3. A: どんなデザートがありますか。
B: _____
C: _____
A: _____
4. A: _____
B: _____
C: あのテーブルの人たちがちょっとうるさいんですが…

アクティビティー　9

店 (Shops and stores)

Refer to Chapter 7, Book 1.

Following the example, tell where you can buy the items listed. Then name more items that are available at the same store.

[例] フレンチ・ロール、クロワッサン、サンドイッチ →
パン屋で買えます。サワードゥブレッドも買えます。

1. ソファー、椅子、テーブル
2. ハイヒール、ブーツ、サンダル
3. アスピリン、風邪薬、目薬
4. スイートピー、カーネーション、チューリップ
5. ペン、ノート、カレンダー
6. テレビ、冷蔵庫、ステレオ
7. バービー人形、ビデオ・ゲーム、プラモデル
8. ブラウス、スカート、スカーフ

Do You Remember?

アクティビティー 10

買い物 (Shopping)

Work in pairs, but do not look at each other's prepared written materials. Student A should write a very specific shopping list of four common items that are available in stationery stores: pens, pencils, notebooks, paper, envelopes, and so on, specifying the size, color, price range, and perhaps brand name of the items.

Student B should prepare an inventory list of the same types of items, including a wide variety of sizes, colors, prices, and brand names. When you have completed your lists, Student A role plays the part of a customer, asking whether Student B has the desired items. Student B then answers, based on the inventory list that he or she has written. Student A should come to a decision about what to purchase and then buy the items.

アクティビティー 11

服 (Clothing)

Refer to Chapter 7, Book 1.

What would you wear on the following occasions? Or what did you wear on the following occasions in the past? Describe your clothing as shown in the example.

[例] 夏、海へ行く時
去年の夏、家のそばの海に毎日行きました。その時はいつも半袖のTシャツを着て、ショートパンツをはいていました。むぎわら帽子(straw hat) をかぶって、サングラスもかけました。時々、サンダルをはきましたが、ほとんど裸足 (barefoot) でした。

1. 結婚式 (wedding ceremony) に行く時
2. 仕事の面接 (job interview) の時
3. スキーに行く時
4. 雨が降って寒い時

アクティビティー 12

夏季クラスを取りたいのですが、... (I would like to take a summer course, ...)

1. Work in pairs. One of you has been awarded a fellowship to take a summer course (夏季クラス) in the Japanese language in Japan this summer. (Congratulations!) You have just found that Saitama College offers a good Japanese course, so you phone the college and obtain information about the course. The other student plays the role of the academic coordinator of

Saitama College's Japanese course. The academic coordinator can refer to the following English brochure, making up additional details, if necessary.

Summer Language Course in Japan

Come to Saitama College and study Japanese this summer!

Special four-week intensive course for college students

Period 1—June 1 through June 30
Period 2—July 1 through July 31
Period 3—August 1 through August 31

- First-year through fourth-year levels
- Small classes
- Class meets six hours a day, five days a week
- Excellent instructors with more than ten years' experience
- Pickup service at Narita Airport
- Dormitory available on campus
- Instructors live with students in the dorm, providing a total immersion environment
- Quiet suburban location
- 35 minutes by train to central Tokyo (service every 10–15 minutes)
- Weekend activities include a festival, excursions, parties, sports events, outings with local people
- Low tuition: 80,000 yen per session, including room and board!

For more information, please write to:
Yoshimi Umeda
Academic Coordinator
Summer Intensive Japanese Program
Saitama College
35 Motohuto 1-chome
Urawa-shi, Saitama-ken 199 Japan
Tel/Fax (0488) 456-9087

2. Saitama College has sent you a brochure and an application form. After reading the brochure, you have decided to go there for your summer course in Japanese. Fill in the following application form in Japanese.

Useful vocabulary

志願者	applicant	出願理由	reason for applying
氏名	full name	現在	present, current
学習	study, learning	推薦状	recommendation
国籍	nationality	厳封のうえ	sealed
その他	other	提出(する)	submission (to submit)
能力	ability		

埼玉学院夏季日本語コースの入学願書

志願者氏名	生年月日：　　　　年　　　月　　　日
	性別　　　　男・女

住所
電話番号：　（　　　　　）

国籍	高校卒業：　　　　　年　　　　月
日本語の学習期間	大学：
高校：　　　　　年間	住所：
大学：　　　　　年間	
その他：	
日本語能力：	現在の日本語の先生または出身校の教員からの推薦状を厳封の上、堤出すること
会話：	
漢字：	推薦者の氏名：
出願理由：	住所：
	電話番号：

志願者のサイン：＿＿＿＿＿＿＿＿＿＿＿＿＿＿＿＿＿＿＿　　　　年　　　月　　　日

1
第一章

旅行
りょこう

Travel

新幹線のホーム
しんかんせん

OBJECTIVES

Vocabulary and Oral Activities

Travel

Vocabulary: Travel

旅行(する)	りょこう(する)	travel (*n.*); (to travel)
出張(する)	しゅっちょう(する)	business trip; (to go on a business trip)
観光旅行	かんこうりょこう	sightseeing trip
見物(する)	けんぶつ(する)	sightseeing (*n.*); (to sightsee)
乗り物	のりもの	vehicles
新幹線	しんかんせん	bullet train
飛行機	ひこうき	airplane
船	ふね	ship
フェリー(ボート)		ferry
泊まる	とまる	to stay overnight
旅館	りょかん	Japanese-style inn

Review: 車、電車、ホテル、バス

文化ノート

りょかん
旅館

旅館 refers to traditional-style Japanese inns—typically, wooden structures where the guests sleep, bathe, and eat in the traditional manner. That is, the guests sleep in ゆかた (*cotton kimono*) provided by the inn, on ふとん (*Japanese bedding*), which are laid out on the 畳 [たたみ] (*reed-mat flooring*); they bathe in a communal bath (usually two baths, actually, segregated by sex), and they eat Japanese breakfasts and dinners served in a central dining room or in their rooms.

アクティビティー　1

この人はどこへ旅行しましたか。(*Where did this person travel?*)

Using the information in these statements, tell what country each person traveled to.

[例] 「東京から京都まで新幹線に乗りました。」 → この人は日本へ旅行しました。

1. 「山登りはたいへんでしたが、アルプスの山はとてもきれいでした。」
2. 「リオのカーニバルで朝まで踊りました (*danced*)。」
3. 「カンガルーをたくさん見ました。」
4. 「エベレストを見ました。」
5. 「ピラミッドを見ました。とても大きいですね。」
6. 「毎晩 (*every night*)、フラメンコを見ました。でも、闘牛 (*bullfight*) は見ませんでした。」
7. 「シベリアは寒かったです。でも、もう一度行ってみたいです。」
8. 「ルーブル美術館 (*art museum*) やエッフェル塔 (*tower*) へ行きました。」

アクティビティー　2

旅行は好きですか。(*Do you like traveling?*)

Answer these questions.

1. 旅行は好きですか。
2. 今まで (*up to now*)、どこへ旅行したことがありますか。
3. その時何日間、旅行しましたか。
4. 誰と旅行しましたか。
5. 出張でしたか。
6. どこか見物しましたか。
7. どんな乗り物で行きましたか。飛行機ですか。車ですか。船ですか。電車ですか。バスですか。
8. 今どこに一番旅行したいですか。

...間

Time unit + 間 (*duration*) indicates a duration or length of time. For example, 三時 (*lit., three hour*) names a specific time, *three o'clock*, whereas 三時間 (*lit., three-hour duration*) refers to the length of time, *three hours.* Similarly, to refer to a duration of weeks, you also must add 間 to the time unit; for example, 六週間 (*six weeks*). For years, months, days, and minutes, however, 間 is optional. Thus 三年 can either name a year (*year 3*) or indicate a duration of time (*three years*), but 三年間 can only mean *three years (in duration).* Likewise, 十五分 means *the fifteenth minute of the hour* as in 二時十五分 (*2:15*) or *fifteen minutes,* but 十五分間 only means *fifteen minutes.*

Study this pair.

弟は平成二年に生まれました。
My brother was born in **Heisei 2** (*i.e., year 2 of the* **Heisei** *era*).
中国に二年(or 二年間)いました。
I was in China two years.

勉 Study Grammar 1.

アクティビティー　3

ダイアログ：旅行したらどうですか。(*How about going on a trip?*)

山口：カワムラさん、来週は学校が休みなんでしょう？
カワムラ：ええ、24日まで休みなんです。
山口：じゃあ、京都へでも旅行したらどうですか。
カワムラ：ううん、それはいい考えですね。前から京都へ旅行したいと思っていたんです。

Practice this dialogue, substituting the following phrases (altered as appropriate) for the underlined portions.

1. 東京見物でもする
2. 上野の美術館にでも行く
3. 新幹線にでも乗ってみる

YAMAGUCHI: Mr. Kawamura, your school is closed for vacation next week, isn't it?　KAWAMURA: Yes, I am off until the twenty-fourth.　YAMAGUCHI: Then why don't you take a trip to Kyoto or somewhere like that?　KAWAMURA: Oh, that's a good idea. I've wanted to take a trip to Kyoto for some time (*lit., from before*).

道南（洞爺・札幌）3日間

札幌
千歳空港
洞爺湖

添乗員同行／2朝食・2昼食・1夕食　　　　　　　　●募集人員35名（最少催行人員20名）

日次	コース（★印の箇所は下車観光となり、それ以外は車窓観光となります）	食事
1	（07:00〜10:00頃） 羽田空港 ──────→千歳空港　　★ノーザンホースパーク Park 　★支笏湖（昼食）　　★登別クマ牧場　　　　洞爺湖（泊）	─ 昼 夕
2	洞爺湖　　★昭和新山　　倶知安　　　　余市 　★小樽（昼食・北一硝子・運河等）　　札幌市内（泊）	朝 昼 ─
3	（出発迄フリータイム）free time until we leave 　　　　　（各自） 札幌市内────────千歳空港──────→羽田空港 　　　　千歳空港集合　　　　　　　　（17:00〜21:00頃）	朝 ─ ─

※出発日により往復の利用航空便の時間帯が変更になる場合があります。

| 宿泊地・利用予定ホテル |

第1日目：洞爺湖温泉／洞爺湖プリンスホテル湖畔亭、洞爺観光ホテルなど
第2日目：札幌／チサンホテルすすきのなど

●出発日：[4月] 24
　　　　　[5月] 16
　　　　　[7月] 17

●旅行代金（お一人様）

	出発日 タイプ	4/24	5/16	7/17、8/23
お と な	4名以上1室（B〜E）	55,800円	68,800円	86,800円
	3名1室（A）	57,800円	70,800円	88,800円
	2名1室（A）	59,800円	73,800円	91,800円
こども		おとなと同じ	おとなと同じ	各16,000円引

でも

でも in the dialogue in **Activity 3** means *something/somewhere/some-one like that.* It is frequently used when making suggestions or offering things to others. With でも, the speaker implies that the hearer can choose from options other than the one specified and thereby avoids giving the impression that the speaker is too pushy or insistent.

> ケーキでも食べませんか。
> *Would you like some cake?* (lit., *won't you eat cake or something like that?*)

> ブラウンさんにでも電話しましょう。
> *Let's call Ms. Brown* (lit., *or someone*).

Note that でも replaces the particles は, が, and を but is appended to other particles.

で is the te-form of the copula (だ/です), and も is the particle meaning *also, even.* In other contexts, でも means *even.*

> 私でもわかります。
> *Even I understand.*

Do you remember how でも attaches to interrogatives? (If not, review Chapter 5, **Grammar 24** in Book 1.)

アクティビティー 4

どこへ行ったらいいですか。(*Where should I go?*)

You are a travel agent. Make suggestions to customers who have expressed the following interests.

[例] サーフィンをしたいんですが、どこへ行ったらいいですか。→
ハワイへ行ったらいかがですか。or ハワイへ行ったらどうですか。

1. おいしいパスタを食べたいんですが、どこへ行ったらいいですか。
2. ソンブレロを買いたいんですが、どこへ行ったらいいですか。
3. 中国語を勉強したいんですが、どこへ行ったらいいですか。
4. スキーをしたいんですが、どこへ行ったらいいですか。
5. キャンプをしたいんですが、どこへ行ったらいいですか。
6. 釣りをしたいんですが、どこへ行ったらいいですか。
7. 有名な絵をたくさん見たいんですが、どこへ行ったらいいですか。
8. 勉強でとても疲れました (*am tired*) から、ゆっくり (*leisurely*) 休みたいんです。

Vocabulary Library

Travel

旅行者	りょこうしゃ	traveler
国内旅行	こくないりょこう	domestic travel
海外旅行	かいがいりょこう	travel abroad
団体旅行	だんたいりょこう	group travel
一人旅	ひとりたび	traveling alone, solo travel

Sightseeing and Vacations

ツアー		package tour
観光(する)	かんこう(する)	sightseeing; (to sightsee)
観光客	かんこうきゃく	sightseer
観光案内所	かんこうあんないしょ	tourist information center
名所	めいしょ	sights (*lit., famous place[s]*)
温泉	おんせん	hot spring
休暇	きゅうか	vacation, holiday
民宿	みんしゅく	Japanese-style bed and breakfast

Loanwords: チャーター、ツアーコンダクター、ヒッチハイク、ユースホステル、リゾート

アクティビティー 5

ダイアログ：観光バスに乗ることにします。(*I will take a sightseeing bus.*)

カワムラ：京都でいろいろなところを見たいんですが、どうしたらいいでしょうか。

山口：京都は広くて、歩くのは大変ですよ。観光バスに乗ったらどうですか。

カワムラ：それはいい考えですね。じゃ、観光バスに乗ることにします。

山口：いろいろなコースがあって、便利ですよ。

Practice the dialogue, and then do the following practice with a classmate as in the example.

[例] おいしい日本料理を食べたいんですが、どうしたらいいですか。→

S1: おいしい日本料理を食べたいんですが、どうしたらいいですか。

S2: 大学の前の和食の店に行ったらどうですか。何でもおいしいですよ。

S1: そうですか。じゃ、そのレストランに行くことにします。

1. おいしいコーヒーを飲みたいんですが、どうしたらいいですか。
2. スペイン語のテープを聞きたいんですが、どうしたらいいですか。
3. この大学のTシャツを買いたいんですが、どうしたらいいですか。
4. 何か食べたいんですが、あまりお金がありません。どうしたらいいですか。
5. 日本語の宿題がたくさんあるんですが、どうしたらいいですか。
6. アルバイトを探しているんですが (*am looking for*)、どうしたらいいですか。
7. ボーイフレンド（ガールフレンド）を探しているんですが、どうしたらいいですか。
8. 日本語をもっと練習したいんですが、どうしたらいいですか。

Transportation and Schedules

Vocabulary: Transportation and Schedules

Buying Tickets

時刻表	じこくひょう	timetable
切符	きっぷ	ticket
予約(する)	よやく(する)	(to make a) reservation

Preparation for a Trip

保険	ほけん	insurance
荷物	にもつ	luggage
つめる		to pack

KAWAMURA: I would like to see many different places in Kyoto. What should I do? YAMAGUCHI: Kyoto is large, so it's hard to walk everywhere (*lit., so walking is awful*). How about taking a sightseeing bus? KAWAMURA: That's a good idea. Then I will (*lit., have decided to*) take a sightseeing bus. YAMAGUCHI: There are a variety of sightseeing routes, so it's convenient.

Transportation

空港	くうこう	airport
港	みなと	harbor, port
停留所	ていりゅうじょ	bus or tram stop
待合室	まちあいしつ	waiting room
乗る	のる	to ride
降りる	おりる	to get off
乗り換える	のりかえる	to transfer
発つ	たつ	to leave
着く	つく	to arrive
止まる	とまる	to come to a stop
遅れる	おくれる	to be late, to be delayed

During a Trip

借りる	かりる	to rent (e.g., a car, bicycle, etc.)
おみやげ		souvenir
雇う	やとう	to hire (e.g., a guide, driver, interpreter, etc.)

Loanwords: トラベラーズ・チェック、スーツケース、パスポート、ビザ、ガイドブック、レンタカー、ガイド

Review: 駅、タクシー、バス停

37 国際線スケジュール（12月1日〜1月31日）

便名	機種	クラス	運航日	出発	到着	便名	機種	クラス	運航日	出発	到着
東京（成田）発着便											
東京（成田）→ ロサンゼルス						→ 東京（成田）					
NH006	B44	FCY	毎日	1800	1030	NH005	B44	FCY	毎日	1230	1700+1
東京（成田）→ ワシントンD.C.						→ 東京（成田）					
NH002	B44	FCY	月水土	1100	0925	NH001	B44	FCY	月水土	1040	1455+1
東京（成田）→ ニューヨーク						→ 東京（成田）					
NH010	B44	FCY	毎日	1100	0915	NH009	B44	FCY	毎日	1100	1455+1
東京（成田）→ (ワシントンD.C. 経由) → オーランド → (ワシントンD.C. 経由) → 東京（成田）											
NH002/US2002	B44/B3	FCY/FY	月水土	1100*0925/1100	1308	US2001/NH001	B3/B44	FY/FCY	月水土	0715*0919/1040	1455+1
NH010/US2010	B44/B3	FCY/FY	火木金日	1100*0915/1100	1345	US2009/NH009	B3/B44	FY/FCY	火木金日	0715*0944/1100	1455+1
東京（成田）→ ロンドン						→ 東京（成田）					
NH201	B44	FCY	毎日	1130	1510	NH202	B44	FCY	毎日	1655	1335+1
東京（成田）→ パリ						→ 東京（成田）					
NH205	B4	FCY	火木金土日	1150	1630	NH206	B4	FCY	火木金土日	1830	1420+1
東京（成田）→ フランクフルト						→ 東京（成田）					
NH209	B4	FCY	月水土	1200	1620	NH210	B4	FCY	月水土	1940	1455+1
東京（成田）→ (モスクワ) → ウィーン						→ (モスクワ) → 東京（成田）					
NH/OS/SU556ⓐ	A310	FCY	月水土	1055 1510/1610	1725	OS/NH/SU555ⓐ	A310	FCY	火金日	1125 1615/1720	0920+1
東京（成田）→ モスクワ						→ 東京（成田）					
NH/OS/SU556ⓐ	A310	FCY	月水土	1055	1510	OS/NH/SU555ⓐ	A310	FCY	火金日	1720	0920+1
東京（成田）→ (ブリスベン) → シドニー						→ 東京（成田）					
NH913	B4	CY	月水木金日	1920	0640+1	NH914	B4	CY	月火木金土	0850	1620
NH923	B4	CY	火土	1920 0500+1/0600+1	0830+1				水日	1000	1730
東京（成田）→ ブリスベン						→ (シドニー) → 東京（成田）					
NH923	B4	CY	火土	1920	0500+1	NH923/NH914	B4	CY	水日	0600 0830/1000	1730
東京（成田）→ グアム						→ 東京（成田）					
NH911	B4	Y	月金	0955	1420 ①	NH912	B4	Y	月金	1600	1830

アクティビティー 6

ダイアログ：お寺を見た後、タクシーで旅館に帰りました。
(After I saw the temple, I returned to the inn by taxi.)

カワムラ：そろそろ昼ごはんにしませんか。

林：昼ごはんを食べる前に、清水寺[1]でも見ませんか。

カワムラ：でも、もうおなかがすいて、歩けません。

林：そうですか。じゃあ、昼ごはんを食べた後、清水寺に行くことに
しましょう。

アクティビティー 7

旅行のスケジュール *(Travel itinerary)*

The following is the itinerary for Linda Brown and Heather Gibson's ongoing three-day trip. At the end of the first day, they wrote down what they had done and what they planned to do for the rest of the trip.

First describe what they did or will do in Japanese.

[例] 今日12時に東京駅を新幹線で発ちました。会津若松に着いた後、タクシーで猪苗代湖に行きました。夕ごはんを食べる前に、温泉に入りました。

TODAY

12:00	bullet train	Left Tokyo
2:45 P.M.		Arrived at Kooriyama
		Got off the train and transferred
2:50 P.M.	electric train	Left Kooriyama
4:20 P.M.		Arrived at Aizuwakamatsu
	taxi	Went to Lake Inawashiro
5:30 P.M.		Arrived at Inawashiro Inn
6:00 P.M.		Took a hot spring bath
7:00 P.M.		Had dinner in their room
10:00 P.M.		Went to bed

KAWAMURA: Shall we have lunch now?   HAYASHI: Before eating lunch, shall we (go) see Kiyomizu Temple (or something like that)?   KAWAMURA: But I am already too hungry to walk.   HAYASHI: I see. Then let's (*lit., decide to*) go to Kiyomizu Temple after having lunch.

[1]Kiyomizu Temple is a famous temple in Kyoto.

TOMORROW

7:00 A.M.		Get up
8:00 A.M.		Have breakfast at the hotel cafeteria
9:00 A.M.		Go fishing
4:00 P.M.		Go to Hotel Lake Hibara
		Stay at Hotel Lake Hibara

THE DAY AFTER TOMORROW

9:00 A.M.	sightseeing bus	See Lake Hibara area
1:17 P.M.	bus	Leave for Hukushima
4:36 P.M.		Arrive at Hukushima Station
4:49 P.M.	bullet train	Leave Hukushima
7:06 P.M.		Arrive in Tokyo
8:00 P.M.		Arrive home

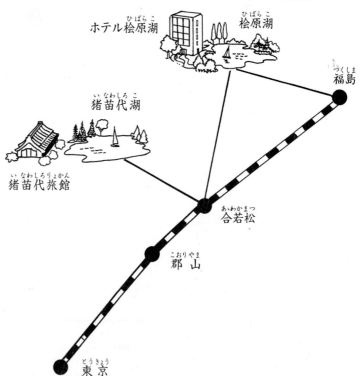

Now answer these questions.

1. 今晩、どこにいますか。
2. 明日、起きた後、何をする予定ですか。
3. 明日、昼ごはんを食べる前に、何をしますか。

Now make up your own questions to ask your classmates.

アクティビティー　8

前ですか。後ですか。(*Is it before or after?*)

Connect the two clauses using 前 or 後 so that the resulting sentence represents a logical sequence.

[例]　（旅行に行く）（トラベラーズ・チェックを買う）　→
旅行に行く前に、トラベラーズ・チェックを買います。
（ホテルをチェックアウトする）（駅へ行く）　→
ホテルをチェックアウトした後、駅へ行きます。

1. （旅館に着く）（お風呂に入る[*take a bath*]）
2. （新幹線に乗る）（切符を買う）
3. （お寺に着く）（写真をとる）
4. （ハワイへ行く）（新しい水着を買う）
5. （旅行に出る）（ガイドブックを買う）
6. （寝る）（家族に絵はがき[*picture postcard*]を書く）
7. （ガイドを雇う）（町を見物する）
8. （時刻表を見る）（切符を買う）

文化ノート

みどりの窓口

Trains are the most popular mode of travel in Japan. An extensive, well-developed national network of train lines run by Japan Railways (JR) plus numerous other private railways make it more convenient to travel by train than by any other means of transportation.

If you travel in Japan, sooner or later you will need to visit the みどりの窓口 (*lit., green window*) that is found at major stations on JR lines. There you can buy JR tickets for long-distance trips one month in advance of the day of travel. In addition, you can purchase commuter passes, package-tour tickets, and plane tickets, and even make hotel reservations. When you make purchases at this window, you must first fill out a ticket request form and then present it to the counter clerk.

Sightseeing and Travel Planning

Study Grammar 4.

アクティビティー　9

ダイアログ：青山神社にはどうやって行きますか。(*How do I get to Aoyama Shrine?*)

カワムラ：すみません。青山神社にはどうやって行きますか。

通行人：ええと、この道をまっすぐ行って、二本目の道を右に曲がります。しばらく行くと、左側にあります。

カワムラ：どうもありがとうございます。

通行人：どういたしまして。

文法ノート

…目

As you have learned, when you count people and things in Japanese, you have to use a counter suffix. Streets, for example, are counted with 本, the counter for long, thin objects: 一本の道 [いっぽんのみち] (*one street*), 二本の道 (*two streets*), etc. Adding 目 to this combination of numeral plus counter allows you to express cardinal numbers (in English, *first, second, third,* etc.): 一本目の道 (*the first street*), 二本目の道 (*the second street*), and so on. Street corners, by the way, are counted with the Japanese ～つ numerals. Thus *five corners* is 五つの角 [いつつのかど], and *the fifth corner* is 五つ目の角. Here are a few more cardinal numbers: 五人目 [ごにんめ] (*the fifth person*), 四軒目 [よんけんめ] (*the fourth building*), and 一番目 (*the first one*).

KAWAMURA: Excuse me. How do I get (*lit., go*) to Aoyama Shrine?　PASSERBY: Uh, go straight up this street, and turn right at the second corner. Keep going, and you will find it on your left. (*lit., Go for a while, and it will be on the left.*)　KAWAMURA: Thank you very much.　PASSERBY: You're welcome.

道_{みち}をたずねる (*Asking the Way*)

ASKING FOR DIRECTIONS

すみません、駅_{えき}へ行く道_{みち}を教_{おし}えてください。

Excuse me, but please tell me how to get to the station. (lit., . . . please tell me the way to the station.)

すみません、駅_{えき}にはどうやって行ったらいいんでしょうか。

Excuse me, how do I get to the station? (lit., . . . how should I go to the station?)

駅_{えき}はどちらでしょうか。

Where is the station?

歩_{ある}いて何分くらいかかるでしょうか。

About how many minutes does it take on foot?

GIVING DIRECTIONS

この道_{みち}をまっすぐ100メートルほど行くと右側_{がわ}にあります。

Go straight up this street about 100 meters and it will be on the right side (of the street).

三つ目_めの角_{かど}を左_へに曲_まがって、角から四軒目_{よんけんめ}の左側_{がわ}です。

Turn left at the third corner, and it is the fourth house from the corner on the right side of the street.

二つ目_めの交差点_{こうさてん}を右_みに曲_まがって、しばらく行きます。

Turn right at the second intersection and go (straight) a bit (lit., for a while).

この道_{みち}をまっすぐ行って、つきあたりを左_ひに曲_まがります。

Go straight down this street and turn left at the T-intersection.

橋_{はしみち}(道)を渡_{わた}って、左に行きます。

Cross the bridge (street) and go left.

歩_{ある}いて5分くらいです。

It takes about five minutes on foot.

私_{わたし}もそちらへ行きますから、一緒_{いっしょ}に行きましょう。

I am going in that direction, so let's go together (and I will show you where it is).

すみません。だれかほかの人に聞_きいてください。

I'm sorry. Please ask someone else.

ASKING WHERE TO GET OFF

美術館_{びじゅつかん}へ行きたいのですが、どこで降_おりたらいいでしょうか。

I would like to go to the art museum. Where should I get off?

16番のバスに乗_のって、4つ目_めの停留所_{ていりゅうじょ}で降_おります。

You take a number 16 bus, and get off at the fourth stop.

アクティビティー 10

地図 (Map)

Look at the map, and explain how to get from point X to the following places.

1. 伊勢丹デパート
2. 丸井旅館
3. 中央公園 (Central Park)
4. 東宝劇場 (Toohoo Theater)
5. 三島神社
6. 仁徳寺
7. 現代美術館 (Modern Art Museum)

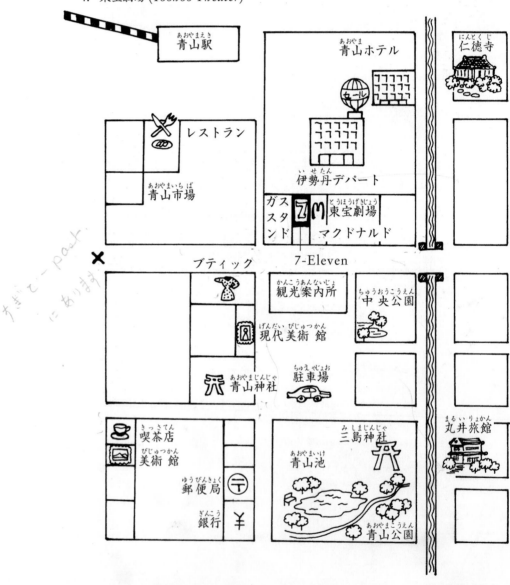

アクティビティー 11

観光案内所 (かんこうあんないしょ) (*Tourist Information Center*)

You are working at a tourist information center. Answer these tourists' questions based on the information in the box.

1. 吉野寺(よしのでら)はどのように行きますか。
2. おみやげを買いたいんですが、...
3. 歌舞伎(かぶき)を見たいんですが、...
4. レストラン・ローマに行きたいんですが、...
5. モダン・アート・ギャラリーへ行く道(みち)を教(おし)えてください。

Sightseeing and Shopping Guide

東急(とうきゅう)デパート　　Walk straight down the road in front of the Tourist Information Center, and you will find it on your left. They sell a lot of good souvenirs.

レストラン・ローマ　　Take a number 30 bus from the bus stop across the street from the Center, and get off in front of Aoyama Post Office. The restaurant is to the left of the post office. Their pasta is the best in town.

モダン・アート・ギャラリー　　It's a fifteen-minute walk to the left down the street in front of the Center; look for a red and green building on your right.

吉野寺(よしのでら)　　It's about twenty minutes by taxi from the Center; it's the most popular tourist attraction in town.

明治劇場(めいじげきじょう)　　Take a number 52 bus across from the Center, and get off at Ginza. It's the brown building across from the Ginza stop. You can see Kabuki theater there.

シティー・ファッション・センター　　Cross the street in front of the Center, and go left for five minutes; they sell inexpensive clothes.

(勉) Study Grammar 5, 6, and 7.

This is a conversation between mother and daughter. わかってる is a shortened form of わかっている (the い is dropped). This shortened form of ている is frequently used in informal speech.

アクティビティー 12

ダイアログ：早(はや)く行きなさい。(*Go now!*)

山口ゆり子：早(はや)く行きなさい。電車(でんしゃ)に遅(おく)れるわよ。

山口さとみ：じゃあ、行ってきます。[1]

YURIKO YAMAGUCHI: Hurry up! (*lit., Go quickly.*) You will be late for your train.
SATOMI YAMAGUCHI: Well, see you later.

[1]Do you remember this set phrase for saying good-bye?

山口ゆり子：あまりお金を使ってはダメよ。
山口さとみ：うん、わかってるわ。

アクティビティー　13

両親の忠告 (*Parents' advice*)

Imagine that you are a parent of a 20-year-old who is going on a trip to Japan with a friend for the first time. Would you give the following pieces of advice? Why or why not?

1. 毎日、うちに電話しなさい。
2. 生水 (*unboiled water*)を飲んではいけません。
3. 毎日うちに手紙を書きなさい。
4. 毎日ビタミンCを飲みなさい (*take*)。
5. お金をたくさん使ってはいけません。
6. 日本人の男の人に気をつけなさい (*watch our for*)。
7. 生の (*raw*) 魚を食べてはいけません。
8. お酒を飲みすぎてはいけません。
9. トラベラーズ・チェックを持って行きなさい (*take*)。
10. 危ない (*dangerous*)ところに行ってはいけません。

勉　Study Grammar 8.

アクティビティー　14

ダイアログ：朝早く起きなければなりませんね。(*We have to get up early in the morning.*)

カワムラ：金沢行きの電車は何時ですか。
　　林：午前6時14分です。

カワムラ：じゃあ、明日の朝は早く起きなければなりませんね。
　　林：ええ、遅くとも5時半には旅館を出なければなりません。

アクティビティー　15

旅行の用意 (*Preparation for a trip*)

What do you have to do to prepare for your trip to Japan? Complete the following sentences using なければなりません。

YURIKO YAMAGUCHI: Don't spend (*lit., use*) too much money.　　SATOMI YAMAGUCHI: Yeah. I know.

KAWAMURA: What time is the train bound for Kanazawa?　　HAYASHI: It's at 6:14 A.M.　　KAWAMURA: Then we have to get up early tomorrow morning.　　HAYASHI: Yes, we have to leave the inn at 5:30 at the latest.

[例]　スーツケース →
スーツケースがないので、買わなければなりません。or
スーツケースを持っていかなければなりません。

Useful vocabulary

パスポートを取る　*obtain a passport*
トラベラーズ・チェックを作る　*buy travelers' checks*
保険に入る　*take out insurance*

1. パスポート
2. 飛行機の切符
3. トラベラーズ・チェック
4. 保険
5. 日本にいる友だち

6. 旅館
7. おみやげ
8. 服
9. ガイドブック

アクティビティー　16

予定通りにいきませんでした。(*Things didn't go as planned.*)

Mr. Takada had several problems on his trip. Describe these problems, following the example.

[例]　　予定　　　　　　　　　　　　　　　実際 (WHAT ACTUALLY HAPPENED)
　　　9時の飛行機に乗る　　　　　　　　空港へ行くバスが遅れた。
　　　　　　　　　　　　　　　　　　　　11時の飛行機に乗った。

→9時に飛行機に乗るつもりでした。でも、空港へ行くバスが遅れたので、11時の飛行機に乗らなければなりませんでした。

予定	実際
1. タクシーで旅館へいく	タクシーがなかった　バスで行った
2. 旅館に泊まる	旅館が満員 (*full*) だった　ホテルに泊まった
3. 9時にお寺を見物する	10時までお寺が閉まっていた (*closed*)　10時まで待った
4. ガイドを雇う	ガイドがいなかった　一人で町を見物した
5. 有名なレストランで昼ごはんを食べる	レストランの予約をするのを忘れた (*forgot*)　ファースト・フードを食べた

Vocabulary Library

Travel by Train

指定席	していせき	reserved seat
自由席	じゆうせき	nonreserved seat
グリーン車	グリーンしゃ	first-class (*lit., green*) car
普通車	ふつうしゃ	regular-class car
喫煙席	きつえんせき	smoking seat
禁煙席	きんえんせき	nonsmoking seat
寝台車	しんだいしゃ	sleeping car
食堂車	しょくどうしゃ	dining car
特急	とっきゅう	express
普通列車	ふつうれっしゃ	local train
ホーム		platform
車掌	しゃしょう	conductor
乗客	じょうきゃく	passenger
待合室	まちあいしつ	waiting room
私鉄	してつ	private railway

Tickets

片道切符	かたみちきっぷ	one-way ticket
往復切符	おうふくきっぷ	round-trip ticket
運賃	うんちん	fare
券売機	けんばいき	ticket vending machine

Lodgings

客室	きゃくしつ	guest room
1泊2食付き	いっぱくにしょくつき	one night's lodging including two meals
宿泊する	しゅくはくする	to stay, to lodge
サービス料	サービスりょう	service charge
空室	くうしつ	vacant room

Loanwords: キャッシャー、キャンセル、シングル、スイート、チェックアウト、チェックイン、フロント、ルームサービス、ダブル、シングル

Travel by Plane

飛ぶ	とぶ	to fly
離陸(する)	りりく(する)	take off; (to take off [*lit., to leave the ground*])
着陸(する)	ちゃくりく(する)	landing; (to land)

Loanwords: スチュワーデス、スチュワード、ターミナル、パイロット、フライト、ウイング(北ウイング、etc.)、カウンター

どちらにしますか。(*Which one do you choose?*)

Tell which of the two options given you would choose in each situation. Why?

1. あさって、日本で会議 (*meeting*) があります。ロサンゼルスから飛行機で行きますか。船で行きますか。

2. 日本人の生活 (*life*) をよく知りたい (*want to know*) です。ホテルにしますか。旅館にしますか。

3. 大阪で今日の午後会議があります。東京から新幹線で行きますか。バスで行きますか。

4. 明日、大阪へ行って、夜帰ってきます。片道切符にしますか。往復切符にしますか。

5. 東京から大阪まで座って行きたいです。指定席にしますか。自由席 (*nonreserved*) にしますか。

6. 一日の旅です。スーツケースを持っていきますか。持っていきませんか。

7. 夜、電車で旅行します。ゆっくり寝たいです。普通席にしますか。寝台車にしますか。

8. お金があまりありません。グリーン車 (*first-class car*) にしますか。普通車にしますか。

9. おなかがすきました。駅弁 (*box lunch*) を買いますか。食堂車に行きますか。

文法ノート

持っていく versus 持ってくる

In Japanese, *to take* (*things*) and *to bring* (*things*) are expressed with the te-form of 持つ (*to hold, to have*) followed by 行く and 来る, respectively. It may help to remember the literal meaning: 持って行く= *to go holding*, that is *to take*.

> プレゼントにネクタイを持って行きました。
> *I took a necktie as a gift.*
> 高田さんはすしを持って来ました。
> *Mr. Takada brought sushi.*

駅弁 _{えきべん} (*Station Box Lunches*)

One of the pleasures of traveling by train in Japan is trying the different box lunches (弁当) sold at each station. On major intercity express trains like the **Shinkansen,** vendors walk up and down the aisles selling standard varieties of 弁当 [べんとう], such as the 幕の内 [まくのうち] 弁当, which was originally sold at **Kabuki** theaters and contains rice and a variety of side dishes, such as pork, broiled fish, and pickled vegetables. The vendors also sell boxes of fried chicken or sandwiches, ice cream bars, and plastic containers of green tea.

幕の内弁当：おいしそうですね。

But you also have the option of buying your lunch from one of the vendors on the station platform, and, if you are traveling on a small, local line, it is your only option. (Don't worry, because Japanese regulations about food preparation and handling are very strict.) The 弁当 sold on the station platforms typically feature foods for which the region is famous. For example, Hiroshima is well known for oysters, so the vendors at Hiroshima Station sell a 弁当 of oysters and rice. Other 弁当 are famous because of the containers that they come in, including, in some cases, ceramic pots that the customer gets to keep. These 弁当 are considered such an essential feature of traveling by train that the monthly national railway schedule indicates which lunches you can buy at each major station.

誰の旅でしょうか。会社の重役ですか。学生ですか。(*Is it a company executive's trip or a student's trip?*)

Discuss in class whether each of the following statements is more characteristic of travel by company executives or travel by students.

1. 秘書 (*secretary*) がホテルを予約します。
2. いつもバックパックを持って旅行します。
3. 時々、ヒッチハイクをします。
4. 観光はあまりしません。
5. 電車はグリーン車 (*first-class car*)、飛行機はファースト・クラスかビジネス・クラスを使います。
6. ジーンズをはいて旅行します。
7. スーツを着て、ネクタイをして、旅行します。
8. ユースホステルをよく使います。
9. いつもいいホテルに泊まります。

日本旅行のスケジュール (*The itinerary of my trip to Japan*)

You are going to Asia soon. The following is your travel itinerary for the Japanese portion of your trip. Answer the questions based on your itinerary.

DATE	
May 11	Fly out of Los Angeles
May 12	Arrive in Tokyo
	Stay in the Miyako Hotel
May 13	See some friends in Tokyo
	Sightseeing in Tokyo
	Stay in the Miyako Hotel
May 14	Go to Kyoto by bullet train (first-class, reserved seat)
	Sightseeing in Kyoto
	Stay in the Higashiyama Ryokan

May 15	Sightseeing in Kyoto by bus
	Stay in the Higashiyama Ryokan
	Go from Kyoto to Izumo[1] by train
	(regular-class, nonreserved seat)
	Sightseeing in Izumo
May 16	Go back to Tokyo by train (sleeping car)
May 17	Leave Tokyo for Taiwan by airplane (business class)

…泊 is a counter for overnight stays. 三泊 means *three overnight stays*, and 一泊する means *to stay over one night*. 泊 has different pronunciations depending on what number precedes it.

1. 何月何日に日本へ発ちますか。
2. 東京に何泊しますか。
3. 東京で何をしますか。
4. 東京では旅館に泊まりますか。
5. 東京から京都へ行く時は、何で行きますか。
6. 京都ではどこに泊まりますか。
7. 京都からどこへ行きますか。
8. そこへ行く時、何を使いますか。
9. 東京へは何で帰りますか。
10. いつ日本を発ちますか。
11. 日本からどこへ行きますか。

Grammar and Exercises

1. Making a Suggestion

カワムラ：静かなところでゆっくりしたいんですが、どこへ行ったらいいですか。
三村：山の温泉へ行ったらどうですか。

---

[1]Located on the Japan Sea coast, Izumo in Shimane Prefecture is the site of Izumo Shrine, which is a famous place where people go to pray for a good marriage.

KAWAMURA: I would like to relax in a quiet place. Where do you think I should go?   MIMURA: How about going to a hot spring resort in the mountains?

カワムラ：でも、お金がかかるでしょう？

三村：では、青山温泉はどうですか。あそこは安いですよ。

町田：ホンコンへ行くんですが、何を着ていったらいいですか。

チン：今とても暑いですから、Tシャツを着ていったらいいですよ。

町田：でも、カジュアルすぎませんか

チン：じゃあ、サマードレスも持っていったらどうですか。

1.1 There are several ways to make suggestions in Japanese. Here are some of the most common ways.

<table>
<tr><td rowspan="3">Ta-form of verb + ら</td><td>いかがですか。</td><td>How about if you (do...)?</td></tr>
<tr><td>どうですか。</td><td>Why not (do...)?</td></tr>
<tr><td>いいと思います。</td><td>It would be good if you (do...).</td></tr>
</table>

Review the たら conditional (Chapter 7, **Grammar 42** in Book 1).

When you would like to ask for a suggestion or someone's advice, the following constructions are used.

どうしたらいいですか。
What should I do?
どうしたらいいでしょうか。
What should I do? (politer)
どうしたらいいと思いますか。
What do you think I should do?
東京駅に行きたいんですが、どうしたらいいですか。　—地下鉄で行ったらいいと思います。
I would like to go to Tokyo Station. How do I get there? (lit., . . . but what should I do [to get there]?) —I think you should go by subway.
来週、友だちがアメリカから来るんですが、どこに連れていったらいいでしょうか。　—新宿に連れていったらどうですか。
My friend is coming from the U.S. next week. Where do you think I should take him or her? —How about if you take him or her to Shinjuku?

KAWAMURA: But that would cost a lot of money, wouldn't it? MIMURA: How about Aoyama Hot Springs? It (lit., that place) is inexpensive, you know.

MACHIDA: I'm going to Hong Kong. What do you think I should wear there? CHIN: It's very hot now, so I think you should wear a T-shirt. MACHIDA: But don't you think it's too casual? CHIN: Then why don't you take a summer dress, too?

連れていく、連れてくる

To take someone and *to bring someone* are expressed with the te-form of 連れる (*to accompany*) plus いく and くる respectively. Thus, 連れていく means *to take someone* (lit., *to go, accompanying someone*), whereas 連れてくる means *to bring someone* (lit., *to come, accompanying someone*). Use 持っていく and 持ってくる only for inanimate objects.

明日映画に連れていきましょう。
I will take you to the movies tomorrow.
デパートに行くんだったら、私も連れていってください。
If you are going to the department store, please take me too.
今夜は高田さんを連れてきました。
I brought Mr. Takada along tonight.

Don't use these verbs if the accompanied person is your social superior because it would sound impolite to do so. In such a case, you should use 一緒に行く or 一緒に来る instead.

パーティーに彼と一緒に行きます。
I will go to the party with my boyfriend.
今日は先生と一緒に来ました。
Today I came with my professor.

1.2 In colloquial speech, the endings of these constructions are often unexpressed. In these cases, the ends of the sentences are pronounced with a rising intonation.

明日のパーティー、何を着ていったらいい？ —赤いワンピースを着て
いったら、どう？
What should I wear to the party tomorrow? —How about wearing (your) red dress?
この漢字が読めないんだけど... —町田さんに聞いてみたら？
I can't read this Chinese character . . . (What should I do?) —How about asking Ms. Machida (to see if she can help you)?

...だけど is a colloquial form of ...だけれども.

練習　　　　　　　　1

Turn the following sentences into suggestions, using たらどうですか。

1. お母さんに手紙を書く
2. あと十五分、三村さんを待つ
3. もう少し早く起きる
4. あのレストランで食事をする
5. 山本さんと話してみる
6. 毎日ジョギングをする

7. お酒をやめる (quit)
8. 水を飲む

9. ここに来る
10. 村山さんに会う

練習　2

Make an appropriate suggestion in response to each comment or question in the first column, choosing from the list in the second column.

1. _____ 銀行へはどう行きますか。
2. _____ この漢字がわからないんですが…
3. _____ ちょっと暑いですね。
4. _____ 京都ではどこへ行ったらいいですか。
5. _____ 朝8時からずっと (without interruption) 働いています。
6. _____ 午後、雨が降るそうです。
7. _____ おなかがすきました。(I'm hungry.)
8. _____ 来週、クラスがありません。

a. ちょっと休んだらどうですか。
b. 辞書をひいて (look up in a dictionary) みたらどうですか。
c. コートをぬいだらどうですか。
d. ガイドブックを見てみたらどうですか。
e. 何か食べたらどうですか。
f. 旅行したらどうですか。
g. 私もわかりません。あのおまわりさん (police officer) に聞いたらどうですか。
h. 傘を持っていったらいいと思いますよ。

練習　3

Make an appropriate suggestion in response to each statement.

[例] 空港に行くんですが、どうしたらいいですか。→
タクシーを使ったらどうですか。

1. のどがかわいたんです (I'm thirsty) が、…
2. この問題がわからないんですが、…
3. いい日本語の辞書を買いたいんですが、どうしたらいいですか。
4. 日本語が上手になりたいんですが、どうしたらいいですか。
5. この町ではどこを見たらいいですか。
6. おいしい日本料理を食べたいんですが、…

2. Deciding to Do Something: …ことにする

2.1 A personal decision is expressed with the following construction.

Verb (plain, nonpast form) ＋ ことにする

(I) will decide to (do . . .)　　*(I) have decided to (do . . .)*

明日から毎日運動_{うんどう}することにします。
I have decided to exercise every day starting tomorrow.

ギブソンさんは、あのセーターを買_かうことにしました。
Ms. Gibson decided to buy that sweater.

アメリカに帰_{かえ}らないことにしました。
I decided not to return to America.

When する is in the nonpast tense, this construction expresses one's decision being made at the time of speech. On the other hand, when する is in the past tense, it expresses a decision made before the time of speech.

2.2 …ことにしている expresses a habit or routine activity; that is, *I have decided to (do something) and I am doing it.*

毎日牛乳_{ぎゅうにゅう}を飲むことにしています。
I make it a rule to drink milk every day.

毎週月曜日にギブソンさんと会うことにしている。
I make it a routine to see Ms. Gibson every Monday.

MIMURA: I hear that you're going to Hokkaido next week.　　CURTIS: Yes. I'm going with Mr. Hayashi.
MIMURA: Are you going by train or by plane?　　CURTIS: We want to see the Seikan Tunnel, so we've decided to go by train.

GIBSON: Ms. Chin, what are you going to do during summer vacation?　　CHIN: I haven't seen my parents for some time, so I've decided to return to Beijing.　　GIBSON: I see. I've decided to stay in Tokyo and work part-time.

[1]The Seikan Tunnel is a 53.9 kilometer underwater tunnel connecting the islands of Hokkaido and Honshu. It was completed in 1988.

It also expresses that someone has decided to do something and is strongly committed to the decision.

あの人とは話さないことにしています。
I am determined not to speak with that person. (or, *I'm not speaking with that person.*)

2.3 Noun + ...にする means *to decide on* (something).

何にしますか。
What will you have (lit., choose)?
タクシーにしますか。バスにしますか。
Shall we go by taxi or bus?

2.4 When a decision is made irrespective of the speaker's intention or will, ことになる is used. See Chapter 7 for details.

来週の水曜日、村山さんと会うことになっている。
It has been decided that I will meet with Ms. Murayama next Wednesday.

練習　　　　　　　　　　　　　1

Fill in the blank space with an appropriate verb from the following list.

Suggested verbs: 食べる、起きる、休む、買う、帰る

1. 今日は頭が痛い (*my head hurts*) ので、学校を（　　　）ことにした。
2. おなかがすいた (*I'm hungry*) ので、昼ごはんを（　　　）ことにします。
3. 毎日朝6時に（　　　）ことにしています。
4. 今日は娘の誕生日 (*birthday*) なので、早く家に（　　　）ことにします。
5. 横井先生がすすめる (*recommend*) ので、その辞書を（　　　）ことにしました。

練習　　　　　　　　　　　　　2

Complete the following sentences with a phrase ending in ことにした or ことにしている.

[例]　日曜日は... →
　　　日曜日は12時に起きることにしている。or デパートへ行くことにした。

1. 私は毎日...
2. 来週の木曜日...
3. 夏休みに...
4. 毎週土曜日...
5. 友だちと...

6. つかれた (*I'm tired*) ので、...
7. 雨が降っているので、...
8. あのレストランはおいしそうなので、...
9. 私の趣味は読書で、...
10. 私はサラダが大好きで、...

Answer these questions using にします, based on the background information in parentheses.

[例]　カーテンの色は赤にしますか。グレーにしますか。(はでな色はあまり好きじゃありません。)　→グレーにします。

1. コーヒーにしますか。アイスティーにしますか。(今日は暑いです。)
2. カーティスさんの誕生日 (birthday) のプレゼントは本にしますか。CD にしますか。(カーティスさんの趣味は読書だそうです。)
3. 夏休みの旅行は北海道にしますか。九州にしますか。(去年北海道へ行きました。)
4. お風呂にしますか。夕ごはんにしますか。(おなかがすいています。[You are hungry.])
5. ビールにしますか。ジュースにしますか。(アルコールはだめなんです。)

3. Saying Whether Something Occurred Before or After: 前 and 後

ギブソン：今日の予定はどうなっていますか。

　　　林：ええと、まず上野へ行きます。上野で買い物をした後、浅草へ行きます。浅草でお寺を見た後、日光へ行きます[1]。

ギブソン：昼ごはんはどこで食べますか。

　　　林：日光へ行く前に、浅草で食べましょう。おいしい天ぷら屋があるんですよ。

カワムラ：林さん、夕ごはんはお風呂の前にしますか。後にしますか。

　　　林：そうですね。夕ごはんを食べてから、入ることにします。

GIBSON: What is scheduled for today?　　HAYASHI: Uh, first we will go to Ueno. After we shop in Ueno, we will go to Asakusa. After seeing a temple in Asakusa, we will go to Nikko.　　GIBSON: Where will we eat lunch?　　HAYASHI: Let's eat in Asakusa before we go to Nikko. There is a good tempura restaurant there.

KAWAMURA: Mr. Hayashi, will you have dinner before or after your bath?　　HAYASHI: Let me see . . . I'll bathe after dinner.

[1]Asakusa is an area of Tokyo. Nikko, known for its brightly colored Toshogu Shrine, is located north of Tokyo.

カワムラ：ぼくは夕ごはんの前に、入ります。夕ごはんの後は、町を散歩するつもりです。

3.1 To say that something happens before or after something else, use the following patterns.

BEFORE
Noun の
Verb (dictionary form) } → 前に

Note that 前 (before) is also used to refer to location (*in front of*) and that the Chinese character 後 is read うし(ろ)—後ろ—when it is used in a positional sense (*behind*). (See Book 1, Chapter 2, **Grammar 8**.)

AFTER
Noun の
Verb (ta-form) } → 後で

海外旅行の前に、パスポートを取った。
Before my trip abroad, I got a passport.
その旅館を予約する前に、ガイドブックで値段を調べて (check) みましょう。
Before making a reservation at that inn, let's check its price in the guidebook.
昼ごはんの後で、その町を見物した。
After lunch, we went sightseeing in that town.
クラスが終わった後、駅に切符を買いに行った。
After class was over, we went to the station to buy tickets.
この神社を見た後で、旅館を探しましょう。
After we've seen this shrine, let's look for an inn.

3.2 As you studied in Chapter 4, **Grammar 49.2** in Book 1, the te-form of a verb + から has a meaning similar to the ta-form of a verb + 後(で).

切符を買ってから、ホームへ行った。
After I bought a ticket, I went to the train platform.
スーツケースをあずけてから、ギフトショップを見てみましょう。
After we check our bags (lit., suitcases), let's take a look at the gift shop.

KAWAMURA: I'll bathe before dinner. After dinner, I'm going to take a walk around town.

3.3 前 and 後 are also used with time expressions. When it directly follows a time expression, 後 can be read ご.

> | Time expression | + | { | 前(に)...ago, ... before |
> | | | | 後(に)... later, ... after, in ... |

いつ北海道へ行ったんですか。—二ヶ月前に行きました。(or 二ヶ月前です。)
When did you go to Hokkaido? —We went there two months ago. (or, Two months ago.)
いつペキンに帰るんですか。—三週間後に帰ります。
When will you return to Beijing? —I'll return in three weeks.

ケ月 (pronounced かげつ) is a counter for counting (not naming) months. (See Chapter 2, **Grammar 9** in Book 1.)
週間 is a counter for weeks.

3.4 前に and 後 で can be used adverbially, meaning *before* and *later*.

そこには前に行ったことがあります。
I have been there before.
その問題は後で話しましょう。
Let's talk about that issue later.

練習　　　　　　1

Choose either the *before* or *after* phrase, whichever best completes the sentence.

1. 席 (*seat*) に、(座る前に、座ってから)、シートベルトをしめました。(しめる = *to fasten*)
2. 切符を予約 (する前に、した後)、旅行のプランをたてました。(プランをたてる = *to make a plan*)
3. 朝 (起きる前に、起きた後)、オレンジジュースを飲んだ。
4. 夜 (寝る前に、寝た後)、テレビを見ます。
5. ホテルにチェックイン (する前に、した後)、部屋 (*room*) に行きました。

練習　　　　　　2

Combine the sentences using the time expressions given. Make any necessary changes to the verb endings.

前に
1. (町を見物する) (フィルムを買った)

2. (ホテルに行く)（明日の飛行機の予約をしましょう）
3. (雨が降る)（駅に着いた）
4. (日本に来る)（町田さんに手紙を書きました）
5. (家に帰る)（家内に電話することにしています）

後

6. (切符を買う)（フライトがキャンセルになった）
7. (神社を見る)（ホテルに行った）
8. (日本語を一年勉強する)（日本に来た）
9. (喫茶店でお茶を飲む)（公園を散歩した）
10. (パスポートを取る [get a passport])（トラベラーズ・チェックを作りました）

~てから

11. (ハワイから帰ってくる)（病気になった）
12. (町田さんに電話する)（買い物に行きましょう）
13. (レンタカーを借りる[rent])（町を見物しました）
14. (東京に着く)（カワムラさんに電話します）
15. (日本を発つ)（ブラウンさんと話しました）

練習　　　　　　3

Answer these questions using the information given in parentheses.

Review how to count days in Chapter 2, **Grammar 9** in Book 1, if necessary.

1. いつ日本に来ましたか。(one year ago)
2. いつアメリカに帰りますか。(three months later)
3. いつ町田さんに会いましたか。(four days ago)
4. いつヨーロッパに発ちますか。(two weeks later)
5. いつ朝ごはんを食べましたか。(thirty minutes ago)

4. と Conditionals

カワムラ：すみません。赤坂神社はどこでしょうか。
通行人：あの角を右に曲がると、銀行があります。銀行の横の道をまっすぐ
　　　　行くと、左側にあります。

KAWAMURA: Excuse me. Where is Akasaka Shrine?　　PASSERBY: Turn right at that corner, and you will see (*lit., there is*) a bank. Go straight down the street next to the bank, and the shrine will be on your left.

カワムラ：どうもありがとうございます。

通行人：どういたしまして。

ブラウン：コンサートのチケットは、どこで買えますか。

林：デパートのチケットのプレイガイド[1]に行くと、買えますよ。

ブラウン：学生割引はあるんですか。

林：ええ、学生証を見せると、安くなります。

Besides たら (review Chapter 7, **Grammar 42**, Book 1), と can be used to mark the end of a conditional clause.

CONDITIONAL CLAUSE (C1)		
Noun + だ／でない I-adjectives (plain, nonpast form) Na-adjectives + だ／でない Verbs (plain, nonpast form)	と、	+ RESULTANT CLAUSE (C2)

The と conditional can be interpreted in either of two ways, depending on whether the second clause is in the present tense or the past tense. In a present-tense sentence, a と conditional expresses the idea that the second clause is a natural or expected consequence of the first clause. It often translates into English *as if* or *when(ever)* and is used in statements about general principles or recurring events and situations.

まだ学生だと、あのバーに入れません。
If you are still a student, you cannot enter that bar.
アパートが駅から遠いと、歩くのは大変でしょう？
If the apartment is far from the station, it would be hard to walk [there],
    wouldn't it?
こんなに不便だと、誰も来ませんよ。
If it's this inconvenient, no one will come.

KAWAMURA: Thank you very much.   PASSERBY: You are welcome.

BROWN: Where can I buy a concert ticket?   HAYASHI: If you go to the Playguide counter in a department store, you can buy one.   BROWN: Is there a student discount?   HAYASHI: Yes, if you show your student ID, your ticket will be cheaper.

[1]プレイガイド is an event ticket sales service, akin to Ticketron in the U.S., with outlets throughout Japan.

冬になると、雪がたくさん降ります。
When winter comes (when it becomes winter), it snows a lot.
夏になると、みんな海に出かけます。
When it gets to be summer, everyone heads for the sea.

In the last two sentences, ~たら would also be grammatical, but the meaning would change slightly. The versions with と can be only general statements of fact; they cannot describe a specific winter or summer. The versions with ~たら, on the other hand, would allow the interpretation that the speaker was talking about a specific winter or summer, most likely this coming winter or summer: *When [this] winter comes, it will snow a lot* or *When [this] summer comes, everyone will head for the sea.* Unlike ~たら, however, と cannot be used if the second clause is a command, request, invitation, prohibition, or expression of will.

宿題が終わると、映画に行きましょう。(ungrammatical)
宿題が終わったら、映画に行きましょう。(grammatical)
When the homework is finished, let's go to the movies.

宿題が終わると、部屋を片付けてください。(ungrammatical)
宿題が終わったら、部屋を片付けてください。(grammatical)
When the homework is finished, please straighten up the room.

In spite of this restriction, however, it is possible to make suggestions using a と construction, usually when expressing some general principle or guideline.

このガイドブックを読むといいですよ。
It would be good if you read this guidebook.
電卓 (calculator) を使うと便利ですよ。
It's [more] convenient if you use a calculator.

When used within a past-tense sentence, と is similar to ~たら in translating as English *when.* Unlike ~たら, however, と is used when the second clause is an event or situation outside of the speaker's control. For this reason, it is often used to describe unexpected events.

その喫茶店に行くと、チンさんがいた。
When I went to the coffee shop, Ms. Chin was there.
その店に行くと、いい家具がたくさんありました。
When we went to that store, we found a lot of good furniture (lit., there was a lot of good furniture).
家に帰ると、三村さんが来ていた。
When I returned home, Mr. Mimura had [already] come.
角を曲がると、子供が車の前に飛び出てきました。
When I turned the corner, a child came dashing out in front of my car.

Join sentences from the two columns using the と conditional.

[例]　夜になります。　　　暗くなります。 → 夜になると、暗くなります。

1. 春になります。
2. カワムラさんの家に行きました。
3. 二十になりました。
4. 寒くなりました。
5. デパートへ行きました。
6. ホームへ行きました。
7. 電車に乗りました。
8. あの角を曲がります。

a. 電車がもう来ていました。
b. 誰もいませんでした。
c. セールをしていました。
d. 少し暖かくなります。
e. お酒が飲めます。
f. セーターを着ます。
g. すぐ (immediately) 席 (seat) にすわりました。
h. スーパーがあります。

練習　　　　　　　2

Give directions from the station to Ms. Machida's house by using the と conditional and the following expressions.

1. この道、まっすぐ、信号 (traffic light)
2. 右に曲がる、すぐ、スーパー
3. 左に曲がる、少し行く、銀行
4. 公園のとなりの道、まっすぐ、大学

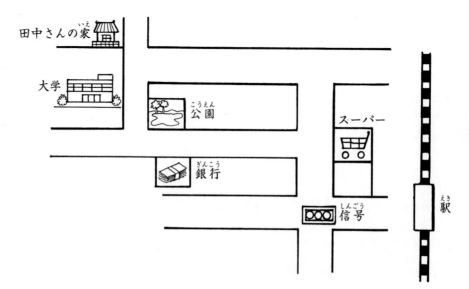

Complete these sentences.

1. 冬が来ると、
2. 雨が降ると、
3. 3時になると、
4. 図書館へ行くと、

5. ここをまっすぐ行くと、
6. マクドナルドへ行くと、
7. 暑いと、
8. 電車を降りると、

5. Commands

山口ゆり子：さとみ、起きなさい。
山口さとみ：お母さん、今何時?
山口ゆり子：もう7時よ。
山口さとみ：まだ7時?

山口ゆり子：大助、部屋の掃除はした?
山口大助：まだだよ。

山口ゆり子：まだ?早く掃除しなさい。洋子さんが来るんでしょう?
山口大助：うん、今するよ。

5.1 Commands to subordinates can be expressed by the following construction:

Conjunctive verb form + なさい

書く → 書き
食べる → 食べ
する → し
来る → 来

+ なさい

YURIKO YAMAGUCHI: Satomi, get up.　SATOMI YAMAGUCHI: Mom, what time is it now?
YURIKO YAMAGUCHI: It's already 7:00.　SATOMI YAMAGUCHI: Still 7:00?

YURIKO YAMAGUCHI: Daisuke, did you clean your room?　DAISUKE YAMAGUCHI: Not yet.　YURIKO
YAMAGUCHI: Not yet? Clean it quickly. Yooko is coming here, isn't she?　DAISUKE YAMAGUCHI: Yes, I'll
clean it now.

もっと野菜を食べなさい。
Eat more vegetables.
変な人には気をつけなさい。
Watch out for strange people.
わかった人は手を上げなさい。
Those who have understood, raise your hands.
答えはここに書きなさい。
Write your answer here.

This is the command form used by parents talking to children, teachers talking to students, and other authority figures giving orders to subordinates.

5.2 The plain equivalent of the なさい command is formed as follows

direct order

CLASS 1 VERBS	CLASS 2 VERBS	CLASS 3 VERBS
Root + the e-column **hiragana** corresponding to the dictionary ending	Root + ろ	Irregular
買う → 買え 書く → 書け 話す → 話せ 立つ → 立て 死ぬ → 死ね 読む → 読め 乗る → 乗れ 泳ぐ → 泳げ	食べる → 食べろ 見る → 見ろ	する → しろ 来る → 来い

u-column	→ e-column
う	→ え
く	→ け
す	→ せ
つ	→ て
ぬ	→ ね
む	→ め
る	→ れ
ぐ	→ げ

This command form, which is called the imperative, sounds very blunt and harsh, so non-Japanese learners would be well-advised to avoid using it for commands and requests. Female speakers do not use it at all.

おい、早く食べろ。
Hey, eat quickly. (not-so-well-educated or angry father to son)

ビールを持って来い。
Bring me beer! (chauvinistic husband to wife; drunk customer to bartender)

When you quote someone's command indirectly, you can use the plain command + と言う. It does not matter what form the original command was in. Even though this command form sounds harsh and masculine when used by itself, its use within indirect quotations is completely acceptable, even for female speakers.

彼は早く起きろと言いました。
He said to get up quickly.
父は息子にもっと勉強しろと言った。
Father told my son to study more.

練習　　　　1

What do you say to these people who are subordinate to you? Answer using …なさい.

[例]　a student who doesn't come to school every day → 毎日学校に来なさい。

　　　1. a child who doesn't drink milk
　　　2. a student who doesn't study at all　　　しなさい)
　　　3. a child who doesn't go to bed
　　　4. a student who doesn't go back home after class
　　　5. a child who doesn't read books at all
　　　6. a student who looks not at the chalkboard, but at a pretty student next to him
　　　7. a child who stays out after 8:00 P.M.

練習　　　　2

Rewrite these sentences by using the plain command form + と言った.

[例]　名前を書く → 名前を書けと言った。

　　　1. ここに来る　　　　4. 勉強する　　　　　　7. お茶を飲む
　　　2. 学校に行く　　　　5. お金をはらう
　　　3. 本を読む　　　　　6. これを買う

6. Admonishment and Prohibition: 〜てはいけない／…な

カワムラ：ここで写真を取りましょうか。
林：ええ。あっ、芝生の中に入ってはいけませんよ。

―――――――――――

KAWAMURA: Let's take a photo here.　　HAYASHI: Yes. Oh, you have to keep off the grass.

カワムラ：中に入っちゃいけないんですか。

林：ほら、「立ち入り禁止」の立て札があるでしょ。

林：あっ、湯船の中で体を洗ってはいけません。

カワムラ：あっ、そうですか。

林：日本のお風呂では、体は湯船の外で洗います。

カワムラ：あっ、あのおじいさんは？

林：おじいさん、湯船の中で入れ歯を洗ってはだめですよ。

言語ノート

おじさん、おばさん、おじいさん、おばあさん

In Chapter 5 of Book 1, you studied the above words, which mean *uncle*, *aunt*, *grandfather*, and *grandmother*, respectively. These words are used not only to refer to family members or relatives but also to refer to or address middle-aged and older people in informal speech. おにいさん and おねえさん are used to refer to young men and women. If you go to Japan during your student years, don't be surprised when small children address you as おにいさん or おねえさん.

6.1 Admonition or warning is expressed by the following constructions.

Te-form of verb ＋ は ＋ {
いけない(いけません)
ならない(なりません)
だめだ(だめです)
こまる(こまります)
}

You must not (do…)

...いけない、...ならない and ...だめだ have a similar meaning, but the sense of prohibition is most strongly expressed by...だめだ, followed by ...ならない and ...いけない in this order. ...こまる expresses prohibition indirectly by saying that the hearer's action will inconvenience the speaker.

一人で町を歩いてはいけません。
You mustn't walk in the town alone.
ここに車を止めてはならない。
You mustn't park (stop) a car.

───────────

KAWAMURA: Can't I go onto the grass?　　HAYASHI: Look! There is a sign saying "Keep Out."

HAYASHI: Oh, you mustn't wash your body inside the bathtub.　　KAWAMURA: Oh, really?

HAYASHI: In Japan, we wash ourselves outside the bathtub.　　KAWAMURA: How about that elderly man?

HAYASHI: Sir! You mustn't wash your dentures in the bathtub.

お酒を飲みすぎてはだめですよ。
You mustn't drink too much sake.

6.2 A negative command is expressed as follows.

Dictionary form of verb + な

Don't . . . .

ここにごみをすてるな。
Don't throw your garbage here.
そんなばかなことはするな。
Don't do such a stupid thing.

The negative command form sounds harsh and strong. It is used only in public signs and by males speaking to family members, close friends, or subordinates. As with the plain command, you may use …な in front of と言う, no matter what the original form of the negative command was, without any unpleasant connotations.

父は私にそんなにたくさん食べるなと言いました。
Father told me not to eat that much.
彼にあまりテレビを見るなと言いましょうか。
Shall I tell him not to watch TV so much?

入っちゃ is a colloquial form of 入っては.

練習　　　　　　1

Rewrite the following sentences using てはいけません。

1. ここでサッカーをする
2. ごみをすてる
3. ロビーをスリッパで歩く
4. ここで泳ぐ
5. たばこをすう (*to smoke a cigarette*)
6. 水を飲む
7. 大きな声 (*voice*) で話す

練習　　　　　　2

What is forbidden in these situations? Complete the following using てはいけません。

1. 教室 (*classroom*) の中で
2. ホテルの部屋の中で
3. 飛行機の中で
4. 日本では
5. アメリカでは
6. 食事の時

7. The Adverbial Use of Adjectives

林：チンさん、昨日はクラスに行きましたか。

チン：ええ。でも、早く帰ったんです。

林：どうしたんですか。

チン：頭が痛かったんです。

山口ゆり子：大助、部屋の掃除したの？

山口大助：うん、したよ。

山口ゆり子：これで掃除したと言うの？

山口大助：うん。

山口ゆり子：もっときれいに掃除しなさい。

文法ノート

Sentence-Final の

The sentence-final particle の, used mainly, but not exclusively, by female speakers and children, indicates (1) mild affirmation, (2) asking a question or asking for an explanation (の is spoken with a rising intonation), (3) persuasion, and (4) explanation. It is one of the informal forms of the …んです construction.

私、このケーキがとても好きなの。
I really like this cake.
何をするの？
What are you going to do?
もっと勉強したらどうなの？
Why don't you study more?
お金がないの。
It's because I don't have any money.

HAYASHI: Ms. Chin, did you go to class yesterday?　　CHIN: Yes, but I left early.　　HAYASHI: What happened?　　CHIN: I had a headache.

YURIKO YAMAGUCHI: Daisuke, did you clean your room?　　DAISUKE YAMAGUCHI: Yes, I did.

YURIKO YAMAGUCHI: Do you call this a clean room? (*lit., This is the condition you call cleaned?*)

DAISUKE YAMAGUCHI: Yes.　　YURIKO YAMAGUCHI: Clean more thoroughly.

The sentence-final particle よ, which is used to give new information, to impose one's opinion, or to emphasize information, may follow の.

私このケーキがとても好きなのよ。
何をするのよ。
もっと勉強したらどうなのよ？
お金がないのよ。

Male speakers usually use のだ instead of sentence-final の, and female speakers may occasionally use のだ, too, especially if they are trying to sound "tough."

You can make adverbs from adjectives in the following way.

ADVERBIAL FORM OF ADJECTIVES

| **I-adjectives** | Root + く | 小さい → 小さく
安い → 安く |
| **Na-adjectives** | Root + に | きれい → きれいに
静か → 静かに |

もう少し小さく切ってください。
Please cut it into smaller pieces.
このソックスはセールの時に安く買いました。
I bought this pair of socks cheaply when there was a sale.
ナイフとフォークをきれいに並べてください。
Please arrange the knives and forks neatly.
ここでは静かに歩きなさい。
Walk quietly here.

練習　　　　　1

Fill in the blanks with the appropriate form of the following adjectives.

Suggested adjectives

遅い (*late*)　　　　　　　早い　　　　　　　　　長い (*long*)
きれい (な)　　　　　　　上手 (な)
静か (な)　　　　　　　　大きい

1. 仕事が終わったら、（　　　）うちに帰るつもりだ。
2. （　　　）ごはんを食べなさい。
3. ちょっとこれは小さすぎますね。もう少し（　　　）書いてください。
4. きたない手 (hands) ですね。（　　　）洗いなさい。
5. 昨日は仕事がたくさんあって、（　　　）うちに帰った。
6. 妹はいつもお風呂に（　　　）入っている。
7. カワムラさんは日本語を（　　　）話せますね。

8. Expressing Obligation or Duty

高田：アメリカへ行く時は、ビザはいりますか。
ブラウン：どれくらいアメリカへ行くんですか。
高田：一ヶ月です。
ブラウン：それじゃ、いりません。三ヶ月以上はビザを取らなくてはなりません。

カワムラ：この電車は京都へ行きますか。
駅員：いいえ、大阪で乗り換えなくてはいけません。
カワムラ：この切符で京都まで行けますか。
駅員：いいえ、大阪でまた切符を買わなくてはだめですよ。

佐野：お出かけですか。
高田：ええ、スーツケースを買わなくてはいけないんです。
佐野：旅行ですか。
高田：ええ、出張でニューヨークへ行かなければならないんです。

TAKADA: When I go to the United States, do I need a visa?　BROWN: How long are you going to be there?
TAKADA: One month.　BROWN: Then you don't need one. If you stay there for more than three months, you have to get a visa.

KAWAMURA: Does this train go to Kyoto?　STATION WORKER: No, you have to transfer at Osaka.
KAWAMURA: Can I go to Kyoto with this ticket?　STATION WORKER: No. You have to buy one again at Osaka.

SANO: Are you going out?　TAKADA: Yes, I have to buy a suitcase.　SANO: Is it for your trip?
TAKADA: I have to go to New York on business.

8.1 An obligation or a duty is expressed by the following construction.

The te-form of the negative, nonpast form (ない form) of verb + は	ならない （なりません） いけない （いけません） だめだ （だめです）

One must . . . One has to . . .

このレンタカーは6時までに返^{かえ}さなくてはいけない。
We have to return this rental car by six o'clock.
早^{はや}く寝^ねなくてはいけませんよ。
You have to go to sleep quickly.
もっと勉強しなくちゃだめだよ。
You have to study more.

For instance, the te-form of the negative, nonpast form 書かない is 書かなくて. Note that ない is an i-adjective and conjugates as such. Note that ならない、いけない、and だめだ are used in the construction expressing admonishment or prohibition. (See **Grammar 6** in this chapter.)

しなくちゃ is a colloquial form of しなくては。

8.2 An obligation or a duty is also expressed by the following construction.

The root of the negative, nonpast form of verbs + ければ +	ならない （なりません） いけない （いけません） だめだ （だめです）

The roots of negative, nonpast forms 書かない, 食べない, しない, and 来ない are 書かな, 食べな, しな, and 来な, respectively. Note that verb forms ending in ない are conjugated like i-adjectives.

夜^{よる}9時までここにいなければなりません。
I have to stay here until nine in the evening.
食堂車^{しょくどうしゃ}は今こんでいますから、少し待^またなければいけません。
The dining car is now crowded, so you have to wait a little.
海外旅行^{かいがいりょこう}にはパスポートを持^もっていかなければならない。
You must carry your passport when traveling abroad.
毎日、歯^はをみがかなければだめですよ。
You must brush your teeth every day.

Note that the root of i-adjectives can be obtained if you delete the final i from their dictionary form. むずかしい → むずかし、赤い → 赤、ない → な

まで versus までに

In Chapter 3 of Book 1, you learned that the particle まで means *until*.
までに (adding the particle に), on the other hand, means *by* or *before*
and is used to indicate the time *by* or *before* which an action or an
event is completed.

一時まで勉強した。
I studied until one o'clock.
三時までにうちに帰らなければならない。
I have to return home before (by) three o'clock.

練習　　　　　　1

Following the example, create a dialogue.

[例]　（今日の午後、映画に行く）（早く家に帰る）→
　　　—今日の午後、映画に行きませんか。
　　　—すみません。早く家に帰らなければならないんです。

1. （来週、うちに来る）（ニューヨークに行く）
2. （明日図書館に行く）（うちにいる）
3. （あさって昼ごはんをいっしょに食べる）（ギブソンさんと話す）
4. （今夜テレビを見る）（宿題をする）
5. （そろそろ帰る）（チンさんを待っている）

練習　　　　　　2

Complete the following using ...なくてはなりません or ...なくてはいけません。

1. 日本へ行く時には、
2. バスに乗る時には、
3. ホテルを予約する時には、
4. ホテルをチェックアウトする時には、
5. 授業中 (*during class*) は、
6. 旅行の前には、
7. 家に帰ってきたら、

Vocabulary

Travel

おみやげ		souvenir
かんこうりょこう	観光旅行	sightseeing trip
きっぷ	切符	ticket
くうこう	空港	airport
けんぶつ(する)	見物(する)	sightseeing (to sightsee)
じこくひょう	時刻表	timetable
しゅっちょう(する)	出張(する)	(to go on a) business trip
ていりゅうじょ	停留所	bus or tram stop
にもつ	荷物	luggage
ほけん	保険	insurance
まちあいしつ	待合室	waiting room
みなと	港	harbor, port
やど	宿	accommodations
よやく(する)	予約(する)	(to make a) reservation
りょかん	旅館	Japanese-style inn

Loanwords: ツアー、ガイド、ツアーコンダクター、スーツケース、トラベラーズチェック、パスポート、ビザ、チケット、スケジュール

Review: ホテル

Transportation

しんかんせん	新幹線	bullet train
のりもの	乗り物	vehicle
ひこうき	飛行機	airplane
ふね	船	ship, boat

Loanwords: タクシー、フェリーボート、レンタカー

Review: 車、電車、バス

Nouns

えはがき	絵はがき	picture postcard
おふろ	お風呂	bath (*especially Japanese-style*)
おんせん	温泉	hot spring
こうさてん	交差点	intersection
ちず	地図	map
はし	橋	bridge
ひだりがわ	左側	left side
みぎがわ	右側	right side
よてい	予定	plan, schedule

Verbs

おくれる	遅れる	to be late
おしえる	教える	to teach, tell
おりる	降りる	to get off (*a vehicle*)
かりる	借りる	to borrow, rent
しまる	閉まる	to shut off, close
たずねる	尋ねる	to ask, inquire
たつ	発つ	to leave
つく	着く	to arrive
つめる		to pack
つれていく	連れていく	to take (*people*)
つれてくる	連れてくる	to bring (*people*)
とまる	泊まる	to stay overnight
のりかえる	乗り換える	to transfer (*from one means of transportation to another*)
まがる	曲がる	to turn (*in a direction*)
もっていく	持っていく	to take (*things*)
もってくる	持ってくる	to bring (*things*)
わたる	渡る	to cross

X を Y につめる　to pack X into Y

Review: 乗る

Adverbs

いそいで	急いで	quickly
はやく	早く	early
まっすぐ		straight
よく		often, well

あと(で)	後(で)	after
～かん	間	during, for
…ことにする		to decide on …
～たらいいとおもいます。	～たらいいと思います	I think it would be good to (do) …
～たらいかがですか。		How about (doing) … ?
～たらどうですか。		How about (doing) … ?
～てから		after (doing)
～てはいけない		must not (do)
～てはこまる		It will cause trouble if you (do)
～てはだめだ		It's forbidden/inappropriate to (do)
～てはならない		must not (do)
～でも		or something like that
～なさい		(*command to subordinate*)
どのように		how, in what way
～なければいけない		must, have to
～なければだめだ		must, have to
～なければならない		must, have to
まえ(に)	前(に)	before
まで		until
までに		by (the time)
…め	…目	*suffix for cardinal numbers (e.g., first, second, third)*

Kanji

Learn these **kanji.**

京 都 社 内 目 所 約 予 車
早 歩 館 乗 待 駅 止 旅 客
寺 神 地 図 曲 海 私

Reading and Writing

Reading 1 北海道の案内

Mr. and Ms. Sano are members of the Nakano Travel Club. Today they received an announcement of a trip to Hokkaido from the club.

Before You Read

1. What information do you think is included in a travel itinerary?

2. The announcement that you will read includes many 漢語 (*Chinese-origin words*). You may not know these words, but you can often figure out their meaning based on your knowledge of related 和語 (*Japanese-origin words*). For example, the Chinese-origin 集合 means *getting together*. The first character is found in the Japanese-origin word 集まる, which also means *to get together*. Now guess the meaning of these 漢語.

    出発　到着　朝食　昼食　夕食　乗船

3. The announcement employs the same abbreviated style you might see in an English itinerary: *You depart Tokyo at 9:00 A.M.* becomes *9:00 A.M. Tokyo departure.* Add appropriate particles and verbs to the following itinerary entries to make complete sentences. By the way, 出発、到着 and 乗船 are nominal verbs.

    午前9時東京出発　　午後10時中野到着　　観光船乗船

Useful vocabulary

みなさん *everyone*, 知らせる *to notify*, 便 *flight number*, 羽田空港 *Haneda Airport*, 千歳空港 *Chitose Airport (near Sapporo)*, 支笏湖 *Shikotsu Lake*, 登別温泉 *Noboribetsu Hot Spring Spa*, 洞爺湖 *Toya Lake*, 市内 *inside the city*, 料金 *fee*, 含む *to include*, 自分で *by oneself*, 払う *to pay*

Now Read It!

中野旅行クラブのみなさんへ

七月の北海道旅行のスケジュールが決まりましたので、お知らせします。

７月１２日	午前８時	中野駅前に集合
	午前８時半	バスで羽田空港へ
	午前１０時４５分	ＡＮＡ１２３便で千歳空港へ出発
	午後１２時１０分	千歳空港到着
	午後１時半	バスで札幌到着
		観光バスで札幌市内見物
	午後６時半	札幌プリンスホテルにチェックイン
７月１３日	午前６時	ホテルで朝食
		朝食の後、チェックアウト
	午前８時	バスで支笏湖へ出発
	午前１０時	支笏湖到着
		観光船乗船
	午後１２時半	昼食
	午後２時	バスで登別温泉へ出発
	午後４時	登別温泉到着
		登別温泉グランドホテルにチェックイン
	午後７時	ホテルで夕食
７月１４日	午前６時	ホテルで朝食
		朝食の後、チェックアウト
	午前８時	バスで洞爺湖へ出発
	午前１０時	洞爺湖到着
	１２時	昼食
	午後１時	バスで函館へ出発
	午後６時半	函館到着
		函館ホテルにチェックイン
	午後７時	ホテルで夕食
７月１５日	午前９時	観光バスで見物
	午後４時	ショッピング
	午後６時１８分	寝台特急「はくつる」で函館を出発
７月１６日	午前７時９分	上野駅に到着

料金は一人７万８千円です。料金は１３日と１４日の食事を含んでいますが、１２日の夕食と１５日の食事は含んでいません。これは自分で払わなければなりません。

昼は暖かいですが、夜は涼しくなるので、セーターかジャケットを持って行ったらいいでしょう。

After You Finish Reading

Trace the route of the trip on the map. Write in the form of transportation that will be used from one place to the next place.

Answer these questions in English.

1. Where will the tour group meet on the morning of July 12?
2. Where will they take a boat ride?
3. What are they going to do in Sapporo?
4. What time will they arrive at Hakodate?
5. By what means of transportation will they return to Tokyo?
6. How much is the fee?
7. Does the fee include all meals?
8. What suggestion is made in the announcement? Why?

The Sanos decided to go on the club trip. Here is a postcard (絵はがき) that Ms. Sano sent to Linda Brown during their travels. Read it and answer the following questions.

ブラウンさん

　今, このはがきを登別温泉のホテルで書いています。おとといの朝, 東京を出発, お昼ごろ千歳空港に着きました。バスで札幌市内を見物して, おとといの夜は札幌に泊まりました。昨日, 札幌からバスで支忽湖に行き, 観光船に乗りました。午後登別に来ました。昨日の夜はホテルの温泉に何度も入りました。今日はこれから洞爺湖へ向かい, その後, 函館に行きます。東京にはあさって帰ります。おみやげを買って帰りますから, 楽しみにしてください。では, また。

7月14日朝

佐野良子
登別にて

1. Where did Ms. Sano write the postcard?
2. When did she arrive there?
3. Where is she going tomorrow?
4. When is she going back to Tokyo?
5. What will she buy for Linda Brown?

What is the most memorable trip you have ever taken? Explain to a classmate in Japanese what you did on that trip.

おんせん
温泉

Japan is sitting on one of the most active geothermal fault zones in the world. As a result, it is home to numerous volcanoes, both active and dormant, and thousands of hot springs. These hot springs have been used for centuries for their purported ability to cure skin ailments, arthritis, stomach problems, infertility, rheumatism, and other maladies, and that tradition continues at the inns and resorts built up around the most popular springs. Today, however, most Japanese see the hot springs simply as places to soak and relax several times daily in between sightseeing, relishing local delicacies, and otherwise enjoying a hard-earned vacation. Hot spring destinations range from touristy spa towns like Atami to remote mountaintop open-air pools with no sign of civilization for miles. The temperature of the water is usually above 40 degrees Celsius and, where possible, you are expected to bathe before entering the communal tub or pool.

おんせん　　　　　　　　ゆ
温泉で：いい湯だな。

Writing 1

1. Using the following information, write a postcard to Henry Curtis.

   You arrived in Kyoto yesterday. Today, you went to temples and shrines south of Kyoto Station. Tomorrow, you will see temples and shrines north of Kyoto Station. The day after tomorrow, you will go to Kyushu. After traveling in Kyushu, you will return home next Wednesday.

2. Write a brief account of the most memorable trip you have ever taken.

Reading 2　トラベルガイド：札幌

Before You Read

Bring a travel guide to class, and check to see what information is included.

Match the words in the first column to related words in the second column.

1. _____ 空港　　a. 食べる
2. _____ 特急　　b. 片道
3. _____ 往復　　c. 冬
4. _____ 旅館　　d. 電話
5. _____ 予約　　e. 泊まる
6. _____ 料理　　f. 飛行機
7. _____ 雪　　　g. 駅

Answer these questions.

1. 長さ(length) is a noun derived from the adjective 長い (long). What does 高さ mean?
2. If 夏まつり means *summer festival,* what does 雪まつり mean?
3. 植物 means *plant* and 動物 means *animal.* 植物園 means *botanical garden.* What does 動物園 mean?
4. You have seen the character 屋 at the ends of words referring to stores and shops. What do you think おみやげ屋 means?

Now Read It!

交通
　　札幌は北海道の真ん中にある、人口百四十万人の美しい町だ。北海道の政治、経済、文化の中心である。東京から飛行機で千歳空港まで1時間15分。千歳から

交通 *transportation*

真ん中 *middle* / 政治 *politics*

経済 *economy* / 文化 *culture*
中心 *center*

バスで1時間。電車で45分だ。上野から寝台特急で12時間。飛行機だと、東京から往復45,000円。寝台特急は往復52,660円だ。

見どころ

見どころ *things to see*

- **大通り公園**
  幅105メートル、長さ3.8キロのグリーンベルト。冬はここで雪まつりがある。

  幅 *width*

- **中島公園**
  札幌駅から地下鉄で4分。豊平川のそばにある緑と水の公園。夏はバラが美しい。

  バラ *rose*

- **時計台**
  札幌駅から歩いて8分。札幌のシンボル。

  時計台 *clock tower*

- **円山公園**
  大通りからバスで15分。高さ220メートルの円山にある公園。動物園、スポーツセンターがある。

- **北海道大学植物園**
  札幌駅から5分

ホテル・旅館

札幌市内にはデラックスホテルからビジネスホテルまで[1]、また日本旅館などが140軒ぐらいある。ユースホステル、民宿もある。駅の中の観光案内所でホテル、旅館を探すことができる。6月から7月は観光客が多いので、三ヶ月位前から予約しなければならない。

民宿 *Japanese-style bed and breakfast /*
観光案内所 *tourist information center*
探す *to look for*

デラックスホテル：札幌グランドホテル、札幌パークホテル、ロイヤルホテル、センチュリーロイヤルホテル、プリンスホテルなど。

ビジネスホテル：ホテルワシントン札幌、札幌ビジネスホテル、ビジネスホテルライラック、サッポロ大通り公園ホテルなど。

旅館：よしのや旅館、北海道旅館、千歳館など。

味

- **ラーメン**
  札幌のラーメンは全国で有名。大通り公園のそばにはおいしいラーメン屋がたくさんある。熊さん（電話011-261-0900）、味の三平（電話011-231-0377）。

  全国 *all over the country*

---

[1]*Business hotels* are "no frills" Western-style hotels aimed at business people. For that reason, most rooms are small, simply furnished singles.

■　ジンギスカン[1]

　ビールを飲みながら、ジンギスカンが食べられるのはサッポロビール園
（電話011-742-1531）

■　北海道料理

　雪国（電話011-221-8286）はカニとさけで有名。

おみやげ

　北海道のおみやげと言えば、じゃがいも、アスパラガス、カニ、スモーク・
サーモンなど。札幌駅のそばにおみやげ屋さんが多い。

年中行事

■　札幌雪まつり

　北海道で一番大きい年中行事。全国から観光客が集まる。大きな雪の像が
大通り公園に並ぶ。

方言

旅行している時には、方言を聞くのも楽しみの1つだ。北海道方言では、「つか
れた」は「こわい」という。「気持ちがいい」は「あずましい」という。「凍る」
は「しばれる」という。

トラベル・コンサルタント田中由子

カニ *crab* / さけ *salmon*

年中行事 *annual event* / 集まる *to get together* / 像 *sculpture*
並ぶ *to be lined up*

方言 *dialect*

つかれた *(I'm) tired* / 気持ちがいい *to feel comfortable, to feel at home* / 凍る *to freeze*

文法ノート

...と言えば

...と言えば means *speaking of . . .* , and it is used to introduce a new topic of conversation or to change the subject.

　—この本、佐野さんのですか。—ええ。ところで、佐野さんと
言えば、もう北海道から帰ってきましたか。
　—*Is this book Mr. Sano's? —Yes. By the way, speaking of Mr. Sano, has he already come back from Hokkaido?*

After You Finish Reading

The city of Sapporo has decided to make up an English-language brochure for foreign tourists based on Ms. Tanaka's travel guide. Please help the city officials prepare the brochure by filling in the missing information in English.

---

[1]ジンギスカン is a mutton dish for which Hokkaido is famous (*lit., Genghis Khan*).

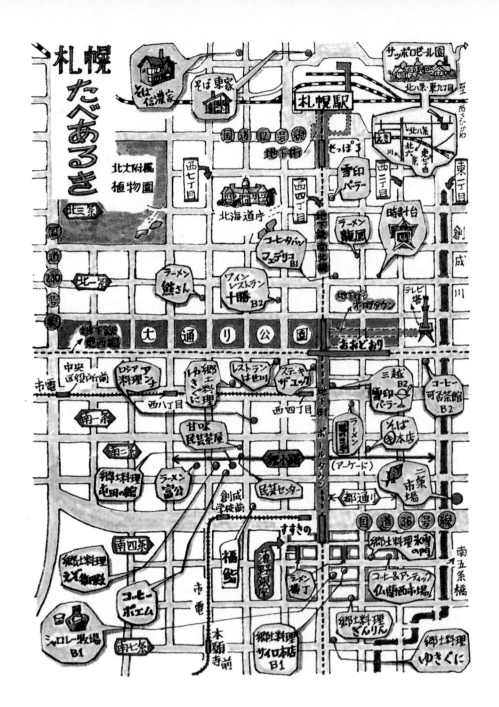

Come to Sapporo

TRANSPORTATION

Sapporo is located in the (   ) part of Hokkaido.
(   ) hour (   ) minutes by (   ) to Chitose Airport from Tokyo, (   ) hours by (   ) from Ueno.

THINGS TO SEE

- Avenue (大通り) Park
  width (   )m, length (   )km. There is a (   ) here in winter.
- Nakajima Park
  (   ) minutes by (   ) from Sapporo Station. The (   ) here are pretty in summer.
- Clock Tower
  (   ) minutes on foot from (   ). This is the (   ) of Sapporo.
- Maruyama Park
  (   ) minutes by (   ) from Avenue Park. Located here are a (   ) and a (   ).
- Hokkaido University (   )
  (   ) minutes from (   ).

ACCOMMODATIONS

There are about (   ) hotels and inns in Sapporo. It's better to reserve them in advance in (   ) and (   ).

FOOD AND SOUVENIRS

As for food, we recommend that you try (   ), (   ), and (   ). For souvenirs, we recommend (   ), (   ), and (   ). There are many souvenir shops (   ) Sapporo station.

言語ノート

ほうげん
方言 (Dialects)

Just as you can often tell whether an American is from New Orleans or New York City based on the way he or she speaks, so too can you often figure out what part of Japan a person is from based on his or her dialect.

The dialects of Japan differ from one another more than the various dialects of English spoken around the world, largely because of a history of geographical barriers, poor transportation, and the policy, in force until the middle of the nineteenth century, of not allowing people to travel outside their home regions.

Some of the differences are in pronunciation: The people of Tohoku (northern Honshu) have trouble distinguishing **shi** from **su** and **chi** from **tsu,** while the people of the Kansai (Kyoto-Osaka-Kobe) area accent words according to a pattern that is almost the exact opposite of that found in the Tokyo-Yokohama area. As in English dialects, there are many differences in vocabulary: Kansai people say おおきに instead of ありがとう and ほんま instead of 本当[ほんとう], while Tohoku people say めんこい instead of かわいい. There are even differences in grammar: Kansai people attach the ending 〜へん to the negative stem instead of using the 〜ません ending, so that わかりません becomes わからへん.

Thanks to Japan's more than 100 years of compulsory education and to the spread of mass communications in the postwar years, you don't have to worry about talking to people as you travel through the country. All schools teach standard Japanese (標準語 [ひょうじゅんご]), which is basically the Tokyo dialect with a few features incorporated from the Kansai dialect. You may find individuals, especially those who grew up before the age of television, whose pronunciation and vocabulary are not what you are used to, but, by and large, the standard language you are learning in *Yookoso!* should serve you well wherever you travel in Japan.

Writing 2

Write a brief description of your community or region such as might be found in a guidebook for Japanese tourists. Include the following. If you don't know some of the things listed, either look up the information or make something up.

1. transportation to your town
2. sightseeing locations you recommend
3. hotels you recommend
4. restaurants you recommend
5. souvenirs you recommend

Language Functions and Situations

Making a Hotel Reservation

<ruby>林<rt>はやし</rt></ruby>さんが<ruby>予約係<rt>よやくがかり</rt></ruby>(*reservation clerk*)に<ruby>電話<rt>でんわ</rt></ruby>をかけています。

<ruby>予約係<rt>よやくがかり</rt></ruby>：プリンセスホテルでございます。

<ruby>林<rt>はやし</rt></ruby>：<ruby>来月<rt>らいげつ</rt></ruby>の13<ruby>日<rt>にち</rt></ruby>の<ruby>予約<rt>よやく</rt></ruby>をしたいんですが。

予約係：かしこまりました。どんな<ruby>部屋<rt>へや</rt></ruby>がよろしいでしょうか。

林：ダブル・ルームはありますか。

予約係：<ruby>申<rt>もう</rt></ruby>し<ruby>訳<rt>わけ</rt></ruby>ありませんが、ダブル・ルームはございません。

林：では、ツイン・ルームはありますか。

予約係：はい、ございます。

林：<ruby>一泊<rt>いっぱく</rt></ruby>いくらですか。

予約係：1<ruby>万<rt>まん</rt></ruby>3<ruby>千<rt>せん</rt></ruby><ruby>円<rt>えん</rt></ruby>です。

林：では、13日に<ruby>一泊<rt>いっぱく</rt></ruby>お<ruby>願<rt>ねが</rt></ruby>いします。

予約係：かしこまりました。お<ruby>名前<rt>なまえ</rt></ruby>とお<ruby>電話番号<rt>でんわばんごう</rt></ruby>をどうぞ。

林：<ruby>林正男<rt>はやしまさお</rt></ruby>です。<ruby>電話番号<rt>でんわばんごう</rt></ruby>は03-3654-7892です。<ruby>午後<rt>ごご</rt></ruby>3<ruby>時<rt>じ</rt></ruby>ごろ<ruby>着<rt>つ</rt></ruby>きます。

予約係：03-3654-7892、<ruby>林正男様<rt>はやしまさおさま</rt></ruby>、8<ruby>月<rt>がつ</rt></ruby>13<ruby>日<rt>にち</rt></ruby><ruby>一泊<rt>いっぱく</rt></ruby>ツインルームですね。お<ruby>待<rt>ま</rt></ruby>ちしております。

<ruby>様<rt>さま</rt></ruby> is an honorific title corresponding to さん、お<ruby>待<rt>ま</rt></ruby>ちしております is a humble form of <ruby>待<rt>ま</rt></ruby>っています。

Mr. Hayashi and a reservation clerk are talking on the phone   CLERK: This is the Princess Hotel. HAYASHI: I would like to make a reservation for the thirteenth of next month (*lit., but... [could you help me?]*).   CLERK: Certainly. What kind of room do you want?   HAYASHI: Do you have a double room with one bed?   CLERK: I am sorry, but we don't have any (available on that day).   HAYASHI: Then do you have a double room with two beds?   CLERK: Yes, we do.   HAYASHI: How much is it per night? CLERK: It's 13,000 yen.   HAYASHI: Then put me down for one night on the thirteenth.   CLERK: Certainly. May I have your name and telephone number?   HAYASHI: I am Masao Hayashi. My telephone number is 03-3654-7892. I will arrive around three o'clock.   CLERK: Your number is 03-3654-7892, Mr. Masao Hayashi, you'll stay one night on October thirteenth, and it's a twin room, right? We are looking forward to your visit. (*lit., We will be waiting for you.*)

Role Play

Work in pairs. One person is a reservation clerk at the Princess Hotel. The other will call the hotel and make a reservation for one or more days between the eleventh and the seventeenth of next month. The reservation clerk will answer based on the following table. The table uses the code ○ for rooms available and ● for rooms unavailable.

TYPES OF ROOM	PRICE PER NIGHT	11日	12日	13日	14日	15日	16日	17日
シングル	8,900円	○	○	○	●	●	○	○
ダブル	13,000円	○	●	○	●	○	●	○
ツイン	14,000円	○	○	●	●	●	○	○
スイート	21,000円	○	○	○	○	○	●	●

Buying a Train Ticket

東京駅で

ブラウン：あのう、次の鎌倉行きの電車は何時でしょうか。

駅員：8時21分です。

ブラウン：鎌倉に着くのは何時ですか。

駅員：10時17分です。

ブラウン：グリーン車はいくらですか。

駅員：運賃とグリーン料金合わせて、片道が1350円、往復は2500円です。

ブラウン：では、往復切符を2枚ください。

駅員：はい、5000円です。

ブラウン：何番線ですか。

駅員：3番線です。

At Tokyo Station   BROWN: Um, at what time does the next train to Kamakura leave?   CLERK: At 8:21. BROWN: What time does it arrive at Kamakura?   CLERK: At 10:17.   BROWN: How much is a first-class (*lit., green*) seat?   CLERK: The total cost of the fare and a first-class seat is 1,350 yen for a one-way ticket and 2,500 yen for a round-trip ticket.   BROWN: Then please give me two round-trip tickets.   CLERK: Yes. That will be 5,000 yen.   BROWN: Which platform does the train leave from? (*lit., What number track is it?*)   CLERK: Platform number 3. (*lit., It's track number 3.*)

Role Play

Work in pairs. Using the table, practice buying a train ticket.

行き先	発	着	番	グリーン車		普通車	
				片道	往復	片道	往復
鎌倉	8:21	10:17	3	1,350	2,500	980	1,760
	9:30	11:28	6				
茅ヶ崎	7:09	9:39	11	2,450	4,700	1,850	3.420
	8:40	11:05	5				
	9:21	11:50	7				
逗子	7:20	10:02	12	2,890	5,550	2,220	4,210
	8:15	10:45	12				
	9:00	11:40	14				

横須賀線時刻表／料金表

行き先 *destination*
片道 *one-way*
往復 *round-trip*

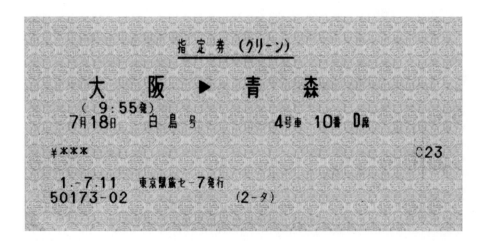

特急・寝台・指定席券申込書

必要なものを記入又つけてください。

お名前	大人 枚	乗車券	片道、往復	駅から
TEL（　）	こども 枚		学割　割引	
			その他	駅まで

| 禁煙車希望 | |

小学生はこどもの欄に記入してください。

第　1　希　望		第　2　希　望		第　3　希　望	
普通車 グリーン車 A　寝　台 B　寝　台	月　日 （列車名） 号	普通車 グリーン車 A　寝　台 B　寝　台	月　日 （列車名） 号	普通車 グリーン車 A　寝　台 B　寝　台	月　日 （列車名） 号
二　階　席 個　室	時　分発 駅から 駅まで	二　階　席 個　室	時　分発 駅から 駅まで	二　階　席 個　室	時　分発 駅から 駅まで
1人用｜2人用 3人用｜4人用		1人用｜2人用 3人用｜4人用		1人用｜2人用 3人用｜4人用	
乗り継ぎ列車	普通車 グリーン車 A　寝　台 B　寝　台	月　日 （列車名） 号	普通車 グリーン車 A　寝　台 B　寝　台	月　日 （列車名） 号	普通車 グリーン車 A　寝　台 B　寝　台	月　日 （列車名） 号
	二　階　席 個　室	時　分発 駅から 駅まで				
	1人用｜2人用 3人用｜4人用					

Listening Comprehension

1. Mr. Kobayashi, a travel agent, is conducting a survey on what kind of vacations people would like to take. Today, he is interviewing Ms. Kikuchi. Fill in the following survey sheet while listening to their conversation.

NAME _____ AGE _____

1. Which country would you most like to visit? _Tai_
2. Why would you like to visit that country? _Pretty place friends say_
3. How would you like to go to that country?

   ☐ by bus   ☐ by train   ☑ by ship   ☐ by car
   ☐ by bicycle   ☐ by plane   ☐ hitchhiking

4. Which city in that country would you most like to visit?
   Bankok.

5. Why? _pretty temples, Shopping – thai silk._

6. How would you like to travel within that country?

   ☐ by bus   ☑ by train   ☐ by ship   ☐ by car
   ☐ by bicycle   ☐ by plane   ☐ hitchhiking

7. What would you like most to do in that country?

   ☑ sightsee   ☐ visit friends   ☐ go camping
   ☑ dine out   ☐ meet local people   ☐ sports
   ☑ other _Shopping_

8. How long would you like to stay there? _1 week_
9. With whom would you like to go?

   ☑ friends   ☐ girlfriend/boyfriend   ☐ classmates
   ☐ family members   ☐ tour group   ☐ alone

10. How often do you take a vacation?

    ☑ once a year   ☐ twice a year   ☐ three times a year
    ☐ more than three times a year

11. How often do you travel for pleasure?

    ☐ once a year   ☑ twice a year   ☐ three times a year
    ☐ more than three times a year. How often? _____

12. How often do you travel on business?

    ☐ once a year   ☐ twice a year   ☑ three times a year
    ☐ more than three times a year. How often? _____

2. Ms. Sakamoto is making a reservation for her trip at a travel agency. Fill in the following table while listening to her conversation with an agent.

DAY	TRANSPORTATION	ACCOMMODATION
1		
2		
3		
4		
5		

2

第二章

家で
いえ

At Home

新しい住宅地
あたら じゅうたくち

OBJECTIVES

Topics

Houses
Furnishings and
  appliances
Household chores

Grammar

9. To do things
   like such and
   such: 〜たり…
   〜たり
10. Expressing a
    purpose:
    …ため(に)
11. Giving and
    receiving

12. Expressing
    permission:
    〜てもいい
13. Negative
    request:
    〜ないで
    ください
14. Offering
    advice:
    …ほうがいい
15. Expressing
    different states
    of actions:
    …ところ
16. Describing a
    preparatory
    action: 〜ておく

Reading and Writing

A letter to the
  aerobics class
A summer home

Language Functions and Situations

Looking for a
  house
Invitations
Offering food to a
  guest
Leave-taking

Vocabulary and Oral Activities

Houses

Vocabulary: Houses

住宅	じゅうたく	residence, housing
マンション		apartment building, condominium
団地	だんち	public housing development, apartment complex
(二)階建て	(に)かいだて	(two-)story
住む	すむ	to reside, live
庭	にわ	garden, yard
戸、ドア	と	door

Rooms in a House

玄関	げんかん	entry hall, foyer
廊下	ろうか	hallway
部屋	へや	room
居間／茶の間	いま／ちゃのま	living room
リビング・ルーム		living room
ダイニング・キッチン		eat-in kitchen (*lit., dining kitchen*)
客間／応接間	きゃくま／おうせつま	sitting room for entertaining guests
寝室	しんしつ	bedroom
浴室	よくしつ	bathing room (*room with a bathtub/shower*)
洗面所	せんめんじょ	washstand (*area with sink for washing hands and face*)
お手洗い、トイレ	おてあらい	rest room, toilet
和室、日本間	わしつ、にほんま	Japanese-style room
洋室、洋間	ようしつ、ようま	Western-style room

Building a House

建てる	たてる	to build
建築家	けんちくか	architect
大工	だいく	carpenter
天井	てんじょう	ceiling
床	ゆか	floor
屋根	やね	roof
階段	かいだん	stairway, steps

Review: アパート、家、…階、壁、キッチン、近所、…軒、狭い、台所、広い、窓

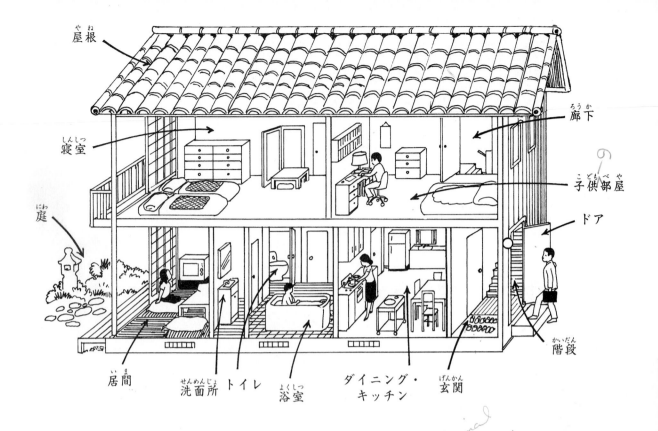

やね
屋根

しんしつ
寝室

にわ
庭

ろうか
廊下

こどもべや
子供部屋

ドア

かいだん
階段

い ま
居間

せんめんじょ
洗面所　トイレ

よくしつ
浴室

ダイニング・
キッチン

げんかん
玄関

文化ノート

ようしつ　わしつ
洋室と和室

Most houses built in Japan in recent years have both Western-style rooms (洋室[ようしつ]) and Japanese-style rooms (和室[わしつ] or 日本間[にほんま]). The Western-style rooms look similar to those found in houses in Western countries, although some minor features of the accessories and decor would be unfamiliar to the foreign visitor. No one may wear street shoes anywhere inside a Japanese house, so everyone wears slippers in the Western-style rooms or in the hallways.

Only stocking feet are permitted inside a Japanese-style room, however, because of the delicate **tatami** (畳[たたみ]) mats that cover the floor. The Japanese-style room is separated from other rooms or

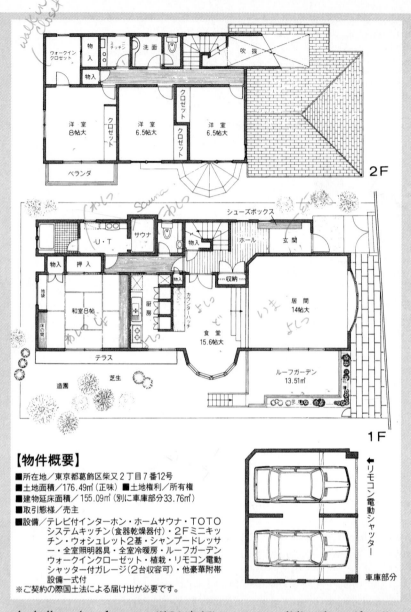

2F

1F

【物件概要】
■所在地／東京都葛飾区柴又2丁目7番12号
■土地面積／176.49㎡（正味）■土地権利／所有権
■建物延床面積／155.09㎡（別に車庫部分33.76㎡）
■取引態様／売主
■設備／テレビ付インターホン・ホームサウナ・ＴＯＴＯ
　システムキッチン（食器乾燥器付）・２Ｆミニキッ
　チン・ウォシュレット２基・シャンプードレッサ
　ー・全室照明器具・全室冷暖房・ルーフガーデン
　ウォークインクローゼット・植栽・リモコン電動
　シャッター付ガレージ（２台収容可）・他豪華附帯
　設備一式付
※ご契約の際国土法による届け出が必要です。

the hallway by a **husuma** (襖[ふすま]), or opaque sliding door. **Shooji** (障子[しょうじ]), which are made of translucent paper stretched over wooden latticework and often mounted on a sliding door, cover the windows or other sources of light. Often there is a **tokonoma** (床の間 [とこのま]), an alcove featuring a decorative scroll and a flower arrangement suitable to the season. The furniture (described more fully in the Culture Note 日本の家具 below) is low to the floor and often adaptable to multiple uses.

Although Western-style hotels and recently built small apartments have Western-style bathrooms, with the toilet, sink, and bathtub all in one room, the traditional preference is for keeping the three functions separate. The room with the deep, gas-heated bathtub is called the 浴室(よくしつ) or the お風呂; the room or area with the sink for washing one's hands and face is called the 洗面所 (せんめんじょ); and the room with the toilet is called the お手洗い(おてあらい) or the トイレ.

アクティビティー　1

ここはどこですか。(*Where is this?*)

In what part of the house are the following statements typically heard?

1. 赤ちゃん (*baby*) が寝ているから、静かにしなさい。
2. 石けん (*soap*) がもうないですよ。
3. ああ、林さん、いらっしゃい。(*Welcome!*)
4. もう8時ですよ。起きなさい。
5. お母さん！紙！
6. きれいな花ですね。
7. どうぞ食べてください。
8. お茶をどうぞ。

マンション

文化ノート

When you ask Japanese people where they live, many will say that they are living in a マンション. Don't think that all of them live in luxurious mansions, because マンション refers to condominiums, in most cases those in high-rise or multistory buildings. Besides マンション, you will see or hear many elegant-sounding foreign words referring to condominiums or housing development projects, such as アビタシオン. Foreign loanwords are used in names of condominiums, and in many product names as well, because they convey an aura of high quality to Japanese ears.

アクティビティー　2

ダイアログ：買い物をしたり、映画へ行ったりしました。(*We went shopping, went to movies, and did other things.*)

ブラウン：町田さん、先週は何をしましたか。

町田：札幌からめいが来たので、一緒に<u>買い物をしたり、映画へ行ったり</u>しました。ブラウンさんは？

ブラウン：私はテレビばかり見ていました。

町田：じゃあ、いい日本語の勉強になりましたね。

Practice the dialogue, substituting the following phrases for the underlined portions.

1. テニスをする、ビデオを見る
2. 話す、料理をする
3. レストランで食事する、ウインドーショッピングする
4. 音楽を聞く、ケーキを作る

文法ノート

ばかり

Noun + ばかり means *only (one thing)*, *nothing (or little else) but (one thing)*. ばかり is different from だけ, which also means *only*, in a significant way. Compare these sentences.

日本語だけ勉強した。
I studied only Japanese.
日本語ばかり勉強した。
I studied only Japanese and nothing else.

The first sentence simply states that the speaker studied only Japanese. The second sentence implies that the speaker studied only Japanese in spite of the fact that he or she should have studied other subjects; it implies that the speaker ignored other subjects. Because of this implication, ばかり is sometimes used to express unfairness, bias, or other negative meanings.

BROWN: Ms. Machida, what did you do over the weekend?　MACHIDA: Since my niece visited (*lit., came*) from Sapporo, <u>we went shopping, went to movies, and did other things</u> together. How about you?
BROWN: I just watched TV.　MACHIDA: Then it was good Japanese language study.

Vocabulary Library

In and Around the House

門	もん	gate
塀	へい	wall
表札	ひょうさつ	nameplate
ベル		doorbell
インターフォン		intercom
鍵(をかける)	かぎ(をかける)	key, lock; (to lock)
郵便受け	ゆうびんうけ	mailbox (*for receiving mail*)
書斎	しょさい	study
勝手口	かってぐち	back (or side) door
流し	ながし	sink
車庫	しゃこ	garage, carport
物置	ものおき	storeroom
柱	はしら	pillar
煙突	えんとつ	chimney

Loanwords: ガレージ、ダイニング・ルーム、ベランダ、バルコニー

アクティビティー 3

何をしますか。(*What do you do?*)

Ask a classmate what people typically do in the following places around the house.

[例]　玄関 → 一玄関で何をしますか。

　　　　　　一靴をぬいだり、はいたりします。or

　　　　　　一あいさつ (*greetings*) したりします。

1. 台所
2. 勉強部屋
3. 客間
4. リビングルーム
5. 庭
6. ベッドルーム
7. 洗面所
8. ダイニングルーム
9. 浴室／お風呂

アクティビティー 4

どんな家に住んでいますか。(*What type of house do you live in?*)

Answer these questions.

1. あなたの家は大きいですか。小さいですか。
2. 新しいですか。古いですか。

3. 何階建てですか。

4. いくつ部屋がありますか。

5. 寝室はいくつありますか。

6. あなたの部屋は何階にありますか。部屋は広いですか。狭いですか。

7. 部屋の天井は何色ですか。壁は何色ですか。

8. あなたの家の隣にはどんな人が住んでいますか。

9. 家のそばにどんな店がありますか。

10. 家から一番近くのバス停まで何分かかりますか。

11. あなたは家やアパートを探したことがありますか。

12. 家やアパートを探す時、どうしますか。

Describing Living Space

Even though there are many Western-style houses and apartments in Japan today, the floor area of a room is always measured by the number of **tatami** mats that would fit into it. A standard **tatami** mat measures about 1 meter by 2 meters, enough space for one person to sleep. The size can vary somewhat by region and depending on the type of building under consideration, but the ratio of length to width is always approximately 2 to 1.

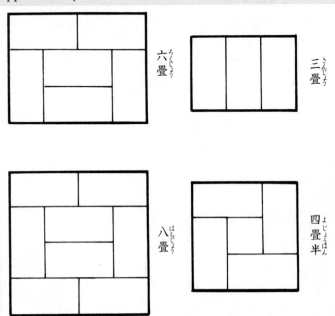

六畳　　三畳

八畳　　四畳半

The most common standard room sizes are 1, 3, 4.5, 6, 8, and 10 mats, although larger rooms do exist. Each number of mats has a standard layout. For example, the **tatami** in a 6-mat room (六畳間[ろくじょうま] or 六畳の部屋[ろくじょうのへや]) are always arranged in a pattern that results in a room measurement of 3 meters by 4 meters, and the 4.5-mat room (四畳半[よじょうはん]) is set up to measure 3 meters by 3 meters. (By the way, 六畳 is a common size for the main room of a studio apartment, and it is not unusual for rooms in boarding houses to be only 四畳半.)

Understanding this system of measurement allows you to read the real estate and rental advertisements in newspapers or in the windows of real estate agents' offices. Roman letters in advertisements refer to either a living room (L) or an eat-in kitchen (DK, from ダイニング・キッチン). A 2DK has an eat-in kitchen and two other rooms. Only the most luxurious houses have separate dining rooms.

アクティビティー　5

私[わたし]のうち、うちの近所[きんじょ] (*My house and my neighborhood*)

Work in pairs. Describe the following to your partner. If necessary, draw a picture.

1. the floor plan of your house
2. who lives in your neighborhood
3. what is in your neighborhood

[例]

1. 玄関[げんかん]を入ると、右に客間[きゃくま]、左に居間[いま]があります。…
2. うちの隣[となり]にはウイリアムさんの家族が住[す]んでいます。…
3. 家を出て右に行くと、セブン・イレブンがありす。…

Vocabulary Library

Real Estate

不動産屋	ふどうさんや	real estate agency or agent
探す	さがす	to look for
新聞広告	しんぶんこうこく	newspaper ad
住宅地	じゅうたくち	residential area
郊外	こうがい	the suburbs
住所	じゅうしょ	address
…部屋	…へや	(*counter for rooms*)

…間	…ま	(counter for rooms)
引っ越す	ひっこす	to move (from one address to another)
土地	とち	land
坪	つぼ	**tsubo** (unit of area equal to 3.3 square meters)
家主	やぬし	property or apartment owner (formal)
大家さん	おおやさん	property or apartment owner (colloquial)
借家人	しゃくやにん	tenant
貸す	かす	to rent out; to lend
借りる	かりる	to rent [from]; to borrow
家賃	やちん	rent (money)
新築	しんちく	newly built
中古	ちゅうこ	secondhand, used
(お)隣	(お)となり	next-door neighbor

Loanwords: コンドミニアム、タウンハウス、モデルルーム

でんき 電気
すいはんき 炊飯器
とけい 時計
のれん
せんぷうき 扇風機
ゆわかしき 湯沸器
でんしレンジ 電子レンジ
るすばんでんわ 留守番電話
でんわ 電話
かびん 花瓶
れいぞうこ 冷蔵庫
そうじき 掃除機

Furnishings and Appliances

Vocabulary: Furnishings and Appliances

Furnishings

家具	かぐ	furniture
本棚	ほんだな	bookshelf
たんす／タンス		chest of drawers, wardrobe
鏡	かがみ	mirror

Review: 椅子、絵、カーテン、机、テーブル

Electric Appliances

電気製品	でんきせいひん	electric appliance
留守番電話	るすばんでんわ	answering machine
電子レンジ	でんしレンジ	microwave oven
冷蔵庫	れいぞうこ	refrigerator
洗濯機	せんたくき	washing machine
エアコン、クーラー		air conditioner
スタンド		floor lamp, desk lamp
掃除機	そうじき	vacuum cleaner
炊飯器	すいはんき	rice cooker
扇風機	せんぷうき	electric fan
ミシン		sewing machine
ストーブ		space heater
電気(をつける／を消す)	でんき(をつける／をけす)	(to turn on/to turn off) a light
スイッチ(を入れる／を切る)	スイッチ(をいれる／をきる)	to turn on a switch

Review: ステレオ、テレビ、電話、時計、ラジオ

アクティビティー　6

どんな家具がありますか。どんな電気製品がありますか。(*What kind of furniture and electric appliances are located here?*)

Tell what furnishings and electric appliances are typically found in the following places.

1. 寝室
2. 浴室
3. 居間
4. 台所
5. 勉強部屋
6. ダイニング・ルーム

Discuss the furnishings and electric appliances you have at home.

アクティビティー 7

こんな時、何が必要ですか。(*What do you need on this occasion?*)

Tell what electric appliance you need on the following occasions.

1. 今日はとてもむし暑いです。
2. 部屋がきたないです。
3. 生の魚がたくさんあります。
4. 父がコーヒーを飲みたがっています。
5. 今夜見たいテレビの映画があります。でも、仕事がありますから、見られません。
6. 私のドレスがしわくちゃ (*wrinkled*) です。
7. ジョギングをしながら、音楽を聞きたいです。
8. 今日はとても寒いです。

11 象印自動コーヒーメーカー「珈琲通」
ECL-A07
9,980円

申込番号	66-5169

コーヒーのおいしさを引き出す、むらしドリップ。お手入れ簡単。「フッ素加工」の保湿プレート。
●サイズ：幅22.5×奥行19×高さ28.5cm ●重量：2kg ●消費電力：(コーヒーメーカー部)100V-650W、(ミル部)100V-130W ●容量：(コーヒーメーカー部)650ml(5カップ)、(ミル部)コーヒー豆35g(5カップ) ●メーカー希望価格：12,800円 001

12 象印氷かき＆クラッシャー「クイックアイス」
BNA-03
8,980円

申込番号	66-5177

冷蔵庫の角氷、バラ氷もそのまま使ってフラッペやクラッシュアイスがあっという間に。
●サイズ：幅22.5×奥行17.5×高さ28.5cm ●重量：1.1kg ●容量：150g/1回・1人前(角氷約10片) ●消費電力：100V-35W ●定格時間：連続10分 ●メーカー希望価格：11,800円 051

13 ブラウンスティックミキサーCAセット
MR-300CA
7,980円

申込番号	66-5185

混ぜる・練る・つぶす・泡立てる・きざむなどが簡単にできます。
●サイズ：長さ31×カッター部直径6.5・グリップ部直径6.3cm、600g(チョッパー)：高さ14.3×直径12cm、360g ●消費電力：91W ●計量カップ、壁掛けホルダー付 ●メーカー希望価格：10,000円 001

14 コロナジャー式電気ポット
DP-S30
10,800円

申込番号	66-5193

沸かしたてのお湯がたっぷり3ℓと便利な沸とうタイプ。上ぶたは着脱式でお手入れも簡単。
●サイズ：幅20.5×奥行28×高さ36.5cm ●消費電力：(湯わかし)700W、(保温)50W ●容量：3.0ℓ ●出湯方式：エアー式 ●120°回転ターンタイプ ●水量計付 ●着脱式上ぶた ●メーカー希望価格：14,800円 001

More Furnishings and Electric Appliances

屑入れ	くずいれ	trash basket
ごみ箱	ごみばこ	wastebasket
引き出し	ひきだし	drawer
棚	たな	shelf

Loanwords:カーペット、クロゼット、ソファー、ブラインド、ベッド

乾燥機	かんそうき	clothes dryer
電球	でんきゅう	light bulb
目覚まし時計	めざましどけい	alarm clock
ガスレンジ		gas stove

Loanwords:アイロン、ウォークマン、オーブン、コーヒーメーカ、
コンピュータ、シェーバー、ジューサー、トースター、ドライヤー、
ミキサー、ヒーター、ビデオレコーダー、CDプレーヤー、リモコン
(*for TV,* air conditioner, *etc.*)

文化ノート

日本の家具

Because a traditional Japanese-style room may be used for many purposes during the day, the furniture is minimal and portable. In recent years, people in Western countries have become familiar with futon-style mattresses, but the Japanese term **futon** actually refers to the entire ensemble of bedding: the folding mattress, or 敷布団 (しきぶとん); the overquilt, or 掛け布団 (かけぶとん); and the pillow, or 枕 (まくら), which is smaller than a Western-style pillow and often filled with rice husks. During the day, the **futon** is stored in the 押入れ (おしいれ), a closet with a sliding door and a single shelf at waist height, but on sunny days people like to air out their bedding in the yard or on the balcony to prevent the growth of mildew.

In a small house or apartment, the same room that serves as the bedroom by night may serve as the living room by day. A short-legged table (座卓 [ざたく]) surrounded by large square **zabuton** cushions (座布団 [ざぶとん]) or legless chairs (座椅子 [ざいす]) is the main furniture in the room. During the cold months, the 座卓 may be replaced by a **kotatsu,** a table with an electric heating element underneath and covered by a quilt and a second tabletop. Many Japanese houses and apartments lack central heating, so the **kotatsu** and ストーブ (*space heaters running on kerosene, natural gas, or electricity*), along with layered clothing, are the principal ways to keep warm.

Many families have a small Buddhist altar (仏壇 [ぶつだん]) somewhere in the house, and some have a Shinto altar (神棚 [かみだな]) as well.

Given the crowded living conditions in modern Japan, storing things is a problem, and the Japanese have devised unique solutions. It is common to see shelves above interior doorways, piled high with all sorts of possessions, placed so that they are not visible to someone glancing casually into the room. The Japanese were also pioneers in the use of closet-organizing equipment.

(勉) Study Grammar 10.

アクティビティー　8

いつ使いますか。何のために使いますか。(*When do you use it? For what purpose do you use it?*)

Useful vocabulary
かわかす *to dry*
縫う *to sew*

[例]　扇風機 → 暑い時、使います。
　　　コーヒーメーカー → コーヒーを作るために使います。

1. 洗濯機
2. ステレオ
3. カメラ
4. シェーバー
5. ヘアードライヤー

6. ワープロ
7. 掃除機
8. トースター
9. ミシン

Vocabulary Library

In a Japanese House

靴箱	くつばこ	shoe cabinet
押入れ	おしいれ	futon closet
座布団	ざぶとん	floor cushion
畳	たたみ	**tatami** (*woven reed*) mat
障子	しょうじ	**shoji** screen (*made of translucent paper*)
ふすま		sliding door of opaque paper
床の間	とこのま	alcove
こたつ		table with built-in heater

アクティビティー　9

ダイアログ：このカメラ、あげましょうか。 (*I will give you this camera.*)

山口：カワムラさんは<u>カメラ</u>を持っていますか。

カワムラ：いいえ。

山口：じゃあ。この<u>カメラ</u>、あげましょうか。

カワムラ：本当^{ほんとう}ですか。

山口：ええ、父から新^{あたら}しいのをもらったので、もうこれはいらないんです。

Practice the dialogue, substituting these items for the underlined word.

1. ワープロ　　　　　　2. ウォークマン　　　　　　3. ヘッドホン

文化ノート

Gift-Giving

Gift-giving is deeply rooted in Japanese life and society. When Japanese people travel, they are expected to bring back souvenirs for virtually everyone they know—this is one reason that Japanese tourists have a reputation for being zealous shoppers. When they visit someone's home, they bring a small gift, usually sweets or some other snack food. After receiving a gift, they have to look for or create an occasion to give a return gift. Even newly married couples are expected to give presents to everyone who attended their wedding and gave them a wedding present. This cycle of gift-giving between two parties can last a lifetime.

During the two big gift-giving seasons, in July (お中元 [ちゅうげん]) and December (お歳暮 [おせいぼ]), the Japanese give presents to all the people who have done favors for them or given them guidance, whether tangible or intangible. Thus they might give a gift to their children's teacher, their own university professor, someone who helped them get a job, their supervisor at work, or the person who introduced them to their spouse.

If you visit a Japanese home, be sure to take a small present. A small souvenir or gift-wrapped candy from your home country will be especially appreciated; or you can buy gift-wrapped packages of sweets, baked goods, or fresh fruit at department stores and special kiosks in train stations. Etiquette requires you to make some dis-

---

YAMAGUCHI: Do you have <u>a camera</u>? KAWAMURA: No. YAMAGUCHI: Well, shall I give you this <u>camera</u>? KAWAMURA: Really? YAMAGUCHI: Yes, I got a new one from my father, so I don't need this one anymore.

paraging remark about the gift as you hand it over, and the recipient will most likely offer a token refusal before accepting. In contrast to the typical Western practice, some Japanese people do not open presents immediately but wait until the giver has left, often placing the present on the family's Buddhist altar (仏壇 [ぶつだん]) temporarily. This way, they believe, the giver will not be embarrassed if the gift turns out to be defective or displeasing to the recipient.

アクティビティー　10

誰にもらいましたか。(*Whom did you receive it from?*)

Recently you moved into a new house and several relatives and friends gave you gifts. Using the following table, explain who gave what to you.

くれた人	ギフト
横井先生	スタンド　Stand
林さん	時計
チンさん	花瓶
おじ　uncle	炊飯器
おば　AUNT	トースター　toaster
大野先生	テーブルクロス　table clothe
両親　parents	テーブル　table
祖母　grandmother	電子レンジ　りょうしん
妹　younger sister	コーヒーメーカー

アクティビティー　11

お歳暮のシーズン (*Year-end gift-giving season*)

According to the following drawing, what did each person give or receive as a year-end gift? Explain in Japanese.

部長 *department head*

調味料↑ ↓そば

高田さん

加山さん　ジュース→　　辞書→　ブラウンさん
　　　　←ビール　ウィスキー←

のり *seaweed*

のり↓ ↑ワイシャツ

鈴木さん

勉 Study Grammar 12 & 13

アクティビティー 12

ダイアログ：ここに置いてもいいですか。(*May I put it here?*)

運送屋：スタンドはここに置いてもいいですか。

町田：いいえ、そこに置かないでください。このソファーの横に置いてください。

運送屋：じゃ、ソファーの横の花瓶はテーブルの上に動かしてもいいですか。

町田：ええ、そうしてください。

アクティビティー 13

引っ越し (*Moving*)

Work in pairs. One of you is in the process of moving into a new house. The other is a mover. The mover asks permission from the new resident before doing anything. The mover's job is to place the following furnishings and appliances in appropriate places in the house on the next page. Now get to work!

MOVER: May I put the floor lamp here?　MACHIDA: No, please don't put it there. Please put it next to this couch.　MOVER: Then may I move the vase that is next to the couch over to the top of the table? MACHIDA: Yes, please do that.

Useful vocabulary

置く　　　*to put, place*
動かす　　*to move* [*something*]
運ぶ　　　*to carry*

ステレオ　　　　　　　　　　テレビ
ソファー　　　　　　　　　　電話
エアコン　　　　　　　　　　テーブル
花瓶
絵　　　　　　　　　　　　　椅子
トースター　　　　　　　　　たんす
鏡　　　　　　　　　　　　　靴箱 (*shoe cabinet*)

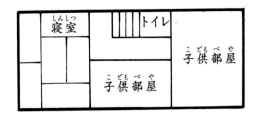

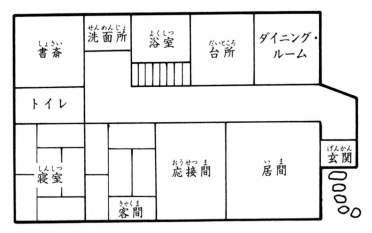

Household Chores

Vocabulary: Household Chores

家事	かじ	housework, household chores
掃除(する)	そうじ(する)	(to do) cleaning
磨く	みがく	to polish: to wipe clean a smooth surface
拭く	ふく	to wipe

洗濯(する)	せんたく(する)	(to do) laundry
洗濯物	せんたくもの	laundry (*things to be laundered*)
干す	ほす	to air-dry (something); to air (something) out
片付ける	かたづける	to straighten (something) up
縫い物(をする)	ぬいもの(をする)	(to do) sewing
アイロンをかける		to iron
庭いじり(をする)	にわいじり(をする)	(to do) gardening
直す	なおす	to repair, mend
手伝う	てつだう	to help, assist

Note the particles: シャツに
アイロンをかける *to iron a shirt*

Note the particles: 林さんの
仕事を手伝う *to help Mr.
Hayashi with his work.*

Review: 料理(する)、洗う、皿、買い物

勉 Study Grammar 14.

アクティビティー 14

ダイアログ：すぐ掃除したほうがいいですよ。(*You should clean it immediately.*)

ギブソン：わあ、すごいほこりですね。
　　林：しばらく掃除していないんです。

ギブソン：すぐ掃除したほうがいいですよ。このにおいは何ですか。
　　林：しばらく皿も洗っていないんです。

ギブソン：早く洗ったほうがいいですよ。

アクティビティー 15

家事！家事！家事！(*Chores! Chores! Chores!*)

What advice will you give in the following situations?

[例]　すごいほこりです。→ 掃除をしたほうがいいですよ。

1. 今夜食べるものがありません。
2. テーブルの上によごれた食器がたくさんあります。
3. 洗濯物がたまりました (*piled up*)。
4. 服がしわくちゃ (*wrinkled*) です。
5. お父さんの靴がきたないです。
6. セーターに穴があいています(*a hole has developed*)。
7. 床に本や新聞がちらかっています (*are scattered*)。
8. 窓ガラスがきたないです。

GIBSON: Wow, look at this dust! (*lit., It is terrible dust, isn't it?*)　HAYASHI: I haven't cleaned [my room]
for a while.　GIBSON: You should clean it immediately. What's this smell?　HAYASHI: I haven't washed
the dishes for a while, either.　GIBSON: You should wash them right away (*lit., quickly*).

Vocabulary and Oral Activities

アクティビティー 16

ダイアログ：部屋の掃除をしているところです。(*I am in the midst of cleaning my room.*)

カワムラ：大助さん、何をしているんですか。
山口：部屋の掃除をしているところです。
カワムラ：ガールフレンドが来るんですね。
山口：よくわかりましたね。
カワムラ：ええ、大助さんはガールフレンドが来る時しか、部屋を掃除しませんからね。

文法ノート

しか...ない

As you already know, you can use だけ to express the concept of *only* or *just.*

> 5ドルだけあります。
> *I have just 5 dollars.*
> カワムラさんだけ来ました。
> *Only Mr. Kawamura came.*
> ギブソンさんだけに会いました。
> *I met only Ms. Gibson.*

Another construction, noun しか... verb ない, also expresses the idea of *only* or *just.* しか replaces the particles は, が, and を. Here are some examples of its use.

> 5ドルしかありません。
> *I have just 5 dollars.*
> カワムラさんしか来ませんでした。
> *Just Mr. Kawamura came.*
> ギブソンさんにしか会いませんでした。
> *I met only Ms. Gibson.*

There is a subtle difference between the two ways of saying *only.* The だけ construction implies that the subject has only a certain amount of something, or did only a certain thing, but that it is sufficient. For example, ギブソンさんだけに会いました implies that you met only

---

KAWAMURA: Daisuke, what are you doing? YAMAGUCHI: I'm in the midst of cleaning my room.
KAWAMURA: Your girlfriend's coming, right? YAMAGUCHI: How did you know? (*lit., You understood well.*) KAWAMURA: Well, you clean your room only when your girlfriend comes.

Ms. Gibson, but she was the only person you were supposed to meet anyway.

The しか…ない construction, on the other hand, implies that whatever the subject did or has is insufficient. ギブソンさんにしか会いませんでした implies that you expected to meet someone else or were expected to meet someone else but for some reason did not.

If you find the negative construction confusing, you may want to think of it as meaning *except*, as in *I don't have anything except 5 dollars. Nobody except Mr. Kawamura came. I didn't meet anyone except Ms. Gibson.*

アクティビティー 17

料理しているところです。(*I am cooking now.*)

Work in pairs. One of you is in the place indicated doing household chores. The other walks in and asks what you are doing there. Answer, following the example.

[例]　台所　→　—台所で何をしているんですか。
　　　　　　　—料理をしているところです。

PLACE	POSSIBLE CHORES
台所	料理をする 皿を洗う
ダイニング・キッチン	テーブルの上を片付ける
居間	アイロンをかける 窓をふく 縫い物をする
洗面所	洗濯をする 鏡を磨く
庭	庭いじりをする 花 (flower) に水をやる 洗濯物を干す
玄関	靴を磨く 掃除をする
家の前	ゴミ (garbage, trash) を出す

Vocabulary and Oral Activities

Now practice following these examples.

　　　—これから何をするんですか。
　　　—家の前に水をまくところです。

　　　—家の前で何をしていたんですか。
　　　—水をまいたところです。

アクティビティー　18

ダイアログ：洗濯をしてくれました。(*She did laundry for me.*)
　　三村：ブラウンさん、風邪をひいて、寝ていたそうですね。
　ブラウン：ええ、一週間寝ていました。
　　三村：それはたいへんでしたね。
　ブラウン：ええ、でも佐野さんの奥さんが洗濯をしたり、食事を作ったりして
　　　　　くれました。
　　三村：そうですか。親切な大家さんですね。

アクティビティー　19

何をしてあげますか。(*What are you going to do for him/her?*)

One of your classmates is sick in bed and has been unable to do any household chores for two weeks. What will you do to help out? Choose from your ill classmate's to-do list, which follows.

[例]　　—オルテガさんは何をしてあげますか。
　　　　—洗濯をしてあげます。

```
TO DO
■ 洗濯をする
■ 買い物をする
■ アイロンをかける
■ テーブルの上を片付ける
■ 花に水をやる
■ 皿を洗う
■ 窓を磨く
■ トイレを掃除する
```

MIMURA: Ms. Brown, I heard that you were in bed with the flu.　　BROWN: Yes, I stayed in bed for a week.
MIMURA: That must have been awful.　　BROWN: Yes, but Ms. Sano did laundry and cooked for me.　　MIMURA: Is that right? She's a good landlady, isn't she?

After each member of the class offers to help, pair up and discuss with a classmate who will do what.

[例] ——誰が掃除をしてくれますか。
　　——ジャクソンさんに掃除をしてもらいます。

Study Grammar 16.

アクティビティー　20

ビールを買っておきましょう。(*I'll buy beer ahead of time.*)

カワムラ：今夜はお客さんが来るんですか。

　山口：ええ、主人の会社の人たち。ビールをたくさん買っておきましょう。

カワムラ：ぼくが買ってきてあげましょう。

　山口：そう、助かるわ。

アクティビティー　21

お客さんが来ます (*Guests are coming.*)

What do you do to prepare for receiving guests at home? Tell what each person in your family (or a typical family) does, choosing from the following list.

窓をふく

客間を掃除する

テーブルの上を片付ける

廊下を磨く

料理をする

座布団を出す

ビールを買う

ビールを冷蔵庫に入れる

KAWAMURA: Are guests coming tonight?　YAMAGUCHI: Yes, some people from my husband's company. I'm going to buy lots of beer.　KAWAMURA: I'll go buy beer for you.　YAMAGUCHI: Really? That would help me out.

Grammar and Exercises

9. To Do Things Like Such and Such: 〜たり … 〜たり

町田：昨日のパーティーはどうでしたか。
ブラウン：とても楽しかったです。歌を歌ったり、踊ったりしました。
町田：カワムラさんも行ったんですか。
ブラウン：ええ、友だちと話したりしていました。
カワムラ：大助さん、会社の仕事のほうはどうですか。
山口：忙しかったり、暇だったりです。
カワムラ：英語の勉強のほうはどうですか。
山口：したり、しなかったりです。

9.1 The 〜たり … 〜たり construction expresses such meanings as *do this, do that, and do others like them; do these things, among other similar activities.* Thus it is used to express only representative actions or states, with the implication that there are additional related actions or states not mentioned explicitly.

Plain Past Verb, + り、	
Plain Past i- or na-adjective + り	} + する or だ

昨日は日本語を勉強したり、部屋を掃除したりしました。
Yesterday, I studied Japanese and cleaned my room, among other things.

Because the plain, past form of many verbs and all adjectives ends in た, this pattern is often called the たり、たり construction.

MACHIDA: How was yesterday's party?   BROWN: It was a lot of fun. We sang songs, danced, and did that sort of thing.   MACHIDA: Did Mr. Kawamura go too?   BROWN: Yes, he was talking with friends and stuff. (*i.e., I saw him there.*)

KAWAMURA: Daisuke, how is your work at the company?   YAMAGUCHI: We're sometimes busy, sometimes not.   KAWAMURA: How is your English study?   YAMAGUCHI: I sometimes study (*lit., do it*) and sometimes don't.

In most cases, two actions or states are expressed in this construction, but you can express more than two (usually three), as shown in the following examples, or only one, as in the last line of the first dialogue. The tense of the actions or states is determined by that of the sentence-final する or だ, whether expressed or implicit.

休みの日は、洗濯をしたり、掃除をしたり、買い物をしたりする。
On my days off, I do laundry, cleaning, shopping, and other such things.

Whatever the number of actions or states, they don't necessarily occur in the order given, unlike the 〜て...〜て construction.

昨日は洗濯をして、掃除をして、それから買い物をしました。
Yesterday, I did laundry, then cleaning, and then shopping. (Also implied is that the speaker didn't do any major activities other than these.)

9.2 When you use the affirmative and negative form of a predicate in this construction, it means *sometimes yes, sometimes no.* When an inconsistent state is described, the copula だ is used in place of する after 〜たり、〜たり.

牛乳は飲んだり、飲まなかったりです。
I sometimes drink milk and sometimes don't.
私の作る料理はおいしかったり、おいしくなかったりだ。
The food I cook is sometimes delicious, sometimes not.

A pair of verbs with contrastive or related meanings is often used in this construction, too, implying that the two actions or states, which are usually opposites, have been alternating.

子供が何度も家を出たり、入ったりしました。
The children kept going in and out of the house.

練習	1

Following the example, complete the sentences using 〜たり...〜たり. Don't forget to omit the incompatible activity.

[例] 東京では（東京タワーを見る、銀座へ行く、シアーズタワーへ行く）しました。→
東京では東京タワーを見たり、銀座へ行ったりしました。

1. 冬は（海で泳ぐ、スキーをする、スケートをする）します。
2. パーティーでは（お酒を飲む、踊る、手紙を書く）した。
3. お客さんが来るので、（部屋の掃除をする、学校へ行く、料理をする）しました。
4. 大学では（クラスに出る、友だちと話す、朝早く起きる）する。
5. 音楽が好きなので、（タイプする、コンサートへ行く、レコードを聞く）します。

6. 自分の (one's own) 部屋でいつも（勉強する、テニスをする、本を読む）
します。
7. 昨日は（晴れる、雨が降る、強い風が吹く）して、ひどい (terrible) お天気
でした。
8. リゾートでは（テニスをする、ゴルフをする、電車に乗る）することが
できます。

<table>
<tr><td>練習</td><td>2</td></tr>
</table>

Following the example, answer these questions.

[例] 毎日、ごはんを食べますか。→
いいえ、食べたり、食べなかったりです。

1. 毎朝、ジョギングをしますか。
2. 毎週、両親に手紙を書きますか。
3. 毎週、うちに電話しますか。
4. 毎日、暇ですか。
5. あの先生はいつもやさしいんですか。
6. いつも早く起きるんですか。
7. この町はいつも静かなんですか。

<table>
<tr><td>練習</td><td>3</td></tr>
</table>

Fill in the blanks using 〜たり...〜たり.

1. 旅行へ行くので、＿＿＿ しました。
2. ＿＿＿ したので、病気になった。
3. 先週の日曜日は、＿＿＿ した。
4. ＿＿＿ したので、疲れました。
5. 京都では ＿＿＿ しました。
6. 日本語のクラスでは ＿＿＿ します。

10. Expressing a Purpose: ...ため(に)

カーティス：三村さん、最近たばこをすいませんね。
三村：ええ、新しいステレオを買うために、お金を貯めているんです。
カーティス：健康のためじゃないんですか。

CURTIS: Mr. Mimura, you aren't smoking cigarettes these days, are you?　　MIMURA: No, I'm saving money in order to buy a new stereo.　　CURTIS: It's not for the sake of your health?

ブラウン：高田さんはどこかへ出かけたんですか。

佐野：ええ、会議に出るために、京都へ行きました。

ブラウン：いつ帰ってくるんですか。

佐野：あさってです。ブラウンさんのために、おみやげを買ってくるって
言っていましたよ。

ブラウン：わあ、うれしい。

10.1 The combination of a noun or verb + the noun ため forms an adverbial phrase expressing purpose.

> Noun + の
> Verb (plain, nonpast) } + ため(に)

in order to [do something]
for the sake of [someone, something]

林さんのために、ケーキを作った。
I made a cake for Mr. Hayashi.

テレビを見るために、居間へ行った。
In order to watch TV, I went to the living room.

The following construction modifies a noun as an adjectival phrase.

> Noun + の
> Verb (plain, nonpast) } + ため + の

for [the purpose of doing something]
for [the sake of someone or something]

これは子供のためのゲームです。
This is a game for children.

これはお茶を飲むための茶わんです。
This is a cup for drinking Japanese tea.

BROWN: Did Mr. Takada go somewhere?　SANO: Yes, he went to Kyoto in order to attend a meeting.
BROWN: When will he come back?　SANO: The day after tomorrow. He said that he would buy a souvenir for you.　BROWN: Wow, I'm glad to hear that.

10.2 ため is a noun meaning *purpose, benefit, reason, cause.* When ため(に) is used to mean *because*, it may be preceded by plain, past, or nonpast forms of verbs and adjectives, or by the pronoun forms of the copula.

試験があった (or ある) ために、コンサートへ行けませんでした。
Because there was an exam, I couldn't go to the concert.
あまりにも高い (or 高かった) ため、そのセーターは買いませんでした。
Because it was too expensive, I didn't buy that sweater.
英語が下手なため、彼の言っていることがわからない。
Because he is bad at English, I cannot understand what he is saying.
あまりにも静かだった (or 静かな) ため、人がいるとは思わなかった。
Because it was so quiet, I didn't think that anyone was there.

When ため is used to express reason or cause, it can be replaced with から or ので in most cases, with little change in meaning other than that ため sounds somewhat more formal.

練習　　　　　　　　　　1

Combine the two sentences using ため(に). (All questions are concerned with purpose.)

[例]　チンさんは昼ごはんを食べます。レストランへ行きました。→
　　　チンさんは昼ごはんを食べるために、レストランへ行きました。

1. フランス語を勉強します。パリへ行くことにしました。
2. 日本語を練習します。日本人の友だちをたくさん作りました。
3. 漢字の意味 (meaning) を調べます (to check)。辞書を使いました。
4. 山本さんに会います。喫茶店で待ちます。
5. スキーをします。北海道へ行きました。
6. トイレを使います。デパートに入りました。
7. コーヒーを飲みます。喫茶店に入りました。

練習　　　　　　　　　　2

Complete these sentences explaining how you would accomplish each purpose or what the result of the reason given would be.

1. 日本語がまだ下手なため、
2. 夕ごはんを作るため、
3. アパートを借りる (to rent) ため、
4. 部屋が狭いため、
5. おいしいコーヒーを飲むため、
6. 雪が降らないため、
7. パーティーをするために、
8. 試験のために、

11. Giving and Receiving

ブラウン：明日は三村さんの誕生日ですね。

町田：そうですね。何かあげますか。

ブラウン：ええ、ネクタイをあげようと思います。

町田：そうですか。じゃあ、私はネクタイ・ピンをあげることにします。

高田：昨日、村山さんの部屋へ行ったら、りんごをくれました。

ブラウン：村山さんはよくいろいろなものをくれますね。

高田：ええ、今度は私も何かあげないといけませんね。

カーティス：今年一年、大野先生にはお世話になりましたね。

チン：そうですね。お礼に何かさしあげましょうか。

カーティス：大野先生はお酒がお好きだから、ウイスキーをさしあげませんか。

チン：それはいい考えですね。

チン：大野先生にウイスキーをさしあげたら、とても喜んで、私たちに辞書を一冊ずつくださいました。

カーティス：本当ですか。

チン：カーティスさん、これはあなたの辞書です。

カーティス：わあ、いただいてもいいんでしょうか。

佐野：ブラウンさん、私が買い物をしてあげますから、寝ていてください。

ブラウン：でも、ご迷惑でしょう。

佐野：洗濯もしてあげますよ。

ブラウン：そんなことまでしてもらってはこまります。

佐野：ブラウンさんはゆっくり休んで、早く元気になってください。

BROWN: Tomorrow is Mr. Mimura's birthday, isn't it? MACHIDA: That's right. Will you give him something? BROWN: Yes, I'm thinking I'll give him a necktie. MACHIDA: Really? Then, I will (*lit., will decide to*) give him a tie pin.

TAKADA: When I went to Ms. Murayama's place (*lit., room*) yesterday, she gave me some apples. BROWN: Ms. Murayama always gives us various things. TAKADA: Yes, next time I (really) must give her something too.

CURTIS: We've been well taken care of by Professor Oono all year. CHIN: We sure have. Let's give him something as a token of our gratitude. CURTIS: Professor Oono likes liquor, so shall we give him whiskey? CHIN: That's a good idea.

CHIN: When I gave the whiskey to Professor Oono, he was very pleased and gave a dictionary to each of us. CURTIS: Really? CHIN: Mr. Curtis, this is your dictionary. CURTIS: Wow! Do you think it's all right to accept (*lit., receive*) this from him?

SANO: Ms. Brown, I'll do the shopping for you, so please stay in bed. BROWN: But it would be too much trouble for you. SANO: I'll do your laundry, too. BROWN: I would feel bad if you did that much for me. SANO: Please rest up and get well soon.

山口さとみ：ねえ、お父さん、新しい靴買ってくれる？

山口健次：先月、買ってやっただろう。

山口さとみ：でも、駅前の靴屋でいいのを見つけたのよ。

山口健次：お母さんに買ってもらいなさい。

ずつ

ずつ preceded by a number + counter or by a word expressing quantity means *each, of each, at a time.*

女子学生と男子学生が、8人ずついます。
There are eight female students and eight male students.
   (*lit., There are eight each of female and male students.*)

みんなにノートを一冊ずつあげよう。
I will give everyone one notebook each.

少しずつわかってきました。
I have come to understand gradually (lit., a little at a time).

11.1 Japanese expressions for giving and receiving are very different from those in English. Suppose that Mr. Mimura gave a book to me. Thus, Mr. Mimura is a giver and I am a receiver. If the giver is the subject, you say

   1. Mr. Mimura gave a book to me.

If the receiver is the subject, you say

   2. I received a book from Mr. Mimura, or
   3. I was given a book by Mr. Mimura.

11.2 In Japanese, there are five verbs corresponding to *to give* and two verbs corresponding to *to receive*. The choice of verbs to describe giving and receiving in Japanese depends on the social relationship between the giver and the receiver, specifically, whether or not they belong to the same social group (family, colleagues, etc.). The constraints on the social relationship can be summarized as follows.

   1. GがRにXをあげる *G gives X to R*

SATOMI YAMAGUCHI: Say, Dad, would you buy me a new pair of shoes?   KENJI YAMAGUCHI: I bought you some last month, didn't I?   SATOMI YAMAGUCHI: I found a good pair in a shoe store in front of the station.   KENJI YAMAGUCHI: Have your mother buy them for you.

The Giver can be anyone (typically, speaker or in-group person). The Recipient cannot include the speaker. The Giver and the Recipient are socially equal.

私はあなた／彼にこの本をあげます。

あなたはこの本を彼にあげますか。

彼は彼女に本をあげました。

2. GがRにXをくれる　*G gives X to R*

The Recipient is the speaker or an in-group person, someone closer to the speaker than the Giver. The Giver is socially equal or inferior to the Recipient.

あなたは／彼は[私に]本をくれました。

彼女は弟に本をくれましたか。

彼もあなたに本をくれました。

in group.
speaker is referenced.

3. RがGに(から)Xをもらう　*R receives X from G*

The Recipient can be anyone. The Giver is socially equal or inferior to the Recipient.

私はあなた／彼に本をもらいました。

あなたも彼から本をもらいましたか。

彼は彼女に本をもらいました。

彼は私からその本をもらったんです。

In Pattern 1, when the Recipient is an in-group superior person or an out-group person, さしあげる is used instead of あげる. In Patterns 2 and 3, when the Giver is an in-group superior person or an out-group person, くださる and いただく are used instead of くれる and もらう, respectively.

私は先生に本をさしあげました。
I gave a book to my professor.

先生は[私に]本をくださいました。
My professor gave me a book.

私は先生から本をいただきました。
I was given a book by my professor.

Because くれる and くださる always mean *give to me* or *give to my group*, you do not have to add 私に unless you are emphasizing the *to me* part.

In Pattern 1, when the Recipient is notably inferior to the Giver, やる is used.

私は犬にドッグフードをやりました。
I gave some dog food to my dog.

ブラウンさんは花に水をやった。
Ms. Brown watered the flowers. (lit., Ms. Brown gave water to the flowers.)

It must be noted that many Japanese consider やる to be a vulgar word, so they use あげる even to dogs or flowers.

Grammar and Exercises

109 百九

11.3 Doing something for the sake or the benefit of someone else is considered in Japanese to be the same as giving and receiving a benefit. Such benefactive acts are expressed by attaching the te-form of verbs to the expressions of giving and receiving in **Grammar 11.2.**

Te-form of verb +
$$\left\} \begin{array}{l} あげる、さしあげる、やる \\ くれる、くださる \\ もらう、いただく \end{array} \right.$$

The choice of verbs follows the same rules as discussed above.

[私は]山本さんの車を洗ってあげました。
I washed Ms. Yamamoto's car for her.

[私は]先生のかばんを持ってさしあげました。
I carried my professor's bag for him.

弟の宿題を見てやりました。
I looked over my brother's homework.

三村さんは日本語を教えてくれました。
Mr. Mimura taught me Japanese.

私は佐野さんにアイロンをかけてもらいました。
I had Ms. Sano do my ironing.

文化ノート

義理

The word 義理 refers to the duties and obligations people have to carry out in order to maintain harmonious relations with others and fulfill their roles in society, whether they like it or not. For example, employees have 義理 toward their employers in the sense that they are expected to work hard, be honest, and always think of the company's interests; the employers have 義理 toward their employees in the sense that they are expected to treat them fairly and look out for their welfare in an almost paternalistic way. 義理 is contrasted with 人情 (にんじょう), which is what people's emotions or gut feelings tell them to do, and which is often in conflict with their social duties.

As a foreign resident or visitor, you are most likely to hear the term 義理 in one of two contexts. The first is in the terms for one's in-laws: 義理の父, 義理の母, and so on, the idea being that people are obligated to treat the family of their spouse the same way that they treat their own family. The second common use of 義理 has developed more recently. Around Valentine's Day, you will hear the term 義理

チョコ. In Japan, Valentine's Day is now a day on which young women give chocolate to their boyfriends, but 義理チョコ is the less expensive chocolate that young women give to their male colleagues at work or their male classmates at school, not because they are romantically interested in them but because they want to maintain a good work relationship.

練習　　　　1

Look at the following picture and complete the following sentences, taking Masao Hayashi's point of view.

[例]　町田さんは、セーターをくれました。

1. カワムラさんは、
2. 横井先生は、
3. 母は、

4. 犬のポチに、
5. 母に、
6. 横井先生に、

7. カワムラさんに、
8. 町田さんに、

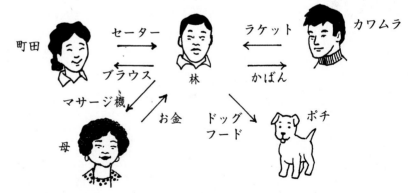

Answer these questions.

9. カワムラさんから何をもらいましたか。
10. 町田さんから何をもらいましたか。
11. 横井先生から何をいただきましたか。
12. お母さんから何をもらいましたか。

Fill in the blanks with the most appropriate verb of giving or receiving.

1. 私は毎年クリスマスには家族にプレゼントをします。去年は父にシェーバーを
（　　　　）。母にはスカーフを（　　　　）。妹にはアイロンを（　　　）ました
し、弟にはラジカセを（　　　　）。家族のみんなも私にプレゼントを（　　　　）。
父は私にペンを（　　　）ましたし、母は時計を（　　　　）。弟からは
スニーカーを（　　　　）。妹からは本を（　　　　）。

2. 先日、私は友人の山下さんから今年の10月に結婚するという手紙を（　　　　）。
山下さんにはいつもお世話になっていますし、私が結婚した時も、トースター
を（　　　）ので、何かいい電気製品を（　　　）つもりです。会社の
佐藤さんに話したら、佐藤さんも何かいい電気製品を（　　　）つもりだと
言っていました。

3. 先日、先生がクラスで日本の映画を見せて（　　　　）。とてもおもしろい映画
でした。それで友だちにその映画について話して（　　　　）。

Answer these questions.

1. 今年のクリスマスに一番もらいたいものは何ですか。
2. 今年のクリスマスにみんなに何をあげますか。
3. お母さんの誕生日に何をあげるつもりですか。
4. 結婚する友だちに何をあげますか。
5. 病気で寝ている友だちに何をしてあげますか。
6. 今、だれかにしてもらいたいことはありますか。

12. Expressing Permission: 〜てもいい

カワムラ：お仕事中ですか。

山口：ええ、明日の用意をしているんです。

カワムラ：テレビを見てもいいでしょうか。じゃまになりませんか。

山口：いいえ、もうすぐ終わりますから。

KAWAMURA: Are you working now?　　YAMAGUCHI: Yes, I am preparing for tomorrow.　　KAWAMURA: May I watch TV? Does it interfere with your work? (*lit, Won't it become a bother?*)　　YAMAGUCHI: No, because I'll be finished soon.

カワムラ：ここに座ってもよろしいですか。
女の人：すみません。連れの者が来ますので、...
カワムラ：じゃ、そちらの席に座ってもよろしいでしょうか。
女の人：ええ、こちらは空いていますよ。

...中

中, attached to a noun, makes a word meaning *in the middle of [something]*, *in progress*. For example,

食事中	*eating now*
工事中	*under construction* (工事 = *construction*)
準備中	*in preparation* (準備 = *preparation*)
営業中	*open for business* (営業 = *business operation*)
会議中	*meeting in progress* (会議 = *meeting*)
話し中	*[telephone] is busy*
使用中	*in use* (使用 = *use*)
仕事中	*working now*
休暇中	*on vacation*
外出中	*out [of the office, etc.]*

高田はただいま会議中です。
Takada is now at a meeting.
仕事中、どうもすみませんが、ちょっとここに来てください。
I am sorry for interrupting your work, but can you come here for a while?

日本料理の店の前で：
準備中です。

KAWAMURA: May I sit here?   WOMAN: Excuse me, my companion is coming, so . . . .   KAWAMURA:
Then may I take that seat?   WOMAN: Yes, this one is free.

Grammar and Exercises

You can often see the sign 準備中 in front of stores and restaurants in Japan. In most cases, they are closed and no one is inside, because this sign is used to mean *closed*.

12.1 When you ask for permission, use the following construction.

$$\text{Te-form of verb} + \text{も} \left\{ \begin{array}{l} \text{いい？} \\ \text{いいですか。} \\ \text{かまいませんか。} \\ \text{いいでしょうか。} \\ \text{よろしいでしょうか。} \end{array} \right\} \begin{array}{l} \text{in increasing} \\ \text{order of} \\ \text{politeness} \end{array}$$

| This も may be dropped.

May I [do something]?

この辞書を使ってもいい？
May I use this dictionary?
たばこをすってかまいませんか。
May I smoke?
2、3日休みを取ってもよろしいでしょうか。
May I take two or three days off?

| The te-form of verb + も means *even if* ... Thus this construction literally means *Is it OK even if . . . ?*

コミュニケーション・ノート

Responding to a Request for Permission

このペンを使ってもいいですか。
May I use this pen?

GRANTING PERMISSION

ええ、どうぞ。
Yes, please.
ええ、けっこうですよ。
Yes, it's all right.
ええ、もちろんです。
Yes, of course.
ええ、ご自由に。
Yes, as you like it.
ええ、どうぞお使いください。
Yes, please use it.

百十四
114

At Home

The affirmative counterpart of the above construction is used to grant permission.

ソファーをここに動かしてもいいですよ。
You may move the couch here.
好きなだけ使ってかまいません。
Please use it as much as you like.

好きなだけ is an idiomatic expression meaning *as much as you like.*

12.2 When this constuction appears before から and is followed by a wish, command, or request, the speaker is stating that he or she is accepting a possibly unfavorable limitation.

高くてもいいから、その絵がほしい。
It's OK even if it is expensive; I want that picture.
水でもいいから、ください。
It's OK even if it is water, so please give it to me.
一度でもいいからあそこへ行ってみたい。
I want to try going there, even if it's just once.

12.3 Interrogatives (such as 何、だれ、いつ、どこ、いつ、どう and いくら) + te-form of the verb + てもいい mean *it is all right no matter what/who/where/when/ how/ how much.*

何を食べてもいいですよ。
You may eat anything.
いつ帰ってもかまいません。
You may leave anytime.
ここは誰が来てもいいです。
Anyone can come here. (lit., It is all right whoever comes here.)

12.4 The negative te-form of a verb followed by (も)いい means *you need not [do something]* or *you don't have to [do something]*; literally, *it is all right if [you don't do something].*

ここはお金を払わなくてもいいです。
You don't have to pay here.

この仕事をしなくてもいいですか。
Is it all right even if I don't do this work?
お母さん、このにんじん、食べなくてもいいでしょう?
Mother, is it OK not to eat this carrot?

練習　　　　　　　　1

Change these sentences to requests for permission, using 〜てもいいですか.

[例]　クレジット・カードを使う → クレジット・カードを使ってもいいですか。

1. お風呂に入る
2. ちょっと遅れる (*to be late*)
3. このビールを飲む
4. ペンを借りる
5. ここに名前を書く
6. 映画に行く
7. ちょっと休む
8. 帽子をかぶる
9. 靴を脱がない
10. 町田さんと話さない

練習　　　　　　　　2

Complete the following sentences by using てもいいですよ.

1. 疲れている時は、
2. おなかがすいた時は、
3. このホテルでは、
4. 家の中では、
5. 雨が降った時は、
6. 病気の時は、
7. 電車が遅れた時は、
8. お金がない時は、

13. Negative Request: 〜ないでください

> カワムラ：林さん、じゃあ、また明日。
> 林：明日? 明日は休みでしょう?
> カワムラ：もう忘れたんですか。明日は三村さんの誕生日パーティーがあるでしょう。
> 林：ああ、ああ、すっかり忘れていました。
> カワムラ：ケーキを買って来るのを忘れないでくださいね。

KAWAMURA: Mr. Hayashi, see you tomorrow.　HAYASHI: Tomorrow? Tomorrow is a holiday, isn't it?
KAWAMURA: You have already forgotten? There is a birthday party for Mr. Mimura tomorrow, isn't there?
HAYASHI: Yes, I had totally forgotten about it.　KAWAMURA: Please don't forget to buy a cake.

カワムラ：ちょっと、すみません。そこに車を止めないでください。
男の人：あっ、すみません。すぐに動かします。

13.1 The following construction is used to express a negative request.

Negative te-form of verb +	くださいませんか ください くれ	in decreasing order of politeness

Please don't [do something]

くれ is used only by male speakers giving orders to close friends, family members, or subordinates.

> それはブラウンさんには言わないでくださいませんか。(very polite)
> *Please don't say that to Ms. Brown.*
> そこにすわらないでください。
> *Please don't sit there.*
> もう電話しないでくれ。
> *Don't call me anymore.*

13.2 In informal speech、ください is often omitted.

> そんなに食べないで。
> *Please don't eat that much.*
> そこで遊ばないでね。
> *Please don't play here.*
> そんなこと言わないでよ。
> *Don't say such a thing.*

It is sometimes easy to confuse the negative te-form of the verb, ~ないで, with the te-form of the ~ない form of the verb, which is ~なくて. The ~ないで form is used mostly in negative commands and in the meaning of *without doing:* 勉強しないで試験を受けた *Took the test without studying.* The ~なくて form is used in other constructions, such as ~なくては いけない, ~なくてもいい, and a few others that you haven't studied yet.

KAWAMURA: Excuse me. Please don't park your car there.　MAN: Oh, I'll move my car immediately.

どうぞ遠慮しないでください。

As you learned before, Japanese people typically refuse when they are first offered food, gifts, and favors. The person who is offering these things then says, どうぞ遠慮しないでください (*Please don't hold back,* or *Please don't hesitate*). Notice how it is used in these situations.

PRESENTING AND ACCEPTING A GIFT

—あのう、これつまらないものですが、どうぞ。
—*Uh, this is a trifling thing, but please accept it.*
—いいえ、そんな...
—*No, this kind of thing . . . [won't do].*
—どうぞ遠慮しないでください。
—*Please take it. (lit., Please don't hold back.)*
—そうですか。では、ありがとうございます。
—*Really? Well, thank you very much.*

OFFERING AND ACCEPTING A MEAL

—なにもありませんが、どうぞ召し上がってください。
—*We don't have anything [special], but please go ahead and eat.*
—いいえ、どうぞおかまいなく。
—*No, please don't trouble yourself over me.*
—どうぞ遠慮しないでください。
—*Please help yourself.*
—そうですか。では、いただきます。
—*Really? Then I will have some.*

召し上がる is the honorific form of 食べる.

どうぞおかまいなく is a phrase used for polite refusals, not for sincere refusals.

練習　　　　　1

Where do you think you would hear these warnings or admonitions?

1. ＿＿ ここに車を止めないでください。
2. ＿＿ ここに入らないでください。
3. ＿＿ たばこを吸わないでください。
4. ＿＿ ごみを捨てないでください。
   (*Please don't litter.*)
5. ＿＿ 座らないでください。
6. ＿＿ ここで泳がないでください。

a. in front of a garage
b. at a filthy beach
c. in a hospital waiting room
d. on a construction site
e. on a just-painted bench
f. in a park

Change these sentences to negative commands by using ～ないでください.

1. 教室の中で、ものを食べる
2. ベッドの中で、たばこを吸う
3. このセーターは洗濯機で洗う
4. ここでお酒を飲む
5. たくさんお金を使う
6. クラスを休む
7. 夜、電話する
8. うちに来る

14. Offering Advice: ...ほうがいい

ギブソン：来月、箱根[1]に行こうと思うんですが、どの旅館がいいですか。
町田：箱根旅館がいいですよ。でも、来月はこみますから、早く予約したほうがいいですよ。
ギブソン：そうですか。電車の切符も早く買ったほうがいいですか。
町田：ええ。

山口：この部屋、昼間でもちょっと暗いんです。どうしたらいいでしょうか。
大工：ううん、この窓をもう少し大きくしたほうがいいですね。
山口：壁の色はどうでしょうか。
大工：そうですね。もう少し明るい色に変えたほうがいいと思います。

The construction on the following page is used to offer advice or make a strong suggestion.

GIBSON: I'm thinking of going to Hakone next month. Which inn [do you think] is good?　MACHIDA: Hakone Inn is good. But it will be crowded next month, so you should make a reservation soon. GIBSON: Is that so? Should I buy a train ticket soon too?　MACHIDA: Yes.

YAMAGUCHI: This room is a bit dark even during the day.　CARPENTER: Umm, it would be better to make this window somewhat larger, wouldn't it?　YAMAGUCHI: How about the wall color?　CARPENTER: Let me see. I think it would be best to change it to a brighter color.

[1]Hakone is a hot spring resort located west of Tokyo.

| Ta-form of verb
Nonpast, negative form of verb | } | + ほうがいい（です） |

You'd better ([not] do something)
It's better for you ([not] to do something)
You'd better not; you shouldn't

電車が来ますよ。急いだほうがいいですよ。
The train is coming. You'd better hurry up.
あの窓にカーテンをつけたほうがいいでしょう。
It would be better to put a curtain on that window.
新しいテレビを買ったほうがいいんじゃありませんか。
Wouldn't it be better for you to buy a new TV set?
あの人とは話さないほうがいいですよ。
It's better for you not to talk with him.
あまりお酒は飲まないほうがいいんじゃありませんか。
It's better for you not to drink too much sake.

Responding to Others' Advice

ACCEPTING ADVICE

ええ、そうですね。
Yes, that's right.
ええ、そうします。
Yes, I will.
それはいい考えですね。
That's a good idea.

REFUSING ADVICE

そうですね。でも...
I see, but...
ええ、そうですが、ちょっと...
Yes, that's right, but...

Turn the following sentences into suggestions by using …ほうがいいですよ.

1. コートを持って行く
2. 窓を閉める
3. 部屋を掃除する
4. バスに乗る
5. 早く家を出る
6. 9時前に着く
7. 古い新聞を捨てる(to dispose of, throw away)

練習　　　　2

Match the situation in the first column with the appropriate advice in the second column.

1. ＿＿ うちはとてもうるさいんです。
2. ＿＿ 頭が痛いんです。
3. ＿＿ 今夜は遅くなります。
4. ＿＿ 迷ってしまいました。 (We've gotten lost.)
5. ＿＿ テストで0点を取りました。
6. ＿＿ 電車に遅れました。
7. ＿＿ 昨日飲みすぎました。

a. アスピリンを飲んだほうがいいですよ。
b. もっと早く起きたほうがいいですよ。
c. もっと勉強したほうがいいですよ。
d. 図書館で勉強したほうがいいですよ。
e. うちに電話したほうがいいですよ。
f. 地図を見たほうがいいですよ。
g. あまり飲まないほうがいいですよ。

練習　　　　3

What kind of advice would you give? Answer by using ほうがいい.

1. 僕は勉強が大嫌いだ。
2. ハンバーガーが大好きで、一日に三つ食べるんです。
3. I hate using Japanese. I won't use Japanese even in my Japanese class!
4. 夕べ、テレビを見すぎて、寝坊しました。
5. 勉強しすぎて、疲れました。
6. 私の部屋はきたなくて… 財布 (wallet) はどこでしょう。
7. コーヒーは一日10杯飲みます。

Useful word: やめる *to stop, quit*

15. Expressing Different States of Actions: …ところ

ブラウン：高田さん、何をしているんですか。

高田：お客さんが来るので、玄関を掃いているところです。ブラウンさんは？

ブラウン：美容院へ行くところです。

高田：ああ、そうですか。

チン：三村さん、今お話してもいいですか。

三村：銀行へ行くところですが、いいですよ。

チン：このレポートを読んでいるところなんですが、
ここの意味がわかりません。教えてもらえますか。

三村：あっ、私もその意味がわからないんですよ。

The noun ところ (*place*), used with different forms of verbs, expresses different states of actions.

You will learn about いた ところだ in Chapter 3.

Dictionary form of verb (nonpast, plain, affirmative)	+	ところだ

to be about to [*do something*]

Te-form of verb + いる	+	ところだ

to be in the process of [*doing something*]

BROWN: Mr. Takada, what are you doing?　TAKADA: A guest is coming so I am in the middle of sweeping the entrance. How about you?　BROWN: I'm just about to go to the beauty salon.　TAKADA: Oh, really? Your hairstyle has changed, hasn't it.

CHIN: Mr. Mimura, is it all right to talk with you now?　MIMURA: I am about to go to the bank, but it's OK.　CHIN: I'm reading this report, but I can't understand the meaning of this part.　MIMURA: Oh, I don't understand its meaning, either.

私は車を洗うところです。
I am about to wash my car.
ブラウンさんはその時、出かけるところでした。
Ms. Brown was about to go out then.
私は部屋を掃除しているところです。
I am in the midst of cleaning the room (or *I am just now cleaning the room*).

The ~ているとことだ construction is similar to the ~ている construction, but it focuses more on the exact point in time. The ~ている form can denote long-term, ongoing processes, as in 英語を勉強している, *I am studying English,* which allows the possibility that the speaker is referring merely to being enrolled in a course. On the other hand, 英語を勉強しているところだ can mean only *I am studying English at this moment.*

練習	1

Following the example, practice using the ところ constructions.

[例]　家を探す (*to look for*) → 家を探すところです。
　　　　　　　　　　　　家を探しているところです。

1. 電気をつける
2. 電気を消す
3. 料理をする
4. 皿を洗う
5. 部屋を片付ける
6. ガラスをみがく
7. ラジオを直す
8. ヒーターを入れる
9. 新しいアパートに引っ越す

練習	2

Fill in the blanks and complete the sentences.

1. 三村さんは学校で（　　　）ところです。
2. 8時に帰った時、父は（　　　）ところでした。
3. 母は台所で（　　　）ところです。
4. ブラウンさんが来た時、居間で（　　　）ところでした。
5. 町田さんが電話をかけてきた時、寝室で（　　　）でした。

16. Describing a Preparatory Action: ～ておく

ブラウン：明日は試験でしょう。

三村：ええ、講義についての質問だそうです。

ブラウン：じゃあ、ノートをコピーしておきましょう。

林：カワムラさん、新幹線の切符、買っておきました。

カワムラ：ぼくは旅館を予約しておきました。

林：これで旅行の準備はできましたね。

カワムラ：ええ。

16.1 The following construction means *to [do something] in advance* or *in preparation for future use.*

Te-form of verb + おく　　(おく itself means *to put, to place*)

---

to do something in advance or ahead of time
to do something with an eye toward the future

クラスの前に教科書を読んでおいた。
I read the textbook before class.(implying preparation for the class)
肉をいためる前に野菜を切っておきました。
I cut the vegetables before stir-frying the meat.
映画を見る前に、コーラとポップコーンを買っておきました。
Before watching the movie, I bought cola and popcorn.
旅行に行くので、スーツケースを出しておこう。
Because I'm going on a trip, I'll get out my suitcase.

BROWN: We have an exam tomorrow, don't we?　MIMURA: Yes, they say that there will be questions about the lectures.　BROWN: Then we'll have to read our lecture notes carefully, won't we?　MIMURA: I will photocopy Ms. Machida's notebook by the end of the day.

HAYASHI: Mr. Kawamura, I bought tickets for the bullet train.　KAWAMURA: I made the inn reservations.
HAYASHI: Now (*lit., with this*) we have finished preparing for our trip.　KAWAMURA: Yes.

16.2 ~ておく is often contracted to ~とく or ~どく in colloquial speech.

これ食べときなさい。
Eat this ahead of time.
これ読んどいたよ。
I read this in advance.

練習	1

Change these sentences by using ~ておく to indicate that the action is being done as preparation for something else.

1. カワムラさんに電話する
2. 高田さんと話す
3. 日本へ行く前に、日本語を勉強する
4. パーティーのためにビールを買う
5. クラスの前にテープを聞く
6. 山本さんに会う前に、写真を見る

練習	2

Match each phrase in Column 1 with the most appropriate sentence ending in Column 2.

1. お酒の好きなお客さんが
   いらっしゃるので、＿＿＿
2. 明日はテストがあるので、＿＿＿
3. パーティーの前に、＿＿＿
4. ブラウンさんに会う前に＿＿＿
5. フランスに行く前に＿＿＿
6. カワムラさんは甘いものが
   好きなので＿＿＿
7. 会議の前に、＿＿＿

a. レポートを読んでおいた。
b. ビールを冷やして (冷やす = *to cool*) おきましょう。
c. 電話をかけておいた。
d. ケーキを買っておいて
   ください。
e. トラベルガイドを買って
   おいた。
f. 漢字を勉強しておいた。
g. ドレスにアイロンをかけて
   おいた。

Complete these sentences by using ておきました. Make as many sentences as you can.

[例]　日本語のテストの前に、→
　　　日本語のテスト前に、漢字を勉強しておきました。
　　　日本語のテストの前に、テープを聞いておきました。
　　　日本語のテストの前に、教科書を読んでおきました。

1. 旅行の前に、
2. お客さんが来るので、
3. 病気にならないために、
4. 取るクラスを決める前に、

5. パーティーをするので、
6. ピクニックに行く前に、
7. 引っ越す前に、

Vocabulary

Housing

いま	居間	living room
おてあらい	お手洗	rest room, toilet
かいだん	階段	stairway, steps
きゃくま、おうせつま	客間／応接間	sitting room for entertaining guests; Western-style room for entertaining guests
げんかん	玄関	entry hall, foyer
けんちくか	建築家	architect
じゅうたく	住宅	residence, housing
しんしつ	寝室	bedroom
すむ	住む	to live, reside
せんめんじょ	洗面所	washstand, area for washing one's face and hands
だいく	大工	carpenter
ダイニング・キッチン		eat-in kitchen (*lit., dining kitchen*)
たてる	建てる	to build
だんち	団地	public housing development, apartment complex
てんじょう	天井	ceiling
と	戸	door
トイレ		toilet, rest room

(に)かいだて	(二)階建て	(two-)story
にほんま／わしつ	日本間／和室	Japanese-style room
にわ	庭	garden, yard
へや	部屋	room
…ま	…間	(*counter for rooms*)
マンション		condominium
もん	門	gate
やね	屋根	roof
ゆか	床	floor
ようしつ／ようま	洋室／洋間	Western-style room
よくしつ	浴室	bathing room

Loanwords: ガラス、ドア

Review:アパート、家、椅子、絵、～階、カーテン、壁、キッチン、近所、～軒、公園、狭い、台所、机、テーブル、庭、広い

Furnishings and Appliances

エアコン		air conditioner
かがみ	鏡	mirror
かぐ	家具	furniture
クーラー		air conditioner
すいはんき	炊飯器	rice cooker
スタンド		floor lamp, desk lamp
ストーブ		space heater
せんたくき	洗濯機	washing machine
せんぷうき	扇風機	electric fan
そうじき	掃除機	vacuum cleaner
たんす／タンス		chest of drawers
でんき	電気	light, electricity
でんきせいひん	電気製品	electric appliance
でんしレンジ	電子レンジ	microwave oven
ほんだな	本棚	bookshelf
るすばんでんわ	留守番電話	answering machine
れいぞうこ	冷蔵庫	refrigerator

Review: ステレオ、テレビ、電話、時計、ラジオ

Household Chores

アイロンをかける		to iron
かじ	家事	housework, household chores
かたづける	片付ける	to straighten [something] up; to clear [something] off
せんたく	洗濯	(to do) laundry

Vocabulary   127 百二十七

せんたくもの	洗濯物	laundry (*things to be laundered*)
そうじ(する)	掃除(する)	housecleaning (to clean)
なおす	直す	to mend, repair
にわいじり(する)	庭いじり(する)	(to do) gardening
ぬいもの(をする)	縫い物(をする)	(to do) sewing
はく	掃く	to sweep
ほす	干す	to air-dry [something]; to air [something] out
みがく	磨く	to polish

Review: 洗う

Verbs

いれる	入れる	to turn on [a switch]	けす	消す	to turn off [a light]
うごかす	動かす	to move [something]	さがす	探す	to look for
おく	置く	to put	つける	付ける	to turn on [a light]
かす	貸す	to lend, rent out	てつだう	手伝う	to help, assist
かりる	借りる	to borrow, rent [from]	はこぶ	運ぶ	to transport, carry [a large object]
きる	切る	to turn off [a switch]			

Review: 開ける

Adjectives

Review: 静か(な)、不便(な)、便利(な)

Grammar

あげる		to give (*to a second or third person*)
いただく		to receive (*from a superior*)
くれる		to give (*to speaker or in-group member*)
さしあげる		to give (*to a superior or outsider*)
しか...ない		only, not except for
...ずつ		each ..., per ...
...ため(に)		for the purpose of, for the sake of
~たり、~たり		[do] this and that
...ちゅう	...中	during, in the middle
~ておく		to do for future use
~てもいい		it is all right if you ...
...ところ		point in time
~ないでください		please don't ...
ばかり		only
...ほうがいい		it's better to ...
もらう		to receive (*from an equal or inferior*)
やる		to give (*to a social inferior*)

Kanji

Learn these **kanji.**

新　開　公　園　住　借　広　直　戸　古　門　室
伝　洗　建　友　貸　階　置　静　庭　不　便　利

Reading and Writing

Reading 1 石黒さんの新しい家

Before You Read

What factors go into your decision to buy a house? Are the factors in the following list important to you?

a. 静かな住宅街にある。
b. いいレストランがそばにある。
c. いい学校がある。
e. 公園がある。
f. 寝室がたくさんある。
g. 2階建てだ。
h. 商店街が近い。
i. 広いリビング・ルームがある。
j. 窓から海が見える。
k. 門がある。
l. 値段が安い。
m. まわりが安全 (safe) だ。
n. プールがある。
o. 駅に近い。
p. 駐車場がある。

Now Read It!

Ms. Ishiguro, a member of the aerobics class that Hitomi Machida attends, has recently moved into a new house. She has invited her classmates to visit her new house, and Hitomi has written a notice to the members about the upcoming visit.

大田区田園調布 *Den'enchoohu, an upscale neighborhood in Tokyo's Oota ward.*

田園都市線 *Den'en Toshi Line (a private train line)*

...ほど *approximately...*

青山カルチャーセンターのエアロビクス・クラスのみなさんへ

　私たちのクラスの石黒さんが、今月８日に大田区田園調布に新しく家を建て、引っ越しました。新しい家は二階建て、３ＬＤＫで、広い庭があります。田園都市線の田園調布駅のそばの、静かな住宅街の中にあります。近くには、スーパーもあって、とても便利です。また、１５分ほど歩くと、谷井神社があって、散歩にもいいところです。

　今月２３日、土曜日にクラスのみなさんを招いて、新しい家を見せてくださるそうです。ご主人が庭でバーベキューをしてくださるそうです。バーベキューは午前１１時から始まります。

　石黒さんの家は田園調布駅から歩いて１０分です。まず、田園調布駅で降りて、北口に出ます。北口の前の道をまっすぐ行くと、川があります。橋を渡ると、前に公園があります。公園の前の道を右に曲がります。しばらく行くと、右側に学校があります。学校の横の道を入り、二つ目の角を左に曲がります。角から３軒目の左側が石黒さんの家です。住所は大田区田園調布３－８－１９です。門のある青い屋根の家です。石黒さんの家の地図は先週火曜日のクラスでみなさん渡しましたが、まだもらっていない人は、私に連絡してください。

　みんなで石黒さんにお祝いの品をさしあげたいと思います。なにかいい考えのある人は、木曜日までに私に知らせてください。

　　　　　　　　　　　　　　　　　　　　　　　　　　　　　　町田ひとみ

お祝の品 *congratulatory present*

After You Finish Reading

1. Ms. Kinoshita has lost the map to Ms. Ishiguro's house. Draw a map for her based on Hitomi's note.

2. Answer these questions in English.
    a. When did the Ishiguros move into their new house?
    b. How many stories does the house have?
    c. What is in the neighborhood?
    d. Is the neighborhood quiet or noisy?
    e. Where is Tanii Shrine?
    f. When are the club members invited to visit the Ishiguros?
    g. What color is the roof?
3. Write a short note in Japanese to Hitomi Machida in which you suggest what to buy as a gift for Ms. Ishiguro. Mention why you think the recommended item would be good.

Writing 1

Write a short note to your friends inviting them to your house. Your invitation should include the following information.

1. You are inviting them to your house next Sunday.
2. The reason is that you moved into a new house last week and would like to show it to them.
3. Give directions to your house.
4. Tell them not to bring anything.

Reading 2 高原の別荘
こうげん　べっそう

Before You Read

Odd man out. Which item in each group doesn't belong? Why?

1. 秋、春、夏、冬、北
2. 暑い、涼しい、遠い、寒い、暖かい
   すず　　とお　　　あたた
3. 二時間、一週間、三ヶ月間、日本間、十分間
4. 寝室、教室、リビングルーム、キッチン、浴室
   しんしつ　きょうしつ　　　　　　　　　　　　よくしつ
5. 窓、天井、壁、床、庭
   まど　てんじょう　かべ　ゆか　にわ
6. 冷蔵庫、オーブン、ガスレンジ、ガレージ、トースター
   れいぞうこ
7. 勉強、買い物、洗濯、掃除、料理
   べんきょう　か　もの　せんたく　そうじ
8. 車、電車、バス、タクシー、飛行機
   くるま　でんしゃ　　　　　　　　　ひこうき

If you had a summer home, where would you like it to be? What kind of summer home would you like to have? Discuss in class.

Now Read It!

Useful vocabulary

高原 *plateau*, 別荘 *vacation home*, 考える *to think, to ponder*, 貸し別荘 *vacation rental*, さらに *furthermore*, 空気 *air*, 全部 *in total*, どの…も *each*, 利用 (する) *make use of*, もちろん *of course*, 美しい *beautiful*, 付く *to be attached*, 大丈夫 (な) *all right, no problem*, 村 *village*, 料金 *charge, fee*, 只今 *right now*, 発売中 *on sale*, …以上 *more than…*, たずねる *to inquire*, こむ *to be crowded*, すぐ *immediately, soon*

今年の夏は高原の別荘で過ごしてみませんか。

夏休みが取れたら、涼しいところでゆっくり休みたいなあ！そう考えているあなた、山川高原の貸し別荘はいかがですか。

東京駅から電車で３時間半、山川駅で降りて、さらに、バスで１時間行くと、青い空、きれいな空気、緑の山があなたを待っています。

山川高原の別荘は全部で２５軒。どの別荘にも寝室が３つ、リビングルーム、キッチン、浴室の広い別荘です。会社のグループで、ご家族で、また友だちとご利用ください。もちろん、お一人でも利用できます。リビングルームの大きい窓からは美しい山中湖が見えます。寝室にはベランダが付いていて、ベランダからは山川高原が見えます。モダンなデザインのキッチンには、冷蔵庫、レンジが付いていますから、料理もできます。スーパーは、バス

で１５分の山川村に３軒ありますから、お買い物も簡単です。別荘には洗濯機も付いていますから、洗濯も大丈夫です。

別荘の料金は一泊１万９千円です。只今、東京から山川までの電車、バス、別荘の料金をパックにした旅行クーポンを発売中です。６月中にこのクーポンを買う

と、便利な旅行バッグをさしあげます。クーポンはお近くの旅行代理店でどうぞ。

６０歳以上の方には、シルバーディスカウントがあります。くわしいことは旅行代理店でおたずねください。７月、８月はとてもこみます。今すぐご予約ください。

After You Finish Reading

Using the advertisement, fill in the missing information in the following English brochure excerpts.

How about spending this summer in a vacation rental in Yamakawa?

It takes about (　　　　　) to get to the summer houses from Tokyo by (　　　　)

and (　　　　　).

(　　　　), (　　　　　), and (　　　　　) await you!

Each spacious house includes these rooms: (　　　　　　　　　　　　　).

The houses afford a view of (　　　　　　　) and (　　　　　　　).

You can do your grocery shopping at (　　　　　　　).

Now on sale is a travel coupon that includes (　　　　　　　).

If you buy the coupon in June, you will receive (　　　　　　　).

People over (　　) years old will receive a discount.

In the months of (　　　　　　) and (　　　　　　　　), the vacation homes tend to fill up

fast, so make your reservation now!

Write a short letter in Japanese to one of your Japanese friends to ask if he or she would like to share a vacation rental in the Yamakawa Highlands this summer. In your letter, write about some of the features of the summer house, where it is located, the rental charge, and when you would like to go there.

Writing 2

You have decided to go to Japan and study the Japanese language for one year. You want to rent out your house while you are gone. Write a short paragraph describing each room and the special features of your house to attract prospective renters.

[例]　にぎやかな町の便利な家に住んでみませんか。
キッチンはモダンなデザインで、いろいろな電気製品があります。
居間は、…

Language Functions and Situations

Looking for a House

久保：あのう、このへんで家を探しているんですが…

不動産屋：ああ、このへんにはいい家がたくさんありますよ。どんな家をお探しですか。

久保：5人家族ですので、大きい家がいいんですが…

不動産屋：じゃ、部屋はいくつぐらいがいいですか。

久保：そうですね。ダイニング・キッチン、居間、それに寝室が3つほしいですね。車があるので、ガレージもほしいですね。

不動産屋：ああ、いい家がありますよ。これがその写真です。

久保：いい家ですね。まだ新しいですか。

不動産屋：ええ。築2年です。

久保：庭はありますか。

不動産屋：ええ、小さいですが、裏庭があります。

久保：駅に近いですか。

不動産屋：ええ、中野駅から歩いて15分です。バス停もすぐそばにあります。

久保：じゃあ買い物も便利ですね。

不動産屋：ええ、近くに商店街がありますから…

久保：学校はそばにありますか。

不動産屋：はい、小学校と中学校までは歩いて10分です。

KUBO: Uh, I'm looking for a house in this neighborhood but . . . (could you help me?).　　REALTOR: Oh, yes. There are many good houses around here. What kind of house are you looking for?　　KUBO: There are five people in my family, so a big house would be good.　　REALTOR: How many rooms do you want? (*lit., About how many rooms is good?*)　　KUBO: Let me see. I would like an eat-in kitchen, a living room, and three bedrooms. I have a car, so I want a garage, too.　　REALTOR: Oh, I have a good house. Here is a photo of it.　　KUBO: What a nice house. Is it new?　　REALTOR: Yes, it is. It was built two years ago. KUBO: Is there a yard?　　REALTOR: Yes. It's small, but there is a backyard.　　KUBO: Is it near a station? REALTOR: Yes, it's a fifteen-minute walk from Nakano Station. There is also a bus stop very close by. KUBO: Is it convenient for shopping?　　REALTOR: Yes. There is a shopping area nearby, so. . .　　KUBO: Are there schools nearby?　　REALTOR: Yes. It is a ten-minute walk to an elementary school and a junior high school.

南向き *facing south*
独身者 *single person*
最適 *most suitable*
日当り良好 *sunny*
水道 *tap water*
~代 *charge*
別 *separate*

立川

3500万円

3寝室（8、6、6畳）、ダイニング・キッチン、庭、ガレージ付。二階建て、南向きベランダあり。

駅まで歩いて10分、バス停、商店街、学校そば。とても便利

中山不動産
立川駅南口

TEL (721) 0808

アパート

二部屋（8畳、6畳)、台所、トイレ、風呂付。独身者に最適。南山駅から歩いて8分、買い物にも便利。静か、南向き。日当たり良好。

月56000円（ガス、水道、電気代別)、礼金2ヶ月、敷金2ヶ月。

電話 (213) 5535 山口

文化ノート

Renting an Apartment in Japan

To rent an apartment in Japan, you must have a lot of cash on hand. In addition to the first month's rent, you must pay the landlord a deposit (敷金[しききん]) in the amount of two or three months' rent and so-called key money (礼金[れいきん]) equal to two or three months' rent. Some of this money goes to the realtor who helped you find the apartment. Therefore, to move into an apartment where the monthly rent is 50,000 yen, you need at least 250,000 yen, 200,000 of which (the deposit and key money) you will never see again. This is tremendously unfair to renters, and makes all renters think twice before moving to another apartment, but it is an established custom in Japan that seems unlikely to change as long as the demand for apartments continues to exceed the supply. Foreigners who plan to stay in Japan for a year or less may be better off in a so-called gaijin house or an apartment hotel. The rents for these are much higher than the rents for apartments of comparable quality, but at least the tenant doesn't have to come up with several months' rent all at once.

Inviting People to Your Home

加藤：来週の日曜日、うちへ来ませんか。

山下：かまいませんか。

加藤：ええ、どうぞ。11時ごろ来てください。

山下：じゃあ、喜んで。

加藤：きたない家ですが。...これ、うちの地図です。

山下：どうもありがとうございます。じゃ、楽しみにしています。

加藤：こちらこそ。

山下：ごめんください。

加藤：はい、どなたですか。

山下：山下です。

加藤：ああ、山下さん。いらっしゃい。お待ちしていました。どうぞお上がり
　　　ください。

山下：失礼します。

加藤：どうぞこちらへ。

山下：お邪魔します。

加藤：どうぞお座りください。

山下：あのう、これ、つまらないものですが、どうぞ...

加藤：いやあ、そんな...

山下：本当にたいしたものじゃありませんが、...

加藤：こんなことをされては困ります。

山下：いいえ、どうぞ...

加藤：そうですか。じゃあ、恐れ入ります。

Role Play

Work in pairs. You have just moved into a new house. Invite your partner to your house. Receive your guest and show him or her the house. Your guest compliments you on the house and other things.

KATO: Won't you come to our house next Sunday? YAMASHITA: Is it all right? (*lit., Don't you mind?*) KATO: No. Please come about 11:00. YAMASHITA: OK, with pleasure. KATO: It's a dirty house, but.... Here is a map to our house. YAMASHITA: Thank you very much. I'm looking forward to it. KATO: I am too. (*lit., I'm the one [who's looking forward to it]*.)

YAMASHITA: Hello! (*lit., Excuse me.*) KATO: Who is it? YAMASHITA: Yamashita. KATO: Oh, Mr. Yamashita. Welcome. I was waiting for you. Please come in. YAMASHITA: Excuse me. KATO: Please [come] this way. YAMASHITA: Excuse me. (*lit., I'll inconvenience you.*) KATO: Please take a seat. YAMASHITA: Well, this is a trifling thing, but please ... [accept it]. KATO: No, that kind of thing ... [won't do]. YAMASHITA: It's really not anything significant, but.... KATO: It's upsetting if you do this sort of thing. YAMASHITA: Oh, no. Please ... KATO: Really? Thank you very much for your kindness.

Offering Food to a Guest

加藤：あのう、何もありませんが、ごはんでもいかがですか。
山下：どうぞご心配なく。
加藤：いいえ、お口に合うかどうかわかりませんが、どうぞ。
山下：こんなことされては困ります。
加藤：どうぞ遠慮しないでください。
山下：そうですか。では、いただきます。

加藤：もう少しいかがですか。
山下：いいえ、もう結構です。たいへんおいしかったです。ごちそうさまでした。

Leave-Taking

山下：あっ、もうこんな時間ですか。そろそろ失礼します。
加藤：まだ、いいじゃありませんか。
山下：いいえ、もう遅いですから。今日はどうもありがとうございました。
加藤：そうですか。じゃ、また、いらっしゃってください。
山下：では、失礼します。さようなら。
加藤：お気をつけて。

Role Play

Work in pairs. The host will offer the visitor a meal. After the meal is over, the visitor will leave.

KATO: Well, we don't have anything [to offer], but how about lunch?   YAMASHITA: Please don't worry about me.   KATO: Oh, no. I don't know if you will like it, but please.   YAMASHITA: It's upsetting if you do this sort of thing.   KATO: Please don't hold back.
YAMASHITA: Really? Then, thank you, I will have some. . . .

KATO: How about a little more?   YAMASHITA: No, thank you. It was really delicious. Thank you very much.

YAMASHITA: Oh, is it already this late? (*lit., . . . this time?*) I must leave (*lit., I will excuse myself soon.*)
KATO: Why don't you stay? (*lit., It's still OK, isn't it?*)   YAMASHITA: No, it's already late. Thank you very much for [inviting me] today.   KATO: I see. Please come again.   YAMASHITA: Excuse me. Good-bye.
KATO: Please take care.

Review

Go over the dialogues in this section and study what set phrases are used in the following situations.

1. inviting people to your house
2. greeting guests at the door, arriving at someone's house
3. asking a visitor to take a seat
4. giving and receiving a gift
5. offering and accepting a meal
6. leave-taking
7. taking one's leave, seeing a guest off

Note that you apologize for both entering the house and taking leave of your host. Also note Kato's ritualized refusal of Yamashita's present, the way both Kato and Yamashita belittle the things belonging to them, Yamashita's initial refusal of the food, and Kato's insistence that Yamashita stay longer.

Listening Comprehension

1. A real estate agent is showing a house to Ms. Swan. Listen to the agent's explanation and write down the features of each part of the house.
2. Mr. and Ms. Yoshioka are talking about what they will give their acquaintances as year-end gifts. While listening to their conversation, write down what they received from other people this summer and what they will give to them this winter.

At Home

3

Automobiles and Transportation

駅のターミナル

OBJECTIVES

Vocabulary and Oral Activities

Cars and Driving

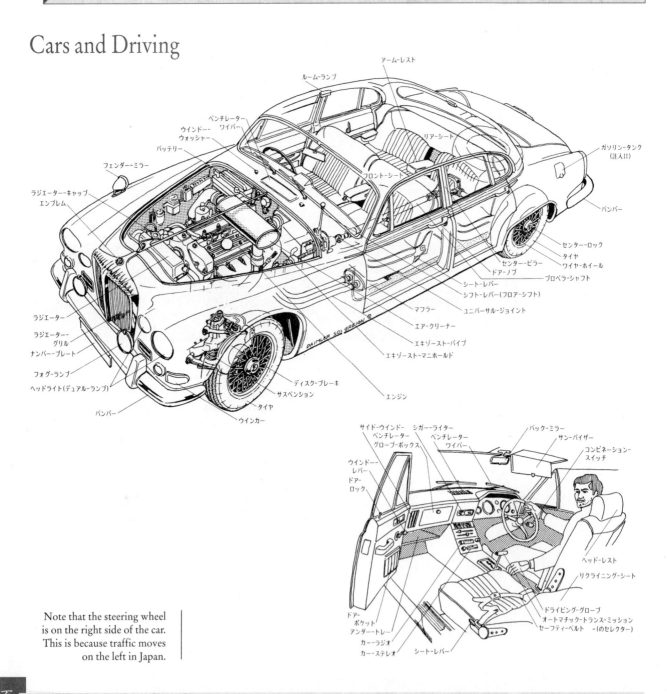

ルームランプ
アーム-レスト
ベンチレーター-ワイパー
ウインドー-ウォッシャー
バッテリー
リアーシート
フロント-シート
フェンダー-ミラー
ガソリン-タンク（注入口）
ラジエーター-キャップ
エンブレム
バンパー
センター-ロック
タイヤ
ワイヤー-ホイール
センター-ピラー
ドアーノブ
プロペラ-シャフト
シート-レバー
シフト-レバー（フロアー-シフト）
ユニバーサル-ジョイント
ラジエーター
ラジエーター-グリル
ナンバー-プレート
マフラー
エアー-クリーナー
エキゾースト-パイプ
エキゾースト-マニホールド
フォグ-ランプ
ヘッドライト（デュアル-ランプ）
バンパー
ウインカー
タイヤ
サスペンション
ディスク-ブレーキ
エンジン

サイド-ウインドー
シガー-ライター
ベンチレーター
バック-ミラー
ベンチレーター-グローブ-ボックス
ベンチレーター-ワイパー
サン-バイザー
コンビネーション-スイッチ
ウインドー-レバー
ドアー-ロック
ヘッド-レスト
リクライニング-シート
ドアー-ポケット
アンダー-トレー
カー-ラジオ
カー-ステレオ
シート-レバー
ドライビング-グローブ
オートマチック-トランス-ミッション
セーフティー-ベルト —（のセレクター）

Note that the steering wheel
is on the right side of the car.
This is because traffic moves
on the left in Japan.

Vocabulary: Cars

自動車	じどうしゃ	automobile, car
道路	どうろ	street, road
交通	こうつう	traffic
(交通)信号	(こうつう)しんごう	traffic light
運転免許(証)	うんてんめんきょ(しょう)	driver's license
運転手	うんてんしゅ	driver
ガソリン		gasoline
止まる	とまる	to come to a stop
アクセル		accelerator
ブレーキ		brake
タイヤ		tire
パンク(する)		(to get a) flat tire
クラクション		horn
チェンジレバー		gear shift lever
ハンドル		steering wheel
エンジン		engine
ラジエーター		radiator
バッテリー		battery
ワイパー		[windshield] wiper
アンテナ		antenna
ナンバープレート		license plate

Review: 車、道、運転(する)、ドライブ(する)、ガソリン・スタンド、駐車場、走る、乗る

アクティビティー　1

何ですか。(*What is it?*)

Connect each word in column A (on the following page) to the appropriate definition in column B.

Useful vocabulary

冷やす　*to cool something*
動かす　*to set in motion, move [something]*
交差点　*intersection*
穴があく　*a hole develops*

	A		B
1.	ガソリン	a.	雨や雪が降っている時に使います。
2.	ワイパー	b.	自動車を止める所です。
3.	信号	c.	車の行く方向をコントロールするために使います。
4.	ハンドル	d.	カーステレオを聞く時に使います。
5.	アクセル	e.	車を動かすために、タンクに入れます。
6.	アンテナ	f.	車のスピードをコントロールする時に使います。
7.	パンク	g.	交差点にある赤、黄色、青のライトです。
8.	駐車場	h.	タイヤに穴があくことです。

Review …ため (Chapter 2, **Grammar 10**) and …時 (Chapter 7, **Grammar 40**, in Book 1).

Vocabulary Library

Actions Involved in Driving

ハンドル（を握る／を切る）	ハンドルをにぎる／きる	(to take the) wheel/(to turn the) wheel
踏む	ふむ	to step on, to pedal
スピードを出す	スピードをだす	to increase speed
ブレーキをかける		to put on the brakes
エンジンをかける		to start the engine
タイヤをかえる		to change a tire
シートベルト		seat belt
締める	しめる	to attach, to buckle up
外す	はずす	to release, undo
クラクション		[automobile] horn
鳴らす	ならす	to sound (*a horn, a bell*)

アクティビティー　2

勉 Study Grammar 17.

ダイアログ：駐車の仕方を教えてくれませんか。(*Won't you teach me how to park a car?*)

ブラウン：日本で車を運転するのはむずかしいでしょうね。

高田：ええ、道が狭いですからねえ。

ブラウン：今度、狭い道での駐車の仕方を教えてくれませんか。

高田：ええ、いいですよ。

BROWN: I guess it's difficult to drive a car in Japan, right?　TAKADA: Yes, that's because the streets are narrow.　BROWN: Won't you teach me how to park a car on a narrow street sometime?　TAKADA: Yes, OK.

Practice the above dialogue by changing the underlined part to the following.

1. 狭い道での運転の仕方
2. 運転免許の取り方
3. オートバイ (*motorcycle*) の乗り方

Driving in Japan

Owning and driving a car in Japan is not a simple matter. To obtain a driver's license (運転免許証 [うんてんめんきょしょう]), you have to go to driving school (自動車学校 [じどうしゃがっこう]). (Because the legal driving age is eighteen, public schools do not offer driving instruction.) After taking a test that covers traffic regulations and basic automobile mechanics and receiving some preliminary instruction from the school, you first get a provisional license. With this in hand, you may practice driving on roads with an instructor until you have successfully passed the driving test.

In many cases, becoming a licensed driver is a lengthy and expensive process, costing as much as several hundred dollars. Furthermore, to register your car, you must bring it to a government-run vehicle checking station and have it checked. This is done every year and is quite costly.

In large cities such as Tokyo, cars parked out in the open on narrow streets (often called 青空駐車 [あおぞらちゅうしゃ]) would keep traffic from moving smoothly. For this reason, you are not allowed to own a car unless you have off-street parking at home. Because of this parking problem, many people don't drive at all even though they have a driver's license. These people are called ペーパードライバー.

On weekends, freeways (高速道路 [こうそくどうろ]) leading to popular leisure destinations are very crowded. Because of this, using the trains and buses is faster and more convenient.

Vocabulary Library

車の部分: Parts of a Car

バックミラー	rearview mirror
フロントガラス	windshield
ボンネット	hood
ハンドブレーキ、サイドブレーキ	parking brake
ウィンカー	turn signal
スピードメーター	speedometer

Loanwords: シートベルト、リクライニングシート、カーステレオ、カーラジオ、クラッチ、ヘッドライト、フェンダー、マフラー、バンパー、トランク、ダッシュボード、グラブコンパートメント

和製英語 (*English Words Made in Japan*)

English-speaking learners of Japanese sometimes believe mistakenly that they can just **katakana**-ize any English word and arrive at the Japanese equivalent. Although this tactic works in many cases, you need to be aware that the Japanese have made up their own words and phrases from English, resulting in words that do not exist in any English-speaking country. These words are called 和製英語, "made-in-Japan English." You have already seen such 和製英語 as パンティストッキング for *panty hose,* and クーラー for *air conditioner,* ガソリン・スタンド for *gas station,* or ワイシャツ for *dress shirt,* all of which were introduced in previous chapters. Other examples include コンセント for *electric outlet,* マスコミ for *mass communication,* カンニング for *cheating* [*on an exam*], and ナイター for *nighttime base-ball game,* among others. Some other examples of 和製英語 related to automobiles are ハンドル for *steering wheel,* ノークラッチ for *auto-matic transmission*, and ドアミラー for *sideview mirror.* Note that many English words entered Japanese from British English: for instance, ボンネット, for *hood* [*of a car*] or ジャンパー for *windbreaker jacket.*

アクティビティー　3

車のマニュアル: 窓の開け方は何ページですか。 (*Manual: On what page are the instructions for how to open the windows?*)

Consult the owner's manual on the next page and ask your partner where to find information on the following aspects of driving a car.

[例]　S1:　窓の開け方は何ページですか。
　　　　S2:　8ページです。

1. 車をコントロールする
2. ボンネットを開ける
3. タイヤを替える
4. ワイパーを動かす
5. 車を止める
6. アンテナを出す
7. ガソリンを入れる
8. ライトをつける

勉 Study Grammar 18.

アクティビティー　4

ダイアログ：乗せてあげましょう。(*I will give you a ride in my car.*)

町田：林さん、ねえ、ねえ、見て！

林：わあ、これが町田さんの新しい車なの？カッコいいなあ。

町田：乗ってみたい？

林：うん、うん。

町田：じゃ、乗せてあげるわ。

MACHIDA: Hey, Mr. Hayashi, look!　HAYASHI: Wow, is this your new car? It looks great.　MACHIDA: Would you like to try going for a ride in it?　HAYASHI: Yes, yes.　MACHIDA: Then I'll give you a ride.

アクティビティー 5

全自動です。(*It's fully automatic.*)

You are a car salesperson. The cars that you sell perform many functions automatically for drivers. Explain them to a potential buyer, basing your explanation on the diagram of the dashboard below.

Useful vocabulary

押す *to push*

[例] シートを前に動かしたいんですが、....
3番のボタンを押すと、動きますよ。

1. 窓を開けたいんですが....
   （　）番のボタンを押すと、（　　　）ますよ。

2. ドアを閉めたいんですが....
   （　）番のボタンを押すと、（　　　）ますよ。

3. 電気を消したいんですが....
   （　）番のボタンを押すと（　　　）ますよ。

4. エアコンを入れたいんですが....
   （　）番のボタンを押すと、（　　　）ますよ。

5. トレイを出したいんですが....
   （　）番のボタンを押すと、（　　　）ますよ。

6. テープを止めたいんですが....
   （　）番のボタンを押すと、（　　　）ますよ。

7. 音楽を変えたいんですが....
   （　）番のボタンを押すと、（　　　）ますよ。

8. シートを上げたいんですが....
   （　）番のボタンを押すと、（　　　）ますよ。

シート	窓	ドア	電気	エアコン	トレイ	テープ	音楽
3 上げる 下げる	5	7	9	11	13	15	
1 2 後ろ	開ける	開ける	付ける	入れる	出す	スタート	17
4	閉める	閉める	消す	切る	入れる	ストップ	チェンジ
	6	8	10	12	14	16	

アクティビティー　6

勉　Study Grammar 19.

窓が開けてあります。(*The window has been opened.*)

Look at the drawing and explain the conditions of the following.

[例]　—窓

窓が開けてあります。

1. 電気
2. 本
3. ドア
4. コンピュータ
5. エアコン
6. 夕ごはん
7. ビール

Use these verbs in your answers. Some will be used more than once.

つける
消す
閉める
出す
作る
開ける

PHOTO：サニー1800スーパーツーリング　タイプS。ボディカラーはダークグレーPM。
（サウンドパッケージ、195/55R15 84Vラジアルタイヤ＆15インチアルミロードホイールはメーカーオプション）

スポーティな走りを予感させる、1800スーパーツーリングTypeS。

〔サニー1800スーパーツーリング　タイプS〕■タイプS専用
装備●リヤスポイラー＆シルスポイラー●ハイマウントストッ
プランプ（トランクリッド組込み）●フォグランプ＆コーナリング
ランプ（フロントエアロバンパー組込み）■1800スーパーツー
リング主要装備●フロントエアロバンパー●オゾンセーフ
オートエアコン●3本スポーク本革巻ステアリング●本革巻
シフトノブ＆縫製シフトレバーブーツ（MT車）●AM/FM電子
チューナーラジオ＋2スピーカー●ATポジションインジケー
ター（AT車）●ワンタッチパワーウインドウ●集中ドアロック
●運転席シートリフター●電動格納式ドアミラー（カラード）
●無段調整式ウォッシャー連動間けつワイパー●トランク
スルー●185/65R14　86Hラジアルタイヤ●14インチフルホ
イールカバー

TypeSはスーパーサルーン（ディーゼルを除く）、1600スーパーツーリング、スーパーサルーンGにも設定がございます。

Car Maintenance and Repairs

（勉）　Study Grammar 20.

アクティビティー　7

ダイアログ：窓を開けようとしたんですが、...(I tried to open the window, but ....)

町田：すみません。ちょっと見てもらいたいんですが...
修理工：どうしましたか。
町田：<u>窓を開けようとしたんです</u>が、<u>開かないんです</u>。
修理工：ちょっと見てみましょう。

MACHIDA: Excuse me, but I'd like to have you look [at my car].　　MECHANIC: What's wrong?
MACHIDA: I tried to <u>open the window</u>, but it doesn't <u>open</u>.　　MECHANIC: Let's take a look at it.

Now practice this dialogue, substituting the following words for the underlined parts of the dialogue. Use the proper verb forms.

1. 窓を閉める、閉まる
2. ワイパーを使う、動く
3. ヘッドライトをつける、つく
4. シートを前に出す、出る
5. ライトを消す、消える
6. ハンドルを回す (to turn)、回る

Vocabulary: Car Troubles and Repair

故障(する)	こしょう(する)	(to have a) mechanical breakdown, (to become) out of order
修理(する)	しゅうり(する)	(to) repair
修理工	しゅうりこう	mechanic
直す	なおす	to fix, repair
部品、パーツ	ぶひん	part (*of a mechanical object*)
オイル		motor oil
交通事故	こうつうじこ	traffic accident
事故を起こす	じこをおこす	to cause an accident
事故にあう	じこにあう	to get involved in an accident
衝突(する)	しょうとつ(する)	collision; (to collide)

Loanwords: サービス・ステーション、メンテナンス、チェックする

Review: ガソリンスタンド

アクティビティー　8

インタビュー (*Interview*)

Walk around the classroom and find people who fit the following statements. You may not ask the same person two questions in a row. Ask for the signature of each person whose situation is described by the statement.

サイン

1. 車がよく故障します。　＿＿＿＿＿＿
2. 毎日、運転する前に、車を点検します。　＿＿＿＿＿＿
3. 車を自分で修理できます。　＿＿＿＿＿＿
4. 自分でオイルをチェックしたことがありません。　＿＿＿＿＿＿
5. 車の修理に一年に500ドル以上使います。　＿＿＿＿＿＿
6. 車のワイパーはこわれていて、動きません。　＿＿＿＿＿＿
7. 去年、交通事故にあいました。　＿＿＿＿＿＿
8. 車はいつもきれいです。　＿＿＿＿＿＿

㊀ Study Grammar 21.

ダイアログ：バッテリーをチェックしたばかりなんですが、…(*I have just checked the battery.*)

町田：エンジンをかけようとしたんですが、かからないんですよ。どこが悪いか
　　　わからないんです。
三村：バッテリーかもしれませんね。
町田：でも、バッテリーは、二日前にチェックしたばかりなんですが…
三村：うん、じゃ、違(ちが)うな。ガソリンは入れてありますか。

Work in pairs. Continue this dialogue with your partner, with the person playing the role of Mimura suggesting other reasons for the car's not starting and the person playing Machida explaining why that isn't the case.

アクティビティー　10

中古車(ちゅうこしゃ)を売ります。(*I'm going to sell my old car.*)

You'd like to sell your old car, but it has the problems listed below. What do you need to do to make it more attractive to a potential buyer?

Review the use of the te-form of verbs + おく in Chapter 2, **Grammar 16.**

[例(れい)]　　—フロントガラスがきたない。→
　　　　　　洗(あら)っておきます。

Useful vocabulary

…にペンキを塗(ぬ)る *to paint* …

1. バッテリーがあがっている (*the battery is dead*)。
2. ラジエーターがこわれている。
3. タイヤがパンクしている。
4. ドアがちょっとさびている (*is rusted*)。
5. ワイパーが動かない。
6. ライトが切れている。
7. スペアタイヤがない。
8. バックミラーがない。

MACHIDA: I tried to start the engine, but it won't start. I don't know what's wrong.　　MIMURA: It could be the battery.　　MACHIDA: But I just checked the battery two days ago.　　MIMURA: Hm, then it's not that. Is there gas in the tank? (*lit., Has gas been put in?*)

Now your car looks new. A prospective buyer is making complimentary remarks and asking questions about it, and you explain what you have done with the car.

[例]　—フロントガラスがピカピカですね。→
　　　昨日洗ったばかりです。

1. バッテリーは新しいんですか。
2. ラジエターは大丈夫ですか。
3. タイヤは大丈夫ですか。

4. ワイパーは動きますか。
5. スペアタイヤはありますか。
6. ライトはつきますか。

アクティビティー 11

車を売ります。(*I'm going to sell my car.*)

You have advertised your car, and a prospective buyer has called you. Answer his or her questions, which appear after the descriptive advertisement. If the necessary information is not included in the advertisement, make up your own answers.

1988 年マツダ・ファミリア67 万円

4ドア、5人乗り、白

5万キロ

サンルーフ、カーステレオ、カーエアコン付

リクライニング・シート

エンジン、水冷4気筒SOHC/1800cc、1992 年オーバーホール

4速、オートマチック

ハイオク・ガソリン使用、タンク70リットル

燃費12km/リットル、とても経済的

タイヤ、新しいタイヤに替えたばかり

---

1. 日本車ですか。
2. 何色ですか。
3. いくらですか。
4. 何人乗りですか。
5. エンジンは新しいですか。
6. 経済的な (*economical*) 車ですか。

7. 運転しやすい (*easy to drive*) ですか。
8. 乗り心地がいい (*comfortable to ride in*) ですか。
9. 何年型の車ですか。
10. トランクは広いですか。

Ask a classmate these same questions about his or her car or about his or her family's car.

Transportation and Traffic in the City

Vocabulary: Vehicles (1)

交通機関	こうつうきかん	means of transportation
オートバイ		motorcycle
モペット		moped
トラック		truck
スポーツカー		sports car
救急車	きゅうきゅうしゃ	ambulance
消防車	しょうぼうしゃ	fire engine
パトカー		patrol car, police car
モノレール		monorail

Review: バス、タクシー、自転車、電車、地下鉄、停留所、乗る

アクティビティー 12

バスをよく使いますか。(*Do you often use a bus?*)

Discuss your use of public transportation by discussing the following issues.

1. あなたの住んでいる町にはどんな交通機関がありますか。
2. あなたはバスをよく使いますか。
3. バスのいい点は何だと思いますか。悪い点は何だと思いますか。
4. どんな時にタクシーを使いますか。
5. このへんのタクシーは高いと思いますか。
6. 車が多いと、どのような問題がありますか。
7. 地下鉄に乗ったことはありますか。
8. モノレールに乗ったことはありますか。

アクティビティー 13

ダイアログ：このバスは江戸博物館へ行きますか。(*Does this bus go to Edo Museum?*)

ブラウン：すみません。このバスは江戸博物館へ行きますか。
運転手：いいえ。江戸博物館へ行くのは5番のバスです。

BROWN: Excuse me. Does this bus go to the Edo Museum?　　DRIVER: No, the bus that goes to the Edo Museum is the Number 5 bus.

ブラウン：ここで乗れますか。

運転手：いいえ、3番乗り場に行って下さい。

ブラウン：ありがとうございます。

Practice the above dialogue by changing the first two underlined parts according to the following information.

1. 東京タワー (Number 7 bus, Stop Number 4)
2. 早稲田大学 (Number 1 bus, Stop Number 1)
3. 池袋駅東口 (Number 2 bus, Stop Number 1)
4. レインボーブリッジ (Number 8 bus, Stop Number 4)

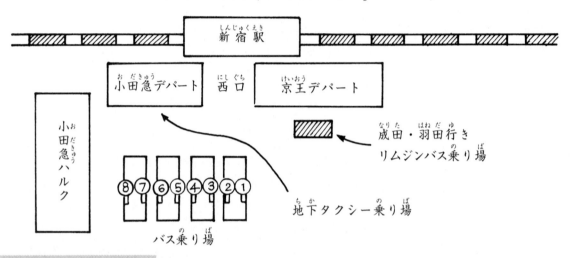

Vocabulary Library

Vehicles (2)

マイクロバス		minibus
ワンマンバス		bus without a conductor
車掌	しゃしょう	conductor
バス・ガイド		bus guide, a person who gives guided bus tours
回数券	かいすうけん	coupon ticket, strip of tickets
定期券	ていきけん	monthly commuter pass
ダンプカー		dump truck

Loanwords: トロリーバス、トレーラー、トラクター、セダン、クーペ、ハッチバック、リムジン、ジープ、バン、ミニバン

Review: 切符

BROWN: Can I get on it here?　　DRIVER: No, go to Stop Number 3.　　BROWN: Thank you.

アクティビティー 14

ダイアログ：あそこで曲がらないで、まっすぐ行ってください。(*Please just go straight without turning there.*)

タクシーの中で

運転手：3丁目1番地はこのへんですかね。

町田：ええと、ここはまだ2丁目ね。

運転手：<u>あそこで曲がりますか。</u>

町田：いいえ、<u>あそこで曲がらないで</u>、もう少しまっすぐ行ってください。

Practice the above dialogue, changing the underlined parts to the following words.

1. ここで止める
2. あそこでUターンする
3. あの道に入る

乗車運賃のご案内

都バス運賃表

	種　別	大人	学生	中学生	小児
普通運賃	一般系統	180円	180円	180円	90円
	学バス系統	150円	150円	150円	80円
	シャトルバス(CH01系統)	160円	160円	160円	80円
定期運賃	都バスフリーカード 1か月	8,100円	6,480円	5,940円	3,240円
	3か月	23,090円	18,470円	16,930円	9,240円
	学バス定期券 1か月	6,750円	5,400円	4,950円	2,700円
	3か月	19,240円	15,390円	14,110円	7,700円

主な回数券

180円×6枚+30円…1,000円　★180円×6枚+30円…1,000円
180円×28枚+90円…4,000円　★180円×19枚+90円…3,000円
★印は民営との磁気付共通回数券
※回数券は、バスの車内でもお買い求めいただけます。

都バスフリーカード

23区内の都バスはこのカード1枚でOK!

大 人	8,100円(1か月) 23,090円(3か月)
学 生	6,480円(1か月) 18,470円(3か月)
中学生	5,940円(1か月) 16,930円(3か月)
小 児	3,240円(1か月) 9,240円(3か月)

● 通勤定期乗車券は、持参人式です。持参人がどなたでも1名様に限りご乗車いただけますので、とてもご利用しやすくなっております。この定期乗車券は、ご希望によりご購入者名として、個人名又は会社名を記載しております。
● フリーカードは、23区内の都バスならどこでも乗り降り自由な乗車券です。
● 新規購入の場合は、有効開始日の前日又は、当日お買い求めいただけます。
● 継続購入の場合は、有効開始日の14日前からお買い求めいただけます。

都営交通相互の連絡定期券

都電・バス連絡定期運賃		
区　分		運　賃
大　人	1か月	13,690円
	3か月	39,010円
	6か月	73,900円
学　生	1か月	10,950円
	3か月	31,200円
	6か月	59,110円
中学生	1か月	10,430円
	3か月	29,730円
	6か月	56,350円

1枚でOK 5%割引

都電、都バス、都営地下鉄のうち2つを2枚の定期券で通勤又は通学している場合は、それぞれの定期運賃から5％割引した額の合算額で連絡定期券をご利用いただけます。

● 都バス・都営地下鉄連絡定期乗車券と都電・都営地下鉄連絡定期乗車券は、都営地下鉄定期券発売所(18か所)で発売中。
● 都電、都バス連絡定期乗車券は、都バス営業所、荒川電車営業所及び交通局協力会主要定期券発売所で発売中。

お子様と都バスに乗車なさるお客様へ

幼児運賃についてのご案内

幼児(1歳以上6歳未満)の都バス運賃は、小学生以上の同伴者1人につき1人に限り無料です。

大人180円　幼児無料　幼児90円
270円

In a taxi DRIVER: Is No. 1, 3-choome (the third district) around here? MACHIDA: Hmm, this is still 2-choome. DRIVER: Do I <u>turn there</u>? MACHIDA: Please just go straight a little more, <u>without turning there</u>.

日本の公共交通機関
(*Public Transportation in Japan*)

Very few Japanese commute to work or school by car unless they live in a small town or in the country. Instead, most people rely on a highly developed, carefully coordinated, well-maintained, virtually crime-free network of buses, JR trains, privately owned railroads, and, in the largest cities, subways.

During the morning and evening rush hours, the trains and subways run as often as every three minutes, and even then they can be packed so tightly that the passengers are unable to move. The system is uncomfortable enough that commuters have dubbed it 通勤地獄 (つうきんじごく), "commuting hell," a takeoff on 受験地獄 (じゅけんじごく), the "entrance examination hell" that high school students endure. Despite the discomforts, this type of commuting has one advantage: the passengers almost always arrive at work or school on time and don't have to worry about getting stuck in traffic.

To save time, most commuters buy either monthly passes (定期券 [ていきけん]) or strips of tickets (回数券 [かいすうけん]), allowing them to pass right through the turnstile (改札口 [かいさつぐち]) without stopping at the ticket machine. For less frequent commuters there are the so-called オレンジ・カード, prepaid cards that allow people to buy tickets at the machines without having to have money on hand.

Fortunately, rush hour is only a small portion of the day, and people who ride the trains and subways during the middle of the day, when they run every eight or ten minutes, can usually find a place to sit.

The bus transportation system is well developed in almost every part of Japan. In addition to 市内バス (しないバス), which run within cities and towns, there are the 長距離バス (ちょうきょりバス), which run between cities. If you need to go to the airport, you may find that a リムジンバス is your most economical option.

You can pick up taxis at taxi stands (タクシー乗り場 [タクシーのりば]) in front of stations or at hotels. Large numbers of taxis constantly cruise the through streets of major cities, so if you are not near a station or hotel, simply go to the nearest busy street and summon a passing cab by raising your hand. Taxis are by far the most expensive form of transportation in Japan, so it is best to avoid them unless you have a lot of heavy luggage or need to get somewhere after midnight, when the public transportation has stopped running.

歩道	ほどう	sidewalk
歩行者	ほこうしゃ	pedestrian
横断歩道	おうだんほどう	pedestrian crossing
交差点	こうさてん	intersection
車道	しゃどう	road
高速道路	こうそくどうろ	freeway
通る	とおる	to pass through, go along
違反(する)	いはん(する)	to violate rules
警察に捕まる	けいさつにつかまる	to be caught by the police
時速	じそく	speed per hour (時速 60 km = 60 kilometers per hour)
制限速度	せいげんそくど	speed limit
駐車禁止	ちゅうしゃきんし	No Parking
近道	ちかみち	shortcut
回り道	まわりみち	detour
工事中	こうじちゅう	under construction
道に迷う	みちにまよう	to lose one's way
道路地図	どうろちず	road map
交通渋滞	こうつうじゅうたい	traffic jam

アクティビティー 15

Review ～はいけません、なさい
in Chapter 1.

交通標識 (*Traffic signs*)
[こうつうひょうしき]

What do you think these signs mean? Some of them may be obvious to you, while others will require some guesswork. Match each sign with the sentence that most closely describes its meaning. For unfamiliar terms, see the Vocabulary Library on the next page.

1. 通ることができません。
2. 自転車は通ることができません。
3. Uターンしてはいけません。
4. 追い越しをしてはいけません。
5. 午前8時から午後8時までは一時間駐車をしてもいいです。
6. ここはバスだけが通ることができます。
7. クラクションを鳴らしなさい。(鳴らす = *to sound*)
8. 真っすぐ行きなさい。
9. 人は通れません。
10. 一度止まりなさい。

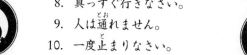

Traffic (2)

一方通行	いっぽうつうこう	one-way traffic
追い越し(する)／追い越す	おいこし(する)／おいこす	passing; (to pass)
Uターン(する)	ユーターン(する)	(to make a) U-turn
Uターン禁止	ユーターンきんし	No U-turn
左側通行	ひだりがわつうこう	driving on the left
ノロノロ運転	ノロノロうんてん	sluggish traffic
酔っぱらい運転(する)	よっぱらいうんてん(する)	drunk driving; (to drive drunk)

Loanwords: ガードレール、インターチェンジ、カーブ、サービスエリア、センターライン、バイパス

アクティビティー 16

何と言いますか。(*What do you say?*)

What do you say to these people? Give a warning by using 〜ないでください。

[例]　—車道を歩いている人 →
　　　車道を歩かないでください。

1. あなたの家のガレージの前に車を止めている人
2. クラクションをうるさく鳴らしている人
3. 一方通行の道に入ってきた人
4. センターラインを越えて (越える = *to go over, go beyond*) 運転している人
5. 狭い道で追い越しをしようとしている人
6. Uターン禁止の道でUターンしようとしている人
7. 自転車しか入れない道を運転している人
8. お酒を飲んで運転している人

アクティビティー 17

運転の準備 (*Preparation for a drive*)

What do you do to prepare for the following driving situations? Discuss in class.

1. コロラドに車で行って、スキーをしようと思う時
2. 夏の暑い時に運転する場合 (*case*)
3. 雨の日に運転する時
4. 長い距離を運転する時

5. 初めての場所 (place) を運転する時
6. 雪が降っている時に、運転する場合
7. 交通渋滞の時に、運転する場合
8. 夜、運転する時

Grammar and Exercises

17. How to Do Something: ～方

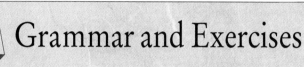

> ブラウン：このシチュー、おいしいですね。
> 山口：どうもありがとう。
> ブラウン：作るのはむずかしいんですか。
> 山口：いいえ、とても簡単よ。
> ブラウン：じゃあ、今度、作り方を教えてください。
>
> 町田：林さん、どうしたの？
> 林：新しい時計を買ったんだけど、アラームのセットの仕方がわからなくて...
> 町田：取り扱い説明書を読んでみたらどう？
> 林：そうだね。

The conjunctive form of a verb followed by ～方 makes a phrase meaning
how to ....

Conjunctive form of verbs + 方

how to [do something] ..., the way of [doing something] ...

BROWN: This stew is delicious. YAMAGUCHI: Thank you very much. BROWN: Is it difficult to prepare? YAMAGUCHI: No, it's very simple. BROWN: Then, please teach me how to prepare it sometime.
MACHIDA: What's the matter, Mr. Hayashi? HAYASHI: I bought a new watch, but I don't know how to set the alarm. MACHIDA: How about reading the instruction manual? HAYASHI: Oh, right.

方 is a noun meaning *method* or *way* in this context, so when you add 方 to a verb, that verb becomes a noun. For this reason, を is replaced by の.

For the formation of the conjunctive form of the verb, refer to Lesson 3, **Grammar 12**, Book 1.

手紙を書く *to write a letter*
手紙の書き方 *how to write a letter*

Here are some sample sentences with verb + ～方.

カワムラさんは、箸の使い方が上手ですね。
Mr. Kawamura, you are good at using chopsticks. (lit., the way of using chopsticks is skillful.)
この漢字の読み方は何ですか。
*What is the reading of this **kanji**? (lit., what is the way of reading this **kanji**?)*
あの人の話し方はちょっと変わっている。
The person's way of speaking is a bit unusual.

練習　　　　　　　　　　　　　1

Answer the questions following the example. Choose whichever of the suggested alternatives you would be more likely to follow.

[例]　着物の着方を知りたい時、どうしますか。
　　　着物の本を読む
　　　日本語の先生に聞く

　　　→ 着物の着方を知りたい時は、着物の本を読みます。

1. ビデオの使い方を知りたい時、どうしますか。
　　マニュアルを見る
　　友だちに聞く
2. マージャンの仕方を知りたい時、どうしますか。
　　日本人の友だちに聞く
　　マージャンの本を読む
3. 漢字の読み方を知りたい時、どうしますか。
　　先生に聞く
　　辞書を引く
4. すきやきの作り方を知りたい時、どうしますか。
　　料理の本を読む
　　日本の友だちに手紙を書いて、聞く

Now see if you can answer giving multiple options and using the ～たり…～たり construction.

Change the verbs in the parentheses to the appropriate form.

1. この漢字の(書く)方がわからないんです。
2. 正しい (correct) タイプの(する)方を教えてください。
3. あの先生は(教える)方が上手ですね。
4. あの人の(歩く)方はおもしろい。
5. 上手な写真の(撮る)方を教えてあげましょう。
6. このワープロの(使う)方、わかりますか。
7. 箸の(持つ)方は、これでいいですか。
8. あの人はコーヒーの(入れる)方にうるさい。(*That person is fussy about how to make coffee.*)

When do you use the following items? Use ～方 in your answers.
1. 車の運転のマニュアル
2. 漢字の辞書
3. 日本語の辞書
4. 料理の本
5. コンピュータのマニュアル

18. Transitive and Intransitive Verbs

山口：ウーン、ウーン。

カワムラ：どうしましたか。真っ赤な顔をして。…

山口：このケチャップの栓が開かないの。

カワムラ：僕が開けてあげましょう。

YAMAGUCHI: (grunt)　　KAWAMURA: What's the matter? Your face is bright red.　　YAMAGUCHI: This bottle of ketchup (*lit., The lid of this ketchup*) won't open.　　KAWAMURA: Well, I'll open it for you.

カワムラ：この部屋、ちょっと暗いね。

町田：ええ。電気をつけてくれる？

カワムラ：うん。あれ、つかないよ。

町田：スイッチがこわれたかしら。

カワムラ：電球がきれたのかもしれないね。

文法ノート

かしら (*I wonder...*)

かしら is an informal sentence-final phrase that female speakers use when wondering about something. This phrase is attached to the informal ending of predicates, nouns, or pronouns.

ギブソンさんはもうデパートへ行ったかしら。
I wonder if Ms. Gibson already went to the department store.
チンさんは病気かしら。
I wonder if Ms. Chin is sick.

In the same context, male speakers use かな or かなあ.

ギブソンさんはもうデパートへ行ったかなあ。
チンさんは病気かな。

Verbs that semantically require a direct object marked by the particle を are called *transitive verbs* (他動詞[たどうし] in Japanese). Transitive verbs represent a situation in which the subject's (doer's) action affects the direct object or the subject acts on the direct object. Verbs that require a subject but no direct object are called *intransitive verbs* (自動詞[じどうし] in Japanese). Intransitive verbs express a situation in which the subject undergoes or performs an action on its own.

In English, the same verb usually functions as either a transitive or an intransitive, depending on the context. In fact, modern English has only three pairs of verbs whose transitive and intransitive forms differ: *rise* and *raise* (*The curtain is rising* and *They are raising the curtain*); *lie* and *lay* (*I will lie down on the bed* and

---

KAWAMURA: This room is a bit dark, isn't it?   MACHIDA: Yes. Would you turn on the light?
KAWAMURA: Yes. (Pause) It doesn't turn on.   MACHIDA: I wonder if the switch is broken.
KAWAMURA: The light bulb may have burned out.

Automobiles and Transportation

I will lay the child down on the bed); and *fall* and *fell* (*The tree is falling* and *They are felling the tree*). In most cases, however, the transitive and intransitive are the same:

1. *They changed the plans.* (transitive)
   The plans changed. (intransitive)
2. *I am walking my dog.* (transitive)
   My dog is walking. (intransitive)

In Japanese, however, there are dozens of transitive and intransitive verb pairs that share the same root but have different endings. The following are some commonly used pairs of transitive and intransitive verbs.

TRANSITIVE VERBS		INTRANSITIVE VERBS	
上^あげる	to raise	上^あがる	to rise, to go up
開^あける	to open [something]	開^あく	to open [by itself]
集^{あつ}める	to gather [things, people] together, to collect	集^{あつ}まる	to gather together, to congregate
出す	to put out, to take out	出る	to come/go out, to appear
始める	to begin [something]	始まる	to begin
入^いれる	to put in, to insert, to include	入^{はい}る	to enter, to be included, to fit inside
返^{かえ}す／帰^{かえ}す	to return, to give back	返^{かえ}る／帰^{かえ}る	to return [home]
間違^{まちが}える	to make a mistake [about something]	間違^{まちが}う	to be in error
見つける	to find	見つかる	to be found
直^{なお}す	to fix	直^{なお}る	to get better
残^{のこ}す	to leave behind	残^{のこ}る	to be left over, to remain
落^おとす	to drop [something]	落^おちる	to fall [from a height]
終^おわる／終^おえる	to end [something]	終^おわる	to [come to an] end
下^さげる	to lower [something]	下^さがる	to go down, to dangle
閉^しめる	to close [something]	閉^しまる	to close
起^おこす	to wake [someone] up	起^おきる	to wake up

TRANSITIVE VERBS		INTRANSITIVE VERBS	
かける	to hang [something]on, to lay [something] on [something else]	かかる	to hang [on a vertical surface], to lean, to take (*time, money, etc.*)
付ける／つける	to attach, to turn [something] on	付く／つく	to become attached, to go on
消す	to extinguish, to put out	消える	to be extinguished, to go off, to disappear
並べる	to line [things] up	並ぶ	to get in line
止める	to stop [something]	止まる	to come to a stop
動かす	to set in motion, to move [something]	動く	to move, to be in motion
乗せる	to put on a vehicle, to give a ride to	乗る	to board a vehicle, to ride
寝かす	to put to bed	寝る	to go to bed, to sleep
なくす	to lose	なくなる	to get lost, to disappear
こわす	to break [something]	こわれる	to become broken
立てる／建てる	to erect, to build	立つ／建つ	to stand, to be built
通す	to send through, to allow to pass through	通る	to pass through, to go along [a road]
回す	to turn [something], to send around	回る	to turn around, to go around
切る	to cut	切れる	to be cut
切らす	to run out of, to use up	切れる	to be used up
変える／かえる	to change [something]	変わる／かわる	to [undergo] change

ブラウンさんは部屋の電気を消しました。
Ms. Brown turned off the room light. (transitive)
急に電気が消えました。
Suddenly the lights went off. (intransitive)

どこに車を止めましょうか。
Where shall we stop (park) the car? (transitive)
家の前に赤い車が止まりました。
A red car stopped in front of the house. (intransitive)

それでは、ミーティングを始めます。
Now we will start the meeting. (transitive)
授業 (class session) は毎日8時に始まります。
Class starts at eight o'clock every day. (intransitive)

The noun or pronoun that is the object of Japanese transitive verb is not always expressed explicitly, so the lack of an expressed direct object does not necessarily mean that the verb in question is intransitive.

このへんに止めますか。
Shall we stop [the car] around here? (transitive)

In the following cases, the verbs are intransitive although the particle を is used.

あの道を通って、公園へ行った。
Going along that street, we went to the park.
三時に家を出ましょう。
Let's leave home at three o'clock.

練習　　　　　　　　　　　1

Is the underlined verb transitive (T) or intransitive (I)? Circle the appropriate letter.

1. T I 　ホテルの前に人が集まっていますよ。
2. T I 　すみませんが、窓を閉めてください。
3. T I 　3時に家を出ましょう。
4. T I 　14日までに本を図書館に返さなければなりません。
5. T I 　パーティーは12時に終わりました。
6. T I 　答えを間違えました。
7. T I 　このお金、なくさないでね。
8. T I 　冬は天気がよく変わる。
9. T I 　公園の中を通って、大学へ行った。
10. T I 　父がドアを直しました。

練習	2

Change the sentences containing transitive verbs to sentences with intransitive verbs and vice versa. Remember to make all the appropriate changes in particles, and be sure that you understand how the two sentences differ in meaning.

[例] 窓が開きました。→ 窓を開けました。

ドアを閉めた。→ ドアが閉まった。

1. 鍵 (*lock*) がかかりました。
2. テレビをつけました。
3. 電気が消えました。
4. 犬を外に出しました。
5. 猫を家に入れた。
6. 髪の色が変わりましたね。
7. 子供をベッドに寝かせた。
8. 日本語の授業が始まった。

練習	3

Fill in the blanks with the appropriate verb in the plain, past form, choosing from the pair of transitive and intransitive verbs provided for each question.

[例] (開く、開ける)
ドアが (　　　)。→ (開いた)
ギブソンさんがドアを (　　　)。→ (開けた)

1. (起きる、起こす) 　　a. 6時になったので、カワムラさんを (　　　)。
　　　　　　　　　　　　b. 今朝、7時半に (　　　)。

2. (落ちる、落とす) 　　a. 風でりんごが木から (　　　)。
　　　　　　　　　　　　b. カワムラさんは棒 (*stick*) を使って、木からりんごを (　　　)。

3. (入る、入れる) 　　　a. 授業 (*class session*) が始まる前に、教室に (　　　)。
　　　　　　　　　　　　b. タンクにガソリンを (　　　)。

4. (こわれる、こわす) 　a. このラジオを (　　) のはだれですか。
　　　　　　　　　　　　b. 昨日、時計が (　　　)。

5. (上がる、上げる) 　　a. 答えがわかったので、手を (　　　)。
　　　　　　　　　　　　b. 先月、ガソリンの値段が1リットル40円 (　　　)。

6. (出る、出す) 　　　　a. 高田さんは暑いので、外に (　　　)。
　　　　　　　　　　　　b. 高田さんは窓から顔を (　　　)。

7. (消える、消す)　　a. 風が吹いて、火 (fire) が（　　）。

　　　　　　　　　　　b. 寝る前に、火を（　　）。

8. (動く、動かす)　　a. 地震 (earthquake) で、家が少し（　　）。

　　　　　　　　　　　b. このソファーをここへ（　　）。

19. Expressing Results and States of Being:
　　　〜てある and 〜ている

　　　山口：ブラウンさんはまだですか。

カワムラ：ええ。もうすぐ来ると思いますが...

　　　山口：寒いから、ヒーターを入れておいた方がいいですよ。

カワムラ：ええ、もう入れてありますよ。

カワムラ：玄関の電気がついていますよ。消しましょうか。

　　　山口：主人がまだ帰って来ていないから、つけてあるのよ。

カワムラ：そうですか。御主人、いつも遅いですね。

　　　山口：毎日だから、もう慣れたわ。

ギブソン：道路地図、買った？

　　　林：うん、もう買ってあるよ。車のチェックもしてあるし、いつでも
　　　　　出られるよ。

ギブソン：ホテルの予約はしてある？

　　　林：ううん。今は部屋がたくさん空いているから、予約はしなくても
　　　　　大丈夫だよ。

Review the use of もう and まだ
　　in Chapter 5, Book 1.

YAMAGUCHI: Isn't Ms. Brown [here] yet?　　KAWAMURA: No, but I think that she'll be here soon.
YAMAGUCHI: It's cold, so you'd better turn on the heater [ahead of time].　　KAWAMURA: It has already
been turned on.

KAWAMURA: The light in the entryway is on. Shall I turn it off?　　YAMAGUCHI: I have it on because my
husband hasn't come back yet.　　KAWAMURA: I see. Your husband always comes home late, doesn't he?
YAMAGUCHI: He's late every day, so I'm used to it.

GIBSON: Have you already bought a road map?　　HAYASHI: Yes, it's been bought. The car's been checked,
too, so we can leave anytime.　　GIBSON: Have hotel reservations already been made?　　HAYASHI: No, we
don't have to make reservations, because there are a lot of rooms available now.

19.1 The te-form of a transitive verb + ある indicates that something is in the state of having already been done with some purpose or for some reason. The agent of the action is commonly omitted, because he or she is unknown, unimportant, or obvious from the context.

Te-form of transitive verb + ある(あります)

Something has been done, someone has done

ラジエターはもう直してあります。
The radiator has already been repaired.
テーブルの上に箸が出してある。
Chopsticks have been put out on the table.
ガレージの前に車が止めてあるので、私の車が出せません。
A car has been parked in front of the garage, so I cannot move my car out.

This construction may mean that something is ready and waiting.

—車はチェックしてある?
Has the car been checked?
—いいや、まだしてない。
No, it has not been checked.

The plain negative form of ある (*to exist*) is ない.

In this construction, the direct object can be marked by either が or を.

カーエアコンがつけてあります。
カーエアコンをつけてあります。
The car air conditioner has been turned on.

19.2 For most of the transitive-intransitive pairs, the te-form of the intransitive verb + いる means that something is in a state brought about by an unidentified individual or by a natural force.

Te-form of intransitive verb + いる(います)

Something occurred and the resulting state still remains.

ヘッドライトがついていますよ。
The headlight is on.
前の車のトランクが開いている。
The trunk of the car in front of us is open.

カーティスさんの車が止まっています。
Mr. Curtis's car has stopped.
何が入っていますか。
What's inside of it?
What's included?

As explained in Chapter 5 of Book 1, the te-form of the verb + いる can also express an action in progress.

あっ、ギブソンさんが昼ごはんを食べていますよ。
Oh, Ms. Gibson is eating lunch.

How do you know which interpretation is correct in a given sentence? The answer lies in the nature of the verb. Verbs such as 食べる, 走る, 見る, 聞く, 書く, 読む, and 作る denote actions that can be continued indefinitely. When you see one of these so-called continuous (継続的 [けいぞくてき]) verbs in the te-form + いる construction, you can be sure that it describes an ongoing action, much like the English present progressive (*is eating, is running*) form. Most transitive verbs are continuous.

The so-called punctual (瞬間的 [しゅんかんてき]) verbs describe either/or situations. From the Japanese point of view, a door that is not completely closed is open, a light that is not completely on is off, and a car that is not completely stopped is moving. When you see one of these punctual verbs in the te-form + いる construction, you can be sure that it describes a state resulting from an action. Almost all the intransitive verbs that have transitive partners are punctual verbs, and there is no short, simple way to describe the transition from one such state to another in Japanese. Thus 閉まっている always means *is closed* and cannot mean *is closing*. A few other common verbs, such as 行く, 来る, 死ぬ, and 結婚する, are also considered punctual, as you learned in Chapter 5, Book 1.

練習   1

Match the following sentences with the drawings on the next page that they best describe.

1. ( ) 電気が消してある。
2. ( ) カワムラさんが電気をつけている。
3. ( ) 電気がついている。
4. ( ) 窓が閉めてある。
5. ( ) ブラウンさんが窓を閉めている。
6. ( ) 窓が開いている。
7. ( ) ビールが出してある。
8. ( ) 三村さんがビールを出している。
9. ( ) ビールが冷蔵庫に入っている。

A.

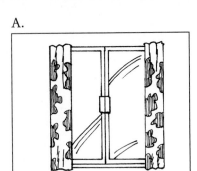

B.

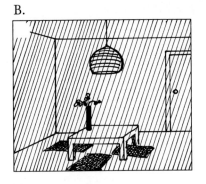

C.

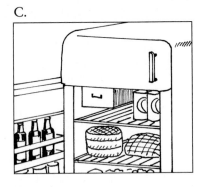

D.

E.

F.

G.

H.

I.

Refer to the drawing to the right, and then complete each sentence by using the te-form of the verbs given + あります or います.

Automobiles and Transportation

1. 部屋の窓が（閉める）
2. 机の上に本が（出る）
3. カーテンが（開く）
4. 壁に絵が（かかる）
5. 机の上に花が（置く）
6. 机の引き出し (drawer) が（閉まる）
7. 机の下にペンが（落ちる）
8. 電気が（つく）
9. 本が（開ける）

20. Expressing an Attempt

大野：三村君、宿題はしましたか。
三村：いいえ。しようとしたんですが、ちょっとむずかしいところがあって...
大野：まだ、していないんですか。
三村：ええ、まだなんです。

町田：三村さん、このビデオのプログラムの仕方、知ってる？
三村：うん、一度したことがあるよ。
町田：今、しようとしているんだけど、なかなかうまくいかないのよ。
三村：取り扱い説明書は読んだ？
町田：ええ。でも、よくわからないのよ。

20.1 The following construction means *to attempt to, try to, be about to....*

Plain, volitional form of the verb + とする／とします

OONO: Mr. Mimura, did you do your homework? MIMURA: No. I tried to do it, but there's a part I just don't get, so (*lit., There's a little difficult place*) . . . OONO: So you haven't done it yet? MIMURA: No, not yet.

MACHIDA: Mr. Mimura, do you know how to program this VCR? MIMURA: Yes, I've programmed it once before. MACHIDA: I've been trying to program it, but it's not going well. MIMURA: Have you read the manual? MACHIDA: Yes, but I still don't get it.

歌を歌おうとしましたが、声が出ませんでした。
I tried to sing a song, but nothing came out (lit., the voice didn't come out).
窓を開けようとしたが、開かなかった。
I tried to open the window, but it didn't open.

To review the volitional form of verbs, refer to Chapter 6, **Grammar 37,** in Book 1.

20.2 You have already learned that the te-form of the verb + みる can sometimes be translated as *try,* so you may be wondering how this new construction is different. Actually, the two constructions are quite different, and the fact that both of them allow the English translation of *try* is just a coincidence. The te-form + みる construction really means *to do something to see what will happen or to see what it is like.* Thus we get sentences like

納豆 (*fermented beans*) を食べてみました。
*I tried eating **nattoo** [to see what it was like].*
ドアを開けてみました。
I opened the door [to see what would happen].

In contrast, the plain, volitional + とする construction often implies that the action was ultimately impossible or futile, especially when it is used in the past tense. In the present progressive tense, the only connotation is that the subject is attempting to do something.

納豆を食べようとしたけれど、まずかったから食べられなかった。
*I tried to eat the **nattoo,** but it was bad-tasting, so I couldn't eat it.*
ドアを開けようとしたけど、鍵がかかっていた。
I tried to open the door, but it was locked.
この小説 (*novel*) を読もうとしています。
I'm trying to read this novel.

The plain, volitional form of the verb + とする construction has an additional use, which is to describe interrupted actions, particularly when the construction appears in its 〜たら form or before 時 or ところ. These are similar to the English *just as I was about to. . . .*

家を出ようとしたら、ブラウンさんが来た。
Just as I was about to leave the house, Ms. Brown came.
お風呂に入ろうとしたところ、電話がなりました。
Just as I was about to get into the bath, the telephone rang.

Automobiles and Transportation

Complete each of these sentences by choosing the best option from among those listed.

1. ＿＿＿が、ガソリンがなかった。
2. ＿＿＿が、雨が降ってきた。
3. ＿＿＿が、鍵がかかっていた。
4. ＿＿＿が、電池 (battery) がなかった。
5. ＿＿＿が、カワムラさんが「食べるな」と言った。
6. 高田さんは山本さんが好きで、＿＿＿。
7. 村山さんのアパートへ行くと、＿＿＿。

a. ウォークマンを聞こうとした。
b. ピクニックに出かけようとした
c. ドレスを着て、どこかへ出かけようとしていた
d. ドライブに行こうとした
e. 彼女を映画に誘おう (invite) としている
f. おととい作ったすしを食べようとした
g. ドアを開けようとした

Change the verbs in parentheses to the plain, volitional form.

1. エンジンを（かける）としたが、かからなかった。
2. 山本さんと（話す）としましたが、忙しくて、話す時間がありませんでした。
3. ホットケーキを（作る）としたが、焦がして (焦がす = to scorch) しまった。
4. そこで本を（読む）としましたが、子供がうるさくて読めませんでした。
5. 散歩へ（行く）としたら、高田さんが来ました。
6. 林さんに（会う）としましたが、どこにいるかわかりませんでした。
7. その近所でアパートを（借りる）としましたが、高くて、やめました。
8. その学生は来年から日本の大学で（勉強する）としています。

Complete the following sentences by changing the verbs in the parentheses to ～ようとする／した or ～てみる／みた.

1. 窓を（開ける）が、どうしても開かなかった。
2. 窓を（開ける）が、外には誰もいなかった。
3. 日本語で手紙を（書く）が、時間がかかりました。
4. 日本語で手紙を（書く）が、時間がありませんでした。
5. 来週、あの新しいレストランへ（行く）。

6. このケーキ、とてもおいしいですよ。ちょっと（食べる）ください。

7. 日本語で（話す）が、ことば (*words*) が口から出て来なかったんです。

8. 日本語で（話す）が、誰もわかってくれなかったんです。

練習　　　　　　　4

Describe what each person or object is trying to do or is about to do by using
〜ようとしている.

[例]　チンさんがバスに乗ろうとしている。

1. カワムラさんは…
2. ブラウンさんは…
3. 町田さんは…
4. 車は…
5. 林さんは…
6. 三村さんは…

21. Expressing a Just-Completed Action: The Ta-Form of the Verb + ばかり／ところだ

山口：カワムラさん、ケーキ、買ってきたんですけど、食べませんか。
カワムラ：残念だな。今、夕ごはんを食べたばかりなんですよ。
山口：そうですか。でも、ほら、小さなケーキだから、食べられますよ。
カワムラ：そうですね。じゃあ、いただきます。

町田：あの方はどなた？
チン：私の友達のリーさん。
町田：中国人の方？
チン：ええ、昨日ペキンから着いたばかりなの。

21.1 The following construction is used when only a little time has passed since something happened.

Ta-form of verb +　ばかりだ(です)
　　　　　　　　　　ところだ(です)

Something has just happened, someone has just done something.

ばかり is a particle meaning *only* or *nothing but what is stated*. (Refer to Chapter 2.), while ところ is a noun meaning *place*, and, by extension, *point in time*.

車にガソリンを入れたばかりです。
I have just put gas in my car.
先週、車のチェックをしたばかりです。
I just had my car checked last week.
このワープロは買ったばかりで、まだ使い方がよくわかりません。
I just bought this word processor, so I don't know how to use it yet.

YAMAGUCHI: Mr. Kawamura, I just bought some cakes (*lit., bought cakes and came back*). Won't you have some?　KAWAMURA: Oh, too bad. I just ate dinner.　YAMAGUCHI: I see, but look, they're small cakes, so I'm sure you can eat one.　KAWAMURA: Do you think so? Then, I'll have some.

MACHIDA: Who is that person?　CHIN: My friend, Ms. Lee.　MACHIDA: Is she Chinese?　CHIN: Yes, she just arrived from Beijing yesterday.

21.2 The ta-form with ばかり and the ta-form with ところ differ slightly in nuance. Here are two contrasting sentences:

> ニューヨークから帰ってきたところです。
> *I have just returned from New York.*
> ニューヨークから帰ってきたばかりです。
> *I have just returned from New York.*

The first sentence implies that the speaker has returned from New York a very short time ago, perhaps even only a few minutes ago, but almost certainly within the same day. The second sentence, however, implies that the speaker returned from New York a relatively short time ago, but the definition of "a relatively short time" varies according to the context. For example, if you were talking about current conditions in New York and you had come back from a trip there ten days before, you could introduce your remarks by saying:

> 十日前にニューヨークから帰ってきたばかりなんですが...
> *I just returned from New York ten days ago, but . . .*

The same sentence with ところ would be ungrammatical, because ten days is too long to be considered a point in time.

練習　　　　　　　　　　1

Match each statement with the person who most likely said it. Choose among the people listed below.

1. マドンナとのインタビューを終えたばかりです。
2. デパートを5軒回って、今帰ってきたばかりです。
3. ビルと話したばかりです。
4. パリへは先月行ってきたばかりです。来月はウィーンへ行くつもりです。
5. その漢字、習ったばかりです。
6. ラビオリを食べたばかりで、おなかがいっぱいです。
7. 「ルーツ」を読んだばかりです。

a. バーバラ・ウォーターズ
b. 日本語を習っている学生
c. 買い物が好きな人
d. 旅行が好きな人
e. イタリアが好きな人
f. アレックス・ヘイリーの本が好きな人
g. ヒラリー・クリントン

Complete these sentences, following the example.

[例] 昼ごはんを食べたところだから、... →
　　　昼ごはんを食べたところだから、おなかがいっぱいです。

1. 運動したところだから...
2. アメリカから来たところだから、...
3. 旅行から帰ってきたところだから、...
4. 新しいスポーツカーを買ったところだから、...
5. コーヒーを飲んだところだから...

Complete these sentences, following the example.

[例] ...なので、疲れています。→
　　　10キロ走ったばかりなので、疲れています。
　　　...なので、ブラウンさんはすぐ出てくるでしょう。→
　　　映画が終わったところなので、ブラウンさんはすぐ出てくるでしょう。

1. ...なので、おなかがすいています。
2 ...なので、部屋がとてもきれいです。
3. ...なので、まだドレスを着ています。
4. ...なので、まだちょっと寒いです。
5. ...なので、今は何も食べられません。
6. ...なので、まだ上手に作れません。

22. Without Doing: 〜ないで

カワムラ：もう8時5分？大変だ。寝坊しちゃった。
　　山口：朝ごはんはテーブルの上よ。
カワムラ：今日は朝ごはんを食べないで、学校へ行きます。
　　山口：朝ごはんを食べないと、体に悪いわよ。

KAWAMURA: Is it already 8:05? Oh, no! I overslept.　　YAMAGUCHI: Your breakfast is on the table.
KAWAMURA: I'll go to school without eating breakfast today.　　YAMAGUCHI: If you don't eat breakfast, it's bad for your health (*lit., body*), you know.

22.1 The negative form (the ない form) of verbs + で, the negative te-form of the verb is used to make an adverbial clause meaning *without doing.* . . .

昨日の夜はぜんぜん寝ないで、宿題をしていました。
Last night I did homework without sleeping at all.

靴を脱がないで、家の中に入ったんですか。
You went into a house without taking off your shoes?

This form is also used for negative commands, as you learned in Chapter 2.

22.2 The ～ないで form can be replaced with the negative te-form, ～なくて, when the following clause expresses emotions, judgments, or reasons. In fact, the alternative with ～なくて is probably more common in these cases.

三村さんと話さなくて、いいですか。
Is it all right not to talk to Mr. Mimura?

人があまり来なくて、さびしいパーティーだった。
Not very many people came, and it was a forlorn party.

22.3 In Chapter 2 you studied the te-form of verbs + おく, which means *do something as a preparation for a future occasion.* The negative of this construction, ～ないで + おく, means *to leave something undone for the time being* or *to leave something undone for a specific reason.*

お父さんのためにそのステーキを食べないでおきました。
I left that steak uneaten for my father [so that he could eat it].

来月旅行にお金を使うので、今月はあまり使わないでおいた。
Because I'll spend money for travel next month, I didn't spend so much money this month.

練習	1

Rewrite these sentences following the example.

[例]　本を（見る）、答えてください。→
　　　本を見ないで、答えてください。

1. となりの人に（聞く）、答えてください。
2. めがねを（かける）、運転した。

YOKOI: Everybody, please try reading this now.　CURTIS: May I use a dictionary?　YOKOI: Please read it without looking things up in a dictionary.

Automobiles and Transportation

3. 顔を（洗う）、学校へいきました。
4. ノートに何も（書く）、聞いていてください。
5. 席に（座る）、立っていた。
6. 電気を（つける）、勉強していました。
7. 傘を（持つ）、家を出ました。
8. そのセーターを（買う）、帰ってきました。

練習　　　　　　　　2

Answer these questions.
1. 何も見ないで、「おんがく」という漢字が書けますか。
2. 三日間何も食べないで、我慢 (endurance) できますか。
3. 誰にも聞かないで、「さんぜんよんひゃくごじゅうはち」が漢字で書けますか。
4. 辞書を引かないで、「高田さんは去年、マダガスカルに旅行しました」の意味がわかりますか。
5. クラスに出ないで、家でテレビを見ていたことがありますか。
6. 一晩中寝ないで、勉強したことがありますか。

練習　　　　　　　　3

Complete each sentence by choosing one appropriate expression from the list below and changing it to the 〜ないで form. Follow the example.

[例]　山口さんは _____ スピーチをしました。すごいですね。（紙を見る）→
　　　山口さんは紙も見ないで、スピーチをしました。すごいですね。

お風呂に入る
さよならを言う
ライトをつける
エアコンを入れる
ごはんを食べる

1. カワムラさんは _____、勉強していますよ。大丈夫ですか。
2. 三村さんは _____、帰りました。失礼な人ですね。
3. あの車は _____、走っています。危いですね。
4. _____、きたないですね。
5. こんなに暑いのに、_____、何しているのですか。

体に悪いわよ

The sentence-final particle わ, not to be confused with は, the topic particle, indicates mild emphasis and is used mostly by female speakers in the Tokyo-Yokohama area. Male speakers in certain other parts of Japan also use it, but in the Tokyo-Yokohama region, it has a definitely feminine flavor. It most commonly appears in informal sentences, where it is one of the features distinguishing the feminine style from the masculine.

大変だ。(masculine)　　　　*It's awful.*
大変だわ。(feminine)

できないよ。(masculine)　　　*I can't.*
できないわよ。(feminine)

The distinctions between masculine and feminine speech are less strict than they used to be, but it is still more acceptable for a female to use slightly masculine speech than for a male to use feminine speech.

The Conjunctive Form of the Verb as a Coordinating Structure

The conjunctive form of verbs (see Chapter 3, Book 1) can be used to connect two clauses.

スイッチを入れ、ライトがつくかどうか確かめます。
I'll put on the switch and check whether or not the light turns on.
一番目の角を左に曲がり、まっすぐ行きます。
Turn left at the first corner and go straight.

Like the te-form of the verb, the conjunctive form is used to express sequential and contrasted actions.

電気を消し、部屋を出た。(sequential actions)
電気を消して、部屋を出た。
I turned off the light and left the room.

私は京都へ行き、村山さんは大阪へ行きました。(contrastive actions)
私は京都へ行って、村山さんは大阪へ行きました。
I went to Kyoto, while Ms. Murayama went to Osaka.

> The conjunctive form of verbs is the form to which ます (non-past, polite affirmative ending) is attached.

The conjunctive form sounds more formal than the te-form, and all in all, it is more common in writing and formal or scripted speech than in everyday conversation. You will often see it in written instructions.

Vocabulary

Automobiles

うんてんしゅ	運転手	driver
うんてんめんきょ(しょう)	運転免許(証)	driver's license
オートバイ		motorcycle
ガソリン		gasoline
きゅうきゅうしゃ	救急車	ambulance
こしょう(する)	故障(する)	(to have a) mechanical breakdown, (to become) out of order
しゅうり(する)	修理(する)	(to) repair
しゅうりや(さん)／メカニック	修理屋(さん)	auto mechanic
しょうぼうしゃ	消防車	fire engine
タイヤ		tire
チェック(する)		(to) check
なおす	直す	to fix, repair
ナンバープレート		license plate
バックミラー		rearview mirror
パトカー		patrol car
パンク(する)		(to get a) flat tire
ハンドル		steering wheel
ぶひん、パーツ	部品／パーツ	part (*of a mechanical object*)
ブレーキをかける		to apply the brakes
フロントガラス		windshield

Loanwords: アンテナ、エンジン、オイル、サービス・ステーション、スポーツカー、トラック、トランク、バッテリー、バンパー、ヘッドライト、メンテナンス、モノレール、モペット、ラジエーター、ワイパー、シートベルト

Review: 運転(する)、ガソリン・スタンド、車、自転車、タクシー、地下鉄、電車、駐車場、停留所、ドライブ(する)、乗る、バス、走る

Traffic

おうだんほどう	横断歩道	pedestrian crossing
こうさてん	交差点	intersection
こうじちゅう	工事中	under construction
こうそくどうろ	高速道路	freeway
こうつう	交通	traffic
こうつうきかん	交通機関	means of transportation
こうつうじこ	交通事故	traffic accident
こうつうじゅうたい	交通渋滞	traffic jam
(こうつう)しんごう	(交通)信号	traffic light
じこにあう	事故にあう	to get involved in an accident
しょうとつ(する)	衝突(する)	collision, (to collide)
じそく	時速	speed per hour
つかまる	捕まる	to be caught
とおる	通る	to pass through, go along
とまる	止まる	to come to a stop
ほこうしゃ	歩行者	pedestrian
ほどう	歩道	sidewalk
まよう	迷う	to get lost
まわりみち	回り道	detour

Review: 道、道路（どうろ）

Verbs: The Transitive and Intransitive Verbs are on pp. 163–164.

Other Words

～かた	～方	how to . . .	つぎに	次に	next
さいごに	最後に	lastly	～ないで		without . . . ing
さいしょに	最初に	first	ばかりだ		to have just done . . .

Kanji

Learn these **kanji.**

自	駐	変	速	信	意
路	教	故	違	号	
交	窓	横	反	走	
通	閉	働	差	帰	
転	消	工	点	注	

Reading and Writing

Reading 1　安全運転
<ruby>安<rt>あん</rt></ruby><ruby>全<rt>ぜん</rt></ruby><ruby>運<rt>うん</rt></ruby><ruby>転<rt>てん</rt></ruby>

Before You Read

1. Connect each noun with a related verb.　_____A

   B

ブレーキ	見る
ガソリン	閉める
バックミラー	かける
ハンドル	回す
シートベルト	入れる
ドア	締める／する
シート	すわる

2. Which of the following factors is most important for you when you buy a car?

   値段が安い
   安全
   経済的 (economical)
   カッコいい
   長持ちする (durable)

Now Read It!

安全な運転の仕方

1. 運転の前

   運転前には、次の点をチェックしましょう。

   a. 運転席でのチェック

   ブレーキペダル、ハンドブレーキ、ガソリンの量、バックミラー、サイドミラー

   b. エンジンルームのチェック

   ブレーキのリザーブタンク、ラジエーターのリザーブタンク　エンジンオイルの量、ファンベルト

次の following / 点 point

運転席 driver's seat

量 amount

c. 車のまわりのチェック

エンジンスイッチを入れ、ウインカー、ブレーキライトがつくかどうか点検しましょう。タイヤのみぞの深さが十分かどうか点検しましょう。定期点検をしたばかりでも、これらの点をいつも点検することが大切です。発車する前には、車の前後に人がいないかどうか、車の下に子供がいないかどうか確かめましょう。

みぞ *[tire] tread* / 深さ *depth*
十分 *sufficient*
定期点検 *regular check up*

発車する *to start a car*

確かめる *to make sure*

2. 車に乗る時

車に乗る時は、後ろから来る車にも注意して、乗りましょう、シートは倒さないで、深く腰かけましょう。シートベルトは必ず締めてください。子供を助手席に乗せるのは危険です。幼児用シートか後部座席に乗せましょう。

注意する *to watch for, be cautious, take care*
倒す *knock over, set back*
腰かける *to sit down, to take a seat*
助手席 *passenger seat* / 幼児 *infant*
後部座席 *rear seat*

衝突時にシートベルトをしていないと……

ハンドルで胸をうつ

フロントガラスにぶつける

車外になげ出される

車内でふりまわされる

3. 車を運転する時

運転する時は、動きやすい服装をしましょう。また、げたやハイヒールなどをはいて、運転してはいけません。ハンドルは両手で握りましょう。発車前に、バックミラーを見て、車の後ろや横がよく見えるか確かめましょう。ドアはロックしてありますか。お酒を飲むと、注意力がにぶります。お酒を飲んで運転するのはやめましょう。また、疲れている時や眠い時は、十分休んでから、運転しましょう。

服装 *clothes* / げた *geta (wooden clogs)*
両手 *both hands*
握る *to grip*

注意力 *attentiveness* / にぶる *to decline*
やめる *to stop, quit* / 疲れる *to get tired*
眠い *sleepy*

After You Finish Reading

The paragraph above mentions things you should watch for (1) before driving, (2) while getting in the car, and (3) while you are driving. In which part do you think the following sentences should be added?

1. ハンドルは10時10分の位置に握ります。
2. シートレバーでシートの前後の位置を変えます。
3. 車を出す前に、バックミラーで車の後ろやまわりの安全をチェックしましょう。
4. フロントガラスはきれいにしておきましょう。
5. ワイパーが古くなっていませんか。
6. 一緒に車に乗っている人もシートベルトを締めなくてはいけません。
7. 雨の日は、道路がすべりやすいです。運転には特に注意しましょう。
8. 長時間休まないで、運転するのは危険です。

The following are things you have to do when changing a flat tire, but they are out of sequence. Arrange them in the correct order. Can you tell which verbs are transitive and which are intransitive by looking at how they are used in the sentences?

( ) ホイルナットをつけます。
( ) エンジンを止め、エマージェンシーライトをつけます。
( ) ハブキャップをとりつけます。
( ) ハブキャップをつけます。
( ) 車から降ります。
( ) ホイルナットを締めます。
( ) ジャッキで車を下げます。
( ) ジャッキで車を上げます。
( ) 道路のはじに車を止めます。
( ) トランクからジャッキ、スペアタイヤを出します。
( ) ホイルナットを緩めます。
( ) サイドブレーキをかけます。
( ) パンクしたタイヤを取り、スペアタイヤをつけます。

Writing 1

You would like to sell your car. Write a short advertisement. Make it as attractive as possible to prospective buyers.

Reading 2　上手なドライブの仕方

Before You Read

1. When you go for a long-distance drive, what do you take along? What do you do before leaving? Discuss in Japanese with your classmates.
2. List three good points and three bad points each of travel by car and travel by air. Compare your answers with those of your classmates.

Now Read It!

上手なドライブの仕方

■ 道路交通情報センター

ドライブする時に一番気になるのは交通渋滞ですね。交通渋滞にあうと、せっかくのドライブのプランも台無し。ドライブの前に道路情報を聞いておきましょう。道路交通情報センターに電話すると、日本中の主な道路の情報、渋滞の情報、交通事故の情報を教えてくれます。東京の電話番号は3581-7611です。

■ JAFの旅行サービス

目的の場所までどのようなコースで行けばいいか、ドライブ・コースを教えてくれるのはJAFの旅行サービスです。ドライブ・プラン、ドライブ・コースの相談にのってくれますし、旅館やホテルの予約もしてくれます。また、車の故障、交通事故、パンクの時には24時間いつでもエマージェンシー・サービスをしてくれます。JAFの電話番号は3436-2811です。

■ レンタカー

どこか遠くへ出かけたい。でも、長時間の運転は疲れるし、途中の交通渋滞はいや。こんな方は、往復はJRを使い、観光地ではレンタカーを借りてはいかがでしょうか。レンタカーは運転免許がある人なら誰でも借りられます。料金もそんなに高くありません。例えば、スターレットが6時間6,900円、カリーナSEが6時間11,000円です。予約はトヨタレンタ予約センター3264-0120に。また、JRの往復料金とレンタカーの料金を一緒にしたレール&レンタカー切符もあります。

■ フェリーボート

九州をマイカーでドライブしたい方には、フェリーが一番。九州まではフェリーでゆっくりと行き、九州に着いたら、マイカーで自由にドライブできます。東京から九州まではオーシャンフェリーで、料金は往復大人が3280円、車は52000円です。予約は3567-0971まで。

気になる *to be worried about, be nervous about*
せっかく *long-awaited, going to all the trouble* / 台無し *totally spoiled*
主(な) *main, major, chief*

情報 *information*

目的 *purpose, objective* / 行けばいい *It would be good to go*

相談 *consultation*

疲れる *to get tired* / 途中 *on the way*
いや(な) *disgusting, disagreeable*
往復 *round trip*
運転免許がある人なら *If it is a person with a driver's license*
料金 *fee*
例えば *for example*
自由に *freely*

せっかく is an adverb that adds the nuance of "having gone to all the trouble" or "having waited this long." It is usually followed by a suggestion of what to do because of this situation.

JAF 仮会員証

振込日より1ヵ月間有効

同居家族一名自署

この仮会員証の提示がなければ会員としてのサービスは受けられません。

裏面受領証に受付局日附印なきもの無効
（入会金・会費は課税対象外）

JAPAN AUTOMOBILE FEDERATION

★会員証はお手もとに届くまで、お振込後3～4週間程かかります。
万一、1ヶ月以上たっても会員証が届かない場合は、お手数ですが、
関東本部会員部（☎03-5976-9730）までご連絡ください。

路上故障にすばやく駆けつける──関東地区主要サービス網

札　幌	011-857-8139	千　葉	043-224-1655
旭　川	0166-53-8828	大　宮	048-651-0111
室　蘭	0143-87-0110	宇都宮	0286-59-3311
帯　広	0155-33-8171	水　戸	0292-31-3271
釧　路	0154-51-2166	群馬中央	0273-63-5141
北　見	0157-61-0521	甲　府	0552-41-0111
函　館	0138-49-5654	長　野	0262-23-1100
東　京	03-5395-0111	新　潟	025-265-0111
横　浜	045-843-7110	沖　縄	098-877-9163

● 高速道路、自動車専用道路で故障の時は、路側の非常電話でJAFにご連絡ください。
（詳しくは、会員証とともにお届けする「JAFサービスガイド」をごらんください。）

こんなに差がある会員と非会員

■高速での事故車けん引（10km）

会員	会員証を提示すれば	けん引料のみ（5kmまで無料）	合計　2,500円
非会員		産業特別料金 基本料金 けん引料 10kmけん引料	合計 16,250円

■キー閉じ込み

会員	会員証を提示すれば		無料
非会員		基本料 5,500円（夜間料金）　作業料 2,200円	合計 7,700円

夜間走行中に車をぶつけてライト部分を破損したので、JAFのサービスカーで10kmけん引してもらった。

ドライブインで、鍵をつけたままドアロックしてしまいました。

『JAFに入っておけばよかったのに！』と困らないために

─────年中無休・24時間安心のＪＡＦ今すぐ入会を─────

●ご入会は簡単です

（この振込用紙に住所＊氏名をご記入の上、最寄りの郵便局＊表記の銀行（本社＊支店）へご持参下さい。）

振込先銀行名及び口座名

第一勧業銀行	（日比谷支店）	東京相和銀行　（虎ノ門支店）
さくら銀行	（東京営業部）	住友銀行　（日比谷支店）
富士銀行	（三田支店）	大和銀行　（神谷町支店）
三菱銀行	（本店）	東海銀行　（三田支店）
あさひ銀行	（本店営業部）	東京都民銀行　（本店）
三和銀行	（虎ノ門支店）	横浜銀行　（東京支店）
八千代銀行	（本店）	

社団法人 日本自動車連盟・普通預金

手数料不要

After You Finish Reading

Fill in the following table in English, basing your answers on the information in the brochure above.

PLACE	FOR WHAT PURPOSES? ON WHAT OCCASIONS?	TELEPHONE NUMBER
		3581-7611
JAF		
		3264-0120
Ocean Ferry		

The following people each have different travel plans. What telephone number should each person call?

1. 林さんと九州に旅行したいんですが、東京から九州までの長い距離を運転するのは疲れますね。
2. 明日、北海道まで車で行きます。途中の道路情報がほしいんですが、…
3. 東京から新潟、金沢へドライブしますが、どんなコースがいいんですか。
4. ドライブの途中なんですが、パンクしてしまいました。タイヤの替え方がわからないんです。
5. これから車で千葉へ行くんですが、途中、事故はありませんか。
6. 車がエンストしてしまいました。どうしたらいいでしょうか。
7. 引っ越しするので、トラックが必要です。
8. ガールフレンドと横浜へドライブしたいんですが、車がありません。

替える *to change*

エンスト *engine stall*

Writing 2

Write out the directions for driving from the campus to your home by car. Then exchange directions with a classmate and see if you can understand each other's directions. If you have a map, try to follow your partner's directions on it.

Language Functions and Situations

Asking for and Giving Instructions

自動車学校で
町田：どうやってバックするんですか。
先生：まず、後ろを見て、車の後ろの安全を確かめます。

MACHIDA: How do I back up?   TEACHER: First, you look back and make sure that it's safe in back.

町田：こうですか。

先生：はい。それから、クラッチを踏み、シフトレバーをRに入れます。

町田：はい、入れました。

はなす to release

先生：クラッチをはなしながら、アクセルをゆっくり踏みます。後ろを見ながら、ゆっくりバックします。

町田：こうですか。

先生：そうそう。ハンドルをしっかり握って...

コミュニケーション・ノート

Asking for and Giving Instructions

どのようにエンジンをかけますか。
How do I start the engine?
どうやってエンジンオイルを替えますか。
How do I change the engine oil?
ガソリンの入れ方を教えてください。
Please show me how to put gas in.
次にどうしますか。
What do I do next?
今度はどうしますか。
What shall I do the next time?

Asking What Something Is For

これは何[のため]に使いますか。
What are we going to use this for?
これは何のためにあるんですか。
What is this for?

Checking If You Are on the Right Track

これでいいですか。
Is it all right like this?
こうですか。
Do you mean like this?

MACHIDA: Like this?   TEACHER: Yes. Then press down the clutch and shift into reverse.   MACHIDA: All right, I've done it.   TEACHER: While releasing the clutch, press down slowly on the accelerator. While looking to the rear, you back up slowly.   MACHIDA: Like this?   TEACHER: Grip the steering wheel firmly.

Language Functions and Situations

189 百八十九

Role Play

Work in pairs, and practice giving each other instructions on how to perform tasks you know how to do.

Cheering Up and Encouraging Others

町田 : 運転免許の試験、ダメだったの。

カワムラ : そう。残念だったね。

町田 : もう、免許取れないんじゃないかしら。

カワムラ : 今度は大丈夫だよ。

町田 : そうかしら。

カワムラ : うん、がんばって。

カワムラ : おにぎりの作り方はこれでいいですか。

山口 : ええ、だんだん上手になってきましたね。

カワムラ : この次はどうするんですか。

山口 : こうやって海苔をまくのよ。

カワムラ : こうですか。

山口 : ええ、その調子、その調子。

MACHIDA: I failed the driving test again.   KAWAMURA: Really? That's too bad.   MACHIDA: I bet I'll never be able to get a driver's license.   KAWAMURA: Next time will be all right.   MACHIDA: I wonder. KAWAMURA: Yes, hang in there.

KAWAMURA: Is this way of making rice balls OK?   YAMAGUCHI: Yes, you have gradually improved. KAWAMURA: What do I do next?   YAMAGUCHI: Wrap them in seaweed like this.   KAWAMURA: Like this?   YAMAGUCHI: Yes, that's the way to go.

Encouraging Words

がんばって(ください)。	*Good luck.* *Try your best.* *Hang in there.*
今度は大丈夫ですよ。	*You'll do OK next time.*
元気を出して(ください)。	*Keep your spirits up.*
気を落とさないで(ください)。	*Don't be discouraged.*
しっかりやってください。	*Do a good job!*
しっかりして(ください)。	*Pull yourself together.*

Giving Assurance

はい、それでいいですね。	*Yes, it's fine like this.*
なかなか上手ですね。	*You're rather good.*
もう一回やってみましょう。	*Let's try again.*
だんだん上手になってきましたね。	*You've gotten better each time.*
その調子、その調子。	*That's the way to go.*

Role Play

Work in pairs. The first student is in one of the following unpleasant situations and explains it to his or her partner. The second student then offers sympathy and encouragement.

a. 日本語の試験で0点を取りました。
b. 交通事故を起こしました。
c. お金をなくしました。
d. 漢字が上手に書けません。
e. 友達のコンピュータをこわしてしまいました。

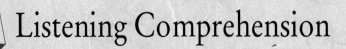

Listening Comprehension

1. Ms. Gibson is trying to buy a used car. She has called three people who have cars for sale. Listen to their phone conversations and fill in the following table in English.

SELLER'S NAME	HOSHI	KUROKAWA	KANEKO
Make			
Year			
Mileage			
How many seats?			
Automatic transmission?			
Horsepower			
Fuel efficiency			
New tires?			
Other features			
Price			

Automobiles and Transportation

2. Mr. Kawamura has witnessed a car accident. Listen as he describes the accident to a policeman. Then draw a diagram of the accident on the following map.

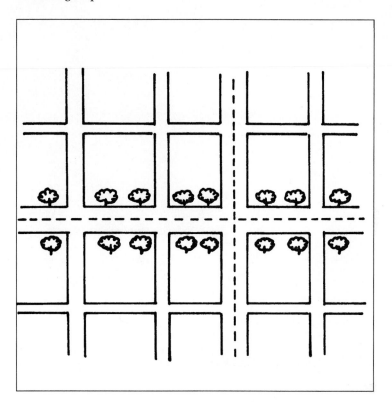

Review
Chapter 1

家族と一緒にカラオケを楽しんでいます。

Culture Reading: Daily Life

After having spent a lot of time talking about your daily activities in Japanese, you may be wondering how Japanese people spend their daily lives. Are the images you see in the American mass media true, or are they just stereotypes? Read the following and discuss in class how the lives of the average Japanese people as described in the survey are different from or similar to your life or the lives of your family members.

日本人の日常生活

　日本人は、どのように一日24時間を使っているのだろうか。NHKの調査によると、日本人は平日は一日平均8時間眠り、食事に1時間40分使っている。仕事は一日8時間ぐらいしている。余暇の時間は7時間半ぐらいである。合計が24時間を超えているのは、テレビを見ながら食事をするからである。46％の人がテレビを見ながら食事をすると答えている。余暇の時間の中で3時間は、テレビを見ている時間である。毎年の調査によるとテレビを見る時間はだんだん増えてきている。

日常生活 *daily life*
NHK (*Nippon Hoosoo Kyookai*)
　Japanese Broadcasting Corporation
調査 *survey, investigation*
…によると *according to …*
平均 *average*
合計 *total*

超える *to exceed*

答える *to answer*

だんだん *gradually*
増える *to increase* (cf. 増やす *increase* [*something*])

サラリーマンが家にいて、起きている時間は平均4時間16分である。家にいる時間が短いのは、「通勤」に時間がかかるからだ。東京のサラリーマンの平均通勤時間は1時間33分で、通勤に2時間以上使っているサラリーマンも20%いる。

平日と違い、週末は眠る時間は、9時間に増え、仕事、勉強、家事の時間は5時間に減る。そして、テレビを見る時間は4時間に増える。中学生の一日の勉強時間は9時間10分、高校生は8時間37分で、大人の一日の仕事時間よりも長く勉強している。日曜日でも一日4時間勉強している。だが大学生は平日でも一日5時間しか勉強していない。交際に1時間7分、レジャーに1時間33分、新聞、本、雑誌に1時間12分使っている。

主婦は家事に一日平均7時間38分使っている。このうち、料理2時間半、掃除1時間、洗濯1時間15分、買い物30分、子供の世話2時間15分となっている。日本人の夫は一日平均、家事に26分しか使っていない。これはこのNHKの調査でも毎年変わっていないようだ。

通勤 *commuting to work*

…以上 *equal to or more than*

減る *to decrease* (cf. 減らす *to decrease [something]*)
中学生 *junior high school student*
高校生 *high school student*

交際 *socializing with friends, peers*

世話 *care, taking care of someone*

夫 *husband*

Oral Activities

アクティビティー 1

単語の復習 (*Vocabulary review*)

For each of the words given below, find two additional words that are somehow related to it. Then explain exactly how the three words are related.

[例]　寝室 → （ベッド、ふとん）寝る時に使います。or
　　　　→ （居間、台所）部屋の名前です。

1. 予約
2. 不動産屋
3. 横断歩道
4. リゾート
5. 運転する
6. 掃除

ロサンゼルス・サンフランシスコ・ホノルル8日間
〈エコノミー／デラックス〉

利用予定ホテル：エコノミー／〔ロサンゼルス〕ハリウッドレガシー、パームホテル　〔サンフランシスコ〕ビバリー・プラザ・ホテル、ホテル・カリフォルニアン　〔ホノルル〕コーラル・リーフ　デラックス／〔ロサンゼルス〕ロサンゼルス・ヒルトン＆タワーズ、ハイアット・オン・ウイルシャー　食事：2昼食　〔サンフランシスコ〕サンフランシスコ・ヒルトン、パーク55　〔ホノルル〕ホリデイ・イン・ワイキキ

		スケジュール	食事
1	夕刻	東京発✈ロサンゼルスへ ─────────〈日付変更線通過〉	機内食
	午前	着後、市内観光 （ロサンゼルス泊）	昼食
2	終日	自由行動 ※オプショナルツアーをお楽しみください。 （ロサンゼルス泊）	
3	午前	ロサンゼルス発✈サンフランシスコへ 着後、市内観光 （サンフランシスコ泊）	昼食
4	終日	自由行動 ※オプショナルツアーをお楽しみください。 （サンフランシスコ泊）	
5	午前	サンフランシスコ発✈ホノルルへ 着後、ホテルへ （ホノルル泊）	
6	終日	自由行動 ※オプショナルツアーをお楽しみください。 （ホノルル泊）	
7・8	午前	ホノルル発✈東京へ ─────────〈日付変更線通過〉	機内食
	午後	着後、空港にて解散	

●最少催行人員2名 ●添乗員は同行しませんが、現地係員がお世話します。●ホテルは同等クラスに変更の場合もございます。
●出発日により、ロサンゼルスとサンフランシスコの日程が入替ることがあります。

ロサンゼルス・ホノルル7日間
〈エコノミー／デラックス〉

利用予定ホテル：エコノミー／〔ロサンゼルス〕ハリウッドレガシー、パームホテル　〔ホノルル〕コーラル・リーフ　デラックス／〔ロサンゼルス〕ロサンゼルス・ヒルトン＆タワーズ、ハイアット・オン・ウイルシャー　〔ホノルル〕ホリデイ・イン・ワイキキ　食事：1昼食

		スケジュール	食事
1	夕刻	東京発✈ロサンゼルスへ ─────────〈日付変更線通過〉	機内食
	午前	着後、市内観光 （ロサンゼルス泊）	昼食
2・3	終日	自由行動 ※オプショナルツアーをお楽しみください。 （ロサンゼルス泊）	
4	午前	ロサンゼルス発✈ホノルルへ 着後、ホテルへ （ホノルル泊）	
5	終日	自由行動 ※オプショナルツアーをお楽しみください。 （ホノルル泊）	
6・7	午前	ホノルル発✈東京へ ─────────〈日付変更線通過〉	機内食
	午後	着後、空港にて解散	

●最少催行人員2名 ●添乗員は同行しませんが、現地係員がお世話します。 ●ホテルは同等クラスに変更の場合もございます。

サンフランシスコ・ホノルル7日間
〈エコノミー／デラックス〉

利用予定ホテル：エコノミー／〔サンフランシスコ〕ビバリー・プラザ・ホテル、ホテル・カリフォルニアン　〔ホノルル〕コーラル・リーフ　デラックス／〔サンフランシスコ〕サンフランシスコ・ヒルトン、パーク55　食事：1昼食　〔ホノルル〕ホリデイ・イン・ワイキキ

		スケジュール	食事
1	夕刻	東京発✈サンフランシスコへ ─────────〈日付変更線通過〉	機内食
	午前	着後、市内観光 （サンフランシスコ泊）	昼食
2・3	終日	自由行動 ※オプショナルツアーをお楽しみください。 （サンフランシスコ泊）	
4	午前	サンフランシスコ発✈ホノルルへ 着後、ホテルへ （ホノルル泊）	
5	終日	自由行動 ※オプショナルツアーをお楽しみください。 （ホノルル泊）	
6・7	午前	ホノルル発✈東京へ ─────────〈日付変更線通過〉	機内食
	午後	着後、空港にて解散	

●最少催行人員2名 ●添乗員は同行しませんが、現地係員がお世話します。 ●ホテルは同等クラスに変更の場合もございます。

アクティビティー　2

飛行機(ひこうき)で旅行(りょこう)します。(*I'm going to travel by plane.*)

Imagine that you are going to take a trip by plane. Number the following activities in the order they would normally occur.

呼(よ)ぶ *to summon*

_____ 電話をかけて、タクシーを呼(よ)ぶ
_____ 飛行機(ひこうき)に乗(の)る

席(せき) *seat* / たずねる *to inquire about*

_____ スチュワーデスに席(せき)をたずねる
_____ 飲み物が出る
_____ 空港(くうこう)に着(つ)く
_____ タクシーに乗(の)る
_____ 飛行機(ひこうき)が離陸(りりく)する
_____ チェックイン・カウンターへ行く

アクティビティー　3

どこに旅行(りょこう)したらいいですか。(*Where should I travel to?*)

If you were a travel agent, what travel suggestions would you make to customers who expressed the following interests? Discuss your ideas in class.

[例(れい)]　—私(わたし)は絵(え)を見るのが好きなんです。
　　　　—パリのルーブルへ行ったらどうですか。

1. 私(わたし)は山に登(のぼ)るのが好きなんです。
2. おいしくて、めずらしい (*rare*) ものを食べたいですね。
3. おもしろい建物(たてもの)を見たいんです。
4. アメリカの歴史(れきし) (*history*) について知(し)りたいんです。
5. スキーが大好きなんです。
6. ギャンブルが好きなんです。
7. バーゲン・ショッピングが趣味(しゅみ)なんです。
8. めずらしい動物(どうぶつ) (*animals*) が見たいですね。

アクティビティー　4

冷蔵庫(れいぞうこ)はありますか。(*Is there a refrigerator?*)

1. Do this exercise in pairs.
   Both students copy the floor plan accompanying this activity. One student "furnishes" his or her rooms by drawing in furniture. The other asks

questions and tries to put the right furniture at the right place in the right room, all without looking at the first person's drawing.

[例] A: 冷蔵庫はありますか。
B: はい、台所にあります。
A: 台所のどこですか。
B: 台所の南側のドアの横です。

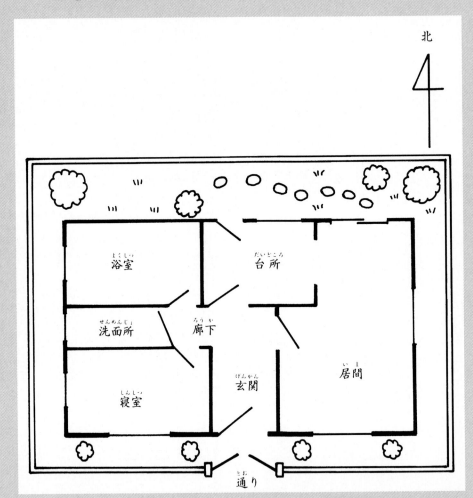

2. Once you have finished placing all your furniture, check your accuracy by comparing drawings. Then discuss how the layout of the rooms could be improved.

[例] ソファーはもう少し前に出した方がいいですよ。ここではテレビがよく見えませんから。ラジオはお風呂場に置かない方がいいですよ。こわれますから。寝室に置いたらどうですか。

アクティビティー 5

和製英語 (*English words made in Japan*)

You have studied many **katakana** words and are gradually learning how the pronunciations of English words are transliterated into Japanese. The following words are all Japanese words derived from English components but are unknown in English-speaking countries. Guess what elements the Japanese created these words from, and choose the most likely meaning for each one from among those listed in the second column.

1. ____ アフターサービス
2. ____ ドア・アイ
3. ____ ワンマンバス
4. ____ ゴールデンアワー
5. ____ ベビーサークル
6. ____ アイスキャンディー
7. ____ キャンピングカー
8. ____ ハンスト
9. ____ カフスボタン
10. ____ レストハウス

a. highway rest stop
b. bus with a driver and no conductor
c. hunger strike
d. door peep-hole
e. playpen
f. travel trailer
g. after-purchase repair and servicing
h. cuff links
i. prime time in television
j. a snack food similar to a Popsicle

アクティビティー 6

贈り物 (*Gifts*)

Of course, you are very creative when choosing a gift for your friends. Work in pairs. First, discuss what you will buy as a Christmas gift for each person listed. Why? How much do you expect to spend on each gift?

国広一郎、60歳の男の人、サラリーマン、音楽が好き
吉村道子、27歳の女の人、キャリアウーマン、旅行が好き
森田明美、32歳の女の人、息子が一人、外国語の勉強が好き
沢井武夫、18歳の男の人、大学生、趣味はウインター・スポーツ
金井由美、7歳の女の子、本を読むのが好き、甘いのもが好き
星野国俊、38歳の男の人、学校の先生、グルメ
花山鈴子、43歳の女の人、先月新しい家を買った

After you decide what you will buy for each person, role play the purchase of each gift, with one of you playing the store clerk and the other playing the customer. Take turns playing the two roles.

東京駅観光案内所 (*Tokyo Station Travel Information Center*)

With a partner, play the roles described.

Student 1: You are a tourist staying in Tokyo, and today you have decided to explore some places outside the city. You are thinking of exploring one of these places on the Yokosuka Line: 川崎大師 (Kawasaki Taishi Shrine), 横浜中華街 (Yokohama Chinatown), 大船撮影所 (Oohuna Movie Studio), 鎌倉大仏 (the Great Buddha of Kamakura), 横須賀マリーンパーク (Yokosuka Marine Park). You're still not quite sure which one you want to go to. Your partner works at the station's tourist information desk. Find out the following from him or her:

> which town to go to and what you can see there
> how frequent the trains are (between 9:00 and 10:00 A.M.)
> train departure times (from Tokyo)
> train arrival times (at your destination)
> whether you have to transfer
> how much the fare is

Student 2: You work at the tourist information center in Tokyo Station. Give your partner the requested information, using the following chart.

STATION	TRAIN 23	TRAIN 26	TRAIN 41	TRAIN 56	TRAIN 58	TRAIN 60	FARE (IN YEN)
Tokyo	9:00		9:20	9:40		10:00	
Kawasaki (shrine)	9:20		9:40	10:00		10:20	210
Yokohama (Chinatown)			9:50			10:30	340
Oohuna (movie studio)		9:35	9:55		10:15	10:35	380
Kamakura (Buddha)		10:00				10:40	670
Yokosuka (Marine Park)		10:15			10:55		830

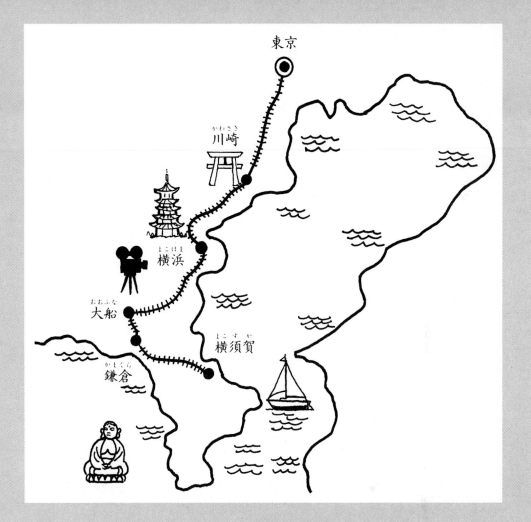

アクティビティー 8

私の夢の家 *(My dream house)*

Work with a partner. One of you is planning your dream house. Tell the other student, who is an architect, your preferences (for example, you would like to have a large window in the living room, you would like to have three bathrooms, and you would like to have a stereo in the bathroom). The architect responds with suggestions and draws a house plan on a piece of paper, according to your instructions.

Show your house plan to another pair of students and explain it to them. Ask for their opinions and suggestions.

軽井沢プリンスホテルです。(*This is the Karuizawa Princess Hotel.*)

Work in pairs. Do not show your partner what you have written down.

Student A: You are a person who wants to spend a few days next week in the mountain resort town of Karuizawa. Figure out exactly what you are willing to spend (between ¥7,000–¥45,000 per night), what sort of room you want, how many people you are going to go with, and when you want to arrive and leave.

Student B: You are the front desk clerk at the Karuizawa Princess Hotel. Decide what rooms are going to be available each night next week. If you want, you may specify that only rooms of a certain price in each category will be available or that the cheap rooms have some disadvantage, such as being next to the elevator. Use the chart below.

INFORMATION FOR STUDENT B (○ VACANCY ● NO VACANCY)

Price/night Date	Japanese Room	Western-style Room			
		Single	Double	Twin	Suite
	30,000 yen/ night	11,000 yen/ night	18,000 yen/ night	21,000 yen/ night	45,000 yen/ night

After going through this once, trade roles. Start your conversation as in the following example:

[例]　B:　もしもし、軽井沢プリンセス・ホテル、予約ですが…
　　　A:　あのう、予約したいんですが、…
　　　B:　何日から、何泊でしょうか。
　　　A:　＿＿＿＿＿
　　　B:　どんなお部屋がよろしいでしょうか。

(Continue the dialogue.)

Interview

In the past three chapters of *Yookoso!* you have expanded your ability to interact with others in Japanese and have begun to talk about travel, housing, transportation, and cars. This activity will help you review these major topics.

In the course of this activity, you will interview a classmate about his or her travel experiences. Find someone in the class with whom you have spoken only infrequently and interview him or her, pretending that you are at a party where you don't know anyone and are making conversation with the person nearest you. Finally, organize the information you have learned about your classmate into a brief oral report about that person's travel experiences.

Situations

First, your instructor will act out the following scenes. Listen carefully to understand how the interactions proceed. Then act out the following situations as fully as possible with a classmate. Use vocabulary that you know.

1. You have just arrived at Hiroshima Business Hotel. Mr. Iwata will visit you at the hotel around 7:00 P.M. Ask the receptionist to call when he arrives. Also ask where the best restaurant near the hotel is and request directions to it. In addition, ask for a wake-up call at 6:00 A.M. tomorrow.

   Useful vocabulary
   モーニングコール *wake-up call*

2. Your travel agent is supposed to have reserved a room for you at the Izumo Hotel. When you arrive at the hotel, they say that there is no reservation under your name. What do you do?

3. You are looking for a place to live. You have answered an advertisement, and the manager is showing you a possible apartment. Find out what kind of stores and services are in the neighborhood.

   Useful vocabulary
   広告 *advertisement*
   新聞 *newspaper*

4. Your car is almost out of gas and needs some repair work. Ask a pedestrian where you can find a gas station and a repair shop.

This Is My Life!: 森下さやか (テレビ・レポーター)

この仕事は大学生の時に、アルバイトで始めました。テレビ・レポーターをしていた私の友だちが病気になって、彼女のピンチヒッターをしたのが最初です。

大学を卒業した後、テレビ・レポーターはやめるつもりでした。子供の時から、グラフィック・デザイナーになりたかったし、大学で勉強していたグラフィック・デザインの仕事をしたかったんです。

でも、テレビの仕事も面白かったので、結局この仕事を続けることにしました。仕事でいろいろな所に行けるので、旅行が好きな私には向いている仕事だと思います。先週は九州に行ってきました。仕事の後は、その土地のおいしいものを食べるのが楽しみです。

ピンチ・ヒッター *replacement* (→ *pinch hitter*)

卒業する *to graduate*
やめる *to stop, quit* [something]

仕事 *job, work*

面白い *interesting, fun*
結局 *in the end, anyway*
続ける *to continue* [something]
いろいろ(な) *various*
向く *to be suitable;* Xに向く *to be suitable for X*
土地 *locale, land*
楽しみ *pleasure, something to look forward to*

仕事でいろいろな人に会えるのも楽しいです。政治家、ビジネスマン、キャリアウーマン、主婦、学生、いろいろな人にインタビューします。

　去年結婚しました。主人は大学のクラスメートでした。サラリーマンです。私は旅行が多いので主人は自分で料理をすることが多いです。私より料理が上手です。

　来年の一月に子供が生まれます。それでテレビ・レポーターの仕事はしばらく休むつもりです。子供が一歳ぐらいになったら、また仕事にもどろうと思っています。

政治家 *politician*

自分で *by oneself*

生まれる *to be born*
しばらく *for a brief period of time*
もどる *to return [a previous location]*

テレビのスタジオ：
ニュースの時間です。

Answer these questions:

1. 森下さんはいつテレビ・レポーターの仕事を始めましたか。
2. 大学では何を勉強しましたか。
3. 子供の時から、何になりたかったですか。
4. なぜ、テレビ・レポーターの仕事を続けることにしましたか。
5. 先週はどこに行きましたか。
6. 仕事の後の楽しみは何ですか。
7. 仕事でどんな人に会いますか。
8. いつ結婚しましたか。
9. ご主人とどこで会いましたか。
10. ご主人のお仕事は何ですか。
11. ご主人が自分で料理をすることが多いのはなぜですか。
12. ご主人は料理がお上手ですか。
13. いつお子さんが生まれますか。

4

第四章

体と健康
（からだ）（けん）（こう）

The Body and Health

毎日、公園でジョギングをしています。
（こうえん）

OBJECTIVES

Topics

Body parts
Feeling and emotions
Health and illness

Grammar

23. Analogy and exemplification
24. Describing attributes: The …は…が construction
25. Talking about appearance: よう, 〜そう, らしい, and みたい
26. Causatives
27. Constructions using interrogatives
28. Expressing expectation: …はず

Reading and Writing

Medical advice
Would you like to try **shiatsu**?

Language Functions and Situations

At a pharmacy
At a clinic

Vocabulary and Oral Activities

Body Parts

Vocabulary: Body Parts (1)

体	からだ	body
頭	あたま	head
顔	かお	face
目	め	eye
鼻	はな	nose
耳	みみ	ear
口	くち	mouth
歯	は	tooth
唇	くちびる	lip
舌	した	tongue
喉	のど	throat
首	くび	neck
肩	かた	shoulder
胸	むね	chest
背中	せなか	back
おなか		belly
腰	こし	waist, hips
腕	うで	arm
肘	ひじ	elbow
指	ゆび	finger
爪	つめ	nail
脚、足	あし	leg, foot
膝	ひざ	knee
毛	け	hair, strand of hair

Review: 髪（かみ）、手

髪（かみ）refers to a person's head of hair, while 毛 can refer to individual hairs, including the hair of animals.

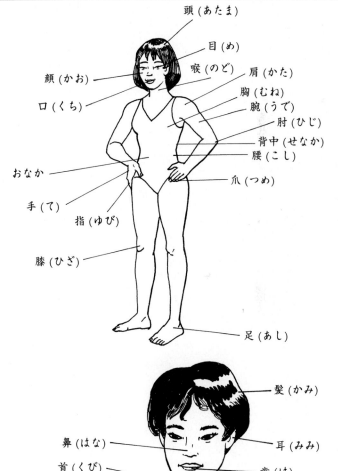

頭（あたま）
目（め）
顔（かお）
喉（のど）
肩（かた）
口（くち）
胸（むね）
腕（うで）
肘（ひじ）
背中（せなか）
腰（こし）
おなか
爪（つめ）
手（て）
指（ゆび）
膝（ひざ）
足（あし）

髪（かみ）
鼻（はな）
耳（みみ）
首（くび）
歯（は）
唇（くちびる）

アクティビティー　1

体のどこを使いますか。(*What part of the body would you use?*)

Tell what part of your body you would use to perform the following actions.

Review 〜時. cf. Chapter 7, **Grammar 40,** in Book 1.

[例]　音楽を聞く →
　　　音楽を聞く時は、耳を使います。

1. 歩く
2. キスをする
3. 本を読む
4. 呼吸する (*to breathe*)
5. においをかぐ (*to perceive a smell*)
6. 考える (*to think*)
7. 人にさわる (*to touch*)
8. ボールを蹴る (*to kick*)
9. ものをかむ (*to bite*)
10. バットを握る (*to grab, to grip*)

アクティビティー　2

体の機能 (*The functions of the parts of the body*)

Tell when you use the following parts of the body.

[例]　口 → 口は何かを食べたり、話したりする時に使います。

Review counters and verbs of existence.

1. 目
2. 足
3. 鼻
4. 手

5. 爪
6. 歯
7. 唇

アクティビティー　3

人間の体 (*Human body*)

Answer these questions.

1. 人間は目がいくつありますか。
2. 耳はいくつありますか。
3. 耳は顔のどこにありますか。
4. 鼻はいくつありますか。

5. 鼻は顔のどこにありますか。
6. 腕は何本ありますか。
7. 手に指は何本ありますか。
8. 足は何本ありますか。

Vocabulary Library

Body Parts (2)

右利き	みぎきき	right-handed
左利き	ひだりきき	left-handed
片〜 (+ name of body part)	かた〜	one [of something that comes in pairs]
両〜 (+ name of body part)	りょう〜	both . . .
髭	ひげ	beard
口髭	くちひげ	moustache
頬／ほっぺた	ほお／ほっぺた	cheek
(お)へそ		navel
手首	てくび	wrist
足首	あしくび	ankle
かかと		heel
足の指	あしのゆび	toe
皮膚	ひふ	skin, skin surface
骨	ほね	bone
筋肉	きんにく	muscle
(お)尻	(お)しり	buttocks

> The difference between the two words for *cheek* is that ほっぺた is more common in everyday conversation.

勉 Study Grammar 23.

アクティビティー　4

宇宙人がやって来た！ (*Extraterrestrials have arrived!*)

A. This is a drawing of an extraterrestrial, an 宇宙人. Describe it in Japanese. Try to use these constructions in your description.

頭はオレンジのような形をしています。

目はチューリップのような形をしています。

B. Work in pairs.

1. Draw an imaginary extraterrestrial. Describe it to your partner in Japanese.
2. Your partner will draw an illustration following your description.
3. Compare the two illustrations.

Useful Vocabulary: Shape

形	かたち	shape, form
丸い	まるい	round
四角い	しかくい	rectangular, square
三角の	さんかくの	triangular
菱形	ひしがた	lozenge, diamond shape
ハート形	ハートがた	heart-shaped

(勉) Study Grammar 24.

アクティビティー　5

ダイアログ：町田さんは指が長いですね。 (*Ms. Machida, you have long fingers, don't you?*)

カワムラ：町田さんは指が長いね。
　　町田：そうですか。気がつかなかったわ。
カワムラ：御家族の皆さんは？
　　町田：うん、そう言えば、家族のみんなも指が長いわね。
カワムラ：遺伝だね。

Practice the above dialogue by changing the underlined parts to the following.

1. 足が大きい
2. 耳たぶ (*earlobe*) が大きい
3. 鼻すじが通っている (*to have a high-bridged nose*)
4. 歯並びがいい (*to have evenly spaced teeth*)
5. 手首が細い (*thin in circumference*)

アクティビティー　6

誰でしょうか。(*Who might it be?*)

Work in pairs. One member of the pair chooses a third classmate but does not reveal that person's identity. The second member of the pair tries to guess the

---

KAWAMURA: Ms. Machida, you <u>have long fingers</u>, don't you?　MACHIDA: Really? I hadn't noticed.
KAWAMURA: How about the members of your family?　MACHIDA: Well, now that you mention it, they <u>have long fingers</u>, too.　KAWAMURA: It's hereditary then, isn't it?

third student's identity by asking questions, using a "Twenty Questions" format. Concentrate on questions about the person's physical appearance.

Sample questions:

その学生は髪が長いですか。

その学生は髪が何色ですか。

Feeling and Emotions

Vocabulary: A Variety of Emotions

気持ち	きもち	feeling, mood, atmosphere
感じる	かんじる	to feel [an emotion]
心	こころ	mind, feeling, "heart"
嬉しい	うれしい	happy, delighted
喜ぶ	よろこぶ	to be delighted
楽しい	たのしい	enjoyable, fun
笑う	わらう	to laugh, smile
悲しい	かなしい	sad
悲しむ	かなしむ	to be sad
寂しい	さびしい	lonely
苦しい	くるしい	oppressively painful
怖い	こわい	frightening, afraid
怖がる	こわがる	to be frightened
恥ずかしい	はずかしい	shameful, embarrassed
泣く	なく	to cry, weep
怒る	おこる	to get angry
怒っている	おこっている	to be angry
驚く	おどろく	to be surprised
心配(する)	しんぱい(する)	worry; (to be worried)
安心(する)	あんしん(する)	peace of mind; (to be relieved)
がっかりする		to be disappointed
びっくりする		to be surprised
困る	こまる	to have difficulty, be troubled

Adjectives describing emotional states, such as 嬉しい and 悲しい, can be used only when talking about your own emotions or when asking another person about his or her own emotions. See Grammar 25 and **26** for details.

アクティビティー　7

どんな気持ちですか。(*How do you feel?*)

A. How do you feel on these occasions?
1. ペットが死んだとき
2. 日本語のクラスでAを取ったとき
3. 誰もあなたに話しかけてくれないとき
4. お金をなくしたとき
5. 人前でころんだ (*trip and fall*) とき
6. 隣の人がうるさいとき

B. Give examples of two occasions on which you might feel these emotions:
1. どんなときうれしいですか。
2. どんなとき悲しいですか。
3. どんなとき寂しいですか。
4. どんなとき楽しいですか。
5. どんなとき苦しいですか。
6. どんなとき怒りますか。
7. どんなとき恥ずかしいですか。

アクティビティー　8

どんな顔をしていますか。(*What kind of face is it?*)

Study Grammar 25.

What emotions do you think each of the following faces expresses? Match each description with the appropriate drawing.

A.

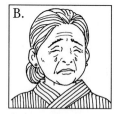
B.

C.

D.

E.

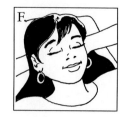
F.

1. _____ 何かを怖そうな顔
2. _____ 驚いているような顔
3. _____ リラックスしているような顔
4. _____ 悲しそうな顔
5. _____ 怒っているような顔
6. _____ うれしそうな顔

Health and Illness

アクティビティー　9

毎日ジョギングをしているようです。(*It appears that she is jogging every day.*)

One of your friends, Ms. Nakayama, seems to be exceptionally healthy. Answer the following questions about her habits and lifestyle by using ようです。

[例]　中山さんは何か運動をしていますか。
　　　—はい、毎日ジョギングをしているようです。

1. タバコを吸いますか。
2. 野菜や果物が好きですか。
3. お酒を飲みますか。
4. 夜遅くまで仕事をしますか。
5. 中山さんの趣味は何ですか。
6. 中山さんは食欲がありますか。
7. 朝ごはんに何を食べますか。
8. 中山さんは一日何時間寝ますか。

アクティビティー　10

体にいいですか。悪いですか。(*Is it good or bad for your body?*)

Tell whether or not the following are good for your body and health.

1. 毎日運動をすること
2. 野菜をたくさん食べること
3. タバコを一日20本吸うこと
4. 週末でも休まないで、一日12時間働くこと
5. 毎日お酒をたくさん飲むこと
6. いつも心配ばかりしていること
7. 朝ごはんを食べないこと
8. 暗いところで本を読むこと
9. アイスクリームをたくさん食べること
10. 一週間シャワーを浴びないこと

Attitudes toward Alcohol, Tobacco, and Drugs

Visitors to Japan today cannot help noticing that drinking plays a prominent role in society. First they notice that beer and other alcoholic drinks are sold in sidewalk vending machines. If they ride the trains or walk through entertainment districts late at night, they see people in various stages of inebriation.

Drinking is a major part of men's socializing, and there are two reasons for this. One is that drinking provides a way for the harried, overworked サラリーマン to unwind and for representatives of different companies to overcome their inhibitions and get to know each other. The other is that Japanese society is extremely tolerant of anything that a drunk person does. For example, if a drunk person says something insulting to a superior, the remark is ignored. The one exception to the overall tolerance for drinking is drunken driving, 酒酔い運転 (さけよいうんてん) or 酔っ払い (よっぱらい) 運転, which is severely punished.

If you go to Japan as a student or on business, you will most likely be asked to go out drinking with friends or colleagues. If you prefer not to drink, you can go along to be sociable and order ジュース or whatever soft drinks the bar has on hand. You never pour your own drink. Instead, people pour drinks for one another and try to make sure that no one's glass or **sake** cup is ever empty. If you have had enough and your companions keep offering, a polite but unmistakable way to refuse further drinks is to leave a full glass untouched.

Tobacco is a profitable government monopoly in Japan, so the government has made almost no efforts to discourage smoking or to accommodate nonsmokers. There are very few nonsmoking areas anywhere, and restaurants with nonsmoking sections are extremely rare.

While Japanese society tolerates and even encourages smoking and drinking, illegal drugs are absolutely forbidden. If you are caught using or even possessing marijuana in Japan, you will be arrested and will have to deal with a criminal justice system in which the accused has few rights. The worst-case scenario is five years in a Japanese prison, as a number of foreign drug users have learned from bitter experience.

アクティビティー 11

お酒をたくさん飲んでいたらしいです。(*It seems that he drank a lot.*)

One of your friends has been hospitalized with multiple health problems. Evidently, he did a lot of things that are bad for one's health. Explain your understanding of what he did or failed to do using ...らしいです。

[例] 運動をしなかったらしいです。

Vocabulary: Sickness and Injuries (1)

病気になる	びょうきになる	to get sick
治る	なおる	to recover
怪我(をする)	けが(をする)	injury; (to get injured)
風邪(をひく)	かぜ(をひく)	(to catch) a cold or the flu
痛い	いたい	painful
頭痛(がする)	ずつう(がする)	(to have a) headache
頭が痛い	あたまがいたい	one's head hurts
腹痛	ふくつう	stomachache
体温	たいおん	body temperature
熱(がある)	ねつ(がある)	(to have a) fever
下痢(をする)	げり(をする)	(to have) diarrhea
吐き気(がする)	はきけ(がする)	nausea; (to be nauseated)
咳(をする)	せき(をする)	(to) cough
医者／医師	いしゃ／いし	medical doctor
看護婦	かんごふ	nurse
入院する	にゅういんする	to be hospitalized
退院する	たいいんする	to get out of the hospital
手術(をする)	しゅじゅつ(をする)	(to perform) surgery
注射(をする)	ちゅうしゃ(をする)	(to give an) injection
レントゲンを撮る	レントゲンをとる	(to take) X rays
受ける	うける	to undergo (*surgery, X rays, an injection*)
薬(を飲む)	くすり(をのむ)	(to take) medicine
アスピリン		aspirin
薬屋／薬局	くすりや／やっきょく	pharmacy

Review: 救急車、健康、病院、病気、休む

アクティビティー 12

どうしますか。(*What are you going to do?*)

Connect the health problems in the first column with the possible solutions in the second column.

1. 頭が痛いです。
2. 下痢をしています。
3. アスピリンがほしいです。
4. 大怪我をしました。
5. 風邪をひきました。

a. 薬局へ行きます。
b. 風邪薬を飲みます。
c. 救急車を呼びます。
d. アスピリンを飲みます。
e. トイレへ行きます。

アクティビティー 13

ダイアログ：病院で (*At a hospital*)

医者：どうしましたか。
林：<u>おなかが痛いんです。</u>
医者：いつからですか。
林：<u>きのう</u>からです。
医者：<u>熱はありますか。</u>
林：<u>いいえ、ありません。</u>

Practice the above dialogue by substituting the following phrases for the underlined portions.

1. 頭が痛い、おとといい、少しあります
2. 咳が出る、先週、37度くらいあります
3. 下痢をしているんです、月曜日、ちょっとあります
4. 吐き気がする、先週、昨日は38度ありました

DOCTOR: What's wrong?   HAYASHI: <u>I have a stomachache.</u>   DOCTOR: Since when?   HAYASHI: Since yesterday.   DOCTOR: <u>Do you have a fever?</u>   HAYASHI: No, I don't.

Vocabulary Library

Sickness and Injuries (2)

患者	かんじゃ	patient
診察(する)	しんさつ(する)	(to perform a) medical examination
体温計	たいおんけい	clinical thermometer
カルテ		patient's chart
血液型	けつえきがた	blood type
ビールス／ウイルス		virus
もどす／はく		to vomit
整形手術	せいけいしゅじゅつ	cosmetic surgery
錠剤	じょうざい	pill
シロップ		syrup, liquid medicine
食前	しょくぜん	before meals
食後	しょくご	after meals
(お)見舞い(に行く)	(お)みまい(にいく)	(to pay) a visit to sick person

アクティビティー 14

頭が痛そうですね。(*He looks as if he has a headache.*)

Connect each statement in the first column with the most appropriate response in the second column.

1. 田中さんは頭が痛そうですね。
2. 苦しそうですね。
3. 外は寒そうですね。
4. 本田さんはうれしそうですね。
5. 金井さんは悲しそうですね。
6. 日本語のテストはむずかしそうですね。

a. いいえ、やさしいですよ。
b. ええ、50万円もらったそうです。
c. ええ、雪が降っています。
d. 風邪をひいたそうです。
e. ガールフレンドにふられた (*was dumped*) そうです。
f. ええ、咳が止まらないんです。

勉 Study Grammar 26.

アクティビティー 15

毎日運動させます。(*I would make him/her exercise every day.*)

If you were a parent of a ten-year-old child, what would you make him or her do to stay healthy? Choose the five items on the next page that you think are most important for parents to insist on.

一日三度食事をさせる。
野菜と果物をたくさん食べさせる。
毎日牛乳を飲ませる。
毎日運動をさせる。
甘いものは食べさせない。
早寝・早起きの習慣 (habit, custom) をつけさせる。
テレビはあまり見させない。
インスタント食品やファーストフードは食べさせない。
あまり勉強させない。
毎日シャワーを浴びさせる。

アクティビティー　16

右手を上げなさい。 (*Raise your right arm [hand]*.)

Work in groups of three. Student A gives Student B a simple command, which Student B then follows. Then Student C describes what Student A ordered Student B to do.

[例]　学生A：左足を上げなさい。
　　　学生B：(左足を上げる)
　　　学生C：AさんはBさんに左足を上げさせました。

Useful Vocabulary: Body Actions (Of course, you can also use the verbs introduced in previous chapters)

掛ける	かける	to hang [something] up
踊る	おどる	to dance
蹴る	ける	to kick
触る	さわる	to touch; Xにさわるto touch X
叩く	たたく	to hit with the hand, to knock
つかむ		to grab, hold, catch
閉じる	とじる	to close (*eyes, books*)
跳ぶ	とぶ	to jump
伸ばす	のばす	to extend or stretch [something]
振る	ふる	to shake [something]
曲げる	まげる	to bend [something]
真似る／真似をする	まねる／まねをする	to imitate
向く	むく	to face toward; Xを向くface toward X
戻す	もどす	to return something to its previous place
渡す	わたす	to hand over

アクティビティー 17

日本語のクラスで先生は学生に何をさせますか。(*What does the instructor make the students do in Japanese class?*)

Discuss these questions in class.

1. 日本語のクラスで先生は学生に何をさせますか。
2. あなたが子供の時、両親はあなたに何をさせましたか。
3. もし、あなたがとなりの人に何でも命令 (*command*) できたら、何をさせたいですか。
4. 子供にさせてはいけないことは何ですか。

勉 Study Grammar 27 and 28.

The counter for pills is ～錠, and the counter for doses of powdered and liquid medicine

アクティビティー 18

ダイアログ：一回に何錠飲むかわかりますか。(*Do you know how many pills to take each time?*)

カワムラ：この薬、何の薬かわかりますか。
山口：ええ、風邪薬ですよ。
カワムラ：一回に何錠飲むかわかりますか。
山口：さあ。説明書が箱の中にあるはずですよ。

アクティビティー 19

とても健康なはずです。(*One can suppose that he is very healthy.*)

Look at the illustrations on the next page and provide an explanation for each case.

[例] ブラウンさんは ＿＿ から、今日は休むはずです。→
ブラウンさんは病気だから、今日は休むはずです。

1. カワムラさんは ＿＿ から、とても健康なはずです。
2. 林さんは ＿＿ から、最近少しやせたはずです。
3. 町田さんは ＿＿ から今日はジョギングをしないはずです。
4. 山口さんは ＿＿ から、お酒をやめているはずです。
5. カーティスさんは ＿＿ から、とても疲れているはずです。

KAWAMURA: Do you know what this medicine is for? YAMAGUCHI: Yes, it's cold medicine.
KAWAMURA: Do you know how many pills to take each time? YAMAGUCHI: I don't know. I suppose there's an instruction sheet inside the box.

Grammar and Exercises

23. Analogy and Exemplification

山口：林さんのニックネームはなぜ「パンダ」なんですか。

カワムラ：パンダのような顔をしているからです。

山口：そうですか。

カワムラ：それに、パンダのように歩くからです。

YAMAGUCHI: Why is Mr. Hayashi's nickname "Panda"?　KAWAMURA: It's because he has a face like a panda.　YAMAGUCHI: I see.　KAWAMURA: In addition, he walks like a panda.

山本：あの人のヘアースタイルは面白いわね。

ブラウン：ええ、ヘアーブラシのような形をしているわね。

山本：髪の色もすごいわね。

ブラウン：ええ、まるでオレンジ・ジュースのような色をしているわね。

Contractions in Colloquial Speech

Just as many English speakers say *gonna* instead of *going to* or *shoulda* instead of *should have* when they are talking informally, Japanese speakers often use shortened or contracted forms in everyday, informal conversation. Here are some of the most common ones:

じゃ for では
学生じゃない for 学生ではない

Verb ちゃ for Verb ては
食べちゃいけない for 食べてはいけない

Verb ちゃう／ちゃった for Verb てしまう／てしまった
閉まっちゃう for 閉まってしまう
忘れちゃった for 忘れてしまった

Noun にゃ for Noun には
日曜日にゃ for 日曜日には

〜なきゃ for 〜なければ
帰らなきゃならない for 帰らなければならない

You may be tempted to use these contractions in your own speech, but they will sound strange unless you are a fairly fluent speaker. However, Japanese people use these contractions all the time in their natural speech, so you need to learn to recognize them when you hear them. Later on, you will find yourself using these forms almost unconsciously. Even so, you should avoid using them in formal situations or when talking to a superior (cf. Chapter 5).

YAMAMOTO: That person's hairstyle is interesting.   BROWN: Yes. It's shaped like a hairbrush.
YAMAMOTO: His hair color is awesome, too.   BROWN: Yes, its color is just like orange juice.

23.1 よう(な) is a na-type adjective used in the following constructions expressing likeness or exemplification.

1	N1 は N2 のようです(だ)	*N1 looks like N2.* *N1 is similar to N2.* *N1 is like N2.*
2	N1 のような N2	*N2 that looks like N1* *N2 that is like N2*
3	N1 は N2 のように V, A	*N1 does something (V) like N2.* *N1 is (adjective) like N2.*
4	V1 ように V2	*... do something (V2) like V1*
5	V ような N	*An N that seems to be V-ing/V-ed*

本がたくさんあって、この家は図書館のようだ。
There are so many books that this house is like a library.
子供のようなことをしてはいけません。
You shouldn't behave like a child.
今日はまるで夏のように暑いですね。
Today is just as hot as summer.
私が発音するように発音してください。
Please pronounce (it) as I pronounce it.
町田さんが言うように、その本は面白かった。
As Ms. Machida says, that book was interesting.

> まるで is an adverb meaning *just, completely* and is used to emphasize similarity.

The na-adjective みたい (it is always written in **hiragana**) can also be used in the above contexts in colloquial speech with the same meaning. ...みたい, like ... よう, can express appearance and conjecture as well as likeness. The pattern is similar to that of よう, with みたい substituting for (の)よう.

> (の)よう can be used in any style of speech.

本がたくさんあって、この家は図書館みたいだ。
This house looks like a library because there are many books.
山本さんは子供みたいにふるまった。
Ms. Yamamoto behaved like a child.
私が発音するみたいに発音して下さい。
Please pronounce it as I pronounce it.

23.2 When you would like to describe the appearances of people and things by comparing them to something else, you can use the following constructions.

Adjective Nのような Nみたいな Vみたいな Vような	顔（かお） スタイル 形（かたち） 色 すがた かっこう	をしている (しています) がする(します)

X has an (adjective) face, style, shape, color, appearance, . . .
X has a face, style, shape, color, appearance, . . . like . . .
X has a face, style, shape, color, appearance that looks as if it . . .

林（はやし）さん、赤い顔（かお）をしていますね。
Mr. Hayashi, your face is red (lit., you have a red face).

その鳥（とり）は青くて、美（うつく）しい色をしている。
That bird is a beautiful blue color.

その赤ちゃんの唇（くちびる）はいちごのような形（かたち）をしていて、かわいいですね。
That baby's lips are shaped like a strawberry, and they are cute.

サンタクロースみたいなかっこうをして、どうしたんですか。
What's going on? You're dressed like Santa Claus.

この水はおかしな味がしますね。
This water has a strange taste.

町田さんの香水（こうすい）はバラの花のようなにおいがしますね。
Ms. Machida's perfume smells like a rose.

外でへんな音（おと）がしていますよ。見てきてください。
I'm hearing a strange sound coming from outside. Can you go check?

ここに立つと、先生になったような気がする。
When I stand here, I feel as if I have become the teacher.

練習　　　　　　　　　1

Fill in the blanks with one appropriate word chosen from the list on the next page.

1. カーティスさんはまるで（　　　）のように、日本語を上手に話しますね。
2. 雨ばかり降（ふ）って、（　　　）のようなお天気だ。
3. チンさんは計算（けいさん）(calculation) が速（はや）くて、（　　　）のようですね。
4. あの人は、大きくてりっぱな、（　　　）のような家に住んでいる。

5. あの絵は何ですか。（　　　）の絵みたいですね。
6. 今日は（　　　）のように暑い。
7. この（　　　）のようなおかしなにおいは何ですか。
8. （　　　）みたいな日本の食べ物が好きですか。
9. 彼女のほっぺたは（　　　）のように赤い。
10. カワムラさんはバスケット・ボールが上手で、（　　　）みたいですね。

夏、マイケル・ジョーダン、日本人、梅雨、ピカソ、ガソリン、すきやき、りんご、コンピュータ、城 (castle)

練習　　　　2

Fill in the blanks with the appropriate forms of よう(だ)、ような、orように.

[例]　私もその(ような)コンピュータがほしい。

1. 先生が書く（　　　）、書きなさい。
2. 今日の（　　　）天気の日には、海岸へ行きたい。
3. それはちょっとむずかしい（　　　）と山本さんは言いました。
4. あなたは氷 (ice) の（　　　）冷たい (cold) 人だ。
5. 私が言った（　　　）しましたか。
6. 子供の（　　　）ことを言ってはいけません。

練習　　　　3

Make up sentences using the following phrases.

[例]　雪のように
　　　→ 町田さんの手は雪のように白い。

1. プロのように
2. 春のような
3. フランス人のように
4. 子供みたいだ
5. 私の言うように
6. 老人 (elderly person) みたいに
7. こわれた (broken) テープレコーダーのように
8. コメディアンのようだ

Fill in the blanks with 形, 色, かっこう, 顔, 味, におい, 音, 気, 感じ, or 気持ち.

1. 村山さん、赤い（　　　）をして、どうしたんですか。
2. あの温泉のお湯は白くて、ミルクのような（　　　）をしています。
3. そんな（　　　）をしていると、風邪をひきますよ。
4. 風邪をひいて、山口さんは青い（　　　）をしている。
5. 日本には富士山のような（　　　）をした山がたくさんある。
6. 冷蔵庫の中はひどい魚の（　　　）がする。
7. このハンバーガーはひどい（　　　）がする！
8. 今日は、何かいいことが起こるような（　　　）がします。
9. 初めて温泉に入って、どんな（　　　）がしましたか。
10. あの人は冷たい（　　　）がする人だ。
11. むこうから人が歩いてくる（　　　）がします。聞こえますか。

24. Describing Attributes: The …は…が Construction

> 佐野：ブラウンさんはいつも髪がきれいですね。
> ブラウン：そうですか。どうもありがとう。
> 佐野：何か秘訣でもあるんですか。
> ブラウン：そうですね。毎日、ブラッシングすることかもしれません。
> 佐野：ああ、うらやましいですね。
> ブラウン：どうしてですか。
> 佐野：私はブラッシングしたくても、もう髪がないんです。

SANO: Ms. Brown, your hair is always pretty.　BROWN: Do you think so? Thank you.　SANO: Do you have any secret [for maintaining it]?　BROWN: Well, it might be brushing it every day.　SANO: I envy you.　BROWN: Why?　SANO: Even if I wanted to brush, I don't have any hair anymore.

三村：チンさんはあそこの看板が見える？

チン：ええ、さくら銀行の看板？

三村：チンさんは目がいいね。

チン：あんな大きな看板が見えないの。

〜ても

The te-form of predicates + the particle も is equivalent to *even if . . . ,
even though . . .*

野口さんに話しても、わかってくれませんよ。
Even if you talk to Mr. Noguchi, he won't understand [your situation.].

あの人はハンサムでも、デートしたくありません。
Even if he is handsome, I don't want to date him.

三村さんが友だちでも、許せません。
Even if Mr. Mimura is my friend, I can't forgive him.

You will learn more about this construction in Chapter 7.

24.1 The following construction is used to describe an essential, permanent (or quasi-permanent) attribute of people and things. This attribute must be something that distinguishes that person or thing from others of its type.

N1	は	N2	が	Adjective

N1's N2 is/are (adjective)
As for N1, its/his/her N2 is (adjective)

村山さんは顔が細長い。
Ms. Murayama's face is long and narrow.

この机は脚が長くて、不安定です。
The legs of this desk are so long that it's unstable.

このステレオは音がとてもいいですね。
This stereo has a very good sound.

MIMURA: Can you see the billboard over there?   CHIN: Yes, it's a Sakura Bank billboard.   MIMURA: You have good eyesight.   CHIN: You can't see that big billboard?

In these examples, N2 is a part of N1. This construction is also used when you have pain in some part of your body.

私は頭が痛い。
I have a headache.

When you ask what part of someone's body hurts, you use どこが痛いんですか. Note that you use どこ, not 何.

24.2 Verbs expressing abilities that are used in this construction are わかる (*to understand, be comprehensible*), 見える (*to be visible*), and 聞こえる (*to be audible*). Another group of verbs that take this construction are those expressing needs and necessity, 要る and 必要だ.

Similarly, おなかがすく (*to get hungry*), 吐き気がする (*to feel nauseated*), 目舞いがする(*to feel dizzy*), and other health-related constructions follow this pattern.

24.3 This …は…が construction is also used with adjectives expressing emotions such as 怖い (*fearful, frightening*) うらやましい (*envious*) 恥ずかしい (*embarrassed, ashamed*), and so on.

私は三村さんがうらやましいですね。
I am envious of Mr. Mimura.

When talking about a third person's emotions, you should use forms such as 怖がる, うらやましがる, 恥ずかしがる, and so on. The idea is that you can't know another person's thoughts or emotions directly, so making direct statements about someone else's feelings is inappropriate. These 〜がる forms have the meaning of *acts frightened, acts envious, acts frustrated, acts embarrassed,* and so on.

ブラウンさんは、暗い所をとても怖がる。
Ms. Brown is very much afraid of dark places.

Incidentally, many of these emotional adjectives can describe either the person who is feeling the emotion or the object of the emotion:

恥ずかしいことをしてしまいました。
I ended up doing something embarrassing.

こんなことをしてしまって、恥ずかしいです。
I'm embarrassed to have ended up doing something like this.

24.4 Finally, the …は…が construction is also used in sentences that single out an individual member of a set of similar items.

すしは、まぐろが一番だ。
As for sushi, tuna is best.

山は、富士山が一番有名だ。
As far as mountains are concerned, Mt. Fuji is the most famous.

Following the example, make up ...は...が sentences. You may have to change the order of the words.

[例] 鼻、象 (*elephant*)、長い → 象は鼻が長い。

着物、たいへん、着る → 着物は着るのがたいへんだ。

1. きりん (*giraffe*)、首、長い
2. 歌、バーバラ・ストライサンド、上手
3. 足、速い、チータ
4. 亀 (*tortoise*)、歩く、のろい (*slow*)
5. イルカ (*dolphin*)、いい、頭
6. 有名、シカゴ、ピザ
7. 村山さん、やさしい、心 (*heart*)
8. 高い、声、チンさん

Answer these questions in Japanese.

1. あなたはこの世 (*in this world*) で何が一番怖いですか。
2. あなたの町は何が有名ですか。
3. 日本語の教科書はどれが一番いいですか。(*It's obvious!*)
4. あなたの好きなレストランは何がおいしいですか。
5. コンパクトな車はどれが一番いいですか。
6. あなたは1キロ先 (*one kilometer ahead*) が見えますか。
7. 日本語は何がむずかしいですか。何がやさしいですか。
8. テレビの番組はどれが一番面白いですか。

25. Talking about Appearance: ...よう, ～そう, ...らしい, and ...みたい

佐野：ブラウンさん、元気がないようですね。
高田：ええ、風邪をひいたみたいです。

SANO: Ms. Brown appears to be unwell.　TAKADA: Yes, she seems to have caught a respiratory infection.

佐野：そうですか。薬を飲んだんでしょうか。
高田：ええ、飲んだみたいですよ。

高田：ブラウンさん、今日は元気そうだね。
ブラウン：うん、昨日飲んだ薬はよく効くみたい。もう、頭痛もないし、咳も
出ないし…
高田：でも、まだ、休んでいた方がいいよ。
ブラウン：ええ、今年の風邪はしつこいようね。

ギブソン：ブラウンさん、風邪をひいていたらしいわよ。
町田：えっ、本当？
ギブソン：ええ、高田さんから聞いたの。もうだいぶよくなったみたいだけど。
町田：みんな風邪をひいているみたいね。横井先生も、今日は休講する
らしいわ。

25.1 In addition to similarity and likeness (cf. **Grammar 23**), the na-type adjectives …よう and みたい are used to express appearance and likelihood.

Noun	の／だった	
Na-adjective	root+な／だった	ようだ／ようです
I-adjective	plain form	みたい／みたいです
Verb	plain form	

It seems that . . . , It looks like . . . , It appears that . . . .

SANO: I see. Has she taken any medicine?   TAKADA: Yes, she seems to have taken some.

TAKADA: Ms. Brown, you look healthy today.   BROWN: Yes, the medicine I took yesterday seems to work well. I no longer have a headache and I'm not coughing anymore.   TAKADA: But you should still be taking it easy.   BROWN: Yes, the flu this year seems to hang on for a long time.

GIBSON: It seems that Ms. Brown has come down with the flu.   MACHIDA: Oh, really?   GIBSON: Yes, I heard it from Mr. Takada. It seems that she has got well already.   MACHIDA: It looks like everyone has the flu. I hear that Professor Yokoi is going to cancel classes today, too.

This construction is usually used to express statements based on the speaker's firsthand, reliable information (mostly, visual information) or his or her reasonable knowledge.

ちょっと早いようですね。まだ、門が閉まっていますよ。
It seems that we are a little early. The gate is still closed.
昨日の試験はやさしかったようです。みんな30分で終わりましたから。
Yesterday's exam seems to have been easy. Everyone completed it in thirty minutes.

This construction is also used to state something indirectly or without committing oneself.

私の言ったことが正しかったようですね。
It appears that what I said was right.

25.2 〜そう, which conjugates like a na-adjective, expresses how someone or something appears to the speaker. In this case, the statement is limited to directly observable things or actions. However, it is not used with adjectives that are always visual, like colors or shapes. It also expresses the speaker's guess or conjecture, and when attached to verbs, it carries the connotation of *looks as if it is about to. . . .* Note that nouns and pronouns cannot be used in front of 〜そう.

Na-adjective	root	
I-adjective	root	〜そうだ／そうです
Verb	conjunctive form	

It seems . . ., It looks . . ., It looks like . . ., It appears . . ., It feels like . . . .
このあたりは便利そうですね。
This neighborhood looks convenient.
時計をもらって、林さんはうれしそうだった。
Receiving a watch, Mr. Hayashi looked happy.
チンさんは今にも倒れそうだった。
Ms. Chin looked as if she was about to fall over at any moment.

The conjunctive form is equivalent to the stem of the ます form.

Note that the adjective いい + そう results in よさそう, *looks good*. The 〜そう form of ない is なさそう, *it looks as if there/it isn't*.

The negative counterpart of this construction is formed in the following way.

The Body and Health

Noun/Na-adjective	1. root + 〜そうではない 2. root + では+ なさそうだ
I-adjective	1. root + 〜そうではない 2. root of the negative form + なさそうだ
Verb	root + 〜そうにない／そうもない

なさそうだ is the combination of the negative ない+そうだ. The negative of いい+ そうだ results in よくなさそうだ.

三村さんはまったく恥ずかしそうではない。
Mr. Mimura doesn't look embarrassed at all.
三村さんはまったく恥ずかしくなさそうだ。
Mr. Mimura looks completely unembarrassed.
あのお客さんは帰りそうにない。
あのお客さんは帰りそうもない。
That guest doesn't look as if he's about to leave.

The adverbial form of this construction, 〜そうに, means *in a manner that looks as if.* . . . For example:

患者は苦しそうに歩いている。
The patient is walking as if in great pain.

25.3 …らしい, which conjugates like an i-adjective, is used in the following construction to express what appears true to the speaker based on information that he or she obtained indirectly, for instance, by reading or hearing it.

Noun	noun/noun + だった	
Na-adjective	root/root +だった	+らしい(です)
I-adjective	plain form	
Verb	plain form	

I hear that . . . , The word is that . . . , I understand that . . . , It says that . . .

三村さんは先週病気だったらしいです。
I understand that Mr. Mimura was sick last week.
台風が来るらしいですよ。
It says that a typhoon is coming.
明日の試験は簡単らしいですよ。
The word is that tomorrow's exam is easy.

Note that 病気 is a noun, not an adjective.

カワムラさんは薬屋へ行くらしい。
It seems that Mr. Kawamura is going to go to the pharmacy.

A negative conjecture is expressed by 〜ない／なかった＋らしい.

その話は本当じゃないらしい。
My understanding is that that story is not true.

…らしい, preceded by a noun, can express that the subject possesses those qualities that are considered essential and natural for his or her role or status. For example, if you say 町田さんは女らしいです, the sentence can mean either *My understanding is that Ms. Machida is a woman* or *Ms. Machida is womanly,* that is, she has those qualities that Japanese culture considers essential for women. Both 女らしい and 男らしい are common expressions in Japanese, because the culture has traditionally had very definite ideas about how men and women should act.

These ambiguous meanings are formally distinguished in the corresponding negative sentences. 町田さんは女らしくない人だ。 *Ms. Machida is not womanly.* 町田さんは女ではないらしい。 *It seems that Ms. Machida is not a woman.*

山口さんはすごく日本人らしい日本人です。
Mr. Yamaguchi is an extremely Japanese Japanese person. (In other words, he fits the common image of a Japanese person.)
それはあなたらしくない。
That's not like you. (In other words, the person being addressed is acting out of character.)

25.4 The following sentences illustrate the differences between でしょう, らしい, 〜そう, and よう.

三村さんは忙しいでしょう。
Mr. Mimura is probably busy.
三村さんは忙しいらしいです。
I heard that Mr. Mimura is busy.
三村さんは忙しそうです。
Mr. Mimura looks busy.
三村さんは忙しいようです。(or 忙しいみたいです。)
It seems that Mr. Mimura is busy [because I heard that he has many things to do].

練習	1

Do you agree with the following statements? Base your decision on the scene depicted in the following drawing.

[例]　今は冬のようですね。→
はい、私もそう思います。外で雪が降っていますから。

この家はアメリカ人の家のようですね。→
いいえ、違うと思います。玄関がありますから。

1. この家には食べ物はないようですね。
2. 子供は本を読むのが好きなようですね。
3. お父さんは仕事を探しているようですね。
4. お母さんは病気のようですね。
5. 外は風が強いようですね。

練習　　　　　　　2

Rewrite these sentences by changing the underlined part to 〜そう(だ).

[例]　おもしろい映画ですね。 → おもしろそうな映画ですね。

　　　雪が降ります。 → 雪が降りそうです。

1. あのコートは高いですね。
2. 山本さんはいい人ですね。
3. 林さんは泣きます。
4. あなたのおじいさんは健康ですね。
5. この宿題は時間がかかります。
6. やさしい試験ですね。
7. カフェテリアには学生がたくさんいます。

練習　　　　　　　3

Fill in the blanks with the correct form of the given words. Be sure to distinguish between the 〜そうだ indicating appearance and the …そうだ indicating hearsay.

1. (雨が降る)
   a. 空が曇って、風が強くなってきました。（　　　）そうです。
   b. 新聞の天気予報によると、明日は（　　　）そうです。

2. (元気)

   a. 山口さんのおばあさんはもう93歳ですが、写真ではとても（　　　）そうです。

   b. さとみさんが言っていましたが、山口さんのおばあさんはとても（　　　）そうです。

3. (いい)

   a. カワムラさんに会いましたが、顔色がとてもよくて、調子が（　　　）そうでした。

   b. カワムラさんに会ったギブソンさんによると、顔色はとても（　　　）そうです。

4. (行きたい)

   a. チンさんははっきりとは言いませんでしたが、私たちと一緒に（　　　）そうでした。

   b. チンさんは私たちと一緒に（　　　）そうです。何度もそう言っていました。

5. (おいしい)

   a. このチーズケーキは大きくて、（　　　）そうですね。

   b. 噂 (rumor) では、あのケーキ屋のチーズケーキは（　　　）そうです。

6. (出かける)

   a. 窓からブラウンさんが見えますが、間もなく（　　　）そうです。

   b. さっき、ブラウンさんが電話してきましたが、間もなく（　　　）そうです。

7. (ない)

   a. 先生は何も言わなかったので、試験は（　　　）そうです。

   b. 三村さんによると、来週は試験が（　　　）そうです。

練習　　　　4

Match each statement in A with the most logical response in B.

A	B
1. おいしそうなケーキですね。	a. 急ぎましょう。
2. 暇そうですね。	b. ちょっと手伝ってもらえますか。
3. 眠たそうですね。	c. スーツケース、私が持ちましょうか。
4. 重そうですね。	d. さあ、聞きに行きましょう。
5. パーティーに遅れそうですよ。	e. 食べてもいいですか。
6. 寒そうですね。	f. ええ、ヒーターを入れてください。
7. 話が始まりそうですよ。	g. 夕べ、何時に寝たんですか。

Respond to these statements by using the words given in the parentheses and
…らしいです。Don't forget to state your source of information or the basis for
your conjecture.

[例]　フランス語の試験はいつですか。(来週) →
　　　来週あるらしいです。カーティスさんがそう言っていました。
　　　ブラウンさんはどこかへ行くんですか。(泳ぐ) →
　　　ええ、泳ぎに行くらしいです。水着を持っていましたから。

1.　ギブソンさんはお休みですか。(病気)
2.　カワムラさん、苦しそうですね。どうしたんでしょう。(風邪をひく)
3.　佐野さんはどんな仕事をしていたんですか。(英語の先生)
4.　このおさしみ、変な味がしますね。(ちょっと古い)
5.　チンさんはどこかへ行くんですか。(ショッピング)
6.　山口さんがいませんね。(忙しい)
7.　カワムラさんはもう起きたんですか。(ジョギング)
8.　山本さんはいくつぐらいですか。(22, 3歳)

Choose the appropriate phrase, either completing the sentence given or making a
statement based on the background information in parentheses.

[例]　(大きいスーツケースを運んでいる人を見ながら)：
　　　(a. 重いそうです　b. 重そうです)ね。
　　　答：b
　　　ボタンを押しても何も出ませんから、このコピーの機械は
　　　(a. こわれているようです。b. こわれているらしいです。)
　　　答：a

1.　(外を見ながら)：
　　　(a. 暑いらしい　b. 暑そう)ですね。
2.　この靴をはいてみましたが、私にはちょっと ____。
　　　(a. 大きいよう　b. 大きそう)です。
3.　(階段の前で)：
　　　三階まで上がるのは(a. 大変そう　b. 大変らしい)ですね。
4.　ニュースによると、北海道はとても ____。
　　　(a. 寒いよう　b. 寒いそう)です。

5. 説明書 (directions) によると、この薬は頭痛にも ＿＿＿。
   (a. いいらしい　b. いいかもしれない)。

6. 今、6時ですよ。あなたの時計は ＿＿＿。
   (a. 遅れているよう　b. 遅れそう)です。

7. ドアが開く音がしたぞ。お父さんが ＿＿＿。
   (a. 帰ってきたそうだ。b. 帰ってきたようだ。)

8. この問題は ＿＿＿。
   (a. むずかしかったらしい　b. むずかしそうだった)
   みんなが間違えている。

26. Causatives

カワムラ：さとみさんはお出かけですか。
　　山口：病院に薬を取りに行かせました。
カワムラ：あっ、大助さんの薬ですか。
　　山口：ええ、風邪がなかなか治らなくて....

　　町田：チンさんにお酒を飲ませたんですか。
　　　林：ええ。
　　町田：ダメですよ。チンさんは顔が真っ赤ですよ。
　　　林：え？チンさんはお酒が飲めないんですか。

カワムラ：郵便局に小包が届いたそうです。
　　山口：そうですか。大助に取りに行かせましょう。
カワムラ：僕に行かせてください。
　　山口：そうですか。じゃ、お願いします。

Many East Asians have a metabolic condition that, among other things, causes their faces to turn bright red when they drink alcohol.

KAWAMURA: Is Satomi out?　YAMAGUCHI: I had her go to the clinic to get medicine.　KAWAMURA: Oh, you mean medicine for Daisuke?　YAMAGUCHI: Yes, his cold just isn't getting better.

MACHIDA: Did you have Ms. Chin drink liquor?　HAYASHI: Yes.　MACHIDA: Her face is really red. HAYASHI: Do you mean that she can't drink?

KAWAMURA: They said that a package has arrived at the post office.　YAMAGUCHI: I see. I'll have Daisuke pick it up.　KAWAMURA: Please let me go.　YAMAGUCHI: Really? Then can you go?

26.1 The following sentences are called "causative sentences," because they refer to making or allowing another person to do something.

> *I made him go to school.*
> *His father let him do whatever he wanted to do.*

In Japanese, sentences like these are built around the following causative verb forms.

	RULES	EXAMPLES
Class 1 verbs	root + a-column **hiragana** corresponding to the dictionary ending + せる	書く → 書かせる
Class 2 verbs	root + させる	食べる → 食べさせる
Class 3 verbs	irregular	来る → 来させる

When the dictionary form ends in う, わ is inserted between the root and せる (cf. 買う, 買わせる).

Note that all causative forms conjugate like Class 2 verbs.

26.2 The causative construction takes different particles depending on whether the verb is an intransitive verb or a transitive verb.

N1 が(は)	N2 に／を	causative form of intransitive verbs

N1 makes N2 do / N1 lets N2 do

N1 が (は)	N2 に	N3 を	causative form of transitive verbs

N1 makes N2 do N3 / N1 lets N2 do N3

For the distinction between intransitive and transitive verbs, refer to Chapter 3.

1a. 山口さんはさとみさんを外へ行かせた。
   Ms. Yamaguchi made Satomi go out.
1b. 山口さんはさとみさんに外へ行かせた。
   Ms. Yamaguchi let / allowed Satomi to go out.

In the first sentence (1a), where the particle を is used, Ms. Yamaguchi forced Satomi to go out against her will. This is usually called the "coercive causative." The second sentence (1b), where に is used, means that Satomi wanted to go out and Ms. Yamaguchi permitted her to do so. Or Ms. Yamaguchi inadvertently let Satomi go out, even though Satomi was supposed to remain inside for some reason. Thus, when the verb is intransitive, the meaning of the sentence differs, depending on whether you use を or に. On the other hand, only one type of causative sentence can be made from a sentence whose verb is transitive.

2a. 山口さんはさとみさんにシチューを作らせた。
Ms. Yamaguchi made Satomi make stew.
Ms. Yamaguchi let Satomi make stew.

This sentence is ambiguous. You must figure out from the context whether or not Satomi wanted to cook.

In causative sentences, N1 must usually be higher in status or age than N2.

先生は二日おきに学生に宿題を出させた。
The teacher made the students turn in homework every other day.

文法ノート

Expressing the Frequency of Actions and Events

Time word + おきに is used to express the frequency of actions and events, meaning *every....*

この薬は三時間おきに二錠飲んでください。
Please take this medicine, two pills every three hours.
カワムラさんは一週間おきに病院へ行く。
Mr. Kawamura goes to the clinic every other week.

In certain limited, impersonal contexts, N2 can be higher than N1.

親にそんなことをさせる子供がいますか！
Is there a child who makes the parents do such a thing?

When talking about having an equal or superior do something, the te-form of the verb + もらう or いただく is more appropriate.

横井先生に読んでいただきましょう。
Let's have Professor Yokoi read it.

cf. Chapter 2.

Study the following examples to get a better idea of the use of the causative.

こんなくだらないことで、私を来させたのですか。
Did you make me come for this trivial thing?

母は娘に着物を着せた。

The mother made her daughter wear a kimono.

The mother let her daughter wear a kimono.

大助さんはだれも自分の部屋に入らせない。

Daisuke doesn't allow anyone to enter his room.

自分 (self, own)

自分 is a reflexive pronoun—that is, it refers back to another noun—corresponding to English *myself, yourself, themselves,* and so on. It usually refers to the subject, almost always a human, and allows you to avoid repeating the same noun in the sentence.

林さんは毎晩、自分で夕ごはんを作ります。

Mr. Hayashi cooks dinner by himself every night.

チンさんは自分のしたことを恥ずかしく思っている。

Ms. Chin is embarrassed about what she did.

あの記憶喪失の患者は、自分の名前も思い出せない。

That amnesia patient can't even recall his own name.

26.3 The te-form of causative verb forms + ください is used to ask a superior for his or her permission to do something or to offer to do something for such a person.

先生、私に黒板を消させてください。

Professor, please let me clean the blackboard.

お父さん、娘さんに会わせてください。お願いです。

Father, please let me see (lit., meet) your daughter. Please!

When you would like to ask not to make you do something, use the negative te-form of causative verbs + ください.

太りますから、あまりたくさん食べさせないでください。

I'll get fat, so please don't make me eat so much.

Asking for and granting permission also can be expressed by using verbs of giving and receiving. For example,

山口さんは僕に掃除機を使わせてくれました。

Ms. Yamaguchi let me use the vacuum cleaner.

Change these sentences to the corresponding causative sentences, framing them as if Mr. or Ms. Yamaguchi is making or letting various people do things.

[例]　私は公園まで歩きました。→
　　　山口さんは私を公園まで歩かせました。
　　　山口さんは私に公園まで歩かせました。
　　　私は歌を歌った。→
　　　山口さんは私に歌を歌わせた。

1. 私はシーツを洗った。
2. 町田さんはアパートに帰った。
3. カワムラさんは日本語を勉強した。
4. 林さんは医者に行きました。
5. 犬は公園を走りました。
6. 山本さんはそこに8時に来た。
7. 村山さんは着物を着た。
8. 私は1時まで待ちました。

Connect the sentences in column A and those in column B to make logical statements.

Useful vocabulary
絶対(に)　*absolutely*
しあわせ　*happy*
やめる　*to quit*
おごる　*to treat someone* [*to dinner, etc.*]

A
1. うちの電話がこわれたんです。
2. 家内が病気なんです。
3. 娘さんを絶対しあわせにします。
4. 簡単にできると思います。
5. もうこんな仕事はきらいです。
6. 山本さんに話があるんです。
7. 父からお金をたくさんもらったんです。
8. あなた一人で話さないでください。

B
a. ここは私におごらせてください。
b. 私にやらせてください。
c. おたくのを使わせてください。
d. 早く帰らせていただきたいんですが。
e. 私にも何か言わせてください。
f. やめさせてください。
g. 結婚させてください。
h. 会わせてください。

Replace the English verbs with the appropriate causative forms.

Useful vocabulary

取りに行く　*to go pick up something*
くわえる　*to hold in one's mouth*
出演する　*to appear on TV, on stage*

僕は佐野さんの家の犬のタローです。佐野さんの御夫妻はいい人たちで、おいしいものを毎日 (1. *eat*) くれます。でも、僕にいろいろなことを (2. *do*)。朝は玄関まで新聞を (3. *go to pick up*)。一日一回、散歩に連れて行ってくれますが、公園ではいつも (4. *run*)。また、ボールを投げて、(5. *go to pick up*)。時々、口にかご (*basket*) を (6. *hold in mouth*) て、近所に買い物に (7. *go*)。僕は買い物へ行くのがあまり好きじゃありません。車が多くて危険だし、空気もあまりきれいじゃありませんから。でも、僕は買い物をする犬として、近所では有名です。佐野さんの御夫妻は僕をテレビのショーに (8. *appear*) たいと思っているようです。

What would you say if someone said the following? Answer using a causative + ください. We'll assume that because of your personality, you are generous and tend to say "yes" to anything.

[例]　誰かこのトラックを運転できる人はいませんか。→
　　　はい、私に運転させてください。

1. 田中さんが駅で待っているんだけど、誰か迎えに行ってくれませんか。
2. 今日の昼ごはんは私が払いましょう。あっ、財布 (*wallet*) を忘れた (*forgot*)。
3. このかばん、ちょっと重いですね。私には持てませんよ。
4. 私が長谷川さんと話すの？あの人と話すのは苦手だな。
5. この車、ちょっと汚いね。
6. このドア、重くて、開きませんね。
7. ああ、おなかがすいた。何か食べる物はありませんか。
8. これを1時までに300部コピーしなくてはならないんです。だれか手伝ってくれませんか。

27. Constructions Using Interrogatives

山口：その薬を飲む前に、説明をよく読んだ方がいいわよ。

カワムラ：ええ。「偏頭痛」っていうのは何ですか。

山口：頭の一部が痛い、とてもひどい頭痛よ。

ブラウン：山本さん、今何時かわかる？

山本：ええ、3時10分前ですよ。

ブラウン：あっ、もう時間だわ。じゃ、また。

山本：あっ、ブラウンさん。どこへ行くかも言わないで、行ってしまったわ。

山本：村山さん、ブラウンさん、どこへ行ったか知っていますか。

村山：いいえ、でも、さっき宮井クリニックがどこにあるか聞いてきたわ。

山本：宮井クリニック？それ、どんな病院。

村山：あら、宮井クリニックがどんな病院か知らないの？有名な整形美容の病院よ。

文法ノート

3時10分前、3時10分過ぎ

In Japanese, as in English, it is possible to express times that are not on the hour or half-hour in terms like *2:50* or *3:10,* and this is what you will usually see on schedules or hear in formal announcements. In everyday conversation, however, English-speakers often say things like *ten minutes to three* or *ten after three.* The same is true of

---

YAMAGUCHI: You'd better read the directions before taking that medicine.   KAWAMURA: What is a "migraine headache"?   YAMAGUCHI: It's a severe headache in which one part of your head hurts.

BROWN: Ms. Yamamoto, do you know what time it is now?   YAMAMOTO: Yes, it's ten minutes to three.   BROWN: Oh, it's time now. Well, see you later.   YAMAMOTO: Oh, that Ms. Brown. She left without even saying where she's going.

YAMAMOTO: Mr. Murayama, do you know where Ms. Brown went?   MURAYAMA: No, but a little while ago, she came asking me where the Miyai Clinic is.   YAMAMOTO: Miyai Clinic? What kind of clinic is that?   MURAYAMA: Oh, you don't know what kind of clinic the Miyai Clinic is? It's a famous cosmetic surgery clinic.

Japanese. To express minutes before the hour, you say x時x分前, as in the following examples.

8時15分前	*quarter to eight*
11時20分前	*twenty minutes to eleven*

To express minutes after the hour, you say x時x分過ぎ.

8時15分過ぎ	*quarter after eight*
11時20分過ぎ	*twenty minutes after eleven*

27.1 When you would like to ask for specific information or clarification about someone or something that the person you are talking to has mentioned, the following construction is commonly used. This pattern is particularly useful for asking for definitions of words that you don't understand.

X	というのは っていうのは とは って	interrogatives interrogative expressions	([の]こと)ですか

「キリキリ」痛むとはどういうことですか。
What does キリキリ痛む *mean?*
大野っていうのはだれ？
Who is Oono? (Who is this Oono person?)
病院に行かないって、なぜですか。
Why is it you say you won't go to a hospital?
昼休みって、何時？
What time is our lunch break?

とは is a shortened form of というのは. っていうのは and って are the colloquial counterparts of というのは and とは, respectively.

27.2 An embedded question is a question placed inside another question or a statement.

Do you know where Mr. Hayashi is from?
I will tell you what it is.

In these two examples, the questions "Where is Mr. Hayashi from?" and "What is it?" are embedded into the main clauses "Do you know . . ." and "I will tell you. . . ." In effect, the first example is two questions. The main clause asks whether the listener knows certain information, while the embedded questions asks where Mr. Hayashi is. The second example is an answer inside a statement. In Japanese, this type of sentence typically takes the following construction.

EMBEDDED QUESTION	MAIN CLAUSE
plain form of predicates + か	plain or polite form

昨日ここに来たのはだれ（だった）か覚えていますか。
Do you remember who the person who came here yesterday was?
どの薬が一番良かったか教えてください。
Please tell me which medicine was best.
山本さんは何時に来るかわかりますか。
Do you know what time Ms. Yamamoto will come?

練習　　　　1

What do you think are the questions that would yield the following answers? Make up questions by using . . . というのは + interrogative + ですか.

[例]　ディズニーランドがあって、観光客が多いところです。 →
　　　アナハイムというのはどんな所ですか。

1. アメリカの副大統領 (*vice president*) です。
2. 有名なコンピュータの会社です。
3. 7月4日です。
4. 風がとても強い所です。
5. スキーが全然できないからです。
6. 牛肉を使った日本の料理です。
7. 野菜を売っている店です。
8. 日本人が年の終わりにあげるおくりものです。

練習　　　　2

The following is the announcement of the wedding of Heather Gibson's sister, as published in a Canadian newspaper. Before she returned to Japan, Ms. Gibson sent this clipping to her landlady, who doesn't read English very well. Pretend that you are another English-speaking tenant of the same apartment building and answer the landlady's questions in Japanese, based on the information contained in the clipping.

Jean Elizabeth Gibson Marries Brian Alexander Wilson

Edmonton– Jean Elizabeth Gibson exchanged wedding vows with Brian Alexander Wilson in a candlelight ceremony at Northland United Church on June 12, with the Rev. John Williams officiating.

The bride, the oldest daughter of John and Marianne Gibson of Edmonton, was born in Vancouver. A graduate of the University of British Columbia, she is a computer programmer with Northern Telecom.

The groom, the only son of William and Molly Wilson, graduated from the University of Toronto and teaches English at Queen Elizabeth High School in Calgary.

The bride's younger sister Heather, who is currently studying in Japan, came home to serve as maid of honor. Other bridesmaids included Ann Marie Parrish and Lori Simms. The bride's attendants wore pale blue, floor-length dresses and carried mixed bouquets of early summer flowers.

The best man was Jason Howard, the groom's college room-mate, and Scott Carey and Gregory Callahan served as ushers.

A reception was held at the Edmonton Hilton Hotel. After a two-week honeymoon in Acapulco, Mexico, the couple will make their home in Calgary.

[例] ギブソンさんのお姉さんはどこの出身かわかりますか。→
はい、わかります。バンクーバーです。
ヘザー・ギブソンさんはいつ日本へ戻る (return) かわかりますか。→
いいえ、わかりません。

1. ギブソンさんのお姉さんはどんなお仕事をしているかわかりますか。
2. お姉さんの御主人はどんなお仕事をしているかわかりますか。
3. お二人はいつ結婚したかわかりますか。
4. お二人はどこで結婚式をあげたかわかりますか。
5. 御主人のルームメートがどんな服を着たかわかりますか。
6. 新婚旅行 (honeymoon) にどこに行ったかわかりますか。
7. 何というホテルに泊まったかわかりますか。
8. お二人はどこに住んでいるかわかりますか。

Make up embedded question sentences by embedding the first question into the second sentence.

[例] チンさんはどこに行きましたか。林さんから聞きました。→
林さんから、チンさんがどこに行ったか聞きました。

1. カワムラさんはどんなワープロを買いましたか。わかりますか。
2. 大学病院はどこにありますか。教えてください。
3. 山口さんは何時に帰りますか。忘れてしまいました。
4. 東京からそこまで電車で何時間かかりますか。時刻表 (timetable) を調べて
おいてください。
5. パーティーに何人の人が出ますか。三村さんに先に (ahead) 電話で知らせて
ください。
6. カーティスさんに何をあげますか。チンさんと相談しておいてください。
7. どんな食べ物がきらいですか。はっきり言ってください。
8. ブラウンさんはなぜクラスに来ませんでしたか。聞くのを忘れました。

28. Expressing Expectation:…はず

林：ブラウンさん、遅いね。今日も休みかな。
カワムラ：ブラウンさん、今日は来るはずだよ。
林：本当?風邪、よくなったのかな。
カワムラ：うん、今朝、電話でそう言っていたよ。

佐野：ブラウンさん、何がそんなにおかしいんですか。
ブラウン：このエッセー、とても面白いんです。
佐野：どれどれ。あ、これ面白いはずですよ。木田洋子のエッセーでしょう?
ブラウン：ええ、彼女のエッセーはいつも面白いですからね。

HAYASHI: Ms. Brown is late, isn't she? I wonder if she'll take today off, too.　　KAWAMURA: I expect her to come today.　　HAYASHI: Really? Did she get over her cold?　　KAWAMURA: Yes, she told me so on the phone this morning.

SANO: Ms. Brown, what's funny?　　BROWN: It's that this essay is so funny.　　SANO: Which one? No wonder it's funny, because it's one of Yooko Kida's essays.　　BROWN: Yes, her essays are always funny.

The following construction is used to express the speaker's expectation that something was, is, will be true. Note that the speaker expresses his or her expectation based on reliable information or because he or she has strong evidence or knowledge for believing it.

Noun	noun + の／だった	
Na-adjective	root + な／だった	はずだ／はずです
I-adjective	plain form	
Verb	plain form	

Note that this construction cannot be used to express what the speaker expects to do or intends to do, although it can be used to express what someone else is expected to do. It can also express someone else's expectation of what the speaker was expected to do. To express one's own intentions or expectations about one's own actions, つもり (cf. Chapter 6, Book 1) is used.

I expect that . . . , it is expected that . . . , I am sure that . . . , ought to . . . , no wonder . . . , is supposed to . . . , I assume that . . .

佐野さんはサラリーマンだったはずだ。
Mr. Sano is supposed to have been a salaried worker.
その近辺は住宅地だから、静かなはずだ。
That neighborhood is a residential area, so it ought to be quiet.
その薬はドイツ製だから、高いはずだ。
Because that medicine is manufactured in Germany, it's natural that it's expensive.

Note that this construction can be used when the speaker has found the reason for something.

手術は成功したから、また目が見えるはずだ。
The surgery was successful, so he must be able to see again.

はず, which is a noun, can be modified by such demonstrative pronouns as その, あんな and the like or can be used to modify another noun (in this case, connected by の), but it cannot be used independently.

ギブソンさんは来ますか。
Is Ms. Gibson coming?
ええ、そのはずです。
Yes, I expect so.
今夜食べるはずのおさしみはどこですか。
Where is the sashimi that we are supposed to eat tonight?

There are two ways to make this construction negative.

1. Plain negative sentence	＋はずだ／はずです
2. Plain sentence	＋はずがない／はずはない

Of the two, the second alternative is the stronger, carrying the connotation of
There's no reason to suppose that . . . or *It's out of the question that . . . .*

高田さんは入院<ruby>入院<rt>にゅういん</rt></ruby>しないはずだ。
We can expect that Mr. Takada won't be hospitalized.
<ruby>高田<rt>たかだ</rt></ruby>さんが<ruby>入院<rt>にゅういん</rt></ruby>するはずはない。
There's no reason to suppose that Mr. Takada will be hospitalized.

練習　　　　　　　　1

Which clause in column A provides evidence or an opinion supporting which
sentence in column B? Connect them.

A

1. もう12月19日だから、
2. カワムラさんの<ruby>靴<rt>くつ</rt></ruby>はまだある
   から、
3. ハンスさんは10<ruby>年間<rt>かん</rt></ruby>日本語を
   勉強していたから、
4. ブラウンさんはここに何度も来て
   いるから、
5. 今日は日曜日だから、
6. クラスは3時間前に終わったか
   ら、
7. 山口さんのおばあさんは<ruby>明治生<rt>めいじ</rt></ruby>ま
   れだから、
8. バーゲンセールの<ruby>時<rt>とき</rt></ruby>に買った
   から、

B

a. もう80<ruby>歳以上<rt>さいいじょう</rt></ruby>のはずです。
b. とても<ruby>安<rt>やす</rt></ruby>かったはずです。
c. <ruby>銀行<rt>ぎんこう</rt></ruby>は<ruby>閉<rt>し</rt></ruby>まっているはずです。
d. <ruby>迷<rt>まよ</rt></ruby>う (*get lost*) はずが
   ありません。
e. 学校は冬休みに入るはずです。
f. まだ学校に行っていないはず
   です。
g. <ruby>漢字<rt>かんじ</rt></ruby>が読めるはずです。
h. 学生はもう<ruby>家<rt>いえ</rt></ruby>に帰ったはず
   です。

練習　　　　　　　　2

Complete the following sentences.

[<ruby>例<rt>れい</rt></ruby>]　＿＿＿＿から、父は<ruby>遅<rt>おそ</rt></ruby>く帰るはずです。→
　　　今日は<ruby>残業<rt>ざんぎょう</rt></ruby>があるから、父は遅く帰るはずです。

1. ＿＿＿＿から、とてもうるさいはずです。
2. ＿＿＿＿から、もう<ruby>着<rt>つ</rt></ruby>いているはずです。
3. ＿＿＿＿から、そんなことできるはずがありません。
4. ＿＿＿＿から、とても<ruby>お金持<rt>かねも</rt></ruby>ちのはずです。
5. ＿＿＿＿から、<ruby>病気<rt>びょうき</rt></ruby>になるはずがありません。
6. ＿＿＿＿から、今日は家にいるはずです。
7. ＿＿＿＿から、あの人は<ruby>知<rt>し</rt></ruby>っているはずです。

8. ＿＿＿＿から、あの人は日本が好きなはずです。
9. ＿＿＿＿から、とても面白いはずです。
10. ＿＿＿＿から、食べたことがないはずです。

練習 3

Answer the following questions by using …はずです, …だろうと思います, or …かもしれません, depending on the degree of certainty in your mind.

[例] カワムラさんは今夜、うちにいるでしょうか。→
今夜はカワムラさんの好きなテレビの番組があるので、うちにいるはずです。
or
カワムラさんは夜、あまり外に出かけないので、いるだろうと思います。or
さあ、よくわかりませんが、いるかもしれません。

1. あなたのお父さんは今、どこにいますか。
2. お母さんは今週、電話してくると思いますか。
3. あなたは日本語のクラスでAが取れると思いますか。
4. 近所のデパートで、来週、バーゲンセールがありますか。
5. 御両親はお元気ですか。
6. 御両親は誕生日に何をくれると思いますか。

Vocabulary

Body, Body Parts

あし	脚、足	leg, foot		け	毛	hair, strand of hair
あたま	頭	head		こし	腰	waist, hips
うで	腕	arm		した	舌	tongue
おなか		belly		せなか	背中	back
かお	顔	face		つめ	爪	[finger or toe] nail
かた	肩	shoulder		のど	喉	throat
からだ	体	body		は	歯	tooth
くち	口	mouth		はな	鼻	nose
くちびる	唇	lip		ひざ	膝	knee
くび	首	neck		ひじ	肘	elbow

みみ	耳	ear		め	目	eye
むね	胸	chest		ゆび	指	finger

Review: 髪、手

Feeling, Emotion

あんしん	安心(する)	peace of mind; (to be relieved)
うれしい	嬉しい	happy, delighted
おこる	怒る	to get angry
おどろく	驚く	to be surprised
かなしい	悲しい	sad
がっかりする		to be disappointed
きぶん	気分	feeling, state of physical well-being
きもち	気持ち	feeling, mood, atmosphere
くるしい	苦しい	oppressively painful
こまる	困る	to have difficulty, be troubled
こわい	怖い	frightening, afraid
こわがる	怖がる	to be frightened
さびしい	寂しい	lonely
しんぱい	心配(する)	worry; (to be worried)
たのしい	楽しい	enjoyable, fun
なく	泣く	to cry, weep
はずかしい	恥ずかしい	shameful, embarrassed
びっくりする		to be surprised
よろこぶ	喜ぶ	to be delighted
わらう	笑う	to laugh, smile
イライラする		to be irritated

Sickness and Injuries

いしゃ／いし	医者／医師	medical doctor
いたい	痛い	painful
うける	受ける	to undergo (*surgery, treatment, etc.*)
かぜ(をひく)	風邪(をひく)	(to catch) a cold or the flu
かんごふ	看護婦	nurse
くすり(をのむ)	薬(を飲む)	(to take) medicine
けが(をする)	怪我(をする)	injury; (to get injured)
げり(をする)	下痢(をする)	(to have) diarrhea
しゅじゅつ	手術	surgery
ずつう	頭痛	headache
せき(をする)	咳(をする)	(to) cough
たいいん(する)	退院(する)	(to get) out of the hospital
たいおん	体温	body temperature

ちゅうしゃ	注射	injection
にゅういんする	入院する	hospitalization; (to be hospitalized)
ねつ	熱	fever
はきけ(がする)	吐き気(がする)	nausea, to be nauseated
びょうきになる	病気になる	to get sick
ふくつう(がする)	腹痛(がする)	(to have a) stomachache
レントゲンをとる	レントゲンを撮る	to take X rays

Loanword: アスピリン
Review: 救急車、健康、病院、病気、休む、薬屋、薬局、直る

Body Actions

かける	掛ける	to hang (something) up
おどる	踊る	to dance
ける	蹴る	to kick
さわる	触る	to touch; X にさわる to touch X
たたく	叩く	to hit with the hand, to knock
ちかづく	近づく	to draw close
つかむ		to grab, hold, catch
とぶ	跳ぶ	to jump
ならぶ	並ぶ	to get in line
のばす	伸ばす	to extend or stretch [something]
ふる	振る	to shake [something]
まねる	真似る	to imitate
わたす	渡す	to hand over

Shape

かたち	形	shape	しかくい	四角い	rectangular, square
かっこう	格好	appearance	まるい	丸い	round
さんかくの	三角の	triangular			

Grammar

〜させる	(causative ending)
〜せる	(causative ending)
〜そう(な)	looking like, looking as if
〜ても	even if
…はず	expectation
みたい(な)	like . . .
…よう(な)	like, appearance
まるで	just like
…らしい	it seems that . . . , the word is that . . .

Kanji

Learn these **kanji**.

体 角 薬 丸 熱
顔 立 頭 持 局
耳 配 鼻 心 御
首 死 歯 苦 式
足 病 指 元
形 痛 毛 院

Reading and Writing

Reading 1 健康相談
<ruby>健康相談<rt>けんこうそうだん</rt></ruby>

Before You Read

In the following magazine article, a professor of medicine answers a question from a reader. Imagine that you have the opportunity to consult a famous medical expert about some health problem. Write a brief question in Japanese, and compare your question with those of your classmates. What seem to be the most common concerns of you and your classmates?

Discuss in class. Which of the following do you try to do in order to maintain or improve your health?

1. 毎日運動をする
2. できるだけ (*as much as possible*) 車を使わないで、歩く
3. 偏食 (*unbalanced diet*) をしない
4. 野菜、果物をたくさん食べる
5. 1日8時間寝る
6. お酒、コーヒーを飲まない
7. たばこを吸わない

What else do you do?

Now Read It!

<ruby>健康相談<rt>けんこうそうだん</rt></ruby>

<ruby>質問<rt>しつもん</rt></ruby>

<ruby>小学生<rt>しょうがっこう</rt></ruby>5年生の<ruby>息子<rt>むすこ</rt></ruby>は<ruby>身長<rt>しんちょう</rt></ruby>146cm、<ruby>体重<rt>たいじゅう</rt></ruby>53kgで、ちょっと<ruby>太り過ぎ<rt>ふと す</rt></ruby>です。先日、<ruby>学校<rt></rt></ruby>の<ruby>定期検診<rt>ていきけんしん</rt></ruby>で、<ruby>血中<rt>けっちゅう</rt></ruby>コレステロールが230ミリグラムもあることがわかりました。コレステロールを<ruby>減らす<rt>へ</rt></ruby>ためには、どのようなことをさせるといいでしょうか。

<ruby>東京都港区<rt>とうきょうとみなとく</rt></ruby>
<ruby>野間<rt>のま</rt></ruby>まり<ruby>子<rt>こ</rt></ruby>(35歳、<ruby>主婦<rt>しゅふ</rt></ruby>)

<ruby>お答え<rt>こた</rt></ruby>

(<ruby>東京大学医学部教授<rt>とうきょうだいがくいがくぶきょうじゅ</rt></ruby>　<ruby>佐藤<rt>さとう</rt></ruby>　<ruby>清先生<rt>きよし</rt></ruby>)

<ruby>日本人<rt></rt></ruby>の<ruby>食事<rt>しょくじ</rt></ruby>は<ruby>健康<rt>けんこう</rt></ruby>にいいので、20年<ruby>前<rt>まえ</rt></ruby>までは日本ではコレステロールはあまり<ruby>問題<rt>もんだい</rt></ruby>になりませんでした。ところが、<ruby>最近<rt>さいきん</rt></ruby>は日本人の<ruby>食生活<rt>しょくせいかつ</rt></ruby>も<ruby>欧米型<rt>おうべいがた</rt></ruby>になり、コレステロールが<ruby>多過ぎる<rt>おおす</rt></ruby>人も<ruby>増えて<rt>ふ</rt></ruby>きました。コレステロールというと、<ruby>中高年者<rt>ちゅうこうねんしゃ</rt></ruby>の<ruby>問題<rt>もんだい</rt></ruby>のように<ruby>考える<rt>かんが</rt></ruby>人が多いようですが、最近は、野間さんの息子さんのように、<ruby>子供<rt>ども</rt></ruby>のコレステロールも<ruby>問題<rt>もんだい</rt></ruby>になっています。では、コレステロールを<ruby>減らす<rt>へ</rt></ruby>ためには、また、<ruby>増やさない<rt>ふ</rt></ruby>ためには、どうしたらいいでしょうか。

<ruby>太り過ぎ<rt>ふと す</rt></ruby>の子供は<ruby>血中<rt>けっちゅう</rt></ruby>コレステロールが高いようですから、<ruby>太り過ぎ<rt>ふと す</rt></ruby>に<ruby>気をつけ<rt>き</rt></ruby>ましょう。そのためには、<ruby>偏食<rt>へんしょく</rt></ruby>させないことが<ruby>大切<rt>たいせつ</rt></ruby>です。また、最近の<ruby>子供<rt>こども</rt></ruby>はハンバーグ・ステーキのような肉料理が好きで、<ruby>野菜<rt>やさい</rt></ruby>を食べさせるのは<ruby>大変<rt>たいへん</rt></ruby>なようですが、野菜、<ruby>果物<rt>くだもの</rt></ruby>、<ruby>海草<rt>かいそう</rt></ruby>などを食べさせてください。

それから、<ruby>毎日運動<rt>うんどう</rt></ruby>させましょう。ジョギングや<ruby>縄跳び<rt>なわと</rt></ruby>のような運動を毎日させ、<ruby>体<rt>からだ</rt></ruby>をフルに<ruby>動かさせて<rt>うご</rt></ruby>ください。体を使う家の<ruby>手伝い<rt>てつだ</rt></ruby>をさせましょう。<ruby>例えば<rt>たと</rt></ruby>、毎日ふとんを<ruby>上げ<rt>あ</rt></ruby>させたり、<ruby>庭<rt>にわ</rt></ruby>の<ruby>掃除<rt>そうじ</rt></ruby>をさせたりするのはどうでしょうか。これだけでも、コレステロールがかなり<ruby>下がる<rt>さ</rt></ruby>ようです。

ストレスもコレステロールを<ruby>上げる<rt>あ</rt></ruby><ruby>原因<rt>げんいん</rt></ruby>らしいことがわかってきました。<ruby>最近<rt>さいきん</rt></ruby>の<ruby>子供<rt>こども</rt></ruby>は<ruby>受験<rt>じゅけん</rt></ruby>のため、学校のほかに、<ruby>塾<rt>じゅく</rt></ruby>へ行ったり、土曜日、日曜日も勉強しているようですが、子供の<ruby>健康<rt>けんこう</rt></ruby>のためにも、時々ゆっくり休ませてあげましょう。

このように<ruby>食生活<rt>しょくせいかつ</rt></ruby>などお母さんやまわりの人の<ruby>協力<rt>きょうりょく</rt></ruby>が一番<ruby>大切<rt>たいせつ</rt></ruby>なようです。

身長 (body) height / 体重 (body) weight / 太り過ぎ overweight
定期検診 regular health checkup
血中 in the blood
減らす to decrease [something]

医学部教授 professor at a medical school

食生活 customary diet
欧米型 European and American style
増える to increase, become greater

増やす to increase [something]

気をつける to watch for, take care
偏食 eating between meals

海草 seaweed

縄跳び jumping rope

ふとんを上げる to put the futons away

原因 cause

受験 preparing for and taking school and university entrance examinations
...のほかに in addition to . . .
塾 cram school

協力 assistance, cooperation
大切(な) important

After You Finish Reading

First let's understand the most essential points in this article.

1. What is the gist of Mrs. Noma's question?
2. Professor Satoo lists four things Mrs. Noma should take care of. What are they? (Hint: He uses causative sentences.)
3. Professor Satoo's response consists of five paragraphs. What is the main topic of each paragraph?
4. Professor Satoo uses よう and らしい several times in his answer. What are the underlying meanings expressed by these forms?

Writing 1

You are writing a regular health column in a local paper in Japan. You have received the following question from one of your readers.

うちの18歳の娘の健康が心配で、質問します。娘は大学受験のため、毎日夜遅くまで勉強しています。朝はごはんも食べないで、学校へ行きます。昼ごはんにハンバーガーやピザを食べているようです。学校から帰ってくると、夕食を10分ぐらいで終えて、すぐ勉強します。夜食には甘いケーキやインスタント・ラーメンばかり食べています。最近、顔色が悪く、とても疲れているようです。どうしたらいいでしょうか。

Respond to this letter. Make several suggestions following the example.

[例]　朝ごはんは毎日食べさせましょう。
　　　甘いケーキは食べさせないでください。

Try to include introductory and closing comments like Professor Satoo's response.

Reading 2　あなたも指圧してみませんか。

Before You Read

Review the body parts listed and illustrated at the beginning of the Vocabulary and Oral Activities section.

In recent years, Japanese finger-pressure therapy (指圧) has become popular in the West. The following passage explains how to do it at home.

Do you have any health problems or any aches and pains? Indicate the places where you have problems. Do any of your problems appear on the following list?

While reading the passage, find what part of your body you should apply finger pressure to in order to treat your problems and the ones listed here.

目の疲れ (*fatigue*), 肩のこり (*stiffness*), 腰の痛み (*pain*) 頭痛 (*headache*), イライラ (*irritability, nervousness*), 食欲不振 (*lack of appetite*), 不眠症 (*insomnia*), 脚のだるさ (*tiredness, languidness*)

Oriental medicine (東洋医学), including **shiatsu,** differs greatly from Western medicine (西洋医学) with regard to its philosophy and methodology. What do you think are the advantages and disadvantages of each approach? Which do you prefer? Why? Discuss in class.

The words and **kanji** for which definitions are given below should be enough to allow you to guess the meanings, and sometimes even the pronunciations, of the undefined words. See how many you can figure out.

両親 (*parents*)　両手 (　　　)　両足 (　　　)　両目 (　　　)

重い (*heavy, serious*)　病気 (　　　)　重病 (　　　)　重体 (　　　)

健康 (*health*)　体 (　　　)　健康体 (　　　)

方法 (*method*)　健康法 (　　　)

調子 (*condition*)　体調 (　　　)

部屋中 (*throughout the room*)　体中 (　　　)

部分 (*part*)　頭 (*head*)　後頭部 (　　　)

左側 (*left side*)　右側 (*right side*)　外側 (　　　)　内側 (　　　)

満足 (*satisfaction*)　不満 (*dissatisfaction*)　規則的 (*regular*)

不規則な (　　　)

飽きる (*to get bored*)　飽きやすい (　　　)

This is the toughest one! (Or maybe it's easy for you.)

二日 (*second day*)　酔い (*drunkenness*)　二日酔い (　　　)

Now Read It!

体がだるくて、疲れが取れない。集中力がなくて、飽きやすい。長時間デスクワークをすると、頭痛がして、肩がこってしまう。いつもコンピュータを使うので、目が疲れてしまう。こんな方はいませんか。

　ちょっとした疲れや痛みも、放っておくと、治りにくくなります。また、これが重病の原因にもなってしまい、たいへん危険です。毎日、ツボを指圧して、あなたも健康体を維持しませんか。ツボを探すのはむずかしそうですが、実はとても簡単です。自宅や学校やオフィスで簡単にできるし、すぐに疲れや痛みがとれるので便利です。

集中力 *concentration*

こる *to become stiff*

ちょっとした *simple, easy*
放っておく *to leave as is, to not deal with*
危険(な) *dangerous*
維持(する) *maintenance; (to maintain)*
ツボ **tsubo,** *pressure point*
実は *actually, to tell the truth*

東洋医学では、健康体を維持するためのエネルギーが体中に流れていると
言います。このエネルギーがスムーズに流れなくなると、疲れや痛みが出て、そ
して、病気になります。エネルギーがスムーズに流れていない部分のツボを指で
押すと、エネルギーの流れがスムーズになります。

では、日ごろのちょっとした疲れ、痛み、ストレスを治すツボを紹介
しましょう。

- 目の疲れ
  両目の外側を押すと、目がスッキリします。
- 首、腕、肩のこりと痛み
  後頭部、首のつけ根、首の横を押します。
- 腰の痛み
  腰を押すだけでなく、足の裏も押します。
- 頭痛
  頭のてっぺん、額、首の後ろを押します。
- 二日酔い
  おへその回りをゆっくりと押します。
- 気分のイライラ
  手首の小指側、耳たぶ、足の裏を押します。
- 下痢
  おへそより15cm下の部分と腰を押します。
- 不眠症
  背中を上から下にゆっくりと押していきます。足の親指のつけ根、頭の
  てっぺんも押します。

指圧は、いつでも簡単にできます。薬を使いませんから、副作用も
ありません。どこでも簡単にできて、時間がかからないので、忙しくて不規則な
生活を送っている現代人には、とても便利な健康法です。あなたも自分のツボを
覚えておいて、ベストな体調を維持しましょう。

流れる *to flow*

日頃 *daily*

スッキリする *to feel refreshed*

つけ根 *base, root*

...だけでなく *not only...*
足の裏 *sole of the foot*

てっぺん *top of the head*
額 *forehead*

耳たぶ *earlobe*

副作用 *side effect*
不規則 *irregular, unstable*
現代人 *people of the modern age*

After You Finish Reading

1. Read the first three paragraphs quickly and give the gist of each paragraph in English.
2. Read the paragraphs in which the writer explains how to do **shiatsu.** Using the following illustrations, indicate where you should press in the various circumstances described.
3. What does the writer want to say most in the last paragraph?

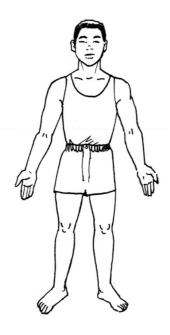
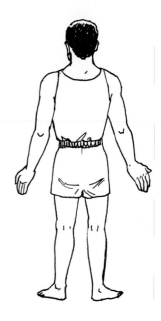

Writing 2

What do you do to maintain your health? Write a short passage on this topic.

Language Functions and Situations

At a Pharmacy

カワムラ：すみません。風邪薬（かぜぐすり）はありますか。
薬屋（くすりや）：どんな症状（しょうじょう）ですか。
カワムラ：頭痛（ずつう）がして、のどが痛（いた）いんです。
薬屋：熱（ねつ）はありますか。

KAWAMURA: Do you have cold medicine?　PHARMACIST: What are your symptoms?　KAWAMURA: I have a headache, and my throat hurts.　PHARMACIST: Do you have a fever?

カワムラ：ええ、7度3分くらいあります。
　　薬屋：せきは出ますか。
カワムラ：いいえ。
　　薬屋：では、この薬がいいでしょう。
カワムラ：そうですか。おいくらですか。
　　薬屋：50錠入りが1500円、25錠入りが800円です。
カワムラ：50錠入りを下さい。
　　薬屋：1日3回食後に3錠ずつお飲み下さい。暖かくして、ゆっくり休んだ方が
　　　　　いいですよ。
カワムラ：ええ、明日は学校を休むつもりです。
　　薬屋：お大事に。

Dialogue Practice

Make up dialogues that start with the following phrases. Be as creative as possible.

1. すみません。頭痛の薬をください。
2. すみません。腹痛の薬をください。
3. すみません。咳止め (*cough suppressant*) のシロップをください。

Role Play

Work in pairs. Practice buying medicine at a pharmacy in the following situations.

1. Your child has a cold. You prefer liquid medicine to pills.
2. You feel fatigued and have a slight headache.
3. You accidentally ate some spoiled food. You have diarrhea.
4. You have a bad cough.

KAWAMURA: Yes. It is about 37.3 degrees.　　PHARMACIST: Are you coughing?　　KAWAMURA: No.
PHARMACIST: Then I recommend this medicine.　　KAWAMURA: I see. How much is it?　　PHARMACIST:
¥1,500 for fifty pills and ¥800 for twenty-five pills.　　KAWAMURA: Please give me the one with fifty pills.
PHARMACIST: Take three pills three times a day after meals. It would be a good idea for you to keep yourself
warm and rest.　　KAWAMURA: Yes, I'm planning to take time off from school tomorrow.　　PHARMACIST:
Take care.

The Body and Health

Health Care in Japan

The kind of situation portrayed in the preceding dialogue is typical of one aspect of health care in Japan. That is, people tend to go to a pharmacist first for everyday ailments, and they consult a physician only if the pharmacist suggests it or the pharmacist's treatment doesn't work. Many people also like to use traditional Chinese medicine (漢方薬 [かんぽうやく]) for minor medical problems.

Most doctors work from their own neighborhood clinics, called either 病院 (びょういん) or 医院 (いいん), and they may even have a few beds on the premises for seriously ill patients. (There are also large institutions called 病院, which are more like what Westerners think of when they hear the term *hospital.*) Patients usually do not make appointments to see their doctor. Instead, they simply go to the clinic and wait. Once they have seen the doctor, they may buy prescription drugs from the doctor's own dispensary.

Almost all Japanese have health insurance, either through their employers or through a government insurance program. Employed people pay insurance premiums through payroll deduction. Others pay in person at their local government office, and these fees are based on income. If you ever live in Japan, you would be well advised to enroll in some kind of health insurance, because the medical fees charged to uninsured people are as high as or higher than those charged in the United States.

医院の入口

Explaining Your Symptoms

(Please refer also to the Vocabulary Boxes in the Vocabulary and Oral Activities section.)

心臓病(にかかる)	しんぞうびょう(にかかる)	(to develop) heart disease
肺病(にかかる)	はいびょう(にかかる)	(to catch) pneumonia
癌(ができる)	がん(ができる)	(to develop) cancer
寒気(がする)	さむけ(がする)	(to have) chills
くらくらする		to feel dizzy
気分が悪い	きぶんがわるい	to feel out of sorts
鼻水が出る	はなみずがでる	to have a runny nose
鼻がつまる	はながつまる	to have a stuffy nose
胸やけ(がする)	むねやけ(がする)	(to have) heartburn
胸が苦しい	むねがくるしい	to have chest pains
息切れする	いきぎれする	to be short of breath
腕に怪我をする	うでにけがをする	to injure one's arm
…がかゆい		. . . is itchy
…の骨を折る	…のほねをおる	to break one's . . . bone
…をねんざする		to sprain . . .
…にやけどする		to get a burn on . . .
…から血が出る	…からちがでる	to bleed from . . .
肉離れを起こす	にくばなれをおこす	to pull a muscle
…にあざができる		to bruise . . .
傷	きず	wound, scar
関節	かんせつ	joints
かぶれる		to get a rash

At a Clinic

先生：どうぞ、そこへかけてください。
チン：はい。
先生：どうしましたか。
チン：食欲(しょくよく)がなくて、夜眠(ねむ)れないんです。
先生：どこか痛(いた)みはありますか。
チン：いいえ。
先生：疲(つか)れやすいですか。
チン：ええ。

DOCTOR: Please take a seat there.　CHIN: Yes.　DOCTOR: What's wrong?　CHIN: I don't have any appetite and I can't sleep at night.　DOCTOR: Do you have any pain?　CHIN: No.

先生：いつごろからそのような症状ですか。

チン：先週くらいからです。

先生：何か心配事はありますか。

チン：いいえ、特に。

先生：そうですか。じゃあ精密検査をしてみましょう。

At a Clinic or Hospital

前にも起こりましたか。

Has this happened before?

これまでに大きな病気をしたことがありますか。

Have you ever been seriously ill before now?

御家族で大きな病気をした方はいますか。

Is there any member of your family who has been seriously ill?

深呼吸をしてください。

Please take a deep breath.

先生、具合はどうでしょうか。

Doctor, how is he/she?

アレルギーはありますか。

Are you allergic to anything?

入浴はしないでください。

Please don't take any tub baths.

ちょっと様子を見てみましょう。

Let's observe your condition for a while.

面会は何時からですか。

What time do visiting hours start?

御見舞に来てくれて、どうもありがとう。

Thank you for coming to visit me while I'm sick.

何かほしいものはありませんか。

Is there anything you want [me to get for you]?

DOCTOR: Do you become tired easily?   CHIN: Yes.   DOCTOR: Since when have you been feeling this way?   CHIN: Since last week.   DOCTOR: Is there anything that you're worried about?   CHIN: Not in particular.   DOCTOR: I see. I'll try giving you a thorough checkup.

Role Play

Work in pairs.

1. One of you has a bad respiratory infection, and the other is a physician. Role play a visit to the doctor's office.
2. One of you has been hospitalized. The other student visits you in the hospital.

Listening Comprehension

1. Ms. Adachi, who has been living in an apartment in a suburb of Tokyo, has been missing for the past two weeks. Even before disappearing, she mostly kept to herself and had little contact with her neighbors. The police had to interview three neighbors to get sufficient information about her. Listen to their descriptions of Ms. Adachi's physical features and personal characteristics, and fill in the following table in English. If one of the neighbors is unable to supply a certain piece of information, put a line (—) in the box.

NEIGHBOR	A	B	C
Name			
Height			
Weight			
Age			
Build			
Hair			
Eyes			
Face			
Voice			
Abilities			
Attitude			
Other Features			

2. It's 7:30 A.M. now. Ms. Yoshimura, a nurse who is just coming off duty, is reporting to the head nurse, Ms. Koyama, about the patients she treated in the emergency room during the night. Listen to their conversation and fill in the following table in English.

	PATIENT'S NAME	WHERE INJURED	HOW INJURED
1.			
2.			
3.			
4.			
5.			
6.			

Life and Careers

職場で：クォリティー・コントロールのディスカッション
しょくば

OBJECTIVES

Topics

From cradle to grave
Careers and
occupations
In the workplace

Grammar

29. Describing a
change in state:
…ようになる
30. Expressing respect
(1): honorific forms
31. Expressing respect
(2): humble forms
32. Passives

Reading and Writing

The work that I have
chosen
The career path of
Mr. Katsuo Sakuma,
company president

**Language Functions
and Situations**

At a job placement
center: Looking for
a job
A job interview

Vocabulary and Oral Activities

From Cradle to Grave

Vocabulary: Life

人生	じんせい	life, human life
生まれる	うまれる	to be born
誕生日	たんじょうび	birthday
赤ちゃん／赤ん坊	あかちゃん／あかんぼう	baby
幼稚園	ようちえん	kindergarten
保育園	ほいくえん	daycare center
小学校	しょうがっこう	elementary school (*grades 1-6*)
中学校	ちゅうがっこう	middle school, junior high school (*grades 7-9*)
高校	こうこう	high school (*grades 10-12*) (*abbreviation of* 高等学校)
生徒	せいと	elementary, middle school, or high school student; pupil
短大	たんだい	two-year college (*abbreviation of* 短期大学)
教育(する)	きょういく(する)	education; (to educate)
入学(する)	にゅうがく(する)	school entrance; (to enter a school)
卒業(する)	そつぎょう(する)	graduation; (to graduate)
若い	わかい	young (*in one's teens or twenties*)
未成年	みせいねん	underage person, minor
就職(する)	しゅうしょく(する)	getting a job; (to get a job)
独身	どくしん	single, unmarried
結婚(する)	けっこん(する)	marriage; (to get married)
Xと結婚する		to marry X
離婚(する)	りこん(する)	divorce; (to get divorced)
中年	ちゅうねん	middle age
退職(する)	たいしょく(する)	retirement; (to retire)
老人	ろうじん	elderly person
年をとる	としをとる	to grow older
死	し	death

Review: 子供、男の子、女の子、大学、大学院、学校、死ぬ

赤ちゃん and 赤ん坊 both mean *baby,* but the first one has a slight honorific connotation, so you would always refer to someone else's baby as 赤ちゃん.

Unlike two-year colleges in North America, Japanese 短期大学 are almost exclusively for young women and offer training in what are traditionally regarded as feminine occupations, such as clerical work, nursery school teaching, and home economics.

人の一生（いっしょう）(*A person's life*)

Tell when the following things happen to people in general.

Review how to express one's age. Cf. p. 64–65, Book 1.

[例]　高校（こうこう）に入学（にゅうがく）する → 15歳（さい）で高校（こうこう）に入学（にゅうがく）します。
　　　高校（こうこう）を卒業（そつぎょう）する → 18歳（さい）で高校（こうこう）を卒業（そつぎょう）します。

- 生（う）まれる
- 高校（こうこう）を卒業（そつぎょう）する
- 幼稚園（ようちえん）に入園（にゅうえん）する
- 大学に入学（にゅうがく）する
- 中年（ちゅうねん）になる

- 結婚（けっこん）する
- 就職（しゅうしょく）する
- 退職（たいしょく）する
- 死（し）ぬ

文化ノート

日本の教育制度（きょういくせいど）—The Japanese Educational System (1): Elementary School

Although kindergartens, 幼稚園 (ようちえん), are not part of the system of compulsory education and also charge tuition, most preschool children attend either public or private kindergartens from age 3 through 5. The emphasis there is on how to work and play amicably in a group setting.

Schooling begins in earnest with elementary school, 小学校 (しょうがっこう), which includes grades one through six. The main task during these first six years of schooling is to give children a grounding in the Japanese writing system. They also receive thorough instruction in other subjects, not only mathematics and science but also music and art. Despite the demanding curriculum, Japanese elementary schools are not grim, harsh places. The school day contains opportunities for hands-on learning, group activities, and recreation.

There are some significant differences between the day-to-day operations of a Japanese school and those of a North American school. For example, the Japanese school year begins in April, with a six-week summer vacation beginning in mid-July, two weeks or so around the New Year's holiday, and a month-long spring vacation in March. Furthermore, school is in session for half a day three out of four Saturdays per month. Another difference is that Japanese schools have little support staff. The students themselves clean the school and school grounds, and although paid staff prepare lunch, students do the actual serving.

しょうがっこう おんがく
小学校の音楽の
時間です。

アクティビティー 2

8歳の時 (*When you were 8 years old, ...*)

Answer these questions.

あなたは8歳の時、
1. どこに住んでいましたか。
2. どの学校に通っていましたか。
3. 学校は好きでしたか。
4. どんなことをするのが好きでしたか。
5. スポーツはしましたか。どんなスポーツをしましたか。
6. 夏休みには何をしましたか。
7. 大きくなったら何になりたいと思っていましたか。

あなたが高校生の時
1. どこに住んでいましたか。
2. 学校は好きでしたか。
3. どんなクラスが好きでしたか。どんなクラスが嫌いでしたか。
4. 放課後 (*after class*)、何をしましたか。
5. たくさん勉強しましたか。
6. デートはよくしましたか。
7. 夏休みには何をしましたか。
8. 将来何になりたい／何をしたいと思っていましたか。

卒業した後 (After graduation)

Answer these questions.

1. 今大学の何年生ですか。
2. いつ卒業するつもりですか。
3. 卒業した後、大学院へ行くつもりですか。
4. 卒業した後、就職するつもりですか。どんな仕事をしたいですか。
5. どこで仕事を探したいですか。
6. 今結婚していますか。独身ですか。
7. もしまだ独身だったら、いつか結婚したいですか。何歳で?
8. 退職した後、何をしたいですか。

Vocabulary Library

More on Life

生年月日	せいねんがっぴ	birth date
年齢	ねんれい	age, age group
産む	うむ	to give birth
妊娠(する)	にんしん(する)	pregnancy; (to get pregnant)
恋愛	れんあい	romantic love
愛する	あいする	to love
見合い結婚	みあいけっこん	arranged marriage
プロポーズ(する)		marriage proposal; (to propose marriage)
婚約(する)	こんやく(する)	engagement; (to get engaged)
婚約者	こんやくしゃ	fiance/fiancee
恋人	こいびと	boyfriend/girlfriend
結婚式	けっこんしき	wedding
新婚旅行	しんこんりょこう	honeymoon
(お)葬式	(お)そうしき	funeral
(お)墓	(お)はか	grave

あなたの略歴 (*Your brief personal history*)

A. Write a brief life history in outline form and explain it in Japanese.

B. Work in pairs. Ask your partner these questions.

1. 生年月日はいつですか。
2. どこで生まれましたか。
3. 幼稚園へ行きましたか。
4. どこの高校を卒業しましたか。
5. この大学に入る前に、ほかの大学へ行きましたか。
6. 独身ですか。今、恋愛していますか。
7. 婚約していますか。結婚していますか。

Greetings on Special Occasions

North Americans like to say something original to express congratulations or sympathy, but Japanese people are content to use the same greetings as everyone else, so don't hesitate to use these phrases on appropriate occasions.

御入学（御出産、御卒業、御就職、御結婚）おめでとうございます。

Congratulations on entering school (childbirth, graduation, getting a job, your marriage).

誕生日おめでとうございます。

Happy birthday.

お喜び申し上げます。

I am very happy for you.

ご愁傷さまです。

My sympathy [at your bereavement].

If you need to congratulate someone and aren't sure of the proper phrase, just say おめでとうございます。

アクティビティー 5

ダイアログ：来週には歩けるようになると思います。(*I think that she'll be able to start walking next week.*)

カワムラ：おばあさんの具合はいかがですか。

山口：ええ、だいぶ良くなりました。昨日から<u>おかゆが食べられる</u>ように
なりました。

カワムラ：それはよかったですね。

山口：来週には歩けるようになると思います。

Practice the dialogue by replacing the underlined part with the following.

1. ジュースが飲める
2. ベッドで起き上がれる(*sit up in bed*)
3. ことばが話せる
4. ごはんが食べられる

アクティビティー 6

子供が話すようになるのは、いつごろですか。(*When do children start speaking?*)

Answer these questions (or work in pairs).

1. 子供が話すようになるのは、何歳ぐらいですか。
2. 赤ん坊が歩くようになるのは、いつごろですか。
3. 文字 (*written symbols*) が書けるようになるのは、何歳ぐらいですか。
4. 一人で自転車に乗れるようになるのは、何歳ぐらいですか。
5. 若い人が異性 (*opposite sex*) を意識する (*to be conscious of*) ようになるのはいつごろですか。
6. この大学で勉強しようと思うようになったのは、いつごろですか。
7. 今勉強していることを専攻しようと思うようになったのはいつごろですか。
8. ひらがなが書けるようになるまで、どれくらいかかりましたか。
9. 簡単な日本語が読めるようになったのは、いつごろですか。
10. 日本語で簡単な手紙を書けるようになったのは、いつごろですか。

Okayu is a rice porridge commonly fed to sick people.

KAWAMURA: How is your grandmother's condition? YAMAGUCHI: It's improved a lot. She was able to start eating **okayu** yesterday. KAWAMURA: That's great. YAMAGUCHI: I think that she'll be able to start walking next week.

日本の教育制度—The Japanese Educational System (2): Secondary Education

After completing elementary school, children proceed to the last three years of compulsory education, junior high school (中学校 [ちゅうがっこう]). Students now have different teachers for different subjects, but instead of moving from classroom to classroom, they stay in one room, and the teachers, who have desks in a central office area, come to them.

During these years, studying takes on increased importance because of the prospect of high school entrance examinations. Public high schools are inexpensive, but there is not enough room for everyone to attend, and certain high schools are known for sending an unusually large percentage of their graduates to prestigious universities, so competition to get into them is fierce. Students who fail to qualify for a public high school may either opt for a private high school, or else spend a year as a 浪人 (ろうにん) studying for another chance at the public high schools.

At the senior high school level, 高等学校 (こうとうがっこう) or 高校 (こうこう), competition intensifies as university-bound students work to pass the entrance exams for the university of their choice. Besides keeping up with their regular homework, many students attend cram schools and devote endless hours to studying old entrance exams. The conventional wisdom is that a student who sleeps only four hours a night is doing the right amount of studying.

As if the long hours of studying were not enough, senior high school students face other restrictions. There are almost no electives in the curriculum. Both junior and senior high schools require uniforms and also specify the acceptable types of hairstyles, shoes, socks, coats, sweaters, and accessories to wear with them. Rules of behavior are strict, covering behavior not only within the school but outside the school as well.

修学旅行で：ハイ、チーズ！

After six grueling years of secondary education, many students enter the university completely burned out. They see their university careers as a four-year vacation and devote most of their energies to their extracurricular activities and social lives.

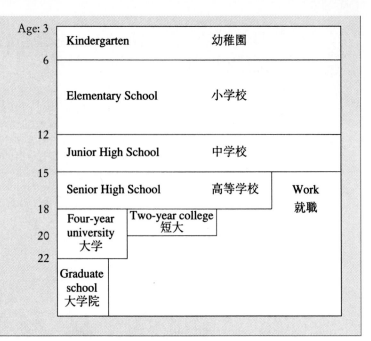

勉 Study Grammar 30.

アクティビティー　7

ダイアログ：部長がお話しになりますか。(*Manager, will you speak to him?*)

高田：部長、田中さんがお見えになりましたが、部長が<u>お話し</u>になりますか。

部長：僕はこれから会議に行かなくちゃならないから、君がかわりに<u>話して</u>くれないかな。

高田：はい、かしこまりました。

部長：うん、よろしく頼んだよ。

Practice the dialogue by changing the underlined parts with the appropriate form of the following verbs.

1. 会う
2. 話を聞く
3. 一緒に昼ごはんを食べる

TAKADA: Manager, Mr. Tanaka has arrived (*lit., has become visible*). Will you <u>talk</u> with him?　MANAGER: I have to go to a meeting now, so will you <u>talk</u> to him for me?　TAKADA: Yes. I will.　MANAGER: All right, please take care of it for me.

Careers and Occupations

Vocabulary: Occupations (1)

職業	しょくぎょう	occupation
会社員	かいしゃいん	company employee
公務員	こうむいん	government employee, civil servant
工員	こういん	factory worker
店員	てんいん	store clerk
事務員	じむいん	office clerk
セールスマン		[outside] salesperson
受付	うけつけ	receptionist
秘書	ひしょ	secretary
タイピスト		typist
銀行員	ぎんこういん	bank employee
技師	ぎし	engineer
教師	きょうし	schoolteacher
コック		cook
弁護士	べんごし	lawyer
新聞記者	しんぶんきしゃ	journalist
電話交換手	でんわこうかんしゅ	telephone operator
建築家	けんちくか	architect
歌手	かしゅ	singer
俳優	はいゆう	actor
女優	じょゆう	actress
美容師	びようし	women's hairdresser
理容師	りようし	barber

教師 is the neutral term for *teacher*, whereas 先生 is honorific. For this reason, teachers in Japan introduce themselves by saying 教師です rather than *先生です, which would sound as if they were showing respect to themselves.

Review: 医者、ウエーター、ウエートレス、運転手、会社、銀行、仕事、スチュワーデス、先生、歯医者、パイロット、働く、大工、看護婦

アクティビティー 8

だれの仕事ですか。(*Whose job is it?*)

Tell who does these things.

[例] 事務所でタイプを打ちます。→ タイピストの仕事です。

1. 料理を作ります。
2. 飛行機の中で飲み物を出します。
3. タクシーを運転します。
4. 病気を治します。
5. 家を建てます。
6. 髪にパーマをかけます。
7. 工場でものを作ります。
8. お金を貸します。

もの *things*

Occupations (2)

裁判官	さいばんかん	judge
科学者	かがくしゃ	scientist
教授	きょうじゅ	college professor
軍人	ぐんじん	military personnel
警察官	けいさつかん	police officer
消防士	しょうぼうし	firefighter
郵便配達員	ゆうびんはいたついん	mail carrier
車掌	しゃしょう	train conductor
駅員	えきいん	station employee
芸術家	げいじゅつか	artist
音楽家	おんがくか	musician
写真家	しゃしんか	photographer
会計士	かいけいし	accountant
通訳	つうやく	interpreter
翻訳者	ほんやくしゃ	translator
作家	さっか	author
スポーツ選手	スポーツせんしゅ	athlete
保母	ほぼ	daycare worker
家政婦	かせいふ	housekeeper, cleaning help
農民	のうみん	farmer
神父	しんぷ	Catholic priest
牧師	ぼくし	Protestant minister
僧侶	そうりょ	Buddhist priest or monk (also お坊さん)
神主	かんぬし	Shinto priest
主婦	しゅふ	housewife
外交官	がいこうかん	diplomat
政治家	せいじか	politician
葬儀屋	そうぎや	funeral director
自由業	じゆうぎょう	self-employed

Loanwords: カーレーサー、デザイナー、テストドライバー、バーテンダー、ファッションモデル、レポーター、コンサルタント、コピーライター、コーチ、ピアニスト、バレリーナ、テレビ・キャスター、アナウンサー

アクティビティー 9

連想 (*Associations*)

With what professions and jobs do you associate these words or phrases? Choose all the jobs that fit the descriptions from the list of occupations.

俳優	大工	警察官
主婦 (主夫)	弁護士	政治家
建築家	バーテンダー	僧侶
銀行員	パイロット	大統領 (*president*)
コック	ヘアースタイリスト	

1. ライセンスが必要である。
2. 責任 (*responsibility*) が大きい。
3. お金がもうかる。(*is earned*)
4. 名誉 (*prestige*) のある仕事である。
5. 8時から4時までの仕事である。
6. つまらない仕事である。
7. 頭が良くなければならない。
8. 前は男しかしなかったが、今は女もする。
9. 前は女しかしなかったが、今は男もする。
10. 力が強くなければならない。

アクティビティー 10

ダイアログ：フランス語の映画をたくさん見るようにしているわ。(*I'm trying to watch a lot of French movies.*)

カワムラ：町田さんは卒業したら、どんな仕事をしたいの。

町田：うーん、フランス語の通訳の仕事をしたいわ。

カワムラ：それで、フランス語のクラスを取っているんだね。

町田：ええ、それにフランス語の映画をたくさん見るようにしているの。

Practice the dialogue by replacing the first and second underlined parts with the following. Make up the third underlined part on your own.

1. 弁護士になる
   法学
2. 建築デザインの仕事をする
   建築学

KAWAMURA: Ms. Machida, what kind of job would you like to do after graduation? MACHIDA: Well, I'd like to work as a French interpreter. KAWAMURA: That's why you're taking French classes. MACHIDA: Yes. In addition, I'm trying to watch a lot of French movies.

アクティビティー　11

責任感 (せきにんかん) (*Sense of responsibility*)

What do you think is the most important responsibility for people who have the following occupations? Discuss in class.

1. 政治家 (せいじか)
2. 弁護士 (べんごし)
3. 看護婦 (かんごふ)
4. 家政婦 (かせいふ)
5. 秘書 (ひしょ)
6. 店員 (てんいん)
7. タクシーの運転手 (うんてんしゅ)
8. 医者 (いしゃ)
9. 日本語の先生

In the Workplace

Vocabulary: Looking for a Job (1)

求人広告	きゅうじんこうこく	help-wanted advertisement
パートタイム		part-time job, part-timer
探す	さがす	to look for
募集(する)	ぼしゅう(する)	recruitment, announcement of an opening; (to recruit)
雇う	やとう	to hire
応募する	おうぼする	to apply for a job, respond to an advertisement
履歴書	りれきしょ	résumé
面接(する)	めんせつ(する)	job interview; (to interview)
推薦状	すいせんじょう	letter of recommendation

Review: アルバイト

アクティビティー　12

仕事 (しごと) を探 (さが) しています。(*I am looking for a job.*)

A. What do you do when you look for a job? Number these activities in the order you would do them.

_____ 履歴書 (りれきしょ) を持って、面接 (めんせつ) に行く

_____ 新聞 (しんぶん) の求人広告 (きゅうじんこうこく) を見る

_____ 会社に電話をかけて、面接 (めんせつ) の日時 (にちじ) を決 (き) める

_____ 人事部 (じんじぶ) の人と面接 (めんせつ) をする

_____ 履歴書 (りれきしょ) の用紙 (ようし) (*résumé paper*) を買う

_____ 新聞 (しんぶん) を買う

_____ 履歴書 (りれきしょ) を書く

When you apply for a job in Japan, you can either send the form shown below to the company you are applying to or take it along to the job interview. The form is called a 履歴書 (りれきしょ), and you can buy it at bookstores or stationery stores. This form has a space to put your photo. See page 318 later in this chapter.

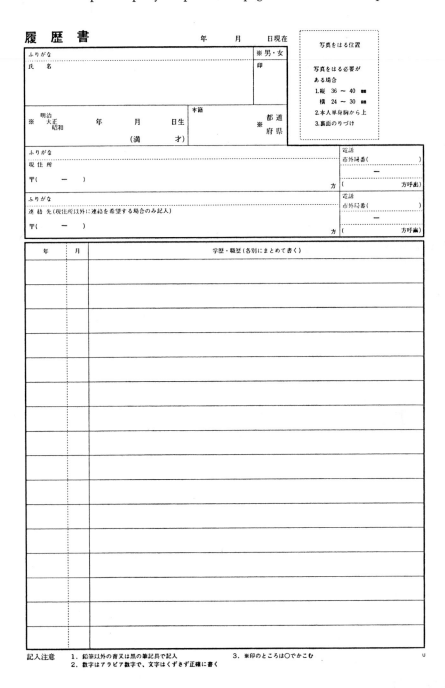

年	月	免 許・資 格

得意な学科	健康状態
趣味	志望の動機
スポーツ	

本人希望記入欄(特に給料・職種・勤務時間・勤務地・その他についての希望などがあれば記入)

家 族 氏 名	性別	年令	家 族 氏 名	性別	年令

通勤時間 約　　時間　　分	扶養家族数 (配偶者を除く)　　人	配偶者 ※ 有・無	配偶者の扶養義務 ※ 有・無

保護者(本人が未成年者の場合のみ記入) ふりがな		電話 市外局番(　)
氏　名	住　所〒(　ー　)	ー (　　　方呼出)

コクヨ

Looking for a Job (2)

失業(する)	しつぎょう(する)	unemployment; (to become unemployed)
応募用紙	おうぼようし	application form
記入(する)	きにゅう(する)	filling in forms; to fill in
経験(する)	けいけん(する)	(to) experience
学歴	がくれき	educational history
職歴	しょくれき	employment history
給料	きゅうりょう	salary
通勤(する)	つうきん(する)	commuting to work; (to commute)
残業(する)	ざんぎょう(する)	overtime; (to work overtime)
休暇	きゅうか	vacation

B. Referring to the personnel ads, tell what information is included in them.

Note that many abbreviations are used in these ads to include a lot of information in a limited space.

募集（男子）

セールス

30歳迄月30万コンピュ
ーターソフト経験不要
東京ソフト(03)5429-9012

募集（女子）

店員

年齢経験不問パート可
時給500円月曜休日
食付山川とんかつ店
青山(03)3123-5678

文化ノート

社会人
しゃかいじん

North American students often joke about entering "the real world" after college or becoming "real people" as opposed to students, but in Japan the division between people who are still in school and people who are out in the working world is very real.

University students are granted a great deal of leeway in their behavior. If they want to dress like the members of their favorite alternative music group, devote their time to video games or shopping, or be less than fastidious in their use of language, no one minds.

This changes abruptly when they take their first full-time job. Now they are 社会人, "society persons," and they are expected to act like adults. They have to dress conservatively, act responsibly, and subordinate their personal inclinations to the good of their employers and families. They may live with their parents until marriage, but the parents are less tolerant of youthful irresponsibility and keep reminding them that they are 社会人 and must behave as such.

Ever since Japanese youth began imitating the fashions and attitudes of the West after World War II, observers have been predicting that "this new generation" will not accept the old rules of behavior. Yet, over the years, a succession of greasers, beatniks, hippies, disco dancers, and punk rockers have traded in their boutique clothes for business suits and quietly turned into 社会人.

アクティビティー 13

ダイアログ：コーヒーをお入れします。(*I will make coffee for you.*)

部長：高田君、疲れたね。ちょっと休もうか。
高田：はい、今、コーヒーをお入れします。
部長：それはありがたいね。
高田：インスタントですが、よろしいでしょうか。
部長：ああ。
高田：砂糖とミルクはお入れしましょうか。
部長：ああ、砂糖をちょっと。

Vocabulary Library

Companies and Offices

The Company and Its Workers

商社	しょうしゃ	trading company
社長	しゃちょう	president of a company
重役	じゅうやく	executive
部長	ぶちょう	department head
課長	かちょう	section chief
係長	かかりちょう	subsection chief
OL	オーエル	female clerical worker (*from* オフィス・レディー)
同僚	どうりょう	colleague
上司	じょうし	superior, supervisor
部下	ぶか	subordinate
先輩	せんぱい	someone who started working for your employer, attending your school, or being involved in an organization or activity before you did
後輩	こうはい	the opposite of 先輩; someone who has been employed, enrolled, or involved for less time than you have
職場	しょくば	workplace

Employees of Japanese companies customarily address their own superiors not by name + さん, but by name + job title or else just by job title. Thus the subordinates of a 課長 named Yamada would call him or her 山田課長 or just 課長, not 山田さん.

MANAGER: Mr. Takada, we're tired, aren't we? Shall we take a little rest?   TAKADA: Yes. I will make coffee for you.   MANAGER: I appreciate that.   TAKADA: It's instant. Is that all right with you?   MANAGER: Yes.   TAKADA: Shall I add sugar and milk for you?   MANAGER: Yes, a little sugar.

株式会社	かぶしきがいしゃ	incorporated company, corporation
企業	きぎょう	enterprise, company
本店	ほんてん	main store, bank headquarters
支店	してん	branch store, bank branch office
事務所	じむしょ	office
工場	こうじょう	factory

Loanwords: ビジネスマン、キャリアウーマン

Review: 会社、会社員、銀行（ぎんこう）、銀行員（ぎんこういん）

Office Equipment

タイプを打つ	タイプをうつ	to type
OA	オーエー	office automation
電卓	でんたく	electric calculator
そろばん		abacus
セロテープ		cellophane tape
ホッチキス		stapler
書類	しょるい	documents, paper
情報	じょうほう	information

Loanwords: タイプライター、テレックス、ファイル、キャビネット、プリンタ、プログラマー、ロッカー、ワープロ (＝ワードプロセッサー)、ファックス (＝ファクシミリ)、コピーマシン

Company Activities

会議	かいぎ	meeting
出張(する)	しゅっちょう(する)	(to take a) business trip
出勤(する)	しゅっきん(する)	to come to work, to show up at work
首になる	くびになる	to be fired
首にする	くびにする	to fire
遅刻(する)	ちこく(する)	lateness; (to be late)
早退(する)	そうたい(する)	to leave early
組合	くみあい	union
スト(ライキ)		strike

アクティビティー 14

お水をお持（も）ちしましょうか。 (*Shall I bring water for you?*)

People in service occupations use a lot of humble language on the job. Here are the neutral forms of some language that service personnel might use in the course of a day. What are the humble forms?

[例]　ウエーター、ウエートレス：

a. お水を持って来ましょうか。→ お水を持ってまいりましょうか。

b. お皿を下げましょうか (*Shall I clear the dishes?*) →
お皿をお下げしましょうか。

1. 洋服屋の店員

a. 試着室 (*fitting room*) へ案内しましょうか。

b. 包みましょうか。(*Shall I wrap it?*)

2. 会社の電話交換手

a. そのように伝えます。(*I'll convey the message.*)

b. 412番につなぎます。(*I'll connect you with number 412.*)

3. ホテルのベルボーイ

a. 荷物を運びます。

b. カーテンを開けます。

4. 空港のカウンターの人

a. 出発 (*departure*) のゲートを教えます。

b. 荷物を預かります。(*I'll take charge of the luggage.*)

5. スチュワーデス、スチュワード：
この飛行機の安全設備 (*safety feature*) を説明します。

㊙ Study Grammar 32.

アクティビティー　15

ダイアログ：ウエーターに水をかけられました。(*I had water spilled on me by a waiter.*)

沢田：高田さん、そのズボン、びしょ濡れ。どうしたの。

高田：喫茶店で、ウエーターに水をかけられたんです。

沢田：まあ。

高田：まわりの人に笑われるし、さんざんでした。

SAWADA: Mr. Takada, those pants are soaking wet. What happened?　TAKADA: At the coffee shop I had water spilled on me by a waiter.　SAWADA: Oh my!　TAKADA: I got laughed at by the people around me. It was tough!

だれが言いましたか。(*Who said that?*)

Each of the people listed below has made a statement about his or her experiences on the job. Match each person with the most appropriate statement.

かむ *to bite* / 追いかける *to chase*

叱る *to scold*

囲む *to surround*

断る *to refuse*

1. 時々、犬にかまれたり、追いかけられたりします。
2. 病気の人がいれば、夜でも病院に呼ばれます。
3. お客さんに笑ってもらうのが、私の仕事です。
4. いろいろな所で、私のサインがほしい人に囲まれて動くこともできません。
5. 注文を間違えて、お客さんに叱られました。
6. みんなによく道を聞かれます。
7. 単位を落とした (*lost points*) 学生に泣かれて、困りました。
8. 玄関のところで、よく断られます。

a. セールスマン
b. 交番のおまわりさん
c. 郵便配達員
d. コメディアン
e. ウエートレス
f. お医者さん
g. 先生
h. スター

Grammar and Exercises

29. Describing a Change in State: ...ようになる

村山：鈴木さん、お子さんはいかがですか。
鈴木：先週から少し歩くようになりました。

───────────

MURAYAMA: Mr. Suzuki, how is your child?　SUZUKI: Last week she finally became able to walk a little.

村山：まあ、そんなに大きくなったんですか。

鈴木：ええ、もうすぐ走れるようになるんじゃないかと思いますよ。

村山：それはもうちょっと先じゃないかしら。

ブラウン：佐野さんはお酒はお飲みにならないんですか。

佐野：ええ、昔はたくさん飲んだんですが、今は全然飲まないようになってから、ずいぶんたちます。

ブラウン：どうしてお酒をおやめになったんですか。

佐野：お酒を飲むと、おなかのこのあたりが痛くなるようになったんです。

ブラウン：肝臓のあたりですね。

The verbal counterpart to the construction adjective + なる is as follows:

The dictionary form of a verb + ようになる (ようになります)
The negative form of a verb

get to be . . . , get so that . . . , become able to . . . , reach the state of . . .

This construction is often translated into English as *start to . . . .* However, verb + ようになる does not denote a situation in which someone starts doing something on a single occasion. Instead it refers to the beginning of a new ability or habit or to a natural development. Here are some examples of the "habit formation" use.

毎日ウエート・トレーニングをするようになりました。
I started doing weight training every day.

コーラをやめて、生ジュースを飲むようになった。
I gave up cola and started drinking fresh juice.

The "ability" use requires either a potential verb or a verb such as わかる or できる that contains the notion of being able to do something.

料理ができるようになりました。
I became able to cook.

ニュース放送 (*broadcast*) がわかるようになって、よかった。
It's good that I have become able to understand the news broadcasts.

MURAYAMA: Oh, my. She has grown that much?　SUZUKI: Yes, I think that she'll be able to run soon. MURAYAMA: I wonder if it won't be a little while.

BROWN: Mr. Sano, don't you drink?　SANO: No. I drank a lot before, but not at all now. It's been a long time since I quit drinking.　BROWN: Why did you quit drinking?　SANO: Whenever I drank, this area of my stomach started hurting.　BROWN: That's around your liver isn't it?

Grammar and Exercises

285

わかる and 知る

While わかる means *to figure out the content of something, to be clear, to be understandable,* 知る means *to find out something or to become acquainted with something or someone.*

> スペイン語がわかりますか。
> *Do you understand Spanish?*
> スペイン語を知っていますか。
> *Do you know Spanish?*

知る, with its basic meaning of *to find out, become acquainted,* is translated as *know* when it appears in its -ている form, (*lit., is in the state of having found out or become acquainted*). This is why you use 知っている for knowing people and being familiar with places and ideas.

> 三村さんを知っていますが、よくわからない人ですね。
> *I know Mr. Mimura, but he is an enigmatic person (person whom I don't understand well).*
> ―カワムラさんの住所を知っていますか。
> *Do you know Mr. Kawamura's address?*
> ―いいえ、知りません。でも、調べれば、わかりますよ。
> *No, I don't. But I'll know (lit., it will be clear) if I check it.*

Both わかりません and 知りません can be used for *I don't know,* but the nuance is quite different. 知りません can imply *I don't know and have no reason to,* so it can sound a bit rude if the question is one that you could be expected to know the answer to. That is why, when you ask a store clerk a question about the merchandise, he or she answers with わかりませんね instead of 知りません. (The ね makes it clear that the meaning is *I don't know,* not *I don't understand you.*)

In fact, saying 知らない directly to another person's face is a way of saying *I disapprove of what you are doing and want nothing to do with you.* Furthermore, since 知る refers to finding out something that you didn't have any reason to know, it sounds odd to use 知りません in reference to something concerning yourself, such as your own future plans or your own wants.

However, 知りません is a perfectly acceptable response when you don't know a person, are unfamiliar with a place or idea, or have no expertise in a certain subject area.

練習　　　　　　1

Connect and complete the sentences.

A

1. 毎日日本語のテープを聞いていた
ので、
2. 病気が治ったので、
3. 12月になって、
4. 近くに図書館ができたので、
5. ガールフレンドができて、
6. 車を買ってから、
7. コーヒーを飲むのをやめてから、
8. あの二人はけんか (quarrel) をし
てから、

B

a. 全然口をきかないように
なった。
b. よく本を借りるように
なりました。
c. 授業 (class session) に出られる
ようになりました。
d. いろいろな所にドライブに行く
ようになった。
e. きちんと髪をとかす (comb)
ようになりました。
f. 毎日、雪が降るようになった。
g. 夜、よく眠れるようになった。
h. 日本語がわかるようになった。

練習　　　　　　2

Complete the following sentences by using …ようになる.

[例]　学校のそばのアパートに移ってから、→
　　　学校のそばのアパートに移ってから、学校に早く行くようになった。

1. 毎日、日本語の新聞を読んでいるので、
2. 春になって、
3. 試験が近づいてきて、
4. 大学を卒業してから、
5. 日本に来てから、
6. 毎日、プールへ行ったので、
7. 一生懸命 (with all one's might) 練習すると、
8. もっと部屋を暖かくすると、

Adjective + する

You have already learned how to use the adjective + なる construction (Chapter 5, **Grammar 31**, Book 1) to mean that something becomes large, expensive, beautiful, or whatever. Adjective + する, refers to causing something to become large, expensive, beautiful, or whatever. As with the adjective + なる construction, i-adjectives go into their -く form, and na-adjectives and nouns go into their に form:

長くする   *to make long*
便利にする   *to make convenient*
グリーンにする   *to make green*

These constructions are sometimes ambiguous, and only the context can clear up the meaning.

きれいにしましょう。
Let's make it beautiful. or
Let's do it beautifully.
はやくしましょう。
Let's make it so that it's fast. or
Let's do it quickly.

However, not every adjective + なる construction has a corresponding adjective + する construction. For example, you often hear things like 食べたくなる *get to want to eat*, but *食べたくする is not used.

30. Expressing Respect (1): Honorific Forms

高田：これは部長がお書きになったんですか。
部長：いやあ、うちの家内が書いたんだ。
高田：奥様、字がお上手ですね。
部長：子供の時に、習字を習っていたそうだよ。

―――――――――――――

TAKADA: Did you write this, director?   DIRECTOR: No, my wife wrote it.   TAKADA: Your wife is good at handwriting.   DIRECTOR: She says that she studied calligraphy when she was a child.

カワムラ：ただいま。

山口：あっ、カワムラさん、横井先生がお待ちですよ。

カワムラ：もっと早く帰るつもりだったんだけど、電車が遅れてしまって。お待たせして、申し訳ないな。

山口：客間で待っていらっしゃるわ。

ブラウン：あのう、これ、京都のおみやげです。お二人で召し上がってください。

佐野：いつもいろいろありがとう。今度からはあまり気を使わないでください。京都はいかがでしたか。

ブラウン：とてもよかったです。写真をたくさんとりましたから、後でお見せします。

佐野：ええ、ぜひ見たいわ。ところで、昨日、三村さんという方がいらっしゃったわよ。

敬語
けいご

The Japanese language has significant built-in indicators of respect to the listener or a third party. The Japanese word for this system of respectful language is 敬語, but we use the English term *honorifics* in this textbook.

The system of 敬語 has many facets. First, we need to make a distinction between politeness and honorifics. The term *polite form* is the usual English translation of 丁寧語 (ていねいご) or 丁重語 (ていちょうご), and it refers to the use of the -ます forms of verbs and the copula です as opposed to plain verbs and the copula だ. It may indicate only that the two speakers don't know each other well, although it plays an important part in the system of honorifics as well.

Because the decision whether or not to use -ます/です forms depends on your relationship to the listener, it is possible to speak honorifically in plain form, such as when talking to a close friend or family member (in the plain form) about your instructor (using honorifics). On the other hand, you may talk to a stranger (in the polite form) about some impersonal topic (with no honorifics necessary).

KAWAMURA: I'm home.　YAMAGUCHI: Oh, Mr. Kawamura. Professor Yokoi is waiting for you.　KAWAMURA: I intended to come back earlier, but the train was late. It's really bad of me to have kept her waiting. YAMAGUCHI: She's waiting in the parlor.

BROWN: Uh, this is a souvenir from Kyoto. Please enjoy it together (*lit., Please the two of you eat it*). SANO: You're always doing nice things for us—thank you. Please don't bother about us next time. How was Kyoto?　BROWN: It was good. I took a lot of pictures, so I'll show them to you later.　SANO: Yes, I would like to see them by all means. By the way, a Mr. Mimura came [to see you] yesterday.

30.1 When you talk about actions or events related to someone superior to you, those actions or events are usually expressed by an honorific form of the verb. There are three ways to make a verb honorific, and the most common and regular is お + conjunctive form of verb + になる(になります).

To review the conjunctive form of the verb, refer to page 177, Book 1. お is a prefix that express politeness.

VERB CLASSES	DICTIONARY FORM	HONORIFIC FORM
Class 1	書く	お書きになる
Class 2	起きる	お起きになる

Caution: Some commonly used verbs, including 見る、着る、いる、ある、来る、and する, do not allow you to form their honorifics in this way. These irregular forms are found in **Grammar 30.2.**

横井先生は黒板に本の名前をお書きになりました。
Professor Yokoi wrote the name of the book on the chalkboard.
今日の午後、社長が皆さんにお話しになります。
This afternoon, the [company] president will speak to you all.

言語ノート

Who Is Superior to You?

It is all very well to say that you use honorifics to people superior to you, but how do you decide who is superior to you? Actually, both personal and contextual factors affect this decision. Unlike the military, a person who is a general in one situation may be a private in another situation.

Personal factors include, for instance, *position within an organization*. Lower-ranking employees use 敬語 (けいご) to their superiors, with the people in each position using 敬語 to the members of the organization who rank above them in the hierarchy. *Age* is another important factor: younger people use 敬語 in speaking to older people. *Length of experience* is another personal factor. Even when two people are at the same rank in the same occupation, the one with the longer experience is usually considered superior to the one with less experience. This is also true among university students, who speak politely to their **senpai,** 先輩, the members of the classes ahead of them and the alumni of their school. A *benefactor-recipient relation* can also influence the use of honorifics. Those who receive a benefit usually use honorifics to those who provide them with benefit. This is why shop clerks use honorifics in speaking to their customers.

Life and Careers

Another important personal factor is *the degree of familiarity in the relationship*. All other things being equal, you will become less formal as you become better acquainted. The *gender of the speaker and the addressee* is also a factor. Female speakers tend to speak more politely and formally than male speakers.

Finally, it is customary to use honorifics *when you don't know the identity of the person you are talking to.* This usage is heard most often in telephone conversations, when the person who answers the phone starts out speaking in honorific language, because he or she does not want to risk being offensive in case it is a high-ranking person on the other end of the line.

One reason for the widespread use of 名刺 (めいし) in Japan is that each 名刺 reveals its owner's organizational affiliation and rank within the organization, thus making the decision about what level of language to use a bit easier.

30.2 There are a number of irregular honorific forms of verbs. These are very commonly used, so you should memorize them.

DICTIONARY FORMS/NONHONORIFIC	IRREGULAR HONORIFIC FORMS
見る	ご覧になる
行く/いる/来る	いらっしゃる おいでになる
言う	おっしゃる
食べる/飲む	召し上がる
する	なさる
着る	お召しになる
くれる	くださる
死ぬ	おなくなりになる
知っている	ご存じだ

社長、この書類はご覧になりましたか。
President, did you take a look at this document?
社長は今日はまだ何も召し上がっていない。
The [company] president has not eaten anything yet today.

横井先生、もうご存じでしょうが、明日チンさんが中国に帰ります。
Professor Yokoi, you probably know this already, but Ms. Chin is going
*   back to China tomorrow.*

いらっしゃる and おいでになる can be used as the honorific form of 行く, いる, and
来る. You have to figure out the meaning based on the context.

横井先生も成田空港までいらっしゃるそうです。
I heard that Professor Yokoi, too, will go to Narita Airport.
横井先生は今研究室にいらっしゃいますか。
Is Professor Yokoi in her office now?

いらっしゃる, くださる, なさる, and おっしゃる conjugate like class 1 verbs, as indicated above. They are irregular, however, in the conjugation of the so-called ます
form and the imperative form.

DICTIONARY FORM	POLITE, NONPAST AFFIRMATIVE	IMPERATIVE
いらっしゃる	いらっしゃいます	いらっしゃい
くださる	くださいます	ください
なさる	なさいます	なさい
おっしゃる	おっしゃいます	おっしゃい

You have already studied the
use of ください Chapter 5,
Book 1 and なさい Chapter 1,
Book 2 in requests and commands.

30.3 The honorific form of the progressive form of verbs (cf. Chapter 5, Book 1)
is commonly expressed by the te-form of verbs + いらっしゃる(いらっしゃいます).

社長は今電話をかけていらっしゃいます。
The [company] president is now making a phone call.

With certain verbs, お + conjunctive form of verbs + だ(です) also expresses an
action in progress.

DICTIONARY FORM	HONORIFIC FORM
書く	お書きだ

社長、田中さんが応接室でお待ちです。
President, Mr. Tanaka is waiting for you at the reception room.

30.4 The honorific forms of adjectives are formed by adding the polite prefix お.

社長_{しゃちょう}はいつもお忙_{いそが}しいので、昼ごはんを召_めし上_あがらない。
Because the president is always busy, he doesn't eat lunch.
先生の奥様_{おくさま}はまだお若_{わか}いですね。先生の生徒_{せいと}さんでいらっしゃったんですか。
Professor, your wife is still young. Was she your student?

佐野_{さの}さんの御主人_{ごしゅじん}はいつもお元気です。
Mr. Sano is always healthy.
部長_{ぶちょう}はゴルフがお上手でいらっしゃいますね。
Manager, you're good at golf, aren't you?

30.5 The polite prefix お, when attached to nouns, expresses politeness, respect, or humbleness, or simply gives the sentence a refined and elegant feel, depending on the context.

先生がお手紙_{てがみ}をくださいました。
My professor wrote a letter to me. (respectful)
お昼御飯_{ごはん}にしましょう。
Let's have lunch. (polite, elegant)

Japanese-origin words usually take this お prefix, whereas Chinese-origin words take another polite prefix 御. This rule applies to na-adjectives as well. Thus Japanese-origin na-adjectives take お, whereas Chinese-origin na-adjectives take 御. Some of the most common Chinese-origin nouns and na-adjectives take お instead of 御.

お勉強、お電話、お買物、お天気、お時間、お料理
お洋服_{ようふく} (*clothes*) お歳暮_{せいぼ} (*year-end gift*)、お返事_{へんじ} (*reply*) お上手_{じょうず}、お元気_{げんき}、お葬式_{そうしき} (*funeral*)

Some words are always used with the polite prefix お or 御. In these words, the prefix is considered a part of the original words and they are not used without the prefix. These include.

御飯_{ごはん} (*rice, meal*)、おなか (*belly*)、おかず (*side dish*)、お守_{まも}り (*good luck charm*)、おみくじ (*a kind of fortune telling*) お転婆_{てんば} (*tomboy*)

30.6 In Book 1, you learned that the copula です is a polite form of だ. An even more polite form is でございます. When used in reference to a person, でございます is humble. (The corresponding honorific form for human subjects is でいらっしゃいます.) Compare:

私は林_{はやし}でございます。
I am Hayashi.

加藤_{かとう}先生でいらっしゃいますか。
Is it you, Professor Katoo?

Note that this formation of honorific i-adjectives is not possible with all i-adjectives. For example, 面白_{おもしろ}い、つまらない、遠_{とお}い、大きい, and so forth don't take the polite prefix お.

お is the polite prefix. ていらしゃる sounds politer than だ, but it is used only in reference to people.

Some na-adjectives do not take the polite prefix お, such as those of foreign origin like ハンサム or those with negative meanings like 下手, 不器用 (*clumsy*), or けち (*stingy, ungenerous*).

These words are fully assimilated to Japanese and are considered to be Japanese-origin words. That's why お is attached.

When used in reference to something nonhuman, でございます simply gives the whole sentence an extra feeling of politeness and formality. (でいらっしゃいます is not used in reference to nonhuman subjects at all.)

30.7 Even the title さん has a more polite form, 様. When referring to a high-ranking person's relatives, you can say お母様, お嬢様, お父様, or 奥様. Employees of high-class stores, restaurants, and hotels may address their customers as お客様.

練習　　　　1

In the following sentences, underline the honorific expressions.

1. 先生は毎日、何時にお出かけになりますか。
2. 社長はどちらの御出身でいらっしゃいますか。
3. もうお帰りですか。もう少し、お待ちになりませんか。
4. 先生が今度お書きになった御本はアメリカの大学についての御本でございますね。
5. 先生がアメリカにいらっしゃってから、何年になりますか。
6. 先生、何を御覧になっているんですか。
7. 社長、もう御存じかもしれませんが、山下さんがお亡くなりになったそうです。
8. 課長のお嬢様は、おしとやか (gentle, refined) でいらっしゃいますね。

練習　　　　2

Change the underlined parts into their honorific forms.

先生、元気ですか。私は元気です。こちらは毎日暑い日が続いています。そちらはどうですか。

慣れる *to get used to*

研究 *research*

　　先生がアメリカへ行ってから、3ケ月になります。そちらの生活にもう慣れたことと思います。毎日、研究に忙しいことと思います。新しい本を書いているのでしょうか。先生が書く本はいつも面白くて、全部読んでいます。今も先生がアメリカ

出す (in this context) *to publish*
考え *idea*
感服する *to be struck with admiration*
心配 *worry*
失礼する (in this context) *to excuse one-self*

へ発つ前に出した本を読んでいます。先生のすばらしい考えに感服しています。奥様はどう過ごしていますか。先日、奥様が病気だと、山田先生が言っていました。心配しています。今日はこのへんで失礼します。

You have been asked to introduce a famous pianist at a banquet, and you show your proposed speech to a Japanese friend, who tells you that the speech is grammatically correct but lacks the proper honorifics. Rewrite this speech so that all the honorifics are in place.

本田先生は1955年6月30日に大阪で生まれました。子供のころから、ピアノを習い、6歳の時にはコンサートでショパンの曲を弾いたそうです。学校で得意な学科は、やはり音楽だったそうです。

ショパン Chopin (name of a composer)
曲 a piece of music, a tune
やはり after all

　　1963年に東京音楽大学に入学しました。大学では、三島花子先生のもとで、ピアノを勉強しました。1967年に大学を卒業すると、すぐヨーロッパに渡りました。1971年にモスクワのチャイコフスキーコンクールで2位になり、1972年のパリ・ピアノコンクールでは優勝しました。1973年にはヨーロッパから帰り、東京、大阪など日本各地でコンサートを開きました。

コンクール a competition
優勝する to win a championship

　　現在は東京とパリに家を持ち、一年の半分は日本、残りの半分はパリに住んでいます。日本とヨーロッパにたくさんの生徒を持ち、ピアノを教えています。

現在 at present / 半分 half
のこり the rest, remainder

　　先生は昨日、ヨーロッパから帰ったばかりです。旅行で疲れている中をわざわざ来てくれました。

わざわざ going to all the trouble

　　今日は「私とショパン」というタイトルで話してくれます。話の後、ショパンの曲も弾いてくれるそうです。

文法ノート

Describing an Effort: ...ようにする

The dictionary or negative form of a verb + ようにする is used to express the idea of making an effort or carrying out actions to make sure that something will happen. Often the most appropriate English equivalent is *be sure to . . .*, especially in commands or requests. Unlike verb + ようになる, verb + ようにする may be used in talking about one-time events.

　　寝る前にストーブなどを消すようにしてください。
　　Before you go to bed, be sure to turn off the space heater and so on.
　　大切な会議ですから、遅れないようにしてください。
　　Because it's an important meeting, make an effort not to be late.
　　同僚達と仲良く (congenially) 仕事をするようにしています。
　　I'm making sure that I work with my colleagues in a congenial manner.

31. Expressing Respect (2): Humble Forms

社長：電話帳、ある？

秘書：電話番号をお調べになるんですか。

社長：うん。田中さんのお宅の電話番号を...

秘書：じゃあ、私がお調べいたします。

面接で

人事部長：お名前をどうぞ。

カワムラ：カワムラと申します。

人事部長：どちらの御出身ですか。

カワムラ：アメリカのカリフォルニア州のロサンジェルスから参りました。

人事部長：学生さんだと伺っていますが、...

カワムラ：はい、東京大学の学生でございますが。

31.1 Humble expressions, or 謙譲語 (けんしょうご), express the lower status of the speaker or his or her in-group member and express respect toward a superior or out-group person. As with the honorific forms, there are both regular and irregular ways to express this linguistic function. This regular form is お + conjunctive form of verb + する (します)／いたす (いたします).

お is the polite prefix. いたす is considered more polite than する.

DICTIONARY FORM	HUMBLE FORM (1)	HUMBLE FORM (2)
書く	お書きする	お書きいたす
借りる	お借りする	お借りいたす

COMPANY PRESIDENT: Do you have a telephone directory?   SECRETARY: Are you going to look for a telephone number?   PRESIDENT: Yes. I would like to check Mr. Tanaka's home phone number. SECRETARY: Then I will check it for you.

At an interview   PERSONNEL MANAGER: May I ask your name?   KAWAMURA: I am Kawamura. PERSONNEL MANAGER: Where are you from?   KAWAMURA: I am from Los Angeles, California, in America.   PERSONNEL MANAGER: I hear that you're a student.   KAWAMURA: Yes, I am a student at the University of Tokyo.

In these formations, the subject's action generally must affect a superior in some way, usually, but not always, implying that the subject does something for the superior person's sake.

社長、私がお手紙をお書きいたします。
President, I will write a letter for you.
社長、高田さんをお呼びいたします。
President, I will summon Mr. Takada for you.

31.2 Some important and commonly used verbs have irregular humble forms. They are

NONHUMBLE FORM	IRREGULAR HUMBLE FORM
いる	おる
する	いたす
行く/来る	参る
言う	申す/申し上げる
借りる	拝借する
会う	お目にかかる
見る	拝見する
飲む/食べる/もらう	いただく
あげる	差し上げる
知っている	存じている
聞く/たずねる (to inquire)	伺う
見せる	お目にかける
思う	存じる
たずねる (to visit)	伺う/お邪魔する

私は大学で日本語を勉強しております。
I am studying Japanese at a university.
先生の誕生パーティーには私も参るつもりです。
I am planning to go to your birthday party, Professor.
どこかで一度お目にかかったことがあると存じます。
I think that I have met you once somewhere.
ちょっと申し上げたいことがあるのですが...
There's something I want to say ....
はい、存じております。
Yes, I know.

31.3 In the case of nominal verbs, the humble form is formed with お or 御 + noun + する（します）／いたす（いたします）.

The selection of お and 御 follows the rules discussed in **Grammar 30**.

社長、レストランは私が御予約いたします。
President, I will make a restaurant reservation for you.
出口まで御案内いたします。
I'll guide you to the exit.

31.4 You can also express humbleness with expressions related to giving and receiving, particularly in cases when a superior or an out-group member clearly received a favor from you, or when you have early received a favor from a superior or out-group person, in which case you use ＋いただく.

私がお嬢さんからのお手紙を読んで差し上げましょう。
I will read the letter from your daughter for you.
先生にその言葉を漢字で書いていただきました。
*I had my instructor write that word in **kanji** for me.*

言語ノート

Honorifics and In-group versus Out-group Distinctions

One characteristic of honorifics in Japanese is the consideration of in-group and out-group. Depending on the situation, you may refer to the same person with either honorific or humble forms.

In the following case, we have two 社員 of roughly equal rank talking to each other about their superior.

社員（平井）：田中課長が明日のパーティに御出席になるかどうか知っていますか。
社員（森山）：ええ、御出席になるとおっしゃっていました。

As employees of the same company, and therefore members of the same in-group, they use honorific language (尊敬語 [そんけいご]) when talking *about* Mr. Tanaka, even if he is not present, because he is superior to both of them in the company hierarchy.

STAFF MEMBER (HIRAI): Do you know if Mr. Tanaka will attend tomorrow's party?　STAFF MEMBER (MORIYAMA): Yes, he said that he would attend.

Next let's consider the case in which Moriyama receives a call from someone outside the company, let's say, Ms. Koshino of Company B.

社員(森山)：もしもし、総務課です。
越野：田中課長をお願いします。
社員(森山)：田中はただいま、席をはずしておりますが、…

Note that Moriyama is not using 尊敬語 to talk about his superior's action while talking to Ms. Koshino, an out-group person. In the third line, Moriyama doesn't attach an honorific title to Tanaka, not even -さん. Also, Moriyama uses the humble form (おります) to talk about his superior's action. This illustrates one of the important rules of Japanese honorifics. You should not use 尊敬語 to talk about your in-group person while talking to an out-group person, even when the in-group person is your superior.

練習　1

In the following sentences, underline the humble expressions.

1. すみません。高田さんにお目にかかりたいのですが…
2. ちょっとお目にかけたいものがあるのですが…
3. このケーキ、いただいてもよろしいですか。
4. コンタクトレンズ、私がお探しいたします。
5. 明日お返ししますから、この辞書を拝借してもよろしいでしょうか。
6. ちょっとおたずねしますが、図書館はどちらでしょうか。
7. お客さまにお知らせいたします。ただいま4階の文房具売場で万年筆をお買いになると、ボールペンを無料で (for free) 差し上げております。
8. 皆様の切符を拝見させていただきます。

練習　2

Rewrite these sentences using humble expressions.

[例]　それは先生から聞きました。→ それは先生から伺いました。

1. 社長、ここで待っています。
2. 先生、私がします。

STAFF MEMBER (MORIYAMA): Hello, this is the general affairs department.　KOSHINO: Section Chief Tanaka, please.　STAFF MEMBER (MORIYAMA): Tanaka has stepped out for a minute. (*Lit., he's away from his seat right now.*)

3. 明日は、七時に来る。

4. 私から奥様に言いましょう。

5. これは先生からもらった辞書です。

6. 山田社長は三年前から知っています。

7. 明日、たずねてもいいでしょうか。

8. 先生のお名前はいつも新聞で見ています。

9. ペンをちょっと借りたいのですが、...

10. あの本は私が社長にあげました。

練習　　　　　　　　　　　　　　3

Change the underlined parts to honorific or humble expressions, whichever is appropriate to the situation.

先生、元気ですか。私も元気です。

　　先生が来月京都に来るのを、妻も私も楽しみにしています。その日は妻が駅まで迎えに行きます。手紙で何時の新幹線で着くか、お知らせください。京都ではどうぞ我が家に泊まってください。私が市内を案内していろいろなところを見てもらおうと思っています。また、めずらしい京都の料理も食べてもらおうと妻と話しています。それから、私の妹も先生にぜひ会いたいと言っています。先日先生の本を読み、感銘し、先生と話したいそうです。どうかよろしくお願いします。先生に会うのは5年ぶりで、いろいろ話すことがありそうです。手紙を待っています。

市内 within the city
我が家 our house

ぜひ by all means

感銘する to be impressed, to be struck with admiration
願う to request
5年ぶり It's been five years since . . .

32. Passives

チン：林さん、どうしたんですか、その腕？

林：昨日、自転車に乗っていたら、車にぶつけられたんです。

チン：本当ですか。大丈夫ですか。

林：ええ、たいしたことないんです。

CHIN: Mr. Hayashi, what happened to your arm?　　HAYASHI: I was hit by a car while riding my bike yesterday.　　CHIN: Really? Are you all right?　　HAYASHI: Yes, it's no big deal.

町田：先輩に夕食に誘われたんだけど、どうしようかしら。

ブラウン：先輩って、だれ？

町田：ほら、同じクラブの木下さんよ。

ブラウン：あの木下さん。チンさんもいつも言い寄られて、困っているんですって。

カーティス：三村君、眠そうだね。

三村：うん、昨日、となりの赤ん坊に一晩中泣かれて、4時まで眠れなかったんだ。

カーティス：大変だったね。

三村：それだけじゃないんだ。やっと眠れたと思ったら、5時に電話で起こされてしまって、それも間違い電話だったんだ。

カーティス：さんざんだったね。

32.1 In both English and Japanese it is possible to restate a situation so that what would normally be the direct object becomes the subject. This kind of a restatement is called *the passive.*

For example, if one of your cousins were a writer, you could hold up one of his or her books and brag

> *My cousin wrote this book.*

In the same situation, however, you could also say

> *This book was written by my cousin.*

The second sentence, in which the usual direct object has become the subject, is a *passive* sentence. The first sentence, with the subject and direct object in their usual roles, is an *active* sentence.

BROWN: I've been invited to dinner by my **senpai.** What should I do?   MACHIDA: Who is that **senpai**? BROWN: You know—Mr. Kinoshita, who's in the same club as I am.   MACHIDA: That Mr. Kinoshita! I hear that Ms. Chin is upset because she's always being approached by him.

CURTIS: Mr. Mimura, you look sleepy.   MIMURA: Yeah, I had the baby next door crying all night and I couldn't get to sleep until four.   CURTIS: That's terrible.   MIMURA: That's not all. Just when I thought I could finally get to sleep, I was awakened by a phone call at five. And it was the wrong number!   CURTIS: That was really harsh.

32.2 The passive is formed in the following manner.

CLASS 1	CLASS 2	CLASS 3
root + the a-column **hiragana** corresponding to the dictionary ending+ れる	root + られる	irregular
書く → 書かされる 買う → 買われる	食べる → 食べられる 見る → 見られる	する → される 来る → 来られる

u-column → a-column
く → か
す → さ
つ → た
ぬ → な
む → ま
る → ら
ぶ → ば
う → わ

Note that when the dictionary ending is う, it changes to わ in the passive form, just as in the negative form. The passive form conjugates like a Class 2 verb.

Many verbs that have passive forms in English do not have passive forms in Japanese. For example, there is no passive form for わかる or 要る.

32.3 The normal sentence pattern is

N1 は／が N2	に から	passive verb form

N1 was V-ed by N2

Here N2 is the agent or causer of an action, while N1 is the patient or recipient of the action.

> 林さんはその男になぐられました。
> *Mr. Hayashi was beaten by that man.*
> このウィルス (virus) は山中博士によって発見 (discover) されました。
> *This virus was discovered by Dr. Yamanaka.*

When the agent is clear from the context or when the agent's identity is unknown or of no particular interest, it does not have to be expressed.

> この家は17世紀に建てられました。
> *This house was built in the seventeenth century.*

It is likely that no one knows anymore exactly who built the house.

You cannot assume, however, that all English passives will correspond exactly to Japanese passives or vice versa. For example, Japanese uses the passive less than

English, particularly if the *agent* is being mentioned directly. The second sample sentence above, for instance, could be restated as

このウイルスは山中博士が発見しました。
Lit., This virus, Dr. Yamanaka discovered it.

particularly in normal conversation, as opposed to formal writing. Another example of the active used where English would have the passive is

その事故で二人の人が死にました。
Two people were killed in the accident. (lit., By means of that accident, two people died.)

If you said 殺されました *were killed* instead of 死にました *died*, it would sound as if the accident killed them on purpose.

32.4 A type of passive that is common in Japanese is the so-called *adversative passive* or *indirect passive*. The implication of this type of sentence is that something happened and the subject was adversely affected by it or was upset about it. Note that the subject doesn't have any control over the action. The direct object of the active counterpart remains the direct object in this construction.

私はどろぼうにステレオを取られました。
(*Lit., I was taken the stereo by a thief.*) *I had my stereo taken by a thief.*
母に日記 (*diary*) を読まれました。
(*Lit., I was read [my] diary by my mother.*) *I had my diary read by my mother.*

32.5 An English passive can be formed only on a transitive verb, that is, a verb with a direct object. A Japanese passive can be formed on an intransitive verb such as 来る or 死ぬ. And the resulting passive sentences are adversative passives.

しつこい (*annoyingly persistent*) セールスマンにうちへ来られました。
(*Lit., I was come to the house by an annoyingly persistent salesman.*) *I had an annoyingly persistent salesman come to the house.*
小さい時に両親に死なれました。
(*Lit., I was died by my parents when I was small.*) *I suffered the death of my parents when I was small.*

Remember to use this construction only when you want to express your displeasure at what has happened. When you are pleased with another person's action or have benefited from it, you need to use a favor construction.

練習	1

Answer the following questions in Japanese.
1. あなたの大学は何年前に誰によって建てられましたか。
2. あなたの町ではどんな新聞がよく読まれていますか。

3. あなたの国ではどんな歌がよく歌われていますか。

4. あなたの州 (state) ではどんなものが作られていますか。

5. あなたの町ではどのテレビ局 (television station) のニュースがよく見られていますか。

6. あなたは人にだまされたことがありますか。(だます = to cheat, deceive)

7. あなたは何かいいことをして、人に感謝されたことがありますか。(感謝する = to thank)

練習 2

Rewrite the following sentences in the passive form.

1. ジェームス・クラベルが「しょうぐん」を書きました。
2. たくさんの人が「しょうぐん」を読んだ。
3. テロリストは村の人を殺した。
4. カワムラさんは三村さんを呼んだ。
5. 日本人がゴッホ (van Gogh) のその絵を買いました。
6. 日本人もこの歌をよく歌います。
7. 日本でもこの番組を放送 (broadcast) しています。

練習 3

Take the active sentence at the beginning of each mini-dialogue, turn it into the passive, and insert it at the proper point in the dialogue.

1. (子供が一晩中泣いた)
   A: 眠そうですね。目も赤いですよ。
   B: ええ、昨日、全然眠れなかったんです。
   A: どうしたんですか。
   B: ＿＿＿＿ んです。

2. (雨が降った)
   A: 先週のピクニック、どうでしたか。
   B: ＿＿＿＿ て、さんざん (terrible) でした。
   A: それは大変でしたね。

3. (みんなが笑った)
   A: 真っ赤な顔して、どうしたんですか。
   B: ＿＿＿＿ んです。
   A: どうしてですか。
   B: バナナの皮ですべって、ころんだんです。

4. (誰も話を聞かない)
   A: ねえねえ、いい話があるの。
   B: ええ、何？
   A: ここじゃダメ。＿＿＿＿ ところに行きましょう。
   B: そんないい話なの？

Vocabulary

Life

あかちゃん	赤ちゃん	baby
うまれる	生まれる	to be born
きょういく	教育	education
けっこん(する)	結婚(する)	marriage; (to get married)
こうこう	高校	high school
こうはい	後輩	a person who started at a job, school, or activity after you did
し	死	death
しゅうしょく(する)	就職(する)	looking for a job; (to look for a job)
しょうがっこう	小学校	elementary school
じんせい	人生	life, human life
せんぱい	先輩	a person who started at a job, school, or activity before you did
そつぎょう(する)	卒業(する)	graduation; (to graduate)
たいしょく(する)	退職(する)	retirement; (to retire)
たんきだいがく	短期大学	two-year college (abbreviation: 短大)
ちゅうがっこう	中学校	middle school, junior high school
ちゅうねん	中年	middle age
としをとる	年をとる	to grow older
どくしん	独身	single, unmarried
にゅうがく(する)	入学(する)	entering a school; (to enter school)
ほいくえん	保育園	daycare center
みせいねん	未成年	a minor, an underage person
ようちえん	幼稚園	kindergarten
りこん(する)	離婚(する)	(to get a) divorce
ろうじん	老人	elderly person
りゅうがく(する)	留学(する)	(to) study abroad
わかい	若い	young

Review: 男の子、女の子、学校、子供、死ぬ、大学、大学院

Occupations

うけつけ	受付け	receptionist
かいしゃいん	会社員	company employee
かしゅ	歌手	singer
きょうし	教師	schoolteacher
ぎし	技師	engineer
ぎんこういん	銀行員	bank employee
けんちくか	建築家	architect
こういん	工員	factory worker
こうむいん	公務員	government employee, civil servant
コック		cook
しょくぎょう	職業	occupation
じょゆう	女優	actress
しんぶんきしゃ	新聞記者	journalist
じむいん	事務員	office clerk
セールスマン		[outside] salesperson
でんわこうかんしゅ	電話交換手	telephone operator
はいゆう	俳優	actor
ひしょ	秘書	secretary
びようし	美容師	women's hairdresser
べんごし	弁護士	lawyer
りようし	理容師	men's hairdresser, barber
レジ		cashier

Review: 医者、ウエーター、ウェートレス、運転手、会社員、銀行、仕事、スチュワーデス、先生、歯医者、パイロット、働く、大工、店員、

Loanwords: タイピスト、ヘアードレッサー、メカニック、

Companies

おうぼ(する)	応募(する)	(to make an) application for a job, response to an advertisement
オーエル	OL	female clerical worker
かかりちょう	係長	subsection chief
かちょう	課長	section chief
きゅうじんこうこく	求人広告	help-wanted advertisement
ししゃ	支社	company branch office
しゃちょう	社長	president (*of a company*)
しょうしゃ	商社	trading company
しょくば	職場	workplace
じゅうやく	重役	executive
じょうし	上司	superior, supervisor

どうりょう	同僚	colleague
ぶか	部下	subordinate
ぶちょう	部長	department head
ぼしゅう(する)	募集(する)	recruitment of employees; (to recruit employees)
めんせつ(する)	面接(する)	job interview; (to interview for a job)
やとう	雇う	to hire
りれきしょ	履歴書	résumé

Review: アルバイト、会社

Loanword: パートタイム

Grammar

お…いたす	regular humble form of verb
お…する	regular humble form of verb
お…だ	honorific form of progressive construction
お…になる	regular honorific form of verb
おいでになる	to come, go (*honorific*)
…ようにする	to be sure to …
…ようになる	to reach the point of … -ing
～られる	passive ending for Class 2 verbs
～れる	passive ending for Class 1 verbs

Kanji

Learn these **kanji.**

校 卒 業 仕 就 職 退 若 老

愛 恋 初 結 婚 式 研 究 医 者

銀 亡 忙 知 存 申 召 様 師

Reading and Writing

Reading 1 　私の選んだ仕事

選ぶ *to choose, select*

Before You Read

Column A is a list of jobs or professions. Column B is a list of types of schooling or training required. Column C is a list of reasons for choosing a job. Match each job in column A with the training required for it and the reason a person might choose it.

[例]　　8 - b - H

A　職業	B　学歴・訓練	C　理由
1. 弁護士	a. 大学の教育学部	A. スターになりたかった
2. コンピューター・エンジニア	b. デザイン学校	B. みんなにおいしい料理を食べてもらいたい
3. 学校の先生	c. 料理学校	C. 弱い人を助けたい
4. ロック歌手	d. 大学の法学部	D. 機械 (machines) が好きだった
5. 会社の社長	e. ギターと歌の練習	E. 父が会社を持っていた
6. コック	f. 水泳とダイビングの練習	F. 海が大好きだ
7. スキューバダイバー	g. 大学の工学部	G. 人に教えることが好きだ
8. ファッション・デザイナー	h. MBA	H. ドレスをデザインするのが好きだった

Now Read It!

Ms. Machida, who is scheduled to graduate this year and is looking for her first job, found the following article in a magazine for job searchers. In the article, three women explain why they choose their current jobs.

いろいろな分野で御活躍なさっている女性に、御自分の仕事についてお話ししていただきました。

分野 *field of endeavor*
活躍する *to play an active role, to be prominent*

留学カウンセラー
佐藤まどかさん （25歳）

短大を卒業した後、英語を勉強するためにボストンに二年間留学しました。日本からたくさんの学生が来ていました。ボストンから帰ってきて、今の会社に就職し、留学カウンセラーの仕事を始めました。自分の経験が生かせる仕事なので、この仕事を選びました。留学を希望する女子学生、OLの方がたくさんカウンセリングを受けにいらっしゃいます。その方々に会って、どんなことを勉強したいかなど希望を伺い、アドバイスして差し上げます。遠くの方からの御質問には、手紙や電話でお答えしています。留学の期間や目的は違いますが、皆さん、大きな夢をお持ちになっているようです。皆さんの夢を実現するよをお手伝いできると思うと、うれしいですね。

経験 experience / 生かす to put to use

希望する to desire, hope for

期間 period, length of time
目的 goal, objective
夢 dream
実現する to realize, to bring to reality

会社社長
林さと子さん （34歳）

　花が嫌いな女性はいないと思います。誕生日や結婚記念日、そして何か特別な日に花をプレゼントされるのは、とてもうれしいことです。最近は、フラワーギフトもポピュラーになってきています。私は子供の時から花が大好きで、花屋になるのが夢でした。高校を卒業するとすぐ、花屋さんに就職しました。そこで、10年間花の勉強をしました。そして、2年前に友人とこの「ローズガーデン」という会社を始めました。フラワーギフトを皆さんのお宅にお届けするのが私どもの仕事です。「わあ、きれいなお花！」とお客様に喜んでいただけた時が、一番幸せです。最近は結婚式やいろいろなパーティーのお花のアレンジメントもさせていただいております。華やかな仕事のように見えますが、なかなか大変な仕事なんですよ。新鮮な花をお届けするために、毎朝早く生花市場に行き、いい

結婚記念日 wedding anniversary

特別な special

届ける to deliver

幸せな happy

華やか spectacular, showy

新鮮な fresh

花を選びます。冬の朝は寒くて、とてもつらいです。まだ独身です。今まで仕事が忙しくて、デートする暇もありませんでした。私の仕事に理解のある男性がいたら、結婚したいと思っています。

弁護士
青山洋子さん (43歳)

　私の父が弁護士でした。子供の時から、父のように弁護士になりたいと思っていました。それで、大学も法学部へ行きました。大学を卒業して、会社のOLをしながら、司法試験の勉強をしました。夜、アパートに帰ってから、朝2時くらいまで勉強しました。OLになって、4年後に司法試験にパスしました。しばらく東京の弁護士事務所で仕事をしました。主に、離婚問題を扱いました。夫に愛人のできた主婦や、夫に捨てられた主婦などのケースをたくさん扱いました。女性の地位を高めなければいけないと考え始めたのはこのころからです。去年、独立して自分の事務所を持ちました。セクハラ・ホットラインを作り、セクハラに悩んでいるOLの皆さんの相談にのっています。私もOLをしていたのでOLの方々の気持ちがよくわかります。去年、アメリカへ行ってきましたが、セクハラについては日本はアメリカに10年以上遅れていると思いました。セクハラをなくして、女性の働きやすい社会を作るのが私の夢です。

つらい *tough, hard to take*

理解 *understanding*

司法試験 *bar exam*

弁護士事務所 *law office* / 主に *mainly*
離婚 *divorce* / 問題 *issue, case*
愛人 *lover* / …を扱う *to deal with . . .*

地位 *position, status* / 高める *to raise*

独立する *to become independent, to start one's own business*
…に悩む *to suffer from . . .*

社会 *society*

After You Finish Reading

Based on the above passage, fill in this table in English.

NAME	OCCUPATION	THE REASON THAT SHE CHOSE THIS OCCUPATION

Writing 1

1. Interview someone who has a job. Ask the person why he or she chose that job. Write down the results of your interview in Japanese.
2. What is your career goal? In Japanese, write down what job you would like to do in the future and why you would like to do it.

Reading 2 佐久間社長の生い立ち

生い立ち *life history, life's path*

Before You Read

Work together as a class. Interview your instructor to find out the following. Do not forget to use honorifics to him or her and his or her family members.

1. Where was he or she born?
2. What kind of work did his or her parents do?
3. What university or college did he or she graduate from?
4. Did he or she study hard as a child?
5. What food does he or she like? What food does he or she dislike?
6. What means of transportation does he or she use to come to school?
7. Does he or she see movies often?
8. How long has he or she been living in this country? (If your instructor was born in this country, ask how long he or she has been living in your community or how long he or she lived in Japan.)

Make up your own questions, too, if you like, but remember to use honorifics.

Now Read It!

The other day Mr. Takada attended a birthday party for Mr. Katsuo Sakuma, president of Sakuma Industries, Inc., 佐久間産業 (さくまさんぎょう), with which Mr. Takada's company has business relations. The following is a brief biography of Mr. Sakuma that Mr. Takada found in the party program.

本日は佐久間産業、佐久間勝夫社長の65歳の誕生パーティーに御出席くださり、まことにありがとうございます。簡単に、佐久間社長の生い立ちを御紹介申し上げたいと存じます。
佐久間社長は昭和5年(1930年)4月15日、山口県下関市でお生まれになりました。佐久間社長のお父様は大きな呉服屋をなさっており、下関でとても有名だったということでございます。佐久間社長も幼年時代は何の不自由もなく、非常に恵まれた環境でお育ちになったそうです。しかし、佐久間社長が12歳の時に、

本日 *today* / 出席 *attendance*

呉服屋 *store selling traditional Japanese-style clothing and accessories*
不自由 *disadvantage*
恵まれる *to be blessed with*
環境 *circumstances, environment*
育つ *to grow up*

お父様が事業に失敗なさり、家と財産をすべてお失いになったそうです。

佐久間社長は小学校を御卒業なさるとすぐ、大阪の薬問屋に見習いとして送られたそうです。朝は4時にお起きになり、店の掃除をなさり、朝御飯の後、重い荷物をお背負いになり、薬を売りに夕方の5時までお歩きになったそうです。給料は全部、下関の御両親と妹さんにお送りになっていたそうです。戦争のため、薬問屋もつぶれ、戦後は靴みがき、大工、掃除夫、ゴミ屋、食堂の店員など、いろいろなお仕事をなさいました。その間に、お金をお貯めになり、昭和30年、25歳の時に東京にお出になり、秋葉原で小さな電器店をお開きになりました。ご自分で本をお読みになり、電気について勉強なさったそうです。昭和33年にポータブル・ラジオを御発明になり、これが「佐久間ラジオ」として有名になりました。昭和35年に工場をお作りになり、ラジオの大量生産をお始めになりました。ポータブル・ラジオはアメリカ、カナダ、ヨーロッパに輸出され、大ヒットしました。その後、佐久間産業は年々大きくなり、現在はラジオのほか、コンピュータ、テレビ、CDプレーヤー、ステレオなどを生産しています。佐久間産業が今日のように世界的な会社になったのも、佐久間社長の御努力の結果です。佐久間社長は昭和31年に友子夫人と御結婚なさいました。お二人の間には息子さんお二人、お嬢さんがお一人いらっしゃいます。佐久間社長は65歳になられた今日も、毎日朝7時に会社にお出になり、夜6時までお働きになるのを日課となさっています。佐久間社長には今後もますます御健康で、御活躍いただきたいと存じます。

事業	enterprise, business
失敗する	to fail
財産	property, assets
全て	all, the whole thing
問屋	wholesaler
見習い	apprentice
荷物	load [to carry]
背負う	to carry on one's back
戦争	war
つぶれる	to go under, to be crushed
戦後	after the war
靴みがき	bootblack, shoe polishing business
掃除夫	sweeper
ごみ屋	garbage collector
貯める	to save up
発明する	to invent
…として	as..., in the capacity of...
大量生産	mass production
輸出する	to export
生産する	to produce
世界的な	worldwide / 努力 effort
結果	result / 夫人 an honorific title for the wife of a prominent man
日課	daily schedule

After You Finish Reading

Answer these questions in English.

1. According to this text, how was Mr. Sakuma's childhood?
2. Explain what happened to Mr. Sakuma at these times.
   a. when he was 12 years old
   b. after he graduated from elementary school
   c. after the war
   d. when he was 27 years old
   e. in **Showa** 30
   f. in **Showa** 33
   g. in **Showa** 35
3. Describe the current situation of Sakuma Industries, Inc.
4. Describe Mr. Sakuma's family.
5. What is Mr. Sakuma's daily routine?

List all the honorific and humble expressions used in the text.

List all the passive forms of verbs used in the text.

Writing 2

Write a short life history of someone you greatly respect. He or she could be a historical figure, celebrity, or someone close to you. Use honorific forms.

Language Functions and Situations

At a Job Placement Center: Looking for a Job

ブラウン：すみません。アルバイトを探しているんですが、…

係員：それでは、まず、この求職票に記入してください。

ブラウン：初めてですので、手伝っていただけますか。

係員：ええ。じゃあ、まず、ここにお名前を書いてください。

ブラウン：はい、ふりがなは必要ありませんね。

係員：ええ、カタカナのお名前ですから。ここに学生番号を書いてください。後は、学部、学年、生年月日と本籍と現住所と電話番号も書いてください。

ブラウン：本籍というのはアメリカの両親の住所でいいんですか。

係員：ええ、そうですね。あとは、今までどのような仕事をしたことがあるかということと、仕事の希望を書いてください。

ブラウン：はい、わかりました。

ブラウン：あのう、全部、記入しました。これでよろしいでしょうか。

係員：はい、結構です。英語を教えるアルバイトを探しているんですね。

ブラウン：ええ。

A person's 本籍 is the municipality where his or her family has their family registry (戸籍), and it may not be the same as the actual residence. Children are usually inscribed in their father's family registry at the local government office, and this process makes them Japanese citizens.

BROWN: Excuse me. I'm looking for a part-time job.   CLERK: Then first please fill out this job application form.   BROWN: This is the first time for me, so can you help me?   CLERK: Yes. Please write your name here.   BROWN: Yes. I don't need to write **hiragana,** do I?   CLERK: No, because it's a name written in **katakana.** Please write down your student number here. Then please write your department, year in school, birth date, legal residence, current address, and telephone number.   BROWN: For legal residence, is my parents' address in America all right?   CLERK: Yes, that's OK. Then please write what job experience you have and what type of job you are looking for.   BROWN: All right.

BROWN: Excuse me. I've finished filling in this form. Is this OK?   CLERK: Yes, this is fine. You're looking for an English teaching job, aren't you?   BROWN: Yes.

係員：ええと、それでは、これはどうですか。渋谷にあるフェニックス英語学校
　　　というところなんですが。時給3800円で、月・水・金の6時から9時まで
　　　ですね。

ブラウン：もう少し時給が高い仕事はありませんか。

係員：そうですね。時給4000円というのがありますが、土、日の仕事ですよ。

ブラウン：それじゃ、ダメですね。

係員：それでは、これがフェニックス英語学校の電話番号ですから、沢井さん
　　　という方に電話してください。

ブラウン：はい、わかりました。いろいろありがとうございました。

係員：どういたしまして。

沢井：はい、フェニックス英語学校です。

ブラウン：沢井さんをお願いします。

沢井：私が沢井ですが、...

ブラウン：私、東京大学のリンダ・ブラウンと申します。大学の学生センターで
　　　そちらの英会話の教師のアルバイトを紹介してもらったんですが...

沢井：ああ、そうですか。では、一度お目にかかって、お話しをしたいので、
　　　こちらに来ていただけますか。

ブラウン：はい。いつお伺いしたらいいでしょうか。

沢井：今日の午後はいかがですか。

ブラウン：授業が3時に終わりますから、4時にはそちらに行けると思いますが...

沢井：じゃ、4時にこちらへ来ていただけますか。

ブラウン：はい、わかりました。よろしくお願いします。

Activity

Fill in the following job search sheet with your own personal information.

CLERK: Let me see. Then how about this job? It's at Phoenix English Language School in Shibuya. The hourly wage is 3,800 yen. You teach from six to nine P.M. on Mondays, Wednesdays, and Fridays. BROWN: Isn't there a job that pays a little bit more? CLERK: There is a job that pays 4,000 yen per hour, but you have to work on Saturdays and Sundays. BROWN: That's not good. CLERK: Then this is the phone number of Phoenix English Language School. Please call Mr. Sawai. BROWN: I see. Thank you very much for your help. CLERK: You're welcome.

SAWAI: Hello. This is Phoenix English Language School. BROWN: May I speak to Mr. Sawai? SAWAI: Speaking. BROWN: I am Linda Brown of the University of Tokyo. I was referred to you by the Student Center about the part-time position teaching English conversation. SAWAI: Oh, I see. Well, I'd like to meet with you, so can you come here? BROWN: Yes. When may I stop by? SAWAI: How about this afternoon? BROWN: My class is over at three, so I think I can arrive at your place by four. SAWAI: Then please come here at four. BROWN: All right.

求職票

受付け日 ＿＿＿＿＿＿＿＿＿

受付け番号 ＿＿＿＿＿＿＿＿＿

氏名	ふりがな

生年月日	大正・昭和・平成　　　年　　　月　　　日
年齢	満　　　　　　　　　歳

本籍	
現住所	郵便番号　〒

電話番号	
学歴	中学・高校・短大・大学　　卒業・中退・ その他（　　　　　　）　　　　在学中
職歴	
家族	あり・なし　　　　　　　人

希望する仕事

希望する給料

希望する勤務地

希望する勤務時間

Work in pairs. One student is looking for a part-time job. Visit the Students' Job Placement Office, where the other student is working as a clerk. Conduct this activity based on these ads from one of Tokyo's English-language newspapers.

English Teacher Wanted. Established, reputable school in Nihonbashi. Applicant must be native speaker with excellent oral and writing skills. ¥4000/hour. Call (03) 3987-6543.

Soccer coach / Cross-country coach / American football coach for international school. Must have university-level playing experience. 3-5 pm Mon thru Fri. ¥3000/hour. Call (03) 5123-4567.

Waiter / Waitress (experienced only) for coffee shop of large hotel. Must be fluent in Japanese and English. Third language (French, German, Chinese) desirable. Evening hours. ¥2000/hour. Call (03) 3012-3456.

Foreign models (male and female) for promotion by new discount store. Experience preferred. Possibility of continuing contract. ¥5000/hour. Call (03) 3210-9876.

Job Interview: At One of Maiko Sushi's Chain Stores

コンコン。（ドアをノックする音）

じんじぶちょう
人事部長：どうぞお入りください。

コリン：失礼致します。はじめまして。私、ジェニファー・コリンと申します。

PERSONNEL MANAGER: Please come in.　　COLLIN: Excuse me. How do you do? I am Jennifer Collin.

人事部長：はじめまして。人事部長の川上義広と申します。履歴書を拝見しましたが、
いくつか質問させていただきます。

コリン：はい。

人事部長：これまでどんな仕事をした経験がありますか。

コリン：マクドナルドでアルバイトをしたことがあります。

人事部長：どれくらいですか。

コリン：ええと、大学1年から3年までですから、ほぼ3年です。

人事部長：どんなお仕事でしたか。

コリン：初めはハンバーガーを作る仕事でしたが、後でアシスタント・
マネージャーになりました。

人事部長：大学の専攻は経営学ですか。

コリン：はい、そうです。マーケティングが専門でした。

人事部長：日本語がとてもお上手ですが、…

コリン：いいえ、まだまだです。

人事部長：日本語はどれくらい勉強なさいましたか。

コリン：アメリカの大学で3年間、勉強しました。その後、日本に来て、2年に
なります。

人事部長：我が社で働いてみたいとお考えになったのはなぜですか。

コリン：おすしのテークアウトのようなファーストフード産業に興味があるから
です。

人事部長：将来の仕事の希望はありますか。

コリン：はい、貴社のチェーン店全体のマーケティング・プランを立てるような
仕事ができればいいと思っております。

人事部長：今日はわざわざ来ていただき、ありがとうございました。

コリン：こちらこそ、どうもありがとうございました。

人事部長：結果は後ほど、電話でお知らせ致します。

コリン：どうぞよろしくお願い申し上げます。

PERSONNEL MANAGER: How do you do? I am Yoshihiro Kawakami, personnel manager. I've seen your résumé, but let me ask you some questions.   COLLIN: All right.   PERSONNEL MANAGER: What job experience do you have?   COLLIN: I worked part-time at McDonald s.   PERSONNEL MANAGER: How long?   COLLIN: Well, I worked from my freshman to junior years, so it's almost three years. PERSONNEL MANAGER: What kind of job was it?   COLLIN: In the beginning, I made hamburgers. Later I became an assistant manager.   PERSONNEL MANAGER: Was your major business management?   COLLIN: Yes, that's right. My specialty was marketing.   PERSONNEL MANAGER: You are very good at Japanese. COLLIN: Oh, no. Still a lot of room to improve.   PERSONNEL MANAGER: How long have you studied Japanese?   COLLIN: I studied it for three years at a university in America. Then I came to Japan and have been here for two years.   PERSONNEL MANAGER: Why do you want to work for our company? COLLIN: I am interested in fast-food industries like take-out **sushi.**   PERSONNEL MANAGER: Do you have any future career objectives?   COLLIN: Yes, I hope that I'll be able to make a marketing plan for your entire chain.   PERSONNEL MANAGER: Thank you very much for coming today.   COLLIN: You're welcome. Thank you very much for your time.   PERSONNEL MANAGER: I will notify you of our decision by phone later.   COLLIN: Thank you for your consideration.

Activity

Based on the example shown below, practice filling in the résumé sheet on pages 277 and 278.

● 履歴書の記入例

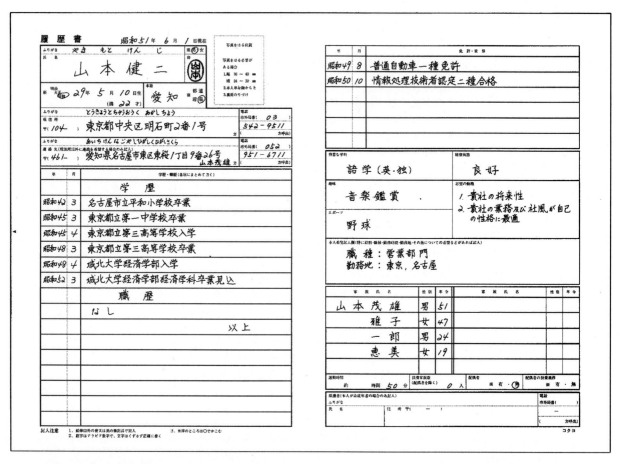

セットされている封筒のうち１枚は、一般にも使用できるよう 履歴書在中 との表示をはずしております。

Discussion

Discuss what questions you would like to ask applicants if you were a personnel manager and what questions you would like to ask a personnel director if you were a job applicant during an interview. Make a list in Japanese.

Role Play

Work in pairs. One student is applying for a job at a company where the other student is personnel manager. Practice conducting a job interview using the résumé you have written. Refer to the questions you listed above. Before conducting the interview, decide what type of business the company is doing and what type of position the job interview is for.

Study Hint

Practicing Japanese Outside of Class

The few hours you spend in class each week are not enough time for practicing Japanese. But once you have done your homework and listened to your tapes until you have them practically memorized, how else can you practice your Japanese outside of class?

1. Practice "talking to yourself" in Japanese as you walk across campus, wait for a bus, and so on. Try keeping a diary in Japanese.
2. Hold a conversation hour—perhaps on a regular basis—with other students of Japanese or with your classmates and a few native speakers.
3. See Japanese-language movies when they are shown on campus or in local movie theaters. The foreign film section of your local video rental store may have subtitled copies of some of the most famous Japanese movies, and if there are a lot of Japanese people in your community, there is probably at least one store that rents nonsubtitled videos of current movies and television programs.
4. Check local bookstores, libraries, and record stores for Japanese-language magazines and music. Comic books and children's books are especially good for beginners. If your local Japanese import store sells educational enrichment workbooks for children, you can challenge yourself with the **kanji** quizzes and other puzzles contained in them.
5. Practice speaking Japanese with a native speaker—either a permanent resident or a Japanese student. (Be patient and persistent, because the Japanese person may not be prepared to hear you speaking Japanese and may also be very determined to speak English as much as possible.) Every bit of practice will enhance your ability to speak Japanese.

Listening Comprehension

1. Ms. Shigeko Takagi, personnel manager of Nihon Export Company, is interviewing Ms. Momoyo Sakamoto, who is applying for a position at the company. Complete Ms. Sakamoto's résumé while listening to the interview.

Momoyo Sakamoto
4-12, Honcho 1-chome
Nakano-ku, Tokyo
164 Japan

Career Objectives:

Education:

Previous Employment:

Special Skills:

Hobbies:

Notes:

---

2. Mr. Komiyama and Ms. Hanamiya are talking about their jobs. Fill in the table while listening to their conversation.

MR. KOMIYAMA		MS. HANAMIYA
	What are their current jobs?	
	What companies are they working for?	
	Why are they working at those jobs?	
	What is one good aspect of their jobs?	
	What is one bad aspect of their jobs?	
	Do they want to change their jobs?	

Communication and Media

日本人はテレビを見るのが大好きです。

Vocabulary and Oral Activities

Telecommunication

Vocabulary: Telephone

電話が鳴る	でんわがなる	the phone rings
電話を切る	でんわをきる	to hang up the phone
内線	ないせん	extension
問い合わせる	といあわせる	to inquire
交換手	こうかんしゅ	telephone operator
電話ボックス	でんわボックス	telephone booth
通話料	つうわりょう	telephone charge
長距離電話	ちょうきょりでんわ	long-distance call
国際電話	こくさいでんわ	international call
コレクトコール		collect call
ダイヤル(を回す)	ダイヤル(をまわす)	(to) dial
プッシュホン		push-button telephone
留守番電話	るすばんでんわ	telephone answering machine
ファックス		facsimile, fax machine
話し中	はなしちゅう	[the line is] busy
間違い電話	まちがいでんわ	wrong number
いたずら電話	いたずらでんわ	annoying call, crank call
伝言	でんごん	telephone message

Review: 電話、(に)電話(を)する、(に)電話をかける、電話番号、電話帳

Refer to Culture Note on p. 22, Book 1. Also refer to the Communication Note on pp. 205-206, Book 1.

文化ノート

公衆電話 (*Public Telephones*)

Although the disparity is less than it used to be, Japanese households are less likely to have a private home telephone than households in North America are, and the reason is cost. Thus you will see more public telephones in a Japanese community than you will in a North American community of comparable size.

Since the early 1980s, residents of Japan have had the option of using debit cards to make local and long-distance phone calls. Referred to as テレホン・カード, these cards, which are about the size of a credit card, are available in denominations of 500 to 1,000 yen and are sold at a variety of outlets, including convenience stores and vending machines.

NTT, the principal telephone and telegraph company, expects to have replaced all other types of phones with card phones by March 1995.

公衆電話で：これ
からお伺いしてよ
ろしいでしょうか。

アクティビティー　1

何ですか。誰ですか。(*What is it? Who is it?*)

Match the following definitions with the appropriate words.

1. 外国に電話すること
2. 電話番号を知りたい時に見る本
3. 電話を受け取る人がお金を払う通話
4. 電話局で電話番号を教えてくれる人
5. 家にいない時にメッセージを取っておいてくれる機械
6. ダイヤルのかわりにボタンが付いている電話
7. 町の中にある誰でも使える電話

a. 交換手
b. 国際電話
c. 公衆電話
d. コレクトコール
e. 電話帳
f. プッシュホン
g. 留守番電話

受け取る *to receive*
通話 *conversation*

取っておく　*to keep, maintain*

X のかわりに　*in place of X*

Communication and Media

アクティビティー 2

よく長電話_{ながでんわ}しますか。(*Do you often make lengthy phone calls?*)

Answer these questions.

1. よく長電話しますか。誰と話しますか。
2. 何分以上の電話が長電話だと思いますか。
3. よく国際電話をかけますか。どの国にかけますか。
4. 電話帳をよく使いますか。それとも、交換手に聞きますか。番号案内は何番ですか。
5. 火事のときの電話番号は何番ですか。
6. 留守番電話を持っていますか。
7. あなたの町の市外局番 (*area code*) は何番ですか。
8. いたずら電話をされたことがありますか。

火事 *fire*

Vocabulary Library

Telephone and Telegram

受話器を取る	じゅわきをとる	to pick up the receiver
かけ直す	かけなおす	to call back
テレホン・カード		prepaid telephone card
携帯電話	けいたいでんわ	cellular phone
通話	つうわ	telephone conversation
ポケベル		beeper
電報(を打つ)	でんぽう(をうつ)	(to send a) telegram

Because many people in Japan do not have telephones, telegrams are used more commonly there than in North America.

勉 Study Grammar 33.

アクティビティー 3

ダイアログ：図書館_{としょかん}に電話すれば、教えてくれるわよ。(*If you call the library, they'll tell you.*)

カワムラ：東京の人口_{じんこう}が知_しりたいんですが、どうすればいいでしょうか。

山口：図書館_{としょかん}に電話すれば、教えてくれるわよ。

カワムラ：図書館_{としょかん}の電話番号_{ばんごう}はわかりますか。

山口：電話帳_{ちょう}を見れば、わかるわ。私が調_{しら}べてあげるわ。

KDD is the largest international phone company in Japan. KDD is an abbreviation of Kokusai Denshin Denwa Gaisha (International Telegraph and Telephone Company). The largest domestic telephone company in Japan is NTT, Nippon Telephone and Telegraph Company.

KAWAMURA: I'd like to know the population of Tokyo. What should I do? YAMAGUCHI: If you call the library, they'll tell you. KAWAMURA: Do you know the library's phone number? YAMAGUCHI: If you look at the directory, you can tell. I'll check it for you.

Practice the above dialogue, substituting the items in column A for the first underlined section and the items in column B for the items in the second and third underlined sections.

	A	B
1.	国際電話料金	KDD
2.	映画の時間	映画館
3.	明日のお天気	天気案内
4.	新幹線の時間	駅
5.	田中さんの住所	田中さんの会社

天気案内 *weather information*

住所 *address*

アクティビティー　4

どうすればいいですか。(*What should I do?*)

Give instructions in response to the questions, forming your answers along the lines of the example.

[例]　この書類を早く日本に送りたいんですが、どうすればいいですか。
（ファックスを使う）→
ファックスを使えばいいですよ。
（フェデラル・エクスプレスで送る）→
フェデラル・エクスプレスで送ればいいですよ。

1. 電車の中に忘れ物をしたんですが、どうすればいいですか。
（駅に電話してみる）（駅に行ってみる）
2. いたずら電話で困っているんですが、どうすればいいですか。
（電話局 [*telephone company*] に電話する）（電話番号を変える）
3. 家にいない時に、電話がたくさんかかってくるんですが、どうすればいいですか。
（留守番電話を買う）（ポケベルを使う）

Now come up with your own solutions for these problems.

4. 娘が長電話をして困っているんですが、どうすればいいですか。
5. 日本語が上手になりたいんですが、どうすればいいですか。
6. 日本の大学で勉強したいので、日本の大学について調べたいんですが、どうすればいいですか。
7. 日本に一年間住みたいんですが、お金がありません。どうすればいいですか。

Now work in pairs. Each of you makes up three questions concerning a problem or puzzling situation, using the form …どうすればいいですか. Then answer each other's questions.

アクティビティー　5

ダイアログ：早く連絡してほしいそうよ。(*He says he wants you to contact him quickly.*)

カワムラ：ただいま。

山口：ああ、カワムラさん。おかえりなさい。林さんからお電話があって、<u>早く連絡してほしい</u>そうよ。

カワムラ：本当？何だろう。

山口：わかんないわ。でも、何だか急いでいたみたい。

わかんない is a contraction of わからない.

Practice the above dialogue, changing the underlined part to the following phrases.

1. 駅前の喫茶店に来る
2. 町田さんの家に電話する
3. すぐにブラウンさんに会う
4. 横井先生のお宅の電話番号を教える

アクティビティー　6

何をしてほしいですか。何をしてもらいたいですか。(*What do you want him or her to do?*)

What do you say in the following situation? Express your request following the example.

[例]　公衆電話で長電話している人がいます。10人以上の人が順番 (*turn*) を待っています。→
「長電話 (*long phone conversations*) は、やめてほしいです。」 or
「長電話しないでほしいです。」

1. 日本語の先生がまた宿題を出そうとしています。他の授業 (*class session*) の宿題がたくさんあります。

2. コンビニの公衆電話から電話しようとしましたが、こまかいお金がありません。

くずす *to change, break*
千円札を百円玉にくずす *to break a 1,000-yen note into 100-yen coins*

3. おなかがとてもすきました。何か食べるものを買いにいきたいんですが、仕事が忙しくて行けません。友達が買い物に行ってくると言っています。

JOHN KAWAMURA: I'm back.　YAMAGUCHI: Welcome back, Mr. Kawamura. There was a call from Mr. Hayashi, and he said he wanted you <u>to contact him quickly</u>.　KAWAMURA: Really? I wonder what it's about.　YAMAGUCHI: I don't know, but he sounded somewhat in a hurry.

4. あなたは真面目な学生です。日本語の授業ではいつも日本語を話すようにしています。でも、あなたの隣の人はいつも英語で話します。
5. また、今日もいたずら電話がかかってきました。
6. またです。あなたの隣の人はいつもあなたのペンを使います。使うだけでなく、いつも持っていってしまいます。

...だけで[は]なく

...だけで[は]なく—the は is optional—means *not only ... [but also]*. Nouns, pronouns, and the plain form of adjectives and verbs may be used before it. The clause following it often contains も also.

カワムラさんはハンサムなだけでなく、とても親切だ。
Mr. Kawamura is not only handsome, he's very kind.
見ているだけでなく、食べてみてください。
Don't just look at it; try eating it.

In ordinary colloquial speech, じゃなくて is often used instead of で[は]なく.

アメリカだけじゃなくてカナダへも行きたいです。
I would like to go not just to America but also to Canada.

Post Office

Vocabulary: Mail and Postal Service (1)

郵便	ゆうびん	mail
郵便を出す	ゆうびんをだす	to mail
X を郵便で送る	X をゆうびんでおくる	to send X by mail
郵便ポスト	ゆうびんポスト	mailbox (*for depositing items to be mailed*)
封筒	ふうとう	envelope
便箋	びんせん	stationery
葉書	はがき	postal card
切手を貼る	きってをはる	to put a stamp on
小包	こづつみ	package
郵便番号	ゆうびんばんごう	postal code (*comparable to the ZIP code in the United States*)
受け取る	うけとる	to receive
はんこ		seal

328

返事(を書く)	へんじ(をかく)	(to write a) reply
配達(する)	はいたつ(する)	delivery; to deliver
船便	ふなびん	surface mail
航空便	こうくうびん	air mail
速達	そくたつ	express mail
書留	かきとめ	registered mail
現金書留	げんきんかきとめ	cash registered mail
あて名	あてな	recipient's address
宅急便	たっきゅうびん	door-to-door package delivery

Review: 絵葉書、(を)送る、切手、住所、手紙、郵便局

Postal Codes

Like most industrialized countries, Japan has postal codes, but they are organized differently from the ones used in North America.

Large cities and areas within large cities have three-digit postal codes, while smaller communities have three-digit plus two-digit codes based on the code of the nearest large post office. Preprinted postcards and envelopes often come with squares printed on them for writing in the postal code, but if you are addressing a plain envelope, write the code preceded by a 〒 symbol before the rest of the address. For example, the postal code for one section of Nakano ward in Tokyo is 165, so a letter addressed to a person living there would bear the code 〒165.

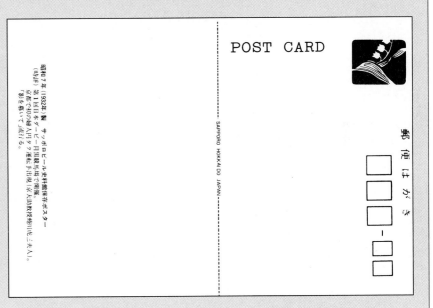

アクティビティー　7

手紙を出します。(*I'm going to mail a letter.*)

You would like to write and mail a letter. Number the following actions in the order that they would normally occur.

___9___ 封筒の重さを計ってもらう
_____ 郵便局に行く
_____ 手紙を書く
_____ 封筒に封をする (*to seal*)
_____ 便箋を折る (*to fold*)
_____ 必要な切手を買う
___1___ 文房具屋に行って、便箋と封筒を買う
_____ 切手を封筒に貼る
_____ 封筒に宛て名を書く
_____ 封筒を郵便ポストに入れる
___5___ 便箋を封筒に入れる

アクティビティー　8

手紙にしますか。電話にしますか。(*Do you do it by mail or by phone?*)

Answer these questions.

1. よく手紙を書きますか。誰に書きますか。
2. よく郵便が来ますか。どんな郵便が来ますか。
3. どんな時に小包を出しますか。
4. 近所に郵便局はありますか。どんな時に郵便局に行きますか。
5. 両親にお金を送ってほしい時、手紙を書きますか。電話をかけますか。
6. 郵便の電話よりいい点は何ですか。
7. 電話の郵便よりいい点は何ですか。
8. あなたの国の切手にはどんな絵がかかれていますか。

アクティビティー　9

ダイアログ：現金書留で現金を送ることはありますか。(*Are there occasions when you send cash by registered mail?*)

ブラウン：山本さんは現金書留で現金を<u>送ることはありますか</u>。

　山本：<u>一年に二・三回ぐらい送ることがあります</u>。

ブラウン：めんどうですか。

　山本：いいえ、簡単ですよ。

ブラウン：じゃあ、今度<u>送り方</u>を教えてくださいね。

Practice the above dialogue, changing the first two underlined parts with the following. Change the last underlined part appropriately.

1. 宅配便でものを送る　　　　　　　　時々送ることがあります
2. 郵便為替でお金を送る　　　　　　　あまり送ったことがありません＿＿
3. テレホンカードを使う　　　　　　　いつも使っています
4. 記念切手を買う　　　　　　　　　　一年に四・五回買うことがあります
5. 電報を打つ　　　　　　　　　　　　最近は打つことが少なくなりました

文化ノート

Special Services at the Post Office

The Japanese postal system offers a service not found in most countries: guaranteed registered mailing of cash (現金書留 [げんきんかきとめ]). However, even though Japan has an enviably low crime rate, people don't just stick the cash into any old envelope and drop it into the nearest mailbox. Instead, they go to the post office, fill out forms, and put the money into a special envelope like the one shown here before handing it over to the postal clerk.

Another service offered by the post office is the postal savings account (郵便貯金 [ゆうびんちょきん]). Before the spread of automatic teller machines, this kind of account offered the advantage of allowing customers to deposit and withdraw money at any post office in the country.

The postal system carries off an impressive feat at New Year's. When people check their mail on New Year's Day, they find all the New Year's cards (年賀状 [ねんがじょう]) that their friends and associ-

---

BROWN: Ms. Yamamoto, are there occasions when you <u>send cash by registered mail</u>? YAMAMOTO: <u>Two or three times a year</u>. BROWN: Is it difficult to send cash by registered mail? YAMAMOTO: No, it's easy. BROWN: Next time, please tell me <u>how to send it</u>.

ates have sent them, bundled and lying in their mailbox. In other words, the post office saves up and sorts all New Year's cards mailed by a certain date so that they may be delivered on the same day throughout the country.

Vocabulary Library

Mail and Postal Service (2)

郵便局員	ゆうびんきょくいん	post office clerk
往復葉書	おうふくはがき	return postal card (*with a pre-paid detachable portion for the recipient's reply*)
年賀状	ねんがじょう	New Year's card
差出人	さしだしにん	sender

Loanword: エアメール

㊙ Study Grammar 35.

アクティビティー　10

クラスメートと先生にインタビューしましょう。(*Let's interview our classmates and instructor.*)

First work in pairs. Ask these questions of your partner and write down his or her answers in column A.

	A	B
1. 一週間に何通ぐらい手紙を書きますか。		
2. 来た手紙は全部読みますか。		
3. 友達からの手紙に返事を書きますか。		
4. 手紙を書くのが好きですか。		
5. 一日に何回電話をかけますか。		
6. 一日にどれくらい電話がかかってきますか。		
7. 留守番電話を使っていますか。		
8. 誰に一番よく電話をしますか。		

Discuss with your partner what forms would be most appropriate for asking questions of a superior, such as your instructor. Then ask your instructor the eight questions, using the proper honorific forms and writing the answers in column B. Discuss in Japanese the comparison between your partner's answers and your instructor's. (Don't forget to use honorifics when discussing your instructor's answers.)

アクティビティー 11

ダイアログ：年賀状のあて名を書かせられるんです。(*I have to address the New Year's cards.*)

高田：ああ、手が痛くてたまらないや。

山本：高田さん、どうしたんですか。

高田：この季節になると、会社の年賀状のあて名を書かせられるんです。

山本：それは大変ですね

Practice the above dialogue, changing the underlined parts with the following.

1. 足　　　会社のカレンダーを配り (*delivery*) に行かされる
2. 目　　　レポートをたくさん読まされる
3. 頭　　　パーティーでお酒をたくさん飲まされる

アクティビティー 12

仕事の不満 (*Dissatisfaction on the job*)

Everyone has some complaints about his or her job. What kinds of complaints do you think these people have? Following the example, write down these people's possible complaints using causative-passive, passive and 〜なければならない。

[例]　外国語の先生
- 学生の下手な外国語を聞かなければならない。
- 学生の下手な作文を読まされる
- 学生の会話の相手をさせられる。
- 学生のいいわけ (*excuses*) を聞かされる

(Hey, we're just kidding!)

1. 電話交換手
2. 秘書
3. タクシーの運転手
4. 家庭の主婦
5. 日本のサラリーマン
6. Choose one occupation not mentioned.
7. What are your complaints as a student of the Japanese language?

TAKADA: My hand hurts so much I can't stand it.　YAMAMOTO: Mr. Takada, what happened?　TAKADA: Around this time of year (*lit., around this season*), I have to address New Year's cards for the company. YAMAMOTO: That's tough.

Media

Newspapers

マスコミ		mass communication
ジャーナリズム		journalism
新聞をとる	しんぶんをとる	to subscribe to a newspaper
…に載る	…にのる	to appear in (*a publication*)
新聞配達	しんぶんはいたつ	paper delivery
新聞記事	しんぶんきじ	newspaper article
広告(する)	こうこく(する)	advertisement; (to advertise)
記者	きしゃ	reporter

Review: インタビュー(する)、新聞、ニュース、～部

Books, Publishing

出版(する)	しゅっぱん(する)	publishing; (to publish)
週刊誌	しゅうかんし	weekly magazine
漫画	まんが	comic book, comic magazine, cartoon
事典	じてん	encyclopedia
小説	しょうせつ	novel
エッセイ		essay

Review: 教科書、～冊、雑誌、辞書、本、本屋、料理の本

Broadcasting

放送(する)	ほうそう(する)	broadcasting; (to broadcast)
NHK	エヌエチケー	Nippon Hoosoo Kyookai 日本放送協会 (*Japan's government-owned radio and television network*)
民放	みんぽう	commercial broadcasting
番組	ばんぐみ	(TV, radio) program
ホーム・ドラマ		soap opera
トーク・ショー		talk show
アニメ		animated cartoon
時代劇	じだいげき	samurai drama
連続ドラマ	れんぞくドラマ	dramatic series, miniseries
教育番組	きょういくばんぐみ	educational program
チャンネル(を変える)	チャンネル(をかえる)	(to change) channels
CM	シーエム	commercial (*from commercial message*)
スタジオ		studio
マイク		microphone
出演する	しゅつえんする	to appear (*as a performer*)
…に出る	(～に)でる	to appear on . . . (*as a performer*)

司会者　　　　　　しかいしゃ　　　　　MC
タレント　　　　　　　　　　　　　　　TV personality
アンテナ　　　　　　　　　　　　　　　antenna
衛星放送　　　　　えいせいほうそう　　satellite broadcast
二カ国語放送　　　にかこくごほうそう　bilingual broadcast

Review: カメラ、カラーテレビ、テレビ、天気予報、ドラマ、ビデオ、ラジオ

Television Stations and Newspapers

NHK, which has both a general-interest and an educational channel, is a semigovernmental network that does not broadcast any commercials and is supported by a monthly fee assessed on all television sets. In each local prefecture, you can usually watch two NHK stations and a few commercial stations that are affiliated with the Tokyo-based networks, but in the past decade, satellite and cable television have been reaching an increasing percentage of the population. Japanese television networks are unusual in that unlike networks in most other countries, they broadcast few American or other foreign series, and some American series that were hits everywhere else in the world have failed to interest Japanese viewers.

Japanese newspapers are divided into nationwide papers (全国紙 [ぜんこくし]) such as *Asahi Shinbun* (朝日新聞), *Yomiuri Shinbun* (読売新聞), and *Mainichi Shinbun* (毎日新聞), which are available throughout the country and carry national and international news, and local papers (地方紙 [ちほうし]), which are available only in a small area and concentrate on local news. In addition, four daily English-language newspapers serve the growing community of foreign residents and are widely available in the larger cities.

9月18日（日曜日）　　　　読売新聞

1 NHKテレビ 03(3465)1111

5.55 天◇N天 2279128
6.15◇漢詩紀行 855296
30 旬の人旬の話 長倉洋一ほ
海◇53生活 91708
00C おはよう日本 N
海外GⅠ初制覇・武豊 278302
▽赤いリンゴが消える？◇自由席 16470
00 小さな旅囲 水ゆたかに慈しむ街 2692
30 週刊こどもニュース 池上彰◇天 62296
00 日曜討論 常任理事国入り・国連総会を前に河野外相に迫る▽軍事的貢献は？ 27586
00 N天◇05S新日本探訪囲 愛媛県 9948012
30S生きもの地球紀行囲 ▽武蔵野の雑木林・都会派のタカ 6982296
11.10経済スコープ 契約社員が雇用変える▽海の新幹線◇天 7937128
00C N 872147
15Sのど自慢 前川清 三船和子~鳥取県大栄町 678895
00C中学生日記 岡本富士太 4447
30 笑いがいちばん プリンプリン爪 83789
00NHKスペシャル囲 「アンデス祈りの山」 877673
50S博物館 8524079
3.05 N 8705321
10S大相撲秋場所 「8日目」 ▽私の選んだ名勝負 瀬戸内寂聴 正面解説・井筒 尾車 向正面解説・入間川 実況・藤沢武 緒方喜治 ~両国国技館 62040499

3 NHK教育テレビ 03(3465)1111

00 高校・化学 4654
30 テレビ体操 238596
40 現役くらぶ囲 「江戸手ぬぐい職人芸」 村野武憲ほ 3755925
7.25S名曲 278302
30 こころの時代 「生きるための知恵⑥法句経に学ぶ」 5987302
8.30趣味の園芸 「ゼラニウム」 柳宗民 487857
55S名園散歩 19383
00 日曜美術館 エゴン・シーレ・家族の肖像「光の詩情・福原信三の世界」 25128
00 将棋講座「淡路仁茂のメディア活用法・ゲームソフト」 275857
20 NHK杯将棋トーナメント・2回戦・第6局 「大内延介×田丸昇」 解説・森雞二 40358321
00 囲碁講座 小山竜吾の入門講座みんなで楽しく覚えよう 556215
20 NHK囲碁トーナメント・2回戦・第6局 「加藤正夫×小県真樹」 解説・武宮正樹 56302079
00S全日本テニス選手権・男子シングルス決勝 「金奉洙×増田健太郎」 実況・高山典久 ~東京・有明コロシアム（録画） 995383
00S芸術劇場・アントニオ・メネセスチェロリサイタル 627050
55 面白動物記 32895
00S母と子のテレビタイム 日曜版 どーなっつ▽お母さん▽英語遊ぼ▽一人▽絵本 44960

4 日本テレビ 03(5275)1111

5.00天◇心の灯囲◇24TV
5.50実戦」門球 7956321
6.15楽しい園芸 741321
30 宗教◇N 86876
00C目がテン 生きている湖・霞ケ浦 2437
30◇遠くへ行きたい 鳥取手仕事の人 87505
00C ザ・サンデー 恐怖・住銀支店長射殺・なぜ狙われる住友▽混む・広猛追臣◇機銃1丁 自衛隊派遣 4442470
9.25S折々の味 281876
30◇波瀾万丈 平尾昌晃スター・没落・作曲家苦労人生告白 3919050
10.25 巨人魔王 282505
30 ワザあり ド迫力・5尺の大太鼓 66012
00C皇室 皇太子ご夫妻の北海道縦断報 9505
30 昼のN 245857
40CTVおじゃマンモス あ然・欽ちゃんに暴言 100万はどうなるのか 仮装大賞にたけし監督作品で挑戦 1261050
00CSスーパージョッキー 超過激水着美女生着替え＆熱湯入りか？千堂あきほも… 14050
00 赤井英和「夏の軌跡」涙の敗北・元木▽都並魂の復活ほ 612128
55 昼のN 10673
00「'94全日空オープンゴルフ」 「最終日」 解説・鷹巣南雄 実況・和久井薫 ~札幌GC輪厚C 923166
4.55ナインティナイン 究極編大魔術 7312321
5.20笑点 落語「ん廻し」小遊三▽大喜利 円楽 歌丸 962234

アクティビティー 13

毎日新聞を読みますか。(*Do you read a newspaper every day?*)

Answer these questions.

1. 新聞をとっていますか。
2. 雑誌をとっていますか。どんな雑誌が好きですか。
3. 教科書以外 (*other than*) の本を読みますか。どんな本を読みますか。
4. よくテレビを見ますか。一日に何時間くらい見ますか。
5. あなたの国で一番人気のある番組は何ですか。
6. コマーシャルをどう思いますか。
7. テレビ番組で暴力 (*violence*) シーンが多すぎると思いますか。
8. 勉強しながら、ラジオを聞きますか。
9. テレビやラジオに出演したことがありますか。

勉 Study Grammar 37.

アクティビティー 14

どんなに言っても、テレビばかり見ています。(*No matter how many times I tell him, he is always watching TV.*)

青山さんはブラウンさんの隣に住んでいます。

ブラウン：息子さん、受験で大変でしょう。
青山：どんなに勉強しろと言っても、テレビばかり見ているんですよ。
ブラウン：息子さん、勉強しなくても、頭がいいから大丈夫ですよ。
青山：そうだといいんですけど。少なくとも1日4時間はテレビを見ているんですよ。

アクティビティー 15

インタビュー (*Interview*)

Walk around the classroom and ask your classmates the following questions. If their answer is はい, ask them to sign on the appropriate blank line. Ask as many people as you can, and don't ask all the questions of just a few people.

Mrs. Aoyama lives next door to Linda Brown.   BROWN: Your son must be working hard for his entrance exams.   AOYAMA: No matter how much I tell him to study, he's always watching TV. BROWN: Even if he doesn't study, he'll be OK because he's smart.   AOYAMA: I hope that's the case. He watches TV for at least four hours a day.

1. どんなに忙しくても、毎日新聞を読みますか。
2. パーティーの途中 (middle) でも、好きな番組を
   見るために家に帰りますか。
3. 少なくとも一日2時間はテレビを見ますか。
4. テレビのコマーシャルは、なくてもいいと
   思いますか。
5. 少なくとも一週間に5時間は本を読みますか。
6. 日本語のいい辞書があったら、いくら高くても
   買いますか。
7. 世界で何が起こっているか知らなくても、
   全然かまいませんか。
8. テレビやラジオがなくても、生活できますか。

Vocabulary Library

Mass Communication (2)

Newspapers

見出し	みだし	headline
社説	しゃせつ	editorial
…欄	…らん	… section
案内広告	あんないこうこく	classified ad
事件	じけん	event, incident
伝える	つたえる	to report, convey information
発表(する)	はっぴょう(する)	(to make an) announcement
英字新聞	えいじしんぶん	English-language newspaper

Loanwords: グラビア、ゴシップ

Books, Publishing

購読(する)	こうどく(する)	subscription; (to subscribe)
文庫本	ぶんこぼん	paperback book
参考書	さんこうしょ	reference book
印刷(する)	いんさつ(する)	printing; (to print)
ページ		page
目次	もくじ	table of contents
索引	さくいん	index
翻訳(する)	ほんやく(する)	translation; (to translate)

Broadcasting

中継(する)	ちゅうけい(する)	(to make a) live, remote broadcast
録音(する)	ろくおん(する)	recording; (to record sound)
録画(する)	ろくが(する)	videotaping; (to videotape)

Loanwords: DJ、ディレクター、バラエティー・ショー、プロデューサー

Japanese Popular Culture (1): 漫画、アニメ

No visitor to Japan can help noticing the proliferation of comic books (漫画) for sale on the newsstands. Some have graphically violent or pornographic illustrations on the covers, so many visitors assume that all the **manga** are equally lurid, but in fact, there are **manga** for every

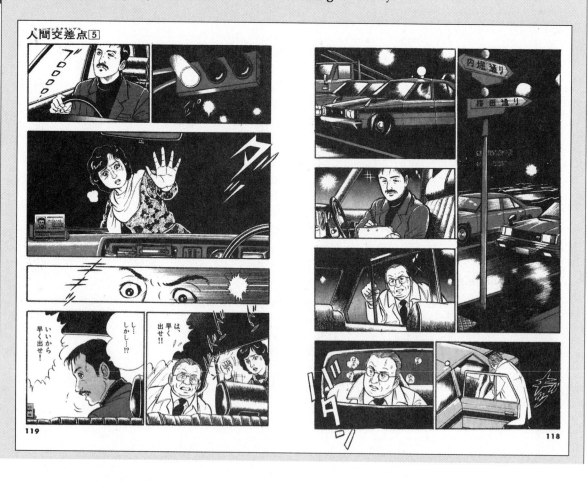

age and interest. Some of the **manga** are humorous, such as *What's Michael?* (ホワッツ・マイケル), a series of stories about cats. Others are serious, such as 人間交差点 (にんげんこうさてん [*Human Intersection*]), a collection of short stories about contemporary social issues. **Manga** are an excellent resource for studying the Japanese language because they are the one place where spoken Japanese is written down verbatim, including slang and contractions.

Closely related to **manga** is **anime** (アニメ), cartoon animation, much of which is based on printed **manga.** Japanese **anime,** particularly the science fiction and fantasy variety, has many fans in other countries. These fans are attracted to the imaginative concepts, technical excellence, and bold design and coloration of the science fiction **anime,** but there are many less flamboyant series that have achieved long-standing popularity within Japan itself, including gentle domestic comedies like *Sazae-san* (サザエさん).

㊉ Study Grammar Note on p. 363.

アクティビティー 16

ダイアログ：新聞で読んだにちがいわよ。(*No doubt they read about it in the paper.*)

ブラウンさんは佐野さんと話しています。「ロマンス」はブラウンさんのアパートの向かいの喫茶店です。

ブラウン：「ロマンス」、今日は人でいっぱいですね。外にも並んでいますよ。
佐野：みんな新聞で読んだにちがいないわよ。
ブラウン：どうしたんですか。
佐野：おいしいコーヒーを出すって、新聞が書いたのよ。

Practice the above dialogue, changing the underlined parts with the following.

1. テレビで見た
   めずらしいコーヒーがあるって、放送した
2. ラジオで聞いた
   今日はコーヒーがただだって、放送した
3. 雑誌で読んだ
   有名なタレントがたくさん来るって、雑誌が書いた

Ms. Brown is talking to Ms. Sano. "Romance" is the name of a coffee shop across the street from Ms. Brown's apartment. BROWN: "Romance" is filled with people today, isn't it? People are even lined up outside, too. SANO: No doubt <u>they read about it in the paper</u>. BROWN: What happened? SANO: <u>The paper reported that they serve delicious coffee.</u>

賛成ですか。反対ですか。 (*Do you agree or not?*)

Do you agree with the following statements? Express your opinion.

1. マスコミの力 (*power*) は大きいから、人の心を簡単に変えてしまうこともある。

2. 新聞やテレビのニュースは、いつも正確で公正 (*impartial*) だ。

3. テレビを見過ぎるのは、健康に良くない。

4. 2010年までには立体 (3D) テレビができているにちがいない。

5. 2010年までには新聞の配達はなくなって、みんなコンピュータでニュースを読むにちがいない。

6. 2010年までには、教科書は全部 CD になっているにちがいない。

Japanese Popular Culture (2): Popular Music

The Japanese are great fans of foreign music, especially classical, jazz, and rock music, and it is also possible to find devoted listeners and performers of country-western, French *chansons,* and even Caribbean salsa. All of these genres exist alongside Japan's own popular music, which is a hybrid of traditional and Western influences and is little known outside of Japan

Japanese folk music is sung in a tight, slightly nasal, highly ornamented vocal style, and this way of singing carries over into **enka** (演歌 [えんか]), the most "Japanese-sounding" of the styles of popular music currently being performed. These songs are most popular among working-class and rural people, so one could say that they are the counterparts of American country-western songs, even though their sound is completely different.

Young teenagers favor the bouncy, upbeat melodies sung by the so-called idol singers (アイドル歌手 [アイドルかしゅ]). These singers, whom the talent scouts choose more for their cute, perky, innocent looks than for their musical ability, are about the age of their fans when they start their careers, and almost all of them are has-beens by the age of nineteen or twenty.

Until about ten or fifteen years ago, almost all Japanese, from small children to elderly people, listened to the idol singers, but the market is much more fragmented now. Older teenagers and university students tend to like either foreign or home-grown rock and alternative music, while people who are past university age may listen to jazz, classical, **enka,** or the many singer-songwriters who sing ballad-style songs while accompanying themselves on the piano or guitar.

演歌歌手：私の心に
雨が降〜る〜

　In recent years three folk traditions have regained small but enthusiastic followings. The first is **taiko** (太鼓 [たいこ]) drumming, which can be heard at festivals, including in Japanese émigré communities abroad. There are even professional **taiko** troupes that tour in Japan and foreign countries. The second is **Tsugaru shamisen** (津軽三味線 [つがるしゃみせん]), a rapid, showy style of playing similar to American bluegrass banjo. The third is Okinawan music, which is similar to Japanese folk music in many ways but heavily influenced by the music of China and Southeast Asia.

　If you ever spend the winter months in Japan, a good way to get an overview of Japanese popular music is to watch NHK's annual New Year's Eve *Red and White Song Contest* (紅白歌合戦 [こうはくうたがっせん]), which features the year's top-selling singers and groups in the various genres.

Grammar and Exercises

33. ば-Conditionals

カワムラ：長野の明日のお天気を知りたいんですが、…

山口：新聞のお天気欄を見れば、書いてありますよ。

カワムラ：ああ、そうでしたね。長野までの道路情報も新聞に書いてありますか。

山口：いいえ、それは177番に電話すれば、教えてくれますよ。

ギブソン：この小包、クリスマスまでにカナダに着くでしょうか。

郵便局員：そうですね。航空便で出せば、間に合うでしょう。

ギブソン：じゃあ、航空便でお願いします。

郵便局員：速達にすれば、もっと早く着きますよ。

林：このへんは便利そうだね。

ブラウン：ええ、その角を右に曲がれば、すぐスーパーだし、左へ曲がれば
コイン・ランドリーもあるし…

林：いい所に住んでるね。

ブラウン：大学にもう少し近ければ、もっといいんだけど。

33.1 You have already learned two constructions, 〜たら and …と, that can correspond to English *if*. The third and last one is 〜ば, which can attach to either
verbs or adjectives. Its uses overlap somewhat with those of both 〜たら and …と,
but in some ways it is more restricted than either of the other forms.

KAWAMURA: I'd like to know tomorrow's weather for Nagano.   YAMAGUCHI: If you look at the weather
section of the newspaper, it's written there.   KAWAMURA: Oh, that's right. Does the paper report the
condition of the road to Nagano?   YAMAGUCHI: If you dial 177, they'll give you the information.

GIBSON: Will this package reach Canada by Christmas?   POSTAL EMPLOYEE: Let me see. If you send it by
airmail, it will be on time.   GIBSON: Then please [send it by] airmail.   POSTAL EMPLOYEE: If you send it
by express, it will arrive sooner.

HAYASHI: This neighborhood looks convenient.   BROWN: Yes, if you turn right at that corner, there's a
supermarket right there. If you turn left, there's a laundromat.   HAYASHI: You live in a good place.
BROWN: It would be better if it were a little closer to the university.

33.2 The ば conditional is formed as follows.

RULE	EXAMPLES
Class 1 verbs: root + the e-column of hiragana + ～ば	洗えば、書けば、読めば、わかれば、待てば、呼べば
Class 2 verbs: root + ～れば	見れば、食べれば、起きれば
Class 3 verbs: change ～る to ～れば	すれば、来れば
Copula and na-adjectives: change だ or です to なら(ば) or であれば	きれいなら、学生なら、便利なら きれいであれば、学生であれば、便利であれば
I-adjectives and negative endings: root + the e-column of hiragana + ～ば	安ければ、むずかしければいかなければ 高くなければ

33.3 The ～ば conditional states a hypothetical condition that is necessary for the resultant clause to come about. The condition has to be something that has not yet occurred and perhaps may not occur but is still necessary for a certain result. Compare the following examples, all of which can be translated as *If it snows, we can go skiing.*

1. 雪が降ったらスキーに行けます。
2. 雪が降るとスキーに行けます。
3. 雪が降ればスキーに行けます。

1 means something like *If or when it snows, we can go skiing;* 2 carries the connotation of *When[ever] it snows, we can go skiing.* However, 3 means something like *If and only if it snows, we can go skiing.* It answers the underlying question, *Under what condition will we be able to go skiing?*

33.4 You have already seen the negative form, ～なければ, in Chapter 1, **Grammar 8,** in the form of the construction ～なければなりません. However, ～なければ used by itself carries the connotation of the English word *unless,* as in the following sample sentences.

あの本を読まなければわかりません。
If you don't read (= Unless you read) that book, you won't understand.
ちゃんと練習しなければ危ないですよ。
If you don't practice (= Unless you practice) properly, it's dangerous.

33.5 Normally, the resultant clause cannot be a command, request, invitation, wish, or expression of intention. If you want to say something like *If I go to*

Kyoto, I think I want to stay in a traditional inn, you need to use the 〜たら form:

もし京都に行ったら、旅館に泊まりたいと思います。

The exception is when the conditional clause is built around an adjective or a non-action verb.

安ければ買いましょう。
If it is cheap, let's buy it.
時間があればシーツなども洗ってください。
If you have time, please wash the sheet, etc., too.

33.6 The construction 〜ばいいです can be used to give advice about some future situation. The meaning is something like *All you have to do is . . . .* This is similar to the 〜たらいいです construction, but it is usually not used to give advice about a current situation.

店員に聞けばいいです。
All you have to do is ask a store employee.
砂糖を入れればいいです。
All you have to do is add sugar.

33.7 You can also express wishes and hopes using the construction 〜ばいいですが/けど/のに. You are literally saying that it would be good if only a certain thing would happen, but the が,けど or のに at the end indicates that this desired thing has, in fact, not happened.

車があればいいのに！
I wish I had a car!
カワムラさんがダンス・パーティーに誘ってくれればいいんだけど…
I wish Mr. Kawamura would invite me to the dance.
満点が取れればいいんですが…
I wish I could get a perfect score.

33.8 An idiomatic use of the 〜ば form is in a construction comparable to the English *the more . . . the . . .* For example:

古ければ古いほどおもしろいです。
The older it is, the more interesting it is.
まじめならまじめなほど上手になります。
The more serious they are, the more skillful they become.
これは使えば使うほど気に入ります。
The more you use this, the more you will like it.

33.9 The irregular 〜ば form of the copula, なら, is used in a variant of the conditional construction. The pattern is verb/adj./noun + なら. In this construction, you are taking the current situation or something that another person has said as the basis for your conjecture. It is comparable to the English *If, as you say, . . .* or *If it is true that . . . .*

鈴木さんが来ないなら、私は帰ります。
If [as you say] Ms. Suzuki isn't coming, I'll go home.
コンピュータが故障しているなら、タイプライターを使いましょう。
If [it is true that] the computer is broken, let's use the typewriter.

This construction is similar in meaning to …のだったら.

33.10 Contrary-to-fact wishes, in which you wish that something had happened, even though it in fact did not happen, are expressed with either the 〜ば or the 〜たら form followed by よかった. The addition of …のですが or のに at the end implies that the speaker is scolding or criticizing another person for having failed to do something.

予約すればよかった。
I wish I had made a reservation.
もっと練習したらよかったのに！
I wish you had practiced more!
行かなければよかった。
I wish I hadn't gone.
何か言ったらよかったのに！
I wish you had said something!

33.11 In the case of contrary-to-fact conditionals, that is, sentences in which you say that if X had happened, then Y would have happened or would happen, but in fact, neither X nor Y happened, the first clause goes into the 〜たら or 〜ば form, and the second clause goes into the past tense + のですが construction. Like the contrary-to-fact wishes in 33.10, this construction makes little sense when translated literally into English, so just learn it as a pattern and don't try to analyze it.

前もって (*beforehand*) こういうことを知っていれば、彼とは結婚しなかったんですが…
If had known these things beforehand, I wouldn't have married him.
もし警察 (*police*) が早く来ていたら、皆助かったのですが…
If the police had come quickly, everyone would have been rescued.

Connect to make meaningful sentences.

A

1. タクシーで行けば、
2. 辞書を引けば、
3. 少し練習すれば
4. お金をあげれば、
5. ロビーに行けば、
6. もう少し待てば、
7. これを食べれば
8. ホットココアを飲めば、
9. もう少し若ければ、
10. 私の部屋がもう少し広ければ

B

a. フランス語で挨拶できますよ。
b. こんな赤い服も着られるんですが;
c. 間に合いますよ。
d. カワムラさんも来るでしょう。
e. 元気になりますよ。
f. みんなに来てもらえるんですが…
g. 体が暖まりますよ。
h. 電話があります。
i. 意味が書いてあります。
j. 喜ぶでしょう。

練習　　　　2

Complete these sentences with a logical conclusion to the condition.

[例]　ビデオを持っていれば、→
　　　ビデオを持っていれば古い映画が見られます。

1. コンピュータを使えば、
2. 今日の新聞を読めば
3. あの人が数学の先生であれば、
4. アパートがもう少し駅に近ければ、
5. 明日、天気が良ければ、
6. 病気でなければ、
7. もう少し安ければ、
8. もっと勉強しなければ、

練習　　　　3

Complete the following dialogues by using the ば-conditional form of an appropriate predicate. Choose from among the predicates listed after the exercise.

[例]　A: 日本に一週間しかいなかったんですか。
　　　B: ええ、もっと時間が＿＿＿、もっといたんですが。→　あれば

1. A: そのブラウス、買わないんですか。
   B: もっと ＿＿＿＿、買うんですが...
2. A: 桜 (cherry blossoms) はまだ咲きません (bloom) か。
   B: ええ、まだです。もう少し暖かく＿＿＿＿、咲くでしょう。
3. A: 次の電車は何時でしょうか。
   B: あそこの時刻表＿＿＿＿、わかりますよ。
4. A: 次にバスに間に合いますか。
   B: 歩けば、ダメでしょうが、＿＿＿＿ 間に合いますよ。
5. A: 頭が痛いんですが、
   B: この薬を ＿＿＿＿、頭痛も直りますよ。
6. A: ケーキ、まだありますか。
   B: もう少し早く＿＿＿＿、あったんですが...
7. A: 前に人がいっぱいいて、パレードが全然見えませんね。
   B: ええ、もう少し背が＿＿＿＿、見えるんですが...
8. A: これから「ニンジャ5」を見に行くんですよ。
   B: ＿＿＿＿、私も来週行きますから、場所を教えてください。

Choices: 見る、暇がある、高い、タクシーで行く、安い、来ている、飲む、なる

練習　　　　　　　4

Make suggestions to the following people by using 〜ばいいですよ。

[例]　頭が痛いんですが、... → この薬を飲めばいいですよ。

1. 日本語の会話が上手になりたいんですが、...
2. おいしい日本料理を食べたいんですが、...
3. ニューヨークへはどうやって行けばいいですか。
4. この町のことをもっと知りたいんですが、どうすればいいですか。
5. アメリカの歴史について知りたいんですが、どうすればいいですか。
6. 電話を付けたいんですが、どうすればいいですか。
7. この本を明日までにワシントンに送りたいんですが、どうすればいいですか。
8. ドライブしたいんですが、車がないんです。;
9. 旅行中なんですが、トラベラーズチェックを落としてしまったんです。
10. 明日試験なんですが、全然勉強していないんです。どうすればいいですか。

34. Wanting to Have Something Done: 〜てほしい

カワムラ：大助さん、ちょっとこの日本語の宿題を見てもらいたいんですが...
大助：ああ、いいよ。日本語ならおやすい御用だ。
カワムラ：特に漢字が正しく書けているか調べてもらいたいんです。
大助：わあ、カワムラさん、上手な日本語を書きますね。

課長：高田君、明日、ちょっと大阪へ行ってほしいんだけど。
高田：はい、新しいプロジェクトの件ですか。
課長：ああ、浪速産業の平井さんと話してきてほしいんだ。
高田：かしこまりました。

鈴木：係長、この書類に判を押していただきたいのですが。
村山：はい、ここですね。
鈴木：それから、今日はちょっと早く帰らせていただきたいのですが...
村山：どうしたんですか。

The following constructions can be used when stating that you would like to have someone do something for you.

(A は)	(B に)	te-form of the verb	ほしい/ほしいです もらいたい/もらいたいです いただきたい/ いただきたいです

For the usage of ほしい, refer to Chapter 6 of Book 1.

A wants to have something done [by B]

林さんと話してほしいんですか。
Do you want me to talk with Mr. Hayashi?
ちょっとテレビをつけてほしいんだけど...
I want you to turn on the TV.

When A and B are obvious from the context, you don't have to express them.

KAWAMURA: Daisuke, I want you to take a look at this Japanese homework.   DAISUKE: Yes, of course. If it's Japanese, it's no problem.   KAWAMURA: I especially want you to check if the **kanji** are written correctly.   DAISUKE: Wow, Mr. Kawamura, you write good Japanese.

MANAGER: Mr. Takada, I want you to go to Osaka tomorrow.   TAKADA: Yes. Is it for the new project?
MANAGER: Yes, I want you to go talk with Mr. Hirai of Naniwa Industries.   TAKADA: Certainly.

SUZUKI: Section Chief, I want you to put your seal to this paper.   MURAYAMA: Yes, here it is.   SUZUKI: Also, I want you to let me leave a little early today.   MURAYAMA: What's going on?

郵便局へ行ってきてもらいたいんですが...
I would like you to go to the post office.
彼にもう少し真剣にこの問題を考えてもらいたい。
I would like him to think about this issue a little more seriously.

もらいたい is the たい form of もらう。 Cf. Chapter 6 of Book 1 and Chapter 1 of Book 2.

The combination of the te-form of the verb and ほしい or もらいたい is used when A's social status is equal or superior to B's. When B's social status is superior to A's, いただきたい must be used.

私たちは先生に参加していただきたいんですが、...
We would like you to attend, please, Professor.

いただく is the humble form of もらう。いただきたい is the たい form of いただく。 Cf. Chapter 6 of Book 1 and Chapter 1 of Book 2.

When A is the third person, the te-form of the verb + もらいたがっている or いただきたがっている is usually used. Alternatively, you may be able to use もらいたいそうだ or いただきたいそうだ.

カーティスさんは林さんにこの葉書を読んでもらいたがっています。
Mr. Curtis would like Mr. Hayashi to read this postcard.

学生たちは横井先生にもテレビに出ていただきたいそうです。
The students would like Professor Yokoi to appear on TV.

When asking someone not to do something, you can use either 〜ないでほしい (です) or 〜てほしくない(です).

仕事中は私用電話をしないでほしいですね。
I want you not to make private calls during working hours.

家族がいることを忘れてほしくないです。
I don't want you to forget that you have a family.

社長にはこのレポートはまだ読んでいただきたくない。
I wouldn't like the company president to read this report yet.

練習	1

Where do you think you hear the following statements? Write down in the parentheses a letter indicating the place.

1. そのお塩、取ってほしいんだけど...（　）
2. これを30部、コピーしてもらいたいんだけど...（　）
3. クラスに遅刻 (tardiness) しないでほしいね。（　）
4. そこを右に曲がってほしいんですが...（　）
5. ちょっと静かにしてほしいんですが...みんな本を読んでいるんですから。（　）
6. このトースター、直してほしいんですが...（　）

a. 図書館
b. タクシーの中
c. 電気屋
d. 会社のオフィス
e. 学校
f. 台所

Complete the following dialogue by using an appropriate verb + 〜てほしい or
〜ていただきたい.

1. A: 林さん、この椅子を ＿＿＿＿。
   B: ええ、いいですよ。どこへ動かしましょうか。
2. A: 先生、この作文を ＿＿＿＿。
   B: どれどれ。ああ、なかなかよく書けていますね。
3. A: すぐ終わりますから、ちょっと ＿＿＿＿。
   B: ええ、結構ですよ。あと何分くらいかかりますか。
4. A: 部長、ここに ＿＿＿＿。
   B: ああ、いいよ。ペンはあるかね。
5. A: ブラウンさん、町田さんに ＿＿＿＿。
   B: はい、わかりました。横井先生、町田さんの電話番号はお持ちですか。
6. A: 高田さん、ちょっと郵便局へ ＿＿＿＿。
   B: あのう、すみませんけど、今、ちょっと手が放せないんですが。
7. A: 部長、午後の会議に ＿＿＿＿。
   B: 悪いけど、午後はちょと。

How would you make a request in the following situation? Answer using
〜てほしい, 〜てもらいたい, 〜ていただきたい, and so on.

1. Ask your friend not to call you after 10 P.M.
2. Ask your professor to teach you how to use a computer.
3. Ask your friend not to move from where he or she is now.
4. Ask your subordinate to come to the office at 7:00 A.M. tomorrow.
5. Ask a stranger on the street to tell you the way to the post office.
6. Ask your superior to give a book to his or her own daughter.

Talking About Occasional Happenings: ...することがある

In Chapter 6 of *Yookoso!*, Book 1, you learned to use the ta-form of
verb + ことがある construction to express the idea that you have had
the experience of doing something. Using the nonpast, plain form of

文法ノート

predicates gives you a construction meaning that you do the action occasionally.

Here are some examples:

> ファースト・フードを食べることがある。
> *I occasionally eat fast food.*
> あの先生でもきびしいことがある。
> *Even that professor is strict from time to time.*

If you substitute も for が, you are admitting that you do the action but implying that this happens only rarely. It is usually followed by an explanation or contradiction.

> ファースト・フードを食べることもありますけれども、たいてい
> 自分で料理します。
> *There are occasions when I eat fast food, but usually I do my own cooking.*

In place of こと, you may use とき *time* or 場合 *case*. The use of 場合 makes the resulting sentence sound formal.

> 家では、ラジオを聞いているときもあります。
> *I occasionally listen to the radio at home.*
> 部長が会議に出席する場合もある。
> *There are occasions when the department head attends meetings.*

When the negative form appears before こと, forms such as these are used.

> 週末は全然勉強しないことがある。
> *I occasionally don't study at all on weekends.*
> あの先生の試験はむずかしくないことがない。
> *There's never a time when that professor's tests aren't difficult.*
> (= *That professor's tests are always difficult.*)

The question form of this construction means *Does it ever happen that . . . ?*

> 横井先生はクラスを休講になさることがありますか。
> *Does Professor Yokoi ever cancel her class?*
> カワムラさんから電話が来ることがある？
> *Do you ever get phone calls from Mr. Kawamura?*

35. Expressing Respect (3): Honorifics

近藤：部長は今日はいらっしゃらないんですか。
高田：ええ、出張で今朝、金沢へ行かれました。
近藤：いつお帰りになりますか。
高田：今夜は金沢に泊まられて、明日の夜、東京に帰られます。会社には
　　　月曜日から出られると思います。

ギブソン：横井先生、質問があるんですが、...
横井：12時にオフィスに来られますか。
ギブソン：ええ。でも、横井先生はお昼御飯を食べられないんですか。
横井：ええ、今ちょっとダイエットをしているところなんですよ。
ギブソン：えっ、先生、そんなにやせていらっしゃって、ダイエットが必要なん
　　　　　です か。

The passive form of the verb can also be used as an honorific. These honorific
forms look exactly the same as the passives you studied in Chapter 5, but no
passive meaning is implied.

Class 1	Root + the a-column of hiragana + れる	書く 読む 買う	書かれる 読まれる 買われる
Class 2	Root + られる	食べる	食べられる
Class 3	Irregular	する 来る	される 来られる

先生は黒板にご自分のお名前を書かれた。
The professor wrote his or her own name on the board.
社長はもうこのレポートを読まれましたか。
President, did you already read this report?

KONDOO: Isn't the department head in today?　TAKADA: No, he went to Kanazawa on business this
morning.　KONDOO: When will he return?　TAKADA: He'll stay overnight in Kanazawa and return to
Tokyo tomorrow night. He'll be back in the office as of Monday.

GIBSON: Professor Yokoi. I have a question.　YOKOI: Can you come to my office at noon?　GIBSON: Yes,
but don't you eat lunch?　YOKOI: No, I'm on a diet now.　GIBSON: What, Professor? Being so slim, is it
necessary for you [to go on] a diet?

佐野さんは窓から外を見られていた。

Mr. Sano was looking out from the window.

部長はこの週末、ゴルフをされますか。

Manager, will you play golf this weekend?

The degree of politeness expressed by this form is not as high as the お + V + になる form and the special honorific forms introduced in Chapter 5. The 〜られる form of a Class 2 verb is ambiguous in that it can express an honorific meaning, a passive meaning, or a potential meaning. The following sentence illustrates the ambiguity.

横井先生はてんぷらを食べられました。

Professor Yokoi ate tempura. (honorific)

Professor Yokoi had [her] tempura eaten [by someone else]. (indirect/adversative passive)

Professor Yokoi could eat tempura. (potential)

In cases like these, you have to figure out the correct meaning from the context.

練習　　　　　　　　　　1

Rewrite the following sentences in their corresponding お + V + になる or special honorific forms.

[例]　山口さん、先に帰られて、結構ですよ。→
山口さん、先にお帰りになって、結構ですよ。

1. 社長は何時にパリを発たれますか。
2. 先生、今日の新聞を読まれましたか。
3. 横井先生はそのことをもう知られているそうですよ。
4. 部長も会議室に来られるようです。
5. 先生もパーティーに行かれないんですか。
6. 社長のお嬢さんが先週、結婚された。
7. 1時のニュースをラジオで聞かれましたか。
8. 社長、奥様にはどのようにして会われたんですか。

練習　　　　　　　　　　2

Rewrite the following sentences using れる/られる honorific forms.

[例]　町田さんに電話しましたか。→ 町田さんに電話されましたか。

1. 山口さんは私の横に座った。
2. 明日の会議に出ますか。

3. 何時の新幹線に乗りますか。
4. カワムラさんと会いますか。
5. もうあのニュースは聞きましたか。
6. ちょっとこのへんを歩きませんか。
7. これでいいと思いますか。
8. 社長はこのペンを使った。

36. Causative-Passives

高田：ブラウンさん、遅くなって、ごめん。
ブラウン：いいえ、私もさっき来たばかりです。
高田：部長の手伝いをさせられていて、遅くなってしまたんだ。
ブラウン：高田さんの部長さんはいろいろなことをさせるんですね。

カワムラ：大助さん、昨日のパーティーはどうでしたか。
山口：いやあ、みんなの前で歌を歌わせられたり、踊りを踊らせられたりして、大変でしたよ。
カワムラ：大助さんは歌も踊りも得意だったんじゃないんですか。
山口：とんでもない！

高田：部長、週末はいかがでしたか。
部長：土曜日は孫をリトルリーグの試合に連れていかせられたし、昨日は家内の買い物に付き合わせられたし…
高田：でも、部長はいつも仕事でお忙しいですから、たまには家族サービスをなさらないと…
部長：まあ、そうなんだが、…

TAKADA: Ms. Brown, I'm sorry for being late.   BROWN: That's OK. I arrived a couple of minutes ago, too.
TAKADA: I was made to help my department head, so I ended up being late.   BROWN: Your department head makes you do all sorts of things, doesn't he?

KAWAMURA: How was the party yesterday?   YAMAGUCHI: Well, I was made to sing a song in front of everybody and to dance. It was terrible.   KAWAMURA: I thought you were good at both singing and dancing.   YAMAGUCHI: No way!

TAKADA: Department Head, how was the weekend?   DEPARTMENT HEAD: I was made to take my grandchild to his Little League game Saturday and to accompany my wife shopping yesterday . . . .   TAKADA: Since you're always busy with your work, you need to do things for your family occasionally.   DEPARTMENT HEAD: Yes, you're right, but . . . .

The passive form of the causative form, generally called the causative-passive form, is used to express the meaning *to be made to do something* [*by someone*].

CLASS	THE FORMATION OF THE CAUSATIVE	EXAMPLES	
Class 1	Root + the a-column of hiragana + せられる	書く	書かせられる
Class 2	Root + させられる	食べる	食べさせられる
Class 3	Irregular	する 来る	させられる 来させられる

In this construction, the person who makes someone do something is marked by に, while the person who is made to do it is marked with は or が.

Xは/が	Yに	(Z を)	Causative-passive verb form

X is caused (forced, made) by Y to do Z

その男に無理やり名前を書かされました。
I was forced by that man to write my name.
嫌だと言ったが、みんなに歌を歌わせられた。
I said that I didn't want to, but I was made by everyone to sing a song.
子供の時、にんじんを食べさせられるのが嫌だったけど、今はにんじんが
　　大好きです。
When I was child, I hated being forced to eat carrots, but now I like them.

When the person who makes someone do something is clear from the context or it is not necessary to identify that person, Y に can be omitted in this construction.

みんなの前で話をさせられた。
I was forced to give a talk in front of everyone.

練習　　　　　　　　1

The following are complaints about three managers from their subordinates. After reading the complaints, complete the table following the example.
[例]　私は田中部長にお弁当を買いに行かせられます。
　1.　私は佐藤部長に私用の (*private*) 手紙をワープロで打たせられます。
　2.　私は田中部長に遅くまで働かされます。

3. 僕は休みの日に山田部長にゴルフに一緒に行かされます。私は佐藤部長に
   パーティーでお酒を無理やり飲まされました

4. 僕は山田部長に机の上の掃除をさせられました。

5. 私は佐藤部長に部長の友人の観光ガイドをさせられました。

6. 私は山田部長にいつもお茶を入れさせらせます。

TANAKA	SATOO	YAMADA
[ex] makes subordinates buy box lunches for him		

練習　　　　　　　　　2

Rewrite the following sentences into the corresponding passive form.

[例]　部長はみんなにカラオケで歌わせた。→
　　　みんなは部長にカラオケで歌わせられた。

残業 *overtime*

1. あの課長はよく残業をさせます。
2. セールスマンは山口さんに事典を買わせた。
3. 母親は子供をおつかい (*errand*) に行かせました。
4. 先生は学生にそのダイアログを暗記 (*memorization*) させました。
5. 先生は日本の歴史に関する (*concerning*) 本を何冊も読ませました。
6. 警官 (*police officer*) は車のトランクを開けさせました。
7. 三村さんはチンさんにすしを食べさせました。
8. 部長は部下にお茶を入れさせました。
9. カワムラさんは林さんにその写真を見させました。
10. 町田さんはカワムラさんをその女の人に会わせた。

Following the example, complete the following causative and corresponding causative-passive sentences.

[例]　（お中元を届ける）
部長は高田さんにお中元を届けさせた。
高田さんは部長にお中元を届けさせられた。

1. （テレビを修理する）
兄は弟に ＿＿＿＿＿。
弟は兄に ＿＿＿＿＿。

2. （サラダを食べる）
母親は子供に ＿＿＿＿＿。
子供は母親に ＿＿＿＿＿。

3. （コピーを取る）
係長は部下に ＿＿＿＿＿。
部下は係長に ＿＿＿＿＿。

4. （ソファーに座る）
彼はカワムラさんを ＿＿＿＿＿。
カワムラさんは彼に ＿＿＿＿＿。

5. （ブラウンさんを呼ぶ）
彼はカワムラさんに ＿＿＿＿＿。
カワムラさんは彼に ＿＿＿＿＿。

Describe the situations shown in the drawings on the next page using causative and causative-passive sentences. Assume that the subject of the passive-causative sentence is unhappy about the situation.

[例]　お母さんは子供に着物を着せました。→
子供はお母さんに着物を着せられました。

1. お母さんは子供に部屋を
   子供はお母さんに部屋を
2. お医者さんは山口さんにお酒を
   山口さんはお医者さんにお酒を
3. 奥さんは御主人にダイヤの指輪を
   ご主人は奥さんにダイヤの指輪を
4. 部長は私に予算 (budget) を
   私は部長に予算を
   (予算を立てる = draw up a budget)
5. 兄は私に郵便局に
   私は兄に郵便局に

Ex.

1.

2.

3.

4.

5.

37. Expressing Concession

カワムラ：このドア、ずっと壊れたままですね。
山口：ええ、大助にどんなに頼んでも、直してくれないのよ。
カワムラ：じゃあ、僕が直しましょう。
山口：そう、じゃ、お願いするわ。

高田：部長、橋本さんのお宅に何度電話しても、誰も出ないんですが...
部長：それはおかしいね。だれか橋本君がどこにいるのか知らないのかね。
高田：それが、だれに聞いてもわからないんです。
部長：それはますますおかしいね。

...まま

まま is a noun expressing that a certain condition or state remains unchanged.

靴のまま、家に入らないで下さい。
Please don't enter the house with your shoes on.
寒かったので、コートを着たままでいました。
I kept wearing my coat because it was cold.
座ったまま、私の話を聞いて下さい。
Please listen to me while [still] seated.

まま also means *exactly as it is.*

見たままを書きなさい。
Write down exactly what you saw.
このままでいいですよ。
It's fine just like this.
そのままで食べてもいいです。
It's all right to eat it like that [just as it is.]

でいる is a variant of だ/です used only in reference to animate subjects and emphasizing their being in a continuous position or state.

KAWAMURA: This door has been damaged like this for a long time.   YAMAGUCHI: Yes. No matter how many times I ask Daisuke, he doesn't fix it for me.   KAWAMURA: Then I'll fix it.   YAMAGUCHI: Really? Please do.

TAKADA: Department Head, no matter how many times I call Mr. Hashimoto's house, no one answers. DEPARTMENT HEAD: That's strange. Is there anyone who knows where Mr. Hashimoto is?   TAKADA: Well, no matter whom I ask, nobody seems to know.   DEPARTMENT HEAD: That's even more strange.

The 〜ても and でも constructions are used to express dependent clauses meaning *even if . . .* or *even though . . . .*

忙しくても、新聞は毎日読む。
Even if I am busy, I read a newspaper every day.
彼はハンサムでも、性格がよくないから好きじゃない。
Even though he is handsome, I don't like him because his personality is not good.
私でも、そのようにしたでしょう。
Even if I were you, I would have done it like that.

When you would like to emphasize the meaning of concession, you can add たとえ *even granting that . . .* , かりに *just supposing* or 万が一 *even in the unlikely event that . . .* Another way to emphasize this meaning is to use a plain predicate + としても.

田村部長が私の上司でも、こんなことは許せない。
Even granting that department head Tamura is my superior, I can't forgive something like this.
万が一我々の計画がうまくいかなくても、誰にも言うな。
In the remote event that our plan doesn't go well, don't tell anyone.
かりにそれが冗談だとしても、そんなことを言ってはいけない。
Even if it is a joke, don't say such a thing.

Interrogatives can be used in this clause to express ideas such as *no matter* (*what, who, when, where, how,* and so on).

誰と話しても、みんながカワムラさんのことをほめる。
No matter whom I talk with, everyone praises Mr. Kawamura.
何を聞いても、林さんはわからないと言うだけだった。
Whatever we asked him, Mr. Hayashi just said he didn't know.
この町は、どこへ行っても清潔です。
This town is clean wherever you go.
どう考えても、その話はおかしい。
No matter how we think about it, that story is strange.
いくら練習しても、上達 (improvement) しません。
No matter how much I practice, I don't improve.

The ても form of some adjectives expressing quantity or time mean *at the very . . . .*

早くても3時まではかかります。
It will take until three o'clock at the earliest.
遅くても朝9時までに家を出なければ間に合わない。
We won't make it unless we leave home by nine in the morning at the latest.

多くても100人くらいしかパーティーに来ないだろう。
At most only one hundred people will come to the party.

This ても construction is semantically close to the use of が or けれども meaning *but*.

手紙を出しても、返事をくれなかった。
Even though I sent him a letter, he didn't reply.
手紙を出したけれども、返事をくれなかった。
手紙を出したが、返事をくれなかった。
I sent him a letter, but he didn't reply.

Note, however, that けれども and が cannot be used with interrogatives. The ても construction can express a hypothetical situation, whereas a sentence containing が or けれども expresses only actions that have already happened or that are relatively certain to happen in the future. Compare:

手紙を出しても、返事をくれないでしょう。
Even if I send him a letter, he probably won't reply.
手紙を出してみるけれども、返事をくれないでしょう。
I'll try sending him a letter, but he probably won't reply.

練習　　　　　　　　　　1

Answer the following questions.

[例] 下手でも、日本語をたくさん使うようにした方がいいですか。→
　　　はい下手でも、たくさん使った方がいいと思います。

1. 日本語の授業 (class session) のない日でも、日本語を勉強した方がいい
　　ですか。
2. どんなに高くても、日本語のいい辞書を買いますか。
3. 勉強が忙しくても、運動はした方がいいですか。
4. どんなに給料が安くても、どんな仕事もきちんとしなければいけません。
5. どんなにむずかしい試験でも、最後まであきらめない(あきらめる = *give up*)
　　でしますか。

練習　　　　　　　　　　2

Complete the following dialogues using verbs or adjectives ending in 〜ても.

[例] A: 明日は雨が降りますよ。
　　 B: 雨が降っても、ジョギングはするつもりです。

1. A: 水はまだ冷たいかもしれませんよ。
　　B: どんなに ＿＿＿＿、サーフィンはできますよ。

2. A: これ、ちょっとまずいですよ。

   B: どんなに ＿＿＿＿、おなかがすいているから、何でも食べますよ。

3. A: カワムラさんは今とても忙しいですよ。

   B: ＿＿＿＿、私には会ってくれますよ。

4. A: 林さんと話してみたらどうですか。

   B: 林さんと ＿＿＿＿、わかってくれませんよ。

5. A: 大学へ行くのはお金がかかりますよ。

   B: どんなに ＿＿＿＿、子供は大学へ行かせたいんです。

6. A: 今日は土曜日ですよ。

   B: ＿＿＿＿、日本の学校では授業があるんですよ。

練習	3

Make sentences using the phrases given and the 〜ても construction. Your sentences do not have to follow the same grammatical pattern as the example.

[例] 苦手/数学のクラスを取る →
　　苦手でも、数学のコースを取らなければいけませんよ。or
　　苦手でも、数学のコースを取らせられますよ。

1. 風邪をひいている/明日会社へ行く
2. きらい/ブロッコリーを食べる
3. 近い/駅までタクシーで行く
4. 前の晩遅く帰ってくる/毎朝ジョギングする
5. 日本人である/漢字を忘れる

練習	4

Complete the following sentences with a logical follow-up to the introductory phrase.

[例] 夏でも、＿＿＿＿。 →
　　夏でも、セーターを着ているんですか。

1. どんなに天気がよくても、＿＿＿＿。
2. お金が全然なくても、＿＿＿＿。
3. どんなにがんばっても、＿＿＿＿。
4. どんなに彼が頼んでも、＿＿＿＿。
5. いくらたくさん運動しても、＿＿＿＿。

Expressing Certain Conviction:
...にちがいない

The ...にちがいない construction is used to express a conjecture of which the speaker is nearly certain.

> カワムラさんはもう今ごろ九州に着いているにちがいない。
> *There is no doubt that Mr. Kawamura has already arrived in Kyushu.*
>
> 新聞記者たちはその警官と話したにちがいありません。
> *The newspaper reporters must have talked with that policeman.*
>
> アラスカはとても寒かったにちがいありません。
> *It must have been very cold in Alaska.*
>
> 祖父は若いころハンサムだったにちがいない。
> *There is no doubt that my grandfather was handsome when he was young.*

The adverb きっと (*undoubtedly, certainly*) is often used with にちがいない.

> 明日はきっと雨が降るにちがいない。
> *It will rain tomorrow for sure.*
>
> チンさんはきっと手紙を書くにちがいない。
> *I am sure that Ms. Chin will write a letter.*

The degree of probability expressed by ...にちがいない is stronger than だろう and かもしれない.

Vocabulary

Telephone

こうしゅうでんわ	公衆電話	public phone
こくさいでんわ	国際電話	international call
ダイヤル(をまわす)	ダイヤル(を回す)	(to) dial
ちょうきょりでんわ	長距離電話	long-distance call

でんごん	伝言	message
でんわボックス	電話ボックス	telephone booth
でんわをきる	電話を切る	to hang up the phone
ないせん	内線	extension
はなしちゅう	話し中	[the line is] busy
プッシュホン		push-button telephone
まちがいでんわ(をする)	間違い電話(をする)	(calling) the wrong number
るすばんでんわ	留守番電話	telephone answering machine

Loanwords: ダイヤル、ファックス、コレクト・コール

Review: 電話、(に)電話をかける、電話番号、電話帳

Postal Service

あてな	あて名	address (*of the recipient*)
げんきんかきとめ	現金書留	registered mail for sending cash
こうくうびん	航空便	air mail
こづつみ	小包	package
たっきゅうびん	宅急便	delivery service
そくたつ	速達	express mail
はいたつ(する)	配達(する)	delivery; (to deliver)
はがき	葉書	postal card
びんせん	便箋	stationery, writing paper
ふうとう	封筒	envelope
ふなびん	船便	surface mail
へんじ(をだす)	返事(を出す)	(to send a) reply
ゆうびん	郵便	mail
ゆうびんばんごう	郵便番号	postal code (*similar to ZIP code*)
ゆうびんポスト	郵便ポスト	mailbox (*for sending letters*)

Review: 絵葉書、切手、住所、手紙、郵便局

Newspaper

こうこく(をだす)	広告(を出す)	(to place an) advertisement
…にのる	…に載る	to appear in, to be covered in (*a newspaper or magazine*)
しんぶんきじ	新聞記事	newspaper article
しんぶんはいたつ	新聞配達	paper delivery
とる	取る	to subscribe (*to a magazine or newspaper*)
マスコミ		mass communication

Review: 新聞、ニュース、〜部

Books, Publishing

げっかんし	月刊誌	monthly magazine
しゅうかんし	週刊誌	weekly magazine
しゅっぱん(する)	出版(する)	publishing; (to publish)
しょうせつ	小説	novel
じてん	事典	encyclopedia
まんが	漫画	comic book, comic magazine, cartoon

Loanword: エッセイ

Review: 教科書、〜冊、雑誌、辞書、本、本屋、料理の本

Broadcasting

アニメ		animation
エヌエチケー	NHK	Nippon Hoso Kyokai
シーエム	CM	commercial (from commercial message)
しゅつえんする	出演する	to appear as a performer
ばんぐみ	番組	[television or radio] program
ほうそう(する)	放送(する)	broadcasting; (to broadcast)
マイク		microphone

Loanwords: AM、FM、アナウンサー、アンテナ、コマーシャル、コメディー、スタジオ、スポンサー、タレント、チャンネル、ドキュメンタリー、エッセイ、ジャーナリズム、ファックス、コレクト・コール

Review: カメラ、カラーテレビ、テレビ、天気予報、ドラマ、ビデオ、ラジオ

Verbs

といあわせる	問い合わせる	to inquire
なる	鳴る	to make a sound, to ring (*telephone or doorbell*)
はる	貼る	to paste

Review: インタビュー(する)、送る

Grammar

…ことがある	there are occasions when …
〜させられる	(*verb causative-passive ending*)
〜せられる	(*verb causative-passive ending*)
〜ていただきたい	to want someone to do … (*humble*)
〜てほしい	to want someone to do …
〜ても	even if …, even though …

〜てもらいたい	to want someone to do . . .
…にちがいない	there is no doubt that . . .
〜ば	(*conditional*)
〜られる	(*honorific ending*)
〜れる	(*honorific ending*)

Kanji

Learn these **kanji.**

刊 雑 誌 記 放 組 試 験 忘 困

調 英 映 画 郵 紙 送 達 宅 重

換 際 留 守 受 取 器 報 文 打

Reading and Writing

Reading 1　手紙の書き方
てがみ

Before You Read

As you learned in Book 1 (pp. 272–274), the standard way of writing letters in Japan is somewhat different from that in Western countries. This reading selection introduces some guidelines for Japanese letter writing found in a book of etiquette published in Japan.

It is customary to refer to the weather or the season in Japanese formal letters. What month do you think each of the following greetings refers to? Assume that these were written by someone in Tokyo.

Month

( ) 桜の季節も間もなくとなりました。

( ) 毎日、雨が降る梅雨の季節となりました。

( ) 毎日暑い日が続きます。

( ) 秋の青空がきれいな季節となりました。

( ) ゴールデンウイークはいかがでしたか。

( ) 遠くに見える山が紅葉で赤く見える季節、いかがお過ごしですか。

過ごす *to pass or spend [time]*

( ) 町はクリスマスのライトでいっぱいですが、

( ) 桜の季節も過ぎて、緑がますます濃くなってきました。

ますます *increasingly*
濃い *thick, deep, intense*

Now Read It!

As Linda Brown's written Japanese improves, she has been trying to write as many letters in Japanese as possible, even though she hasn't always fully understood the rules of Japanese letter writing. Fortunately, she has found a short article about letter writing in this week's edition of 週刊毎朝.

週刊毎朝1994年1月18日家庭欄

　最近は何でも電話ですませるようになり、手紙を書くことが少なくなりました。しかし、手紙は書かれた会話。友人から手紙を受け取ると、うれしいものです。手紙でなければ伝えられないこともあります。直接言いにくいことも手紙では書きやすいものです。電話では言い間違いや、聞き間違いで、誤解することもあります。手紙なら、何度でも読み直しができます。

　今日は上手な手紙の書き方をエチケット評論家の吉田美鈴さんにまとめていただきました。

1. まず、手紙を出す相手によって、フォーマルに書くかカジュアルに書くか決めましょう。目上の人に書く時には、あらたまったスタイルで書きます。

2. 手紙は「拝啓」のような頭語で始まり、「敬具」のような結語で終わるのが基本的な形式です。この形式をしっかり覚えましょう。

3. 形式も大切ですが、あまり形式的すぎると、つまらない手紙になってしまいます。心をこめて、素直に書きましょう。また、ふだんあまり使わない言葉ばかりを使うと、ぎこちない手紙になります。自分の言葉で簡潔に書きましょう。

すませる *to get along, manage*

直接 *directly*

言い間違い *slip of the tongue*
聞き間違い *error in listening*
誤解(する) *misunderstanding; (to misunderstand)*
評論家 *critic, commentator*
まとめる *to summarize, compile*

相手 *partner or counterpart in a mutual activity*
決める *to decide*
あらたまる *to become formal*

基本的(な) *basic* / 形式 *form*
覚える *to learn, to memorize*

心をこめる *to be sincere, to show feeling*
素直(な) *gentle, mild* / ふだん *usually*
ぎこちない *clumsy*
簡潔 *concise*

4. 手紙では「です」、「ます」のような丁寧語を上手に使いましょう。

5. お祝い、お礼、お見舞い、おわびや返事はすぐ書きましょう。遅れたら、そのおわびや理由を忘れないようにしましょう。

6. 急ぐときは、葉書を使ったらいいでしょう。でも、プライベートなことを書いてはいけません。あらたまった時には、手紙のほうがいいでしょう。

7. 便箋は白かグレー、クリーム色にしましょう。目上の人にはカラフルな便箋やイラストが入った便箋を使うのは失礼です。

手紙は人と人の心をつなぐ大切な手段です。マナーを守って、あなたの心の伝わる手紙を書きましょう。

お祝い *congratulations*
お見舞い *checking up on someone's well-being*
おわび *apology* / 理由 *reason*

失礼(な) *impolite, rude*

つなぐ *to link* / 手段 *means, way*
守る *to keep, maintain*

After You Finish Reading

1. As you read the rules for letter writing, you undoubtedly noticed that some of the rules are different from the rules for writing letters in English. List the differences that you noticed, and then make a second list of the similarities. Are there any Japanese rules that are completely irrelevant for English?

2. You are a student at a university in Japan, and a classmate from Thailand, who has not lived in Japan as long as you have, asks you the following questions on how to write a letter in Japanese. Since the Thai student does not speak English, you have to answer in Japanese.

   a. 保証人 (*visa guarantor*) に手紙を書きたいんですが、グリーンの便箋しかないんです。このグリーンの便箋を使ってもいいですか。

   b. 3ヶ月前に友だちから本をもらいましたが、まだ、お礼の手紙を書いていません。どうしたらいいでしょうか。

   c. 2ページも手紙を書いて、書き間違いをしてしまいました。どうすればいいですか。

   d. 字が下手なので、手紙を書くのはきらいです。何でも電話でいいでしょう。

Writing 1

You are asked by a magazine for international students to write a short article about the etiquette of making a phone call. Following the example of the above article, start your essay with a short introduction about telephone calls. Then give some suggestions such as these.

Useful vocabulary

正ただしく *correctly*

はっきり(と) *clearly*

- Do not call early in the morning or late at night.
- Dial directly.
- Avoid lengthy phone calls.
- Write down what you want to say on a piece of paper in advance.
- Always put a memo pad and a pen near the phone.
- Speak clearly.
- Avoid difficult words.
- Use **aizuchi** often on the phone.

Reading 2　ラジオの番組案内

Before You Read

What TV programs do you watch? Discuss in class what programs people watch in respect to each of the following genres.

ニュース番組

メロドラマ

コメディー

ドキュメンタリー

トーク・ショー

音楽番組

スポーツ番組

アニメ

Now Read It!

Linda Brown received the following announcement from FM フジ, of which she is a regular listener.

さわやかな春の季節となりましたが、みなさまいかがお過ごしでしょうか。いつも FM フジ78 をお聞き下さり、まことにありがとうございます。FM フジの来月の番組案内をお届け致します。毎週日曜日朝6時から7時までお送りしております、「サンデー・モーニング・アワー」は来月はバロック音楽の特集です。

月曜日から金曜日の朝6時から9時までお送りしております「おはようフジ」は4月1日から武藤洋子さんをホステスに迎え、内容も新しく、お送り致します。最新のニュースの他、高速道路情報、JR、私鉄、バスの情報、天気予報もあります。これまで毎週月曜日から金曜日の9時から11時までお送りして

さわやかな *fresh, refreshing*

案内 *guidance, information*
届ける *to deliver*
特集 *special feature, special collection*

迎える *to receive [a visitor], greet, look forward to*
内容 *contents*

おりました「日本の歌」は来月から午後1時から2時に移ります。これまで通り、お楽しみください。そのかわり今度新しく「悩みごと相談室」が始まります。悩みごとがおありの方は、東京(03) 3874-2301 までお電話ください。

モデレーターは FM フジの今野道子アナウンサーです。悩みごとのおありの方は、一人で悩んでいないで、お気軽にお電話ください。ウイークデーのお昼の一時、お好きな歌でお楽しみになりませんか。11時から1時までは「リクエスト・ミュージック・タイム」です。歌謡曲、ロック、民謡、何でもかまいません。お聞きになりたい曲がありましたら、東京 (03) 3874-2203 までお電話下さい。皆様のお相手は伊藤国年さんと大山由美子さんです。これまで皆さんにご好評いただいた「あなたと映画を」は3月で終わり、ウイークデーの午後2時から3時までは4月1日から「加納太郎のズバリ聞きます」が始まります。小説、エッセイのベストセラーで有名な加納太郎氏が政治家、会社経営者、タレントの方々にインタビューします。午後3時から6時まではこれまで通り「トワイライトフジ」でお楽しみください。パーソナリティーは FM フジの小林光夫アナウンサーと友野優子アナウンサーです。二人の楽しい話と音楽で楽しい一時をお送りください。また、この番組では皆様からのお電話もお待ちしております。みんなに聞いてもらいたい、とっておきの話、面白いお話がありましたら、東京 (03) 3874-2301 までお電話ください。そして6時から7時までは「ニュースセンター」です。国外、国内の最新のニュースをお送りします。ニュースキャスターは小森宏さん。スポーツは酒井幸太郎アナウンサー、お天気は徳川ゆり子アナウンサーです。4月15日からは毎晩7時から「プロ野球 中継」が始まります。放送カードは新聞などでお知らせします。

　週末の新しい番組を二つご紹介します。土曜日の午後2時から4時までは世界のアーチストのライブコンサートをお送りする「ワールドライブ」です。毎週世界の有名アーチストのライブコンサートの模様をお伝えします。日曜日の午後10時から11時までは新しく「サイエンス・テクノロジー・トゥデイ」が始まります。現在、サイエンス、テクノロジーの世界で何が起こっているかをお知らせ致します。どうぞこれからも今まで同様、FMフジをあなたの生活のパートナーとして、ダイヤルをお合わせください。

そのかわり in its place, instead of it
悩みごと worries, personal problems
相談室 consultation room

気軽に feeling free, without hesitation

歌謡曲 popular song
民謡 traditional Japanese folk song

好評 popularity, favorable comment

ズバリ boldly, decisively

氏 Mr., Ms. (formal)
政治家 politician
会社経営者 company manager

とっておき best, treasured, valuable

Some super-polite forms are used in this announcement, including - ます forms before nouns and 〜ましたら instead of 〜たら.

中継 live remote broadcast

模様 situation, appearance

起こる to happen, take place
同様 in the same way

After You Finish Reading

Fill in this broadcast schedule for FMフジ's coming new season, using the above announcement as a guide.

	WEEKDAYS	SATURDAY	SUNDAY
6–7 A.M.			
7–8 A.M.			
8–9 A.M.			
9–10 A.M.			
10–11 A.M.			
11–12 noon			
12–1 P.M.			
1–2 P.M.			
2–3 P.M.			
3–4 P.M.			
4–5 P.M.			
5–6 P.M.			
6–7 P.M.			
7–8 P.M.			
8–9 P.M.			
9–10 P.M.			
10–11 P.M.			

Writing 2

Some people who have just moved to Tokyo and are unfamiliar with the local radio stations have asked your advice about what radio programs to listen to. Answer in Japanese, because all these people are either Japanese or newly arrived from non-English-speaking countries. (Don't forget to mention the time and the day of the week for each program. Use the information in the reading selection.)

1. 僕はプロ野球の大ファンなんですよ。
2. 私は45歳の主婦です。うちの15歳の娘のことですが、夜の1時や2時まで外で遊んでいて困っています。
3. 私は70年代のディスコミュージックが好きなんですが、最近のラジオではあまり聞かなくなりました。聞きたい曲がいくつかあるんですよ。
4. 僕の夢は科学者になることなんだ。いろいろな科学の本を読んで、勉強しているんだ。
5. 私はケニーGのファンです。あのサックスの音はいいですね。
6. 私は家で仕事をしていますが、3時頃になると、眠くなります。何か面白い番組はありませんか。

Language Functions and Situations

Making a Phone Call

吉野：もしもし、東京ファッション営業部です。
高田：あのう、石山部長をお願いします。
吉野：おそれいりますが、どちら様でしょうか。
高田：SONYの高田と申します。
吉野：SONYの高田様ですね。少々お待ちください。

石山：お電話かわりました。石山です。
高田：SONYの高田です。先日はどうも。
石山：いいえ、こちらこそ。

YOSHINO: Hello, this is the Sales Department of Tokyo Fashion.　TAKADA: Uh, [may I talk to] Mr. Ishiyama (*lit., Manager Ishiyama*), please?　YOSHINO: I beg your pardon, but [may I ask] who's calling? TAKADA: I am Takada of SONY.　YOSHINO: Mr. Takada of SONY, I see. Please wait a moment.

ISHIYAMA: This is Ishiyama speaking.　TAKADA: This is Takada of SONY speaking. Thank you very much for the other day.　ISHIYAMA: Oh, thank *you*.

高田：新しいプロジェクトの件でお話をしたいと思いまして…明日の午後、そちらにお伺いしてもよろしいでしょうか。

石山：明日の午後ですか。ええと、2時以降でしたら、大丈夫です。

高田：それでは、明日2時半にそちらに伺わせていただきます。

石山：それではお待ちしております。

高田：それでは、また明日。失礼します。

石山：じゃあ、失礼します。

吉野：もしもし、東京ファッション営業部です。

高田：あのう、石山部長をお願いします。

吉野：あいにく石山は今、席をはずしておりますが、…

高田：では、伝言をお願いします。

吉野：かしこまりました。どうぞ。

高田：私、SONY営業部の高田洋一と申します。高田は「高い低い」の高に、田んぼの「田」、洋一は太平洋の「洋」に「一番」の「一」です。

吉野：はい。

高田：今月24日午後6時から我が社の銀座ショールームで新しいビデオカメラの発表パーティーを行ないますので、是非御出席くださるようお願いしたくて、お電話致しました。後ほど、改めてお電話差し上げるとお伝えください。

吉野：はい。かしこまりました。

高田：じゃ、失礼いたします。

吉野：失礼いたします。

TAKADA: I'd like to talk with you about the new project. May I visit you tomorrow afternoon?
ISHIYAMA: Tomorrow afternoon? Let me see. If it's after two o'clock, it's OK.   TAKADA: Then I will be there at 2:30.   ISHIYAMA: I'm looking forward to your visit.   TAKADA: Then I'll see you tomorrow. Good-bye.   ISHIYAMA: Good-bye.

YOSHINO: Hello, this is the Sales Department of Tokyo Fashion.   TAKADA: Uh, [may I talk to] Mr. Ishiyama (*lit., Manager Ishiyama*), please?   YOSHINO: I'm sorry, but Ishiyama is away from his desk just now.   TAKADA: Then may I leave a message?   YOSHINO: Yes, please.   TAKADA: I am Yooichi Takada of the Sales Department of SONY. Takada is written with the 高 of high and low and the 田 of rice paddy. Yooichi is written with the 洋 of Pacific Ocean and the 一 of No. 1.   YOSHINO: Yes.   TAKADA: We're going to have a party to announce our new video camera at our Ginza Exhibit Hall starting at 6 P.M. on the 24th of this month. I'm calling Mr. Ishiyama to ask him to please be sure to attend the party. Please tell him I will call him again later.   YOSHINO: All right.   TAKADA: Well, good-bye.   YOSHINO: Good-bye.

Talking on the Phone

Always use honorifics as you begin a call to someone else's home or business, because you don't necessarily know who the person on the other end of the line is. Once you find out whom you are talking to or once the person you want to speak to comes to the phone, you can adjust the level of your speech accordingly. If you do not identify yourself at the beginning of the call, the person at the other end of the line is certain to ask you this or something like it:

> どちら様でしょうか。
> *May I ask who's calling?*
> ブラウンと申します。
> *My name is Brown.*
> 失礼ですが、どちらのブラウンさんですか。
> *I am sorry, but which Ms. Brown?*

In a business or professional situation, you should always identify yourself by your job affiliation. If you do not, you are likely to hear something like the above question. Answer with (*the name of your company, school, or occupation*) + の + (*your name* [*without any title*]) です.

Remember that when talking on the phone you should always refer to an in-group member without any honorific title and with humble language.

One way to give a message is to state briefly what you want to tell the person, end with ...から or ので, and follow up with そうおっしゃってください or そう伝えてください. For example, if you want to leave a message that you have postponed tomorrow's meeting until ten o'clock, you could say:

> 明日の会議のことなんですが、かってながら10時に変更いたしましたので、そうおっしゃってください.
> *It's about tomorrow's meeting, and even though it's inconsiderate of us, we've changed it to ten o'clock, so please tell* [*him/her*] *that.*

And remember that on the phone or off, it is polite to conclude a request with

> よろしくお願いいたします。
> *Please take care of it for me.*

Role Play

Working with a partner, practice the following situations. (For 1, 2, and 3, one student must prepare a message in advance for the other student to take in Japanese.)

1. Call the Yoshioka residence and ask for Mrs. Yoshioka, who happens to be out. Leave a message for her.
2. Call Mr. Takahashi, who is the manager of the Sales Department, ABC Automobiles (ABC自動車). He has momentarily left his seat. Leave a message for him.
3. Call Professor Yokoi's residence. Unfortunately, she is not at home. Leave a message.
4. Call your friend and ask him or her to do something with you this weekend.

コミュニケーション・ノート

よろしく

よろしく is the adverbial form of the adjective よろしい, which is a more formal version of いい, so it literally means *well*. It is used in a variety of common courtesy expressions, all of which have to do with treating the speaker or some third person well. As you learned in Book 1, the expression どうぞよろしくお願いします is used when introducing oneself. When people join any kind of a group in Japan, whether it is a club, a class, or the staff of a company, they give a brief self-introduction in front of everyone, stating their name, background, hobbies and interests, and perhaps their reasons for joining the group. Then they end their presentation with どうぞよろしくお願いします.

This phrase is also the usual conclusion to a request for a favor or a request for someone to take care of something or someone. For example, if you asked your instructor for a letter of recommendation, you would conclude the conversation with どうぞよろしくお願いいたします, the most humble form of this already humble expression.

A superior asking a subordinate to take care of something would use not どうぞよろしくお願いします but よろしく頼(たのむ)よ (male speaker) or よろしく頼むわね (female speaker).

If the two parties are somehow taking care of or doing favors for each other, as when entering into a business relationship, then the second party replies to どうぞよろしくお願いいたします with こちらこそ, an expression that indicates that the polite phrase applies equally to the first party.

When asking someone to give your regards to a third person, use the expression X-さんによろしくお伝(つた)えください. When speaking in informal style, you may leave off the お伝えください.

At the Post Office

郵便局員：次の方。

カワムラ：すみません。この小包を九州へ送りたいんですが。

郵便局員：壊れ物は入っていますか。

カワムラ：いいえ。

郵便局員：ええと、1キロですから、800円です。

カワムラ：何日くらいで着きますか。

郵便局員：そうですね。2～3日で着くでしょう。

カワムラ：それから、この現金書留もお願いします。

郵便局員：ええと、2万円だから、370円です。

カワムラ：それから、70円切手5枚と200円切手2枚ください。

郵便局員：これだけですか。

カワムラ：はい、そうです。

郵便局員：全部で1920円です。

カワムラ：はい、2000円。

郵便局員：おつりの80円と現金書留の領収書です。ありがとうございました。

Role Play

Working in pairs, practice the following situations.

1. You are living in Japan and would like to mail a Japanese doll as a Christmas gift to your friend in the United States. Go to the post office and mail it.
2. You have decided to apply for a job at a Japanese company and have just finished writing your application. The deadline is the day after tomorrow. Mail your application by special delivery mail.
3. You would like to send money to a friend living in Hokkaido. Go to the post office and mail it.

CLERK: Next please.　KAWAMURA: Excuse me. I would like to send this package to Kyushu.
CLERK: Anything fragile inside?　KAWAMURA: No.　CLERK: Well, it weights one kilo, so it's 800 yen.
KAWAMURA: How many days does it take?　CLERK: Let me see. Two or three days.　KAWAMURA: And I would like to mail this by cash registered mail.　CLERK: Well, the amount is 20,000 yen, so the postage will be 370 yen.　KAWAMURA: May I have five 70-yen stamps and two 200-yen stamps?　CLERK: Anything else?　KAWAMURA: That's it.　CLERK: 1,920 yen altogether, please.　KAWAMURA: Out of 2,000 yen.　CLERK: Here are your change of 80 yen and the receipt for your cash registered mail. Thank you very much.

Listening Comprehension

1. You will listen to a telephone conversation. In this call, the person with whom the caller wanted to talk was not at her desk, so he left a message. Write down the content of the message.
2. You will listen to a TV announcement, in which an announcer describes some programs they will broadcast later on today. Fill in the schedule, based on her description.

12:00 noon	
1:00 P.M.	
2:00 P.M.	
3:00 P.M.	
4:00 P.M.	
5:00 P.M.	
6:00 P.M.	
7:00 P.M.	
8:00 P.M.	
9:00 P.M.	
10:00 P.M.	
11:00 P.M.	
12:00 midnight	

3. You will hear conversations between a post office clerk and five different customers. Write down what each customer sent and how much the total postage was.

	ITEM(S) MAILED	POSTAGE
Customer 1		
Customer 2		
Customer 3		
Customer 4		
Customer 5		

第七章　自然と文化

しぜん　ぶんか

Nature and Culture

宮島の厳島神社
みやじま　いつくしまじんじゃ

OBJECTIVES

Topics
Geography
Environment and
Nature
Culture and Customs

Grammar
38. Expressing a speaker's emotional involvement: ...ものだ
39. Various uses of よう
40. It's all right not to: 〜なくてもいい

41. Coming to a conclusion: ...わけだ
42. Even though: ...のに

Reading and Writing
Letter to the editor: No to the golf course!
A book review

Language Functions and Situations
Presenting opinions clearly and logically

Vocabulary and Oral Activities

Geography

Vocabulary: Geography

大陸	たいりく	continent
島	しま	island
火山	かざん	volcano
谷	たに	valley
湾	わん	bay
海岸	かいがん	beach, shore
滝	たき	waterfall
石	いし	stone
岬	みさき	cape, promontory
流れる	ながれる	to flow
湖	みずうみ	lake
池	いけ	pond
平野	へいや	plains
丘	おか	hill
森	もり	forest
林	はやし	woods
木	き	tree
面積	めんせき	area, land area

Review: 山、海、川、地図

アクティビティー　1

インタビュー (*Interview*)

Interview one of your classmates. For each question, add one related question of your own.

1. 海のそばに住んでいますか。きれいな海岸がそばにありますか。湾はありますか。
2. 今まで見た湖で、一番大きいのはどの湖ですか。
3. どの山脈が一番きれいだと思いますか。

4. 火山が噴火 (erupt) しているところを見たことがありますか。
5. 山や森の中でキャンプをしたことがありますか。どこでしましたか。
6. 人の住んでいない島に一人で住まなくてはならなくなったら、どんな
   ものを持っていきますか。

アクティビティー 2

どこにありますか。(*Where are they?*)

John Kawamura is spending a few days on the islands of Kuroiwa and Akaiwa.
Here is a map of the islands, with only a few features labeled. Read the following
descriptions, and draw and label the geographical features described at the correct
places on the map.

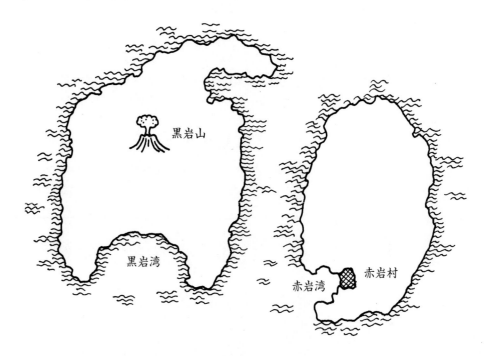

黒岩山

黒岩湾

赤岩湾　赤岩村

1. 黒岩山は黒岩島の真ん中にあります。高さは980mで、そんなに高く
   ありませんが、火山です。
2. 黒岩湖は黒岩山の南にあります。
3. 赤岩湖は赤岩島の北の方にあります。村から北に歩いて、30分ぐらいのところ
   です。赤岩湖の南は森になっています。
4. 黒岩村は黒岩湾に面して (*facing on*) います。村の南には黒岩海岸が広がって
   (*spread out*) います。

5. 黒岩村のすぐ北には大きな林があります。この林は黒岩の林と呼ばれています。林の北側には広い丘が広がっています。この丘は黒岩の丘と呼ばれています。黒岩の丘の真ん中に黒岩沼 (*marsh*) があります。

6. 赤岩湖から南に赤岩川が流れています。赤岩川は村の中を通って、赤岩湾に流れています。

7. 黒岩川は黒岩湖から北に流れています。黒岩川の周りは黒岩谷と呼ばれています。黒岩谷の真ん中に黒岩滝があります。黒岩滝は高さ3mの小さな滝です。

8. 黒岩島の北には黒岩岬があります。黒岩岬は険しい (*steep*) 崖 (*cliff*) になっています。

アクティビティー　3

ダイアログ：午後、登ることになっています。(*It is planned that we will climb it in the afternoon.*)

カワムラ：明日の予定はどうなっていますか？

　ガイド：朝8時に船で、黒岩島に向かうことになっています。

カワムラ：黒岩山には登らないんですか。

　ガイド：ええ、午後、登ることになっています。

Here is Kawamura's schedule for the trip. Explain it in Japanese.

[例]　明日の夜は黒岩山でキャンプをすることになっています。

12日午前	船で黒岩島に向かう
12日午後	黒岩山に登る
12日夜	黒岩山でキャンプをする
13日午前	黒岩滝を見る
13日午後	赤岩島に戻る
	赤岩湾で泳ぐ

KAWAMURA: What are tomorrow's plans like?　GUIDE: We're supposed to head for Kuroiwa Island by boat at eight in the morning.　KAWAMURA: Won't we climb Mt. Kuroiwa?　GUIDE: Yes, it is planned that we will climb it in the afternoon.

13日夜	赤岩海岸でバーベキュー・パーティーをする
14日	東京に戻る

You are the guide for John Kawamura's tour group. For a variety of reasons, it has become necessary to change the original schedule. Write down a new schedule in the following chart and explain why each change is necessary.

[例] 明日は台風が来るそうですから、一日中赤岩島旅館にいることに
なっています。

	NEW SCHEDULE
12日	台風が来るそうですから、一日中赤岩島旅館にいることに なっています。
13日	
14日	

文法ノート

Decisions Made by Others: ...ことになる

The ...ことになる construction is used to express the idea that something has been decided on or happens due to circumstances beyond the speaker's control.

三村さんは4月から貿易会社で働くことになりました。
It was decided that Mr. Mimura will work for a trading company starting in April.

このアパートは家賃が高いので、間もなく引っ越すことになる でしょう。
Because the rent for this apartment is high, we will probably have to move out soon.

今日は天気が悪いので、ピクニックは中止することになった。
Because the weather is bad today, it was decided to call off the picnic.

When a decision was made at some time in the past and that decision is still in effect, になっている (になっています) is used instead of になる (になります).

Vocabulary and Oral Activities

383

三百八十三

明日のクラスでは、カワムラさんが平安時代の建築について発表することになっています。

Mr. Kawamura has to report on the architecture of the Heian Era in tomorrow's class.

3時に山本さんに会うことになっていたが、急用ができてしまった。

It had been arranged that I should see Ms. Yamamoto at three, but some urgent business came up [so I didn't see her].

Because of its time implications, ことになっている is sometimes used to express a custom, regularly scheduled event, rule, or expectation.

上級フランス語のクラスではフランス語しか使わないことになっています。

As a rule, we use only French in our advanced French class.

ここでは靴を脱ぐことになっているので、みなさん、よろしく。

Here you have to take off your shoes, so everyone, please do so.

The ことになる construction is used when you don't have to specify who made a decision or you would rather not mention the decision maker specifically. The superficially similar construction ことにする (cf. Chapter 1, **Grammar 2**), however, requires that you state specifically who made the decision. The distinction is similar to the distinction between *We decided to leave* and *It was decided that we should leave* in English. For this reason, it sounds strange to use the plain, nonpast form of the verb + ことにする when the subject of the sentence is not directly involved in the decision making.

今度、ニューヨークに行かされることにしました。

I have decided to be made go to New York. (sounds strange)

今度、ニューヨークに行かされることになりました。

It has been decided that I will be made go to New York.

If you used the plain, nonpast form of the verb + ことになる even when you are the decision maker, you sound humbler than when you use ことにする.

来週から隣りに引っ越してくることになりましたので、どうぞよろしくお願いいたします。

It has been decided that we will be moving in next door starting next week, so please be kind to us.

The use of a ます/です form before ので is a feature of super-polite speech.

Vocabulary Library

More on Geography

海峡	かいきょう	channel, straits
赤道	せきどう	equator
岩	いわ	rock outcropping
水平線	すいへいせん	horizon
地理	ちり	geography
世界	せかい	world
北極	ほっきょく	North Pole
南極	なんきょく	South Pole
太平洋	たいへいよう	the Pacific Ocean
大西洋	たいせいよう	the Atlantic Ocean
インド洋	インドよう	the Indian Ocean
国	くに	country, nation
州	しゅう	state (*in the U.S.*), province (*in Canada*)
地球	ちきゅう	earth
星	ほし	star
太陽	たいよう	sun
月	つき	moon
宇宙	うちゅう	outer space, the universe

Loanword: ジャングル

勉 Study Grammar 38.

アクティビティー　4

ダイアログ：黒岩湾でよく魚をとったものです。(*I used to fish in Kuroiwa Bay.*)

ブラウン：黒岩島に新しいレジャーランドができたそうですね。

佐野：ええ、昔とすっかり変わってしまったらしいですよ。

ブラウン：佐野さんは黒岩島によく行くんですか。

佐野：子供のころはよく行ったものです。黒岩湾でよく魚ををとったもんですよ。

BROWN: I heard that there's a new resort development (*lit., leisure land*) in the Kuroiwa Islands.　SANO: Yes, it seems that the islands have really changed drastically since the old days.　BROWN: Do you go to Kuroiwa Island often?　SANO: When I was a child, I went there often. I used to fish in Kuroiwa Bay.

アクティビティー　5

開発！開発！開発！ (*Development! Development! Development!*)

Shortly after John Kawamura's visit, a billionaire bought the Kuroiwa and Akaiwa Islands and transformed them into a resort development. The chart shows what has become of various areas of the islands. The drawings show some of the things people used to do in these places before the recreational facilities were built. Complete the chart in Japanese.

THEN	NOW	WHAT DID PEOPLE USED TO DO THERE?
赤岩の丘	ゴルフ場	野菜や果物を作ったものです。
赤岩湾	マリンランド	
黒岩山	ハングライダー場、ボートと乗り場	
赤岩の森	別荘 (*vacation homes*) とテニス・コート	
黒岩村の小学校	レジャーランドの本部 (*main office*)	

Nature and Culture

Environment and Nature

Vocabulary Library

The Environment

環境	かんきょう	environment
公害	こうがい	public nuisance, pollution
汚染(する)	おせん(する)	pollution; (to pollute)
保護	ほご	protection, preservation
破壊	はかい	destruction, damage
自然	しぜん	nature
産業	さんぎょう	industry
節約(する)	せつやく(する)	saving, economizing; (to save, economize)
ごみ		garbage, trash
資源	しげん	resources
もったいない		wasteful

Loanwords: アスベスト、オゾン、フロン・ガス、グリーン・ハウス・エフェクト、スモッグ、リサイクルする

文化ノート

こうがい
公害 *(Pollution)*

From the early 1960s to the mid-1970s, the Japanese economy made remarkable progress, but during this period the rapid, unregulated development of heavy and manufacturing industries brought about several serious incidents of mass poisonings from toxic waste. The most notorious incident occurred at Minamata in Kyushu, where many residents suffered brain damage after eating fish contaminated with mercury-laden wastes from a local factory. Air pollution, water pollution, sinkholes caused by the overuse of underground water, and noise pollution from traffic and construction became problems. The increased urbanization of the country led to the destruction of fields, hills, and forests to build housing and infrastructure.

Thanks to the advancement of environmental protection technology and the strict enforcement of environmental protection laws, the situation is improving. For example, households are required to separate their burnable and nonburnable refuse in order to facilitate recycling. Taxis now run on propane instead of gasoline, leading to a decrease in auto emissions, and the government encourages the building of train and subway lines out into the suburbs so that residents are not dependent on their cars. People who visited Tokyo twenty years ago used to tell of air pollution so bad that it gave them sore throats, but pollution of that severity is rare in the 1990s.

勉 Study Grammar 39.

アクティビティー　6

ダイアログ：大切にするように言いましょう。(*I will tell him to make better use of it.*)

カワムラ：こんないい紙を捨てるんですか。

山口：そうね。もったいないわね。大助だわ。

カワムラ：この紙なんか、ほとんど何も書いてありませんよ。

山口：大助にもっと紙を大切にするように言いましょう。

アクティビティー　7

何と言いますか。(*What would you say?*)

What are you going to say to the following people? Answer in Japanese following the example.

[例]　ジュースの空き缶 (*empty can*) を捨てている人 →
空き缶をリサイクルするように言います。

1. いつも食べ物を残す人
2. どこへ行くのにも車を使う人
3. いつもハンバーガーばかり食べている人
4. いつも文句 (*complaint*) ばかり言っている人
5. ものぐさ (*lazy*) な人
6. 誰とも付き合わない人 (...と付き合う = *to associate with.* ...)
7. 好き嫌いの激しい (*having too strong likes and dislikes*) 人

KAWAMURA: Are you going to throw away such good paper?　YAMAGUCHI: You're right. What a waste. It's Daisuke [who is doing that].　KAWAMURA: This paper has almost nothing written on it. YAMAGUCHI: I'll have to tell Daisuke to make better use of paper.

Vocabulary: Animals, Birds, and Insects

動物	どうぶつ	animal
動物園	どうぶつえん	zoo
飼う	かう	to raise or keep an animal
かわいがる		to treat with affection, to make a pet of
餌	えさ	animal food, bait
犬	いぬ	dog
猫	ねこ	cat
猿	さる	monkey
狐	きつね	fox
兎	うさぎ	rabbit
鼠	ねずみ	mouse, rat
馬	うま	horse
牛	うし	cow, cattle
豚	ぶた	pig
羊	ひつじ	sheep
熊	くま	bear
象	ぞう	elephant
虎	とら	tiger
鹿	しか	deer
鯨	くじら	whale
鳥	とり	bird
翼	つばさ	wing
ニワトリ		chicken
あひる		duck
七面鳥	しちめんちょう	turkey
インコ		parakeet
鳩	はと	pigeon, dove
鶴	つる	crane
蛙	かえる	frog
蛇	へび	snake
虫	むし	insect
蜂	はち	wasp
蜜蜂	みつばち	bee
蚊	か	mosquito
蝿	はえ	housefly
ごきぶり		cockroach
蝉	せみ	cicada
蝶	ちょう	butterfly

The terms 七面鳥 and ニワトリ refer to live birds only. When cooked Western style, the meat is referred to as ターキー and チキン. When cooked Japanese or Chinese style, chicken meat is referred to simply as 鳥.

The Japanese regard the buzzing and humming of the cicadas as one of the most significant signs of summer.

Loanwords: ペット、ゴリラ、チンパンジー、オランウータン、スカンク、ペリカン、パンダ、ライオン、カナリア

<ruby>何<rt>なん</rt></ruby>ですか。(*What is it?*)

What animal or insect does each of the following statements describe?

1. アフリカやインドにいる<ruby>鼻<rt>はな</rt></ruby>の<ruby>長<rt>なが</rt></ruby>い<ruby>動物<rt>どうぶつ</rt></ruby>です。
2. サンクスギビングに<ruby>食<rt>た</rt></ruby>べる<ruby>鳥<rt>とり</rt></ruby>です。
3. この<ruby>虫<rt>むし</rt></ruby>にさされる (*be stung*) と、とてもかゆい (*itchy*) です。
4. <ruby>花<rt>はな</rt></ruby>の<ruby>蜜<rt>みつ</rt></ruby> (*honey, nectar*) を<ruby>集<rt>あつ</rt></ruby>める<ruby>虫<rt>むし</rt></ruby>です。
5. この<ruby>動物<rt>どうぶつ</rt></ruby>から<ruby>取<rt>と</rt></ruby>る<ruby>液体<rt>えきたい</rt></ruby> (*liquid*) を<ruby>飲<rt>の</rt></ruby>んだり、それでアイスクリームやヨーグルトを<ruby>作<rt>つく</rt></ruby>ります。
6. <ruby>一番<rt>いちばん</rt></ruby>大きい<ruby>哺乳動物<rt>ほにゅうどうぶつ</rt></ruby> (*mammal*) です。
7. <ruby>車<rt>くるま</rt></ruby>が<ruby>発明<rt>はつめい</rt></ruby> (*invent*) される<ruby>前<rt>まえ</rt></ruby>に、<ruby>人<rt>ひと</rt></ruby>はこの<ruby>動物<rt>どうぶつ</rt></ruby>に<ruby>乗<rt>の</rt></ruby>って<ruby>旅行<rt>りょこう</rt></ruby>しました。

Now make up several "guess what" questions about animals and try them out on your classmates.

どんな<ruby>動物<rt>どうぶつ</rt></ruby>が<ruby>好<rt>す</rt></ruby>きですか。(*What animal do you like?*)

Discuss in class.

1. どんな<ruby>動物<rt>どうぶつ</rt></ruby>が好きですか。<ruby>何<rt>なに</rt></ruby>か<ruby>動物<rt>どうぶつ</rt></ruby>を<ruby>飼<rt>か</rt></ruby>っていますか。
2. <ruby>猫<rt>ねこ</rt></ruby>と<ruby>犬<rt>いぬ</rt></ruby>とどちらが好きですか。どうしてですか。
3. <ruby>人間<rt>にんげん</rt></ruby> (*humans*) が<ruby>肉<rt>にく</rt></ruby>を<ruby>食<rt>た</rt></ruby>べる<ruby>動物<rt>どうぶつ</rt></ruby>にはどんなものがありますか。
4. <ruby>人間<rt>にんげん</rt></ruby>を食べたり<ruby>殺<rt>ころ</rt></ruby>したり (*kill*) する<ruby>動物<rt>どうぶつ</rt></ruby>には、どんなものがありますか。
5. <ruby>人間<rt>にんげん</rt></ruby>に<ruby>役<rt>やく</rt></ruby>に<ruby>立<rt>た</rt></ruby>つ (*useful*) <ruby>動物<rt>どうぶつ</rt></ruby>にはどんなものがありますか。
6. <ruby>動物園<rt>どうぶつえん</rt></ruby>で<ruby>人気<rt>にんき</rt></ruby>のある (*popular*) <ruby>動物<rt>どうぶつ</rt></ruby>は<ruby>何<rt>なん</rt></ruby>ですか。
7. <ruby>足<rt>あし</rt></ruby>の<ruby>速<rt>はや</rt></ruby>い<ruby>動物<rt>どうぶつ</rt></ruby>にはどんなものがありますか。<ruby>飛<rt>と</rt></ruby>ぶのが<ruby>速<rt>はや</rt></ruby>い<ruby>鳥<rt>とり</rt></ruby>にはどんなものがありますか。

<ruby>動物園<rt>どうぶつえん</rt></ruby> (*The zoo*)

A. You have been appointed director of your city's new zoo (<ruby>動物園長<rt>どうぶつえんちょう</rt></ruby>). The following is the layout of your zoo. You have purchased, borrowed from other zoos, or received the following animals as donations. You also have some money to buy more animals or birds of your choice. How will you assign these animals and the new animals to the cages and enclosures?

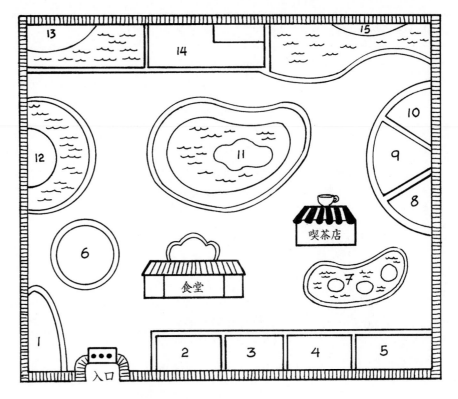

Animals: パンダ、カバ (*hippopotamus*)、チンパンジー、ライオン、キリン (*giraffe*)、ペリカン、イルカ (*dolphin*)、ワニ (*crocodile*)、狼 (*wolf*)、兎 (*rabbit*)、狐 (*fox*)

Try to satisfy at least the following conditions.

1. 池が必要な動物と鳥は、池のある檻 (*cage*) に入れる。
2. 動物園の入口の近くには、子供が好きな動物を入れる。
3. 動物園の入口には、子供が怖がる (*to be scared*) 動物は入れない。
4. 食堂や喫茶店のそばの檻には、静かな動物を入れる。
5. 全ての檻に動物を入れる。

After you decide what animal you would put in each enclosure, explain your plan, including the rationale behind it, and your purchase plan, to your classmates.

勉 Study Grammar 40.

B. Look at your classmate's plan and make comments.

1. 場所を変えたほうがいいのは、どの動物ですか。
2. 場所を変えなくてもいいのは、どの動物ですか。
3. 新しく買う動物について、意見 (*opinion*) はありますか。

植物	しょうぶつ	plant
草	くさ	grass
盆栽	ぼんさい	**bonsai** (*artificially dwarfed trees grown in containers*)
桜	さくら	cherry tree
梅	うめ	plum tree
菊	きく	chrysanthemum
咲く	さく	to bloom
生える	はえる	to grow, flourish (*plants and trees*)
枯れる	かれる	to wither, die (*plants and trees only*)
葉／葉っぱ	は／はっぱ	leaf
花粉	かふん	pollen
土	つち	soil
種	たね	seed
植える	うえる	to plant
松	まつ	pine tree
杉	すぎ	Japanese cedar

The importance of the cherry blossom in Japanese culture is well known, and the chrysanthemum and pine also play prominent roles in traditional symbolism.

Loanwords: カーネーション、ダリヤ、ブーケ、チューリップ
Review: 花、木、庭、花屋

アクティビティー 11

どんな花が好きですか。(*What kind of flower do you like?*)

1. どんな花が好きですか。
2. 母の日にはどんな花をあげますか。
3. ほかにどんなときに花をプレゼントしますか。あなたはよく花をプレゼントしますか。
4. 花粉アレルギーですか。
5. あなたの家に庭はありますか。どんな花や木がありますか。
6. 果実がなる木にはどんなものがありますか。
7. どんなくだものを食べますか。

Plants (2)

植木	うえき	potted plant
芝生	しばふ	lawn
花壇	かだん	flower bed
石庭	せきてい	rock garden
竹	たけ	bamboo

京都の石庭

勉 Study Grammar 41.

アクティビティー 12

ダイアログ：それで早く咲いた
わけですね。(*That's why they've bloomed early, isn't it?*)

山口：いやあ、きれいですね、あの桜は。

カワムラ：ええ。でも、桜の見ごろはまだじゃないんですか。

山口：ええ。でも、<u>今年は冬がとても暖かった</u>から...

カワムラ：ああ、それで<u>早く咲いた</u>わけですね。

Practice the above dialogue, substituting the following expressions for the underlined parts.

1. 今年は冬がとても寒かった
   こんなに遅い
2. 今年の春は暖かい
   もう満開 (*in full bloom*) な

YAMAGUCHI: Hey, aren't they pretty, those cherry blossoms?　KAWAMURA: Yes, but isn't the best time to see cherry blossoms later on? (*lit., Isn't it not yet?*)　YAMAGUCHI: Yes, but the winter <u>this year was very warm</u>. . . .　KAWAMURA: Oh, that's why they've <u>bloomed early</u>, isn't it?

Japanese Poetry

Japanese poems, including the earliest known examples, are structured very differently from those found in English or other European languages. They are organized according to syllable count, typically in lines of either five or seven syllables.

By the Heian period (796–1185), one form, the **waka** (和歌), with its 5-7-5-7-7 pattern of syllables, predominated. Composing **waka** was a favorite pastime of the aristocrats, and a necessary social skill learned in childhood. People included original poems in their diaries and personal letters and especially admired the ability to make up impromptu poems in response to the events of the moment.

The next development in Japanese poetry was the **renga** (連歌), or "linked verse," a popular pastime from the fourteenth century on. **Renga** were always composed by two or more people, who took turns writing alternating sets of 7-7 and 5-7-5 lines. Any two adjacent sets of lines had to amount to a coherent poem, so participants enjoyed giving one another difficult lines to add to.

In the seventeenth century, poets began to write 5-7-5 poems outside the context of **renga,** and this was the origin of the style of poetry known in the West as **haiku** (俳句). The object of a **haiku** is to capture the essence of a sight or a moment, all in seventeen syllables. The poem must refer to nature in some way, but mere description does not make a good **haiku.** The best **haiku** either point out a little-noticed but significant detail of the sight described or hint at its emotional or philosophical significance.

Haiku is still a living tradition in Japan, and foreign poets, including those from English-speaking countries, have experimented with the form as well.

Culture and Customs

Vocabulary: Culture and Customs

文化	ぶんか	culture
歴史	れきし	history
時代	じだい	era, period
社会	しゃかい	society
習慣	しゅうかん	habit
守る	まもる	to observe (*a custom*), to obey (*a rule*), to protect

みっともない		unseemly, improper, disreputable
おとなしい		proper, well-behaved, mild mannered
頑張る	がんばる	to do one's best, to hang in there, to come out of a difficult situation all right
我慢する	がまんする	to put up with an unpleasant situation without complaint
お辞儀をする	おじぎをする	to bow
正座(する)	せいざ(する)	sitting traditional style; (to sit traditional style) (*on one's heels and keeping one's back straight*)
宗教	しゅうきょう	religion
神	かみ	god, divine being
信じる	しんじる	to believe
仏教	ぶっきょう	Buddhism
仏像	ぶつぞう	Buddhist statue
菩薩	ぼさつ	bodhisattva (*a kind of Buddhist supernatural being, the most famous being Kannon, the goddess of mercy, and Jizoo, the guardian of dead children*)
神道	しんとう	Shintoism
鳥居	とりい	gate of a Shinto shrine
祭り	まつり	festival
御輿	みこし	portable shrine carried during festival processions
キリスト教	キリストきょう	Christianity
ユダヤ教	ユダヤきょう	Judaism
イスラム教／回教	イスラムきょう／かいきょう	Islam
儒教	じゅきょう	Confucianism
興味(がある)	きょうみ(がある)	interest; (to be interested)

Loanwords: タブー、マナー、エチケット

「ワッショイ、ワッショイ」
お祭りで御輿をかつい
でいます。

アクティビティー 13

ジェパディー (*Jeopardy*)

What questions would yield the following answers? Use words from the preceding vocabulary box.

1. 床の上にすわる時、この姿勢 (*position*) をとります。
2. 挨拶 (*greeting*) する時、これをします。
3. 大変なことがあってもあきらめない (*not give up*) こと。
4. 神社の前にある大きい物。
5. 面白いと思って、もっと知りたいという気持ち。
6. 寺の中、または寺の周りにある物。
7. ヨーロッパから入ってきた宗教。
8. エチケットを守る人はみんなにこう言われるでしょう。
9. 大変なことがあっても、文句 (*complaint*) を言わないこと。
10. 日本だけの宗教。

Now make up more questions on Japanese history and culture based on your personal knowledge, outside reading, or even the 文化ノート in this textbook. See if you can stump your classmates and instructor.

アクティビティー 14

習慣、慣例、エチケット (*Customs, formalities, etiquette*)

Discuss in class.

1. あなたの国 (文化) にあって、他の国 (文化) にない習慣にどんなものがありますか。
2. あなたの国 (文化) にはどんなタブーがありますか。
3. 食事をするときにはどんなエチケットを守る必要がありますか。日本ではどんなエチケットを守る必要があるか知っていますか。
4. 他人の家を訪ねる (*visit*) ときには、どんなエチケットを守らなければなりませんか。
5. 日本人はお正月には神社にお参りし、お葬式はお寺でします。結婚式をキリスト教の教会であげる人もたくさんいます。あなたの国にも、宗教に対してこういう態度 (*attitude toward*) を取る人はいますか。

Taboos

Every culture has its own ideas about which actions are socially acceptable and unacceptable. For example, the Japanese consider it rude to blow one's nose in public. Instead, people who have colds or allergies just sniff, sometimes very loudly, until they can get away and blow their noses in private.

There are two taboos connected with chopsticks, both of which derive from Japanese funeral customs. One is that you must never stick your chopsticks upright in your rice bowl but always lay them on the 箸置き (はしおき) or on the edge of the bowl. Another is that you must never pass food from one set of chopsticks to another.

The idea behind the well-known rule about taking your shoes off before entering a house or temple is that you should not bring the dirt of the outside world into the building, so Japanese people do not go barefoot outside, even in the hottest weather. After all, if you have been walking outside barefoot, you have nothing to take off when you go into the house!

In connection with this rule, be careful how you dress in hot weather. Both men and women should wear at least a tank top and loosely cut shorts in public on casual occasions, no matter how hot and humid the weather gets. Keep in mind that what seems like a casual occasion to a North American may be a formal or semiformal occasion by Japanese standards, so if in doubt, ask.

When you take a Japanese-style bath, never bring soap into the tub, because that ruins the bath for everyone else, and your hosts will have to refill and reheat the entire tub. Always wash and rinse yourself completely before getting into the tub to soak, and never let your hair or your washcloth touch the water.

Many North Americans like to be thought of as friendly, and once they have learned how to speak in the plain form, they want to use it with everyone because they think it sounds friendlier. This is inappropriate, because using plain form says either "we are intimates" or "you rank below me," and if neither is the case, the use of the plain form is offensive. When people rank above you, you cannot use the plain form to them, no matter how much you like them or how long you have known them.

There are other taboos, but these are the ones that foreign visitors are most likely to violate. If you are about to face an unfamiliar formal situation, such as a wedding or a funeral, ask someone about the expected etiquette ahead of time. When potentially tricky situations come up unexpectedly, do what the people around you do, especially if there is someone of your age and sex to imitate.

If you respect these and other cultural differences, your stay in Japan will go much more smoothly and you will not offend people accidentally.

勉 Study Grammar 42.

アクティビティー 15

ダイアログ：あんなにいやだって言っていたのに (*Even though you said that you didn't want to . . .*)

山口：どうしたんですか。鏡に向かって。

カワムラ：林さんとギブソンさんの結婚式のスピーチの練習をしているんです。

山口：あれ、<u>あんなにいやだって言っていた</u>のに、スピーチするんですか。

カワムラ：ええ、二人とも親友ですから。

Practice the dialogue again, replacing the the underlined part with the following expressions.

人前で話すのは嫌いだといつも言っている

人前で話すのは苦手な

アクティビティー 16

なぜですか。(*Why is it?*)

Why do you think the following happened? Discuss in class.

1. 私は日本に住んでいるアメリカ人です。先日、友人の家に夕食に招かれました。(*was invited*) とてもおいしいとほめた (*praised*) のに、友人は「まずいものばかりですみません」と言いました。日本人は不思議 (*weird*) ですね。

2. 私は日本の会社に勤めているアメリカ人です。私の同僚はいつも「肩が痛い」とか「腰が痛い」とか言っています。それなのに、誰も会社を休みません。そんなに体の調子が悪いのなら、会社を休めばいいのに、と私は思うんですが...

3. 日本に住んでいるカナダ人です。先日日本人の友人の家に招かれました。夕食の後、友人の家族に「年はいくつか」とか「ボーイフレンドはいるか」とか

YAMAGUCHI: What are you doing facing the mirror?　KAWAMURA: I'm practicing the speech for Gibson and Hayashi's wedding.　YAMAGUCHI: What? Even though <u>you said that you didn't want to</u> (*lit., That it was that distasteful*), you're giving a speech?　KAWAMURA: Yes, because they're both my friends.

いろいろプライベートなことを聞かれました。そんなこと聞かなくてもいいのに、と思いました。

4. 私は先月から日本の大学に留学しています。講義 (lectures) の時間は先生だけが話して、学生は全然質問しません。アメリカの大学では授業でいろいろなディスカッションがあるのに、日本の大学ってつまらないですね。

5. 私は日本の会社にコンピュータを売る交渉 (negotiations) をしています。相手の会社の課長さんは、私の会社のコンピュータはとてもいいから、部長さんと話してみると言いました。昨日、電話すると、まだ部長さんと話していないと言われました。私は売れる可能性 (possibility) はまだあると思うのですが、日本人の友人は交渉はダメだったと言います。どうしてわかるんですか。

Grammar and Exercises

38. Expressing a Speaker's Emotional Involvement: ...ものだ

カワムラ：このへんは家が多いですね。
山口：10年前はこのへんは野原だったんですがね。
カワムラ：本当ですか。
山口：ええ、子供の頃はここでよく虫を取ったものですよ。

ブラウン：あら、佐野さん、かわいいお子さんですね。
佐野：長女の子供なんですよ。
ブラウン：こんにちは。
子供：...
佐野：人に会ったら、きちんと御挨拶するものですよ。

KAWAMURA: There are a lot of houses around here.　YAMAGUCHI: Ten years ago, this area was an open field, but ...　KAWAMURA: Really?　YAMAGUCHI: Yes, when I was a child, I used to catch insects around here.

BROWN: Oh, Ms. Sano, that's a cute child.　SANO: It's my oldest daughter's child.　BROWN: Hello.
CHILD: ...　SANO: When you meet people, you're supposed to greet them properly.

林：三村、ハワイに行っていたんだって？

三村：ああ、サーフィンしてきたんだ。

林：僕もハワイでサーフィンしてみたいもんだなあ。

三村：あれえ、林、サーフィン、できたの。

山口：さとみ、今日は学校へ行かないの。

さとみ：ええ、だって、授業がないんだもの1

山口：じゃあ、庭の掃除、手伝ってくれる？

さとみ：ダメよ。今、本を読んでいるんだもの。

山口：よく、そんなことが言えたものね。漫画を読んでいるんじゃない？

38.1 The following construction is used to express a speaker's strong emotional involvement with an event. Depending on the exact circumstances, it can have any one of a number of English translations.

Verb	Plain form	
I-adjective	Plain form (dictionary form/ta-form)	ものだ (ものです)
Na-adjective	Dictionary form + だ or だった	
Noun	Noun + な/だった	

should . . . , used to . . . , because . . .

As mentioned in the note on p. 402, the original meaning of もの is *tangible* or *visible thing*. When used as a sentence ending, もの expresses an event or a situation as if it were a tangible thing or a vivid experience. Depending on context, it expresses different types of emotions, including desire, reminiscence, excuse, admonition, command, conviction, or exclamation.

HAYASHI: Mimura, I hear you've been to Hawaii and back.   MIMURA: Yes, I went there and did some surfing (*lit., I surfed and came back*).   HAYASHI: I sure would like to try surfing in Hawaii.   MIMURA: Wow, Hayashi, can you surf? (*lit., Is it that you are able to surf?*)

YAMAGUCHI: Satomi, aren't you going to school today?   SATOMI: Yeah, because there's no class, you see.
YAMAGUCHI: Well, will you help me clean up the yard?   SATOMI: Uh-uh. (*Lit., No good.*) Because I'm reading a book now.   YAMAGUCHI: You have a lot of nerve saying that. (*Lit., You're someone who could say that well.*) Aren't you reading a comic book?

38.2 The plain past form of the verb + ものだ is used when the speaker is reminiscing about the way things used to be.

子供の頃、あそこでよく遊んだものです。
When I was a child, I used to play there a lot.
学生の時、毎日のようにパチンコをやったものです。
When I was a student, I used to play pachinko almost every day.

38.3 At other times, もの seems to add nothing more that emotional intensity to the statement.

私もその山に登ってみたいものだ。
I also want to try climbing that mountain!

38.4 This construction is also used in making generalizations, particularly when the speaker is expressing a strong impression.

友達はいいものだ。
A friend is a good thing [to have].
困った時には、誰かがきっと助けてくれるものだ。
When you're in a tight spot, someone will certainly help you out.

38.5 ものだ is also used to express what one must do or should do. The negative form, ものではない, expresses what one should not do.

大人だったら、そんなことを言うものではない。
If you are an adult, you shouldn't say such things.

In more formal speech or writing, もの can be replaced with べき. The formal negative of べきだ is べからず, which is sometimes seen on signs.

教育制度 (*educational system*) を改革 (*reform*) するべきだ。
We ought to reform the educational system.
飲むべからず。 (sign on an outdoor water faucet in a park)
Do not drink.

38.6 At times, ものだ functions like から *because*. The difference is that ものだ is used when the speaker is making an excuse or trying to justify an action or an opinion. ものだ and から are sometimes used together.

子供が病気なもので、早く帰らせてください。
Because my child is sick, please let me go home early.
明日は早いものですから、今日はこれで失礼します。
I have an early morning tomorrow, so I'll take my leave for today.

38.7 The construction ものか is a protest against undesirable conditions or against what the speaker feels to be unreasonable expectations. It is not a very polite way to express one's displeasure, so it should be used with caution. It can carry the meaning of the English expression *Do you expect me to . . . ?*

そんな馬鹿なことがあってたまる (*put up with*) ものか。
Do you expect me to put up with that kind of nonsense?
あんな卑怯な男と話すものか。
Do you expect me to talk with that mean and sneaky man?

38.8 In colloquial speech, もの is often contracted to もん.

昔は10円でいろんなものが買えたもんだ。
In the old days, you used to be able to buy a lot of things with ten yen.

言語ノート

こと and もの

こと as a noun means *phenomenon, concept, act, matter, incident*—in other words, it is often translated as the English word *thing*, but it always refers to something intangible and abstract, particularly if it is general or unspecified. For this reason, こと is often called a pseudo-noun.

そのことがあってから、三村さんは私と口をきいてくれません。
Since that incident occurred, Mr. Mimura won't speak to me.
町田さんが面白いことを言っていましたよ。
Mr. Machida said an interesting thing.
木村先生のことを思い出しました。
I recalled [*things about*] *Professor Kimura.*

In contrast, もの refers to a concrete thing or person, not an idea or action. The following sentences illustrate the difference.

それは面白いことだ。
それは面白いものだ。

Both sentences can be translated into English as *That's an interesting thing,* but the first one refers to an event, a situation, a piece of news, a subject of discussion, or something else intangible. The second sentence refers to a piece of artwork, a book, a new gadget, an exotic plant, or anything else that a person can see and touch.

Complete the following dialogues, choosing an appropriate answer from the list.

1. —もう遅いですし、彼は来ない
　　かもしれませんよ。
　　帰りましょうか。

2. —山本さん、今夜どこかへ
　　行きませんか。

3. —三村さんが新しい車を買った
　　そうですよ。

4. —カーティスさんのスピーチ、
　　素晴らしかったですね。

5. —子供のころはどんなことを
　　しましたか。

6. —あんな人、もう大嫌いです。

a. 本当ですか。早く見てみたい
　　ものですね。

b. 彼に会わないで帰るもの
　　ですか。

c. そんなこと言うものでは
　　ありません。

d. 明日の朝早く北海道に発つ
　　もので、ちょっと…

e. アメリカ人で、よくあれだけ
　　日本語を話せるものですね。

f. よく海や川で泳いだものです。

Complete the following dialogues by using …ものだ.

[例]　—どうして遅れたんですか。
　　　—目覚し時計が鳴らなかったものですから。

1. —あの海岸へ行ったことがありますか。
_____

2. —あんな馬鹿なことをしてすみません。
_____

3. —ブラウンさん、日本語がすっかり上手になりましたね。
_____

4. —あの家、大きくていいですね。
_____

5. —あの人、プレゼントをもらっても何も言いませんね。
_____

Both . . . and

English speakers sometimes have trouble with the concepts of *also* or *both . . . and* in Japanese, because English grammar allows the speaker to place these elements freely in the sentence. However, Japanese handles the concept of *is also* or *is both . . . and* by splitting だ/です into its original components of で and ある/あります and putting a も in between. Adjectives go into their く form followed by もある/あります。

「朝日」はビールの名前ですか。

ええ、それに新聞の名前でもありますよ。(grammatical)

*ええ、新聞の名前もです。(ungrammatical)

—*Is Asahi the name of a beer?*

—*Yes, it's also the name of a newspaper.*

39. Various Uses of よう

<table>
<tr>
<td>

おつまみ are small portions of things like **yakitori**, salads, peanuts, tofu with shaved ginger and soy sauce, dried cuttlefish, eggplant roasted with miso sauce, and similar snacks served along with alcoholic beverages. They have to be ordered individually.

</td>
<td>

町田：おつまみがもっといるわね。

ブラウン：さっきウェーターにもっと持ってくるように頼んだわ。

町田：あらあら、林さん、あんまり食べていないわね。

ブラウン：もっと食べるようにすすめたら。

山口：大助、急ぎなさい。遅れますよ。

大助：寝坊しないように目覚まし時計をセットしたのになあ。

山口：富田さんの家はどこか知っているの？

大助：うん。迷わないように地図で調べておいたよ。

</td>
</tr>
</table>

MACHIDA: We need more snack foods, don't we? BROWN: I just told the waiter to bring some more.
MACHIDA: Oh, look, Mr. Hayashi hasn't eaten very much, has he? BROWN: How about suggesting that he eat more?

YAMAGUCHI: Daisuke, hurry up. We'll be late. DAISUKE: And here I set the alarm clock so as not to oversleep! YAMAGUCHI: Do you know where Mr. Tomita's house is? DAISUKE: Yeah. I checked the map ahead of time, so not to get lost.

39.1 In the following construction, …ように is used to report the content of a request, a suggestion, or advice.

Clause ending in the plain, nonpast form of a verb	ように	Verbs expressing a command, request, suggestion, advice, etc.

to tell/ask/suggest that someone do …

カワムラさんにすぐ横井先生とお話しするように言ってください。
Please tell Mr. Kawamura to talk with Professor Yokoi soon.
三村さんに図書館の前で待つように言われた。
I was told by Mr. Mimura to wait in front of the library.
部屋の中でタバコを吸わないように、あの人たちに頼みましょう。
Let's ask those people not to smoke in the room.
カーティスさんに、あまり仕事をし過ぎないように忠告した方がいいですよ。
It would be best to warn Mr. Curtis not to overwork.

に after 三村さん in the second example is the marker of an agent in a passive sentence.

As seen in the above examples, the person to whom a command or request is given is marked by the indirect object marker に.

This construction is called an indirect command, and it is a paraphrase of a direct quotation of a command. For example, instead of saying

カワムラさんに、すぐ横井先生にお話しするように言ってください。
Please tell Mr. Kawamura to talk with Professor Yokoi soon.

you could tell the person the exact words to say:

カワムラさんに「すぐ横井先生にお話してください」と言ってください。
Please say to Mr. Kawamura, "Talk to Professor Yokoi soon."

Unless you really care about the exact words the person uses to convey your message, the indirect command form is more natural.

39.2 In the following construction, …ように is used to express a purpose or the manner in which something is to be done.

The plain, nonpast potential form of a verb/ the plain, nonpast form of a potential verb	ように	Clause
The plain, nonpast, negative form of a verb		

… so that …, … in such a way that …

日本語が上達するように、毎日練習している。
I'm practicing so that I can improve my Japanese.
子供でも使うことができるように、操作が簡単になっている。
The handling of it has become so simple that even a child can use it.
みんなに聞こえるように、マイクを使って話した。
I spoke using a microphone so that everyone could hear.

Note that a purpose is also expressed by …ために (Chapter 2, **Grammar 10**). The difference between …ように and …ために is that the latter expresses a far stronger sense of purpose than the former. Using …ために indicates that the speaker believes that the action or situation described in the first clause will take place for sure.

会議に出るために、大阪へ行った。
*会議に出るように、大阪へ行った。(ungrammatical)

In this example, the principal objective of the speaker's going to Osaka was to attend the conference, so only …ために is grammatical.

風邪を引かないように、コートを着た。
*風邪を引かないために、コートを着た。(ungrammatical)

By wearing a coat, the speaker might somehow avoid catching a cold, but that is by no means a foolproof method of preventing illness, and the speaker might catch a cold anyway. In this case, then, …ように is more appropriate.

練習　　　　　　　　1

Fill in the blanks with the appropriate word from the list. Each word will be used once.

1. ＿＿＿＿に薬を飲むように言われました。
2. ＿＿＿＿にスピード違反しないように注意されました。
3. ＿＿＿＿が学生にもっと勉強するように言った。
4. ＿＿＿＿に切符を見せるように言われた。
5. ＿＿＿＿にノートを貸してくれるように頼まれました。
6. ＿＿＿＿にメニューを持ってくるように頼んだ。
7. ＿＿＿＿は部下に明日早く会社に来るように命じた (gave an order)
8. ＿＿＿＿は口をもっと大きく開けるように言った。

a. ウエイター
b. 先生
c. おまわりさん
d. 駅員
e. お医者さん
f. 部長
g. 歯医者さん
h. クラスメート

Fill in each blank with the most appropriate phrase from the list, first changing it from the direct quotation to the indirect quotation form.

[例] 町田さんに ＿＿＿＿ 言われたが、中を見てしまった。
　　 h. 箱の中に何が入っているか見ないように

1. 母に ＿＿＿＿ 頼まれたのを、忘れてしまいました。
2. アメリカ人の友人に ＿＿＿＿ 頼みました。
3. となりの部屋の人に ＿＿＿＿ 言われたので、テレビの音を小さくした。
4. お医者さんが ＿＿＿＿ おっしゃったので、コーヒーに砂糖を入れないようにしている。
5. スチュワーデスが ＿＿＿＿ 言うと、乗客みんなそうした。
6. タクシーの運転手は ＿＿＿＿ 言われると、すぐ高速道路に入った。
7. 後ろの人に ＿＿＿＿ 言われたので、そうした。

a. シートベルトをお締めください。
b. 静かにしてください。
c. 英語の宿題、手伝ってくれないかなあ。
d. もう少し急いでくれませんか。
e. あまり甘いものは食べない方がいいですよ。
f. 学校の帰りにレタスを買ってきてね。
g. 座ってくれませんか。
h. 箱の中に何が入っているか見ないでくださいね。

Connect each item in A with the most appropriate sentence ending in B.

A

1. 遅れないように
2. 祖母でも読めるように
3. 部屋の中に日が入らないように
4. はっきり聞こえるように
5. 誰も入ってこないように
6. ぐっすり (soundly) 眠れるように
7. 彼に知られないように
8. 誰も気付かないように

B

a. 大きな声で話してください。
b. 大きな字で手紙を書いた。
c. ドアの鍵をかけた。
d. 黙って (not talk) いてください。
e. 窓から外に出た。
f. 早くうちを出た。
g. ホット・ミルクを飲みなさい。
h. カーテンを閉めてください。

Choose the most appropriate verb for each sentence from the list. In some cases, you will have to use the negative form.

1. 猫が外に（　　　）ように、ドアを閉めた。

2. （　　　）ように、シチューを冷蔵庫に入れました。

3. 他人の心 (heart, feelings) を（　　　）ように、言葉には気をつけなさい。

4. 誰にも（　　　）ように、静かに教室の中に入った。

5. 8時までに仕事が（　　　）ように、一生懸命 (with all my might) 働いた。

6. 病気が早く（　　　）ように、うちでゆっくり寝ていた。

7. 誰もそれに（　　　）ように、紙を貼って (affix) おきましょう。

8. 帽子が風で（　　　）ように、手でおさえた (hold down)。

a. 傷つける (to hurt feelings)

b. 腐る (to be spoiled)

c 治る

d. 飛ぶ

e. 終わる

f. 出る

g. 触る (touch)

h. 気付かれる (be noticed)

Complete these sentences with something that makes sense.

1. 頭痛が早く治るように、＿＿＿＿＿＿＿＿＿＿＿＿＿＿＿＿＿＿＿＿＿＿。

2. 両親が喜ぶように、＿＿＿＿＿＿＿＿＿＿＿＿＿＿＿＿＿＿＿＿＿＿＿＿。

3. 日本語が上手に書けるように、＿＿＿＿＿＿＿＿＿＿＿＿＿＿＿＿＿＿＿。

4. ストレスがたまらない (not accumulate) ように ＿＿＿＿＿＿＿＿＿＿＿＿＿＿。

5. 早く新しい車が買えるように、＿＿＿＿＿＿＿＿＿＿＿＿＿＿＿＿＿＿＿＿。

40. It's All Right Not to... : ～なくてもいい

On trash collection days, people bring their refuse to designated ゴミ捨て場, found every block or so in residential neighborhoods.

The チリ紙交換 goes around neighborhoods in a loudspeaker truck collecting newspapers and magazines for recycling. People who hand over paper to be recycled receive tissues or toilet paper in return.

カワムラ：古い新聞がたまりましたね。ゴミ捨て場に出してきましょうか。

山口：ああ、その新聞は出さなくてもいいのよ。

カワムラ：どうしてですか。

山口：チリ紙交換に出すのよ。

大助：ああ、こんな雨の日に映画を見に、わざわざ銀座まで行くなんて…

さとみ：行きたくなければ、無理に行かなくてもいいのよ。

大助：そうか。じゃあ、行くのはよすか。

さとみ：でも、加代子さんも来るのよ。

大助：それをなぜ早く言わないんだ。さあ、仕度しないと遅れるぞ。

高田：部長、この書類、中島さんにお送りした方がいいでしょうか。

部長：何の書類？

高田：シンガポールのプロジェクトのレポートです。

部長：中島さんはプロジェクトに関係 (connection) していないから、お送りすることはないだろう。

The concept *it is all right not to do, one does not have to do* can be expressed with the following construction.

Verb I-adjective Na-adjective/noun	negative stem + Root + く dictionary form/ noun + で (は)	なくて (も) いい

does not have to . . . , it is all right not to . . . , it is not necessary to . . . ,
even if . . .

KAWAMURA: The old newspapers have accumulated, haven't they? Should I go put them out at the collection site (*lit., put them out and come back*)?   YAMAGUCHI: Oh, it's all right not to put them out.
KAWAMURA: Why is that?   YAMAGUCHI: We're going to put them out for the paper recycler.

DAISUKE: Oh, the idea of going all the way to the Ginza to see a movie on a rainy day like this!   SATOMI: If you don't want to go, you don't have to force yourself.   DAISUKE: Really? Well, should we give up [the idea of] going?   SATOMI: But Kayoko is coming, too.   DAISUKE: Why didn't you say so earlier? Come on, if we don't get ready, we'll be late.

TAKADA: Department Head, it would probably be best to send these documents to Mr. Nakajima.
DEPARTMENT HEAD: What documents?   TAKADA: The report about the Singapore project.   DEPARTMENT
HEAD: Mr. Nakajima has no connection with that project, so there's no need to send them to him.

おなかがいっぱいなら、無理して食べなくてもいいです。

If you're full, you don't have to force yourself to eat.

大きくなくてもいいから、会社の近くに家を借りたい。

I want to rent a house near my job even if it's not large. (lit., Because it's all right if it's not large, I want to rent a house near the company.)

それほどハンサムでなくてもいいから、優しい男に人と結婚したい。

I want to marry a kind man, even if he's not particularly handsome. (lit., Because it's all right if he's not particularly handsome, I want to marry a kind man.)

Remember that 〜なくてはいけない/ならない (cf. Chapter 1, **Grammar 6**) means *must* or *have to.* A meaning similar to that of 〜なくてもいい can be expressed by the following constructions.

Verb, i-adjective	The nonpast, plain form	必要はない
Na-adjective, noun	Root/noun + である	(必要はありません)

It is not necessary to . . . , There is no need to . . .

風邪はもう治りましたから、薬を飲む必要はありません。

Because I have recovered from my cold, there's no need to take medicine.

どんなにうるさくても眠れますから、周りが静かである必要はない。

I can fall asleep no matter how noisy it is, so it's not necessary for my surroundings to be quiet.

This construction sounds more formal than ...なくてもいい。

Note that ...必要がある means *it is necessary to . . . .*

我々は省エネに協力する必要がある。

It is necessary for us to cooperate in saving energy.

Another construction that expresses lack of necessity is the nonpast, plain form of the verb + ことはない (ことはありません).

そんな悪い男の言うことなんか聞くことはありません。

You don't have to listen to what a terrible man like that says.

あんな小さい犬なんて怖がることはないよ。

There's no need to be afraid of a little dog like that.

The literal meaning of both なんか and なんて is *and so on* or *and things like that,* but they can sometimes be used to express a vague contempt.

練習　1

Connect each item in A with the most appropriate sentence ending in B.

A	B
1. お金はお母さんからいただきましたから、	a. 手紙は出さなくてもいいよ。
2. 今日はすることが全然ないから、	b. 買い物に行かなくてもいい。
3. コーヒーはブラックが好きだから、	c. 払わなくても結構です。
4. 高田さんとはもう話したから、	d. 熱くなくてもいいです。
5. 食べる物はたくさんあるから、	e. 家はそんなに広くなくてもいい。
6. 誰も怒っていないんだから、	f. 砂糖は入れなくてもいいよ。
7. 本を読んでいるんじゃないから、	g. ペンでなくてもいいです。
8. 夫婦二人だけだから、	h. 電気はそんなに明るくなくてもいい。
9. 鉛筆しかないなら、	i. 泣かなくてもいい。
10. お茶であれば、	j. 来なくてもいい。

練習　2

Try to imagine who might have said the following sentences to whom. Be creative.

1. もう明日から会社に出て来なくてもいいわよ。
2. そんなに大きな声で話さなくてもいいですよ。
3. ドルでなくてもいいですよ。日本の円でも大丈夫です。
4. そんなことを言うなら、食べなくてもいい。
5. もう我慢 (patience, putting up with something) しなくてもいいです。よかったですね。

41. Coming to a Conclusion: ...わけだ

三村：林さん、最近ウキウキしているみたいだけど、どうしたんですか。
町田：あれ、知らなかったの？林さんとギブソンさん、結婚するんですよ。
三村：そんなわけだったんですか。
町田：ええ、ギブソンさんがようやく「イエス」と言ってくれたから、ウキウキしているわけですよ。
ブラウン：高田さん、見ませんでしたか。
佐野：高田さんなら、朝早く会社に出て行きましたよ。ニューヨークへ行くのが一ヶ月も早くなったんですよ。
ブラウン：ああ、それで昨日の夜も、引っ越しの準備をしていたわけですね。
佐野：大変ですね、エリート社員は。

41.1 The noun わけ means *reason, circumstance,* or *meaning* as shown in the following examples.

なぜ怒っているんですか。わけを聞かせてください。
Why are you angry? Please tell me the reason.

わけも分からずに、余計なことは言わないでください。
Don't say more than you have to (lit., Don't say excessive things) without understanding the circumstances.

わけの分からないことを言うのはやめてください。
Stop saying things that don't make any sense.

わけが分からない is an expression meaning *nonsensical.*

41.2 The following construction is used to express the speaker's judgment that a certain circumstance took place as a natural consequence of something. The fact or information that the speaker used to make that judgment is explicitly expressed (in S1 below). The information that allows the speaker to make the conclusion can be either auditory or visual. Sometimes the exact nuance is impossible to translate into English and corresponds to the tone of voice that English speakers use when they have just realized something.

MIMURA: Mr. Hayashi seems to be in a very cheerful mood lately. What's going on?   MACHIDA: Oh, didn't you know? Mr. Hayashi and Ms. Gibson are going to get married.   MIMURA: Is that what it was? MACHIDA: Yes, Ms. Gibson finally said yes, so that's why he's in such a cheerful mood.

BROWN: Haven't you seen Mr. Takada?   SANO: If it's Mr. Takada [you're wondering about], he went to work early this morning. His going to New York was moved up a month (*lit., became as much as a month earlier*).   BROWN: Oh, that's why he was making preparations for moving last night.   SANO: It's tough being an employee of a top company.

S1,	S2	
	Plain form of verb and i-adjectives	わけだ (わけです)
	Root of na-adjective + な/だった	
	Noun + という/だった	

It's that . . . , The fact is that . . . , You could say that . . . , So that's why . . .

ストライキだから、電車が走っていないわけですね。
There's a strike, so that's way the trains aren't running, isn't it?

試験があったんですか。それで、徹夜したわけですか。
You had a test? Is that why you pulled an all-nighter?

私に頼みたいことがあって、あんなに親切だったわけですね。
It's because he had something that he wanted to request of me that he was so nice.

家計は母が全てやりくりしています。母は我が家の大蔵大臣というわけです。
As far as household accounts are concerned, my mother manages everything. You could say that Mother is our finance minister.

41.3 わけで, the te-form of わけだ, is used in conjunction with demonstrative pronouns to form introductory phrases similar in meaning to the English *for this reason, for that reason.*

途中で交通事故がありまして、そんなわけで遅れました。
On the way there was a traffic accident, and for that reason I was late.

子供が病気なんです。そういうわけで、今日は行けません。
My child is sick. For that reason, I can't go today.

~ありまして is the super-polite form of あって. People often use these sorts of super-polite forms when speaking to their superiors.

Ending a sentence with the plain form of the predicate + というわけだ is another way of stating a consequence or explaining a situation. It is very similar to the …のだ construction.

秘密にしてくれと言われたので、誰にも言わなかったというわけです。
Because I was told to keep it a secret, I didn't tell anyone.

まだ、誰も知らないというわけだ。
The fact is that no one knows yet.

41.4 わけではない is used in negative sentences to focus the negation, particularly when it is necessary to negate someone else's partially correct supposition. For example, suppose that an acquaintance notices that you no longer take your morning run. The acquaintance says something indicating an assumption that you've given up running because you don't like it. In fact, you like running very much, but your doctor has told you to give it up in favor of low-impact activities. In such a situation you might be tempted to say

*嫌いだからやめませんでした。

However, this means something like *Because I hate it, I didn't quit*, which sounds strange. What you should say in this situation is

嫌いだからやめたわけではありません。
It isn't the case that I quit because I hate it.

Here are more examples.

三村さんの責任だと言っているわけではありません。
I'm not saying that it's Mr. Mimura's responsibility.

言いわけをするわけではありませんが、お金が足りなかったのです。
It's not that I'm making excuses, but I didn't have enough money.

41.5 The nonpast, plain form of verb + わけに (は) いかない means *it won't do to . . . , one ought not to . . . , it wouldn't be right to. . . .*

あなたからこんな大金をもらうわけにはいかない。
It wouldn't be right for me to receive this large amount of money from you.

町田さんに全部払わすわけにはいかなかった。
It wasn't right to make Ms. Machida pay for the whole thing.

練習　　1

Connect each item in A with the most appropriate sentence ending in B.

A	B
1. 泳ぐのが好きだから、	a. コックになったわけです。
2. お酒が飲めないので、	b. そんなにやせているわけですね。
3. ワープロが使えないので、	c. 日に焼けた (got sunburned) わけですね。
4. 料理が好きだったから、	d. 毎日、プールへ行くわけですね。
5. 家を買うために、	e. 黒板に大きな字で書いているわけですね。
6. 目が悪い人がいるから、	f. お金を貯めているわけだ。
7. 外でずっと働いていたので、	g. 何でも手書き (handwritten) なわけです。
8. あまり食べないから、	h. パーティーに出るのがおっくう (tiresome) なわけです。

Complete these sentences by using ...わけだ.

[例] 料理をするのが嫌いだから、_____。→
料理をするのが嫌いだから、いつもレストランで食事するわけですね。

1. 日本語が上手になるように、
2. 宿題がむずかしいから、
3. 日本の文化に興味 (interest) があるので、
4. 今年は長い休みが取れたから、
5. まだ学生だから、
6. 貝に対して (toward) アレルギーがあるから、

42. Even Though: ...のに

ブラウン：村山さん、お出かけですか。

村山：ええ、ちょっと会社へ。

ブラウン：今日は日曜日なのに、お仕事ですか。

村山：ええ、うちの会社は今が一番忙しい時期なんです。

さとみ：お母さん、一万円、貸してくれる？

山口：この間、おこづかいをあげたばかりなのに、また？

さとみ：新しい服を買ったりして、全部使っちゃったのよ。

山口：あんなにおこづかい、無駄使いしちゃだめだって言ったのに...

さとみ：もう無駄使いしないから、お願い！

ギブソン：井戸の水はおいしいわね。

町田：ええ、こんな水が東京でも飲めたらいいのに。

ギブソン：ええ、そうね。

BROWN: Mr. Murayama, are you going out?   MURAYAMA: Yes, to the company for a little while.
BROWN: Even though today is Sunday, you're going to work?   MURAYAMA: Yes, for our company, now is the busiest time.

SATOMI: Mom, will you lend me 10,000 yen?   YAMAGUCHI: Again? Even though I just gave you your allowance recently?   SATOMI: I used up my allowance buying new clothes and stuff.   YAMAGUCHI: Even though I told you that it's no good to waste your allowance like that?   SATOMI: I'm not going to waste it anymore, so please!

GIBSON: Well water is delicious, isn't it?   MACHIDA: Yes, it would be good if we could drink this kind of water in Tokyo.   GIBSON: Yes, that's for sure.

山口：あらあら、カワムラさん、ビッショリ濡れてしまって。

カワムラ：ええ、駅を出てしばらくしたら、雨が降ってきちゃって。

山口：傘を持っていけばよかったのに。

カワムラ：あんなによく晴れていたので、傘はいらないと思ったんですが。

42.1 のに, which combines the nominalizer の and the particle に, expresses meanings such as *inspite of the fact that, contrary to the fact that, even though,* and *although.* The form is constructed as follows.

	S1		
Verbs	Plain form		
I-adjectives	Plain form	のに	S2
Na-adjectives	Dictionary form + な Dictionary form + だった		
Nouns	Noun + な Noun + だった		

Even though S₁, in spite of the fact that S₁, although S₁, contrary to the expectation that S₁

In this construction, the speaker is expressing disbelief, regret, sorrow, surprise, protest, reproach, sarcasm, or frustration that the situation is not turning out or has not turned out as expected.

まもなくお客さんがいらっしゃるのに、まだそんな格好をしているんですか。

Even though the guests are coming any minute, you're still dressed like that?

彼にプレゼントをあげたのに、お礼の手紙も電話もない。

In spite of the fact that I gave him a present, he neither [sends] me a thank-you letter nor phones me.

あんなにむずかしい試験だったのに、全員が満点を取った。

Even though it was such a difficult test, everyone got a perfect score.

YAMAGUCHI: My, my, Mr. Kawamura, you're soaking wet!   KAWAMURA: Yes, just a little bit after I left the station, it started raining.   YAMAGUCHI: You should have taken an umbrella.   KAWAMURA: Since [the sky] was really clear, I thought I didn't (*lit., don't*) need an umbrella.

In conversations, S2 is not often expressed when it is understandable from the context.

> A: カワムラさん、うちにいなかったよ。
> *Mr. Kawamura wasn't at home.*
> B: せっかく行ったのに？
> *Even though you went to all the trouble of going there?*

Also のに can be added to a sentence to express resentment or disappointment when a promise is broken or one's expectations are otherwise unmet. In these cases, the English equivalent does not necessarily express the idea of *even though*. In fact, the English equivalent is most often an exclamation beginning with *but*.

> あれほど遊園地に連れて行ってくれるって言っていたのに。
> *But he kept saying that he would take us to the amusement park!*
> こんなことになるとは思っていなかったのに。
> *But I never thought it would come to this!*

Because of the nature of the speaker's involvement discussed above, S2 cannot be a wish, command, request, offer, statement of permission, or statement of intention. In such cases, けれど（も）is used instead of のに。

> ちょっと寒いけれど/*のに、外に出ましょう。
> *It's a bit cold, but let's go outside.*
> つまらないものだけれど/*なのに、持っていってください。
> *It's an insignificant thing, but please take it.*
> 遠いけれど/*のに、明日そこに行ってみるつもりです。
> *It's far, but I intend to try going there tomorrow.*

42.2 のに is used in contrary-to-fact conditionals to express the speaker's regret about some desirable situation that will most likely not happen or that the speaker wishes would have happened.

Conditional (…と、〜たら、〜ば)	いい／よかった	＋のに

To review the conditionals, refer to Chapter 7, **Grammar 42**, in Book 1 for 〜たら; Chapter 1, **Grammar 4,** in Book 2 for …と; and Chapter 6, **Grammar 33,** in Book 2 for 〜ば。

> *It would be good if . . . , I wish it would happen that . . . , It would have been good if . . . , I wish it would have happened that . . .*

Note that this construction is used with the actions of people other than the speaker.

> 横井先生ともっと（お話しすれば、お話ししたら）よかったのに。
> *You should have spoken more with Professor Yokoi.*
> 1日が30時間（あれば、あったら）いいのに。
> *I wish there were thirty hours in a day.*

もう少しお金を貯めて (おいたら、おけば) よかったのに。

You should have saved up a little more money.

そんな馬鹿なこと (言わなければ、言わなかったら) よかったのに。

They shouldn't have said such stupid things.

When things that the speaker did are expressed, のに is dropped or is replaced with …んですが (んだが) or …んですけど (…だけど).

夏の間にもっと海に (行っておけば、行っておいたら) よかったんですが…

I should have gone to the coast more during the summer.

The conditional with …いいのに is often used to give suggestions, but it should be used with caution, because it sounds a bit as if the speaker is scolding the person for doing or having done something contrary to the suggestion.

もっと御飯を食べたらいいのに。

You ought to eat more rice. (The implication is that the person is eating or has eaten something else.)

あんな男とは付き合わなければいいのに。

You shouldn't associate with that kind of man. (The implication is that associating with him has had some undesirable consequence.)

42.3 There is also a のに construction that is used to express the process required to accomplish some goal. In some cases, it is easily confused with the のに construction meaning *even though*.

S1		
Nonpast, plain verb (= dictionary form)	のに	S2

In order to do . . . , For the purpose of doing . . .

天ぷらを揚げるのに、油が必要です。

*In order to deep-fry **tempura** you need oil.*

昔はアメリカに行くのに、船で3ヶ月かかりました。

In the old days it took three months by ship to go to America.

カワムラさんを説得するのに協力してください。

Please cooperate with me in order to persuade Mr. Kawamura.

きれいな漢字を書くのには筆が一番です。

*In order to write beautiful **kanji**, a writing brush is best.*

だが is considered a masculine form, so female speakers would be well advised to use だけど, which is gender neutral, instead.

Connect each item in A with the most appropriate sentence ending in B.

A

1. 波が高いのに、
2. 学生なのに、
3. 日本語を1年しか勉強しなかったのに、
4. お金があまりなかったのに、
5. ラッシュアワーの時間なのに、
6. もう12時になるのに、
7. 英語を読むのは上手なのに、
8. あの子はさっきまで (*until a little time ago*) は静かだったのに、

B

a. 高いフランス料理の店に入ってしまいました。
b. 父はまだ帰ってこない。
c. 話すのは全くだめだ。
d. 今はとてもうるさい。
e. あまり混んでいません。
f. たくさんの人が泳いでいる。
g. 漢字がたくさん読める。
h. あまり勉強しない。

練習　　　　　2

Complete these sentences.

1. もう梅雨の季節なのに、＿＿＿＿＿＿＿＿＿＿＿＿＿＿＿＿＿＿
2. あの家にはガレージがあるのに、＿＿＿＿＿＿＿＿＿＿＿＿＿＿
3. コートを着ているのに、＿＿＿＿＿＿＿＿＿＿＿＿＿＿＿＿＿
4. 先月、お金を払ったのに、＿＿＿＿＿＿＿＿＿＿＿＿＿＿＿＿
5. ＿＿＿＿＿＿＿＿＿＿＿＿＿＿＿＿＿、テレビばかり見ている。
6. ＿＿＿＿＿＿＿＿＿＿＿＿＿＿＿＿、富士山は見えない。
7. ＿＿＿＿＿＿＿＿＿＿＿＿＿＿＿、まだ怒っているようだ。

練習　　　　　3

Complete the dialogues on the next page by filling in the blanks with sentences selected from among the following options.

a. 海のそばのホテルは、空室が全然ありませんでした。
b. 駅から歩いて45分もかかるとは知らなかった。
c. 先生の声が小さいので、おっしゃっていることが聞こえなかったよ。
d. この本、田中さんが来週 必要なんだ。
e. 来週、一週間休みを取りたいんだ。
f. ああ、疲れた。

1. A: _____
   B: タクシーで来ればよかったのに。
2. A: _____
   B: 少し休むといいのに。
3. A: _____
   B: 予約しておいたらよかったのに。
4. A: _____
   B: 速達で送ればいいのに。
5. A: _____
   B: 部長にお願いしたらいいのに。
6. A: _____
   B: もっと前に座ればよかったのに。

Vocabulary

Geography and Environment

いけ	池	pond
いし	石	stone
おか	丘	hill
かいがん	海岸	beach, shore
かざん	火山	volcano
かんきょう	環境	environment
き	木	tree
こうがい	公害	pollution
しぜん(の)	自然(の)	nature, (natural)
しま	島	island
せつやく(する)	節約(する)	economizing, careful use; (to economize, to use carefully)
たいりく	大陸	continent
たに	谷	valley
ながれる	流れる	to flow
はやし	林	woods
みずうみ	湖	lake
もり	森	forest
わん	湾	bay

Review: 海、川、山、地図

Animals and Insects

うさぎ	兎	rabbit
うし	牛	cow, cattle
うま	馬	horse
か	蚊	mosquito
かう	飼う	to keep, have, raise (a pet)
かえる	蛙	frog
かわいがる		to love, caress, pet
きつね	狐	fox
くじら	鯨	whale
くま	熊	bear
ごきぶり		cockroach
さる	猿	monkey
しか	鹿	deer
せみ	蝉	cicada
ぞう	象	elephant
とら	虎	tiger
とり	鳥	bird
どうぶつ	動物	animal
どうぶつえん	動物園	zoo
ニワトリ		chicken
はち	蜂	bee
はと	鳩	pigeon, dove
ぶた	豚	pig
へび	蛇	snake
むし	虫	insect

Loanwords: ペット、ゴリラ、パンダ、ライオン
Review: 犬、猫

Plants

うえる	植える	to plant
うめ	梅	plum tree
かれる	枯れる	to wither, die
きく	菊	chrysanthemum
くさ	草	grass
さく	咲く	to bloom
さくら	桜	cherry tree
しょくぶつ	植物	plant
たね	種	seed

つち	土	soil
は	葉	leaf
ぼんさい	盆栽	**bonsai**
まつ	松	pine tree

Loanwords: カーネーション、ダリヤ、ブーケ
Review: 花、木、庭、花屋

Culture and Customs

エチケット		etiquette
しゃかい	社会	society
しゅうかん	習慣	habit
しゅうきょう	宗教	religion
しんじる	信じる	to believe
しんとう	神道	Shintoism
じだい	時代	era, period
ぶっきょう	仏教	Buddhism
ぶんか	文化	culture
まもる	守る	to observe (*a custom*), to obey (*a rule*), to protect
れきし	歴史	history

Loanwords: タブー、マナー

Miscellaneous

おじぎ (をする)	お辞儀 (をする)	(to) bow
がまんする	我慢する	to put up with an unpleasant situation without complaint
がんばる	頑張る	to do one's best, to hang in there, to come out of a difficult situation all right
きょうみ (がある)	興味 (がある)	interest, (to be interested)
ひつよう (な)	必要 (な)	necessary
もったいない		wasteful

Grammar

あるいは	or perhaps
…ことになる	to be decided that …
そして	and (*connecting verbs*)
それで	and then, therefore
それとも	or alternatively
つまり	that is to say …
ところが	but on the contrary …
ところで	by the way …
～なくてもいい	it's all right not to …

...のに	although ..., even though ...
まず	first of all
または	or
...ものだ	*(adds emotional force)*
...わけだ	So it's that ...

Kanji

Learn these **kanji.**

然	森	馬
化	世	虫
島	界	頼
村	球	植
湖	昔	咲
川	害	必
州	例	要
石	他	習
岩	最	慣
林	犬	練

Reading and Writing

Reading 1 ゴルフ場建設反対
<ruby>じょうけんせつはんたい</ruby>

Sakura-machi is a small town in a southern prefecture whose main industries are agriculture and fishing. A development company is planning to develop a golf course in the town with backing from the prefectural government. The following is a letter from a resident that appeared in the local paper.

Before You Read

Read the following brief description of Sakura-machi to understand its natural environment.

桜町は県の南部にある小さな町である。町は太平洋に面し、砂浜の海岸が広がっている。桜町沖では漁業がさかんで、かつお、まぐろなどが取れる。また、最近はハマチ、アサリ、真珠の人工養殖も行っている。町の北には標高459mの森口山がある。森口山から町には森口川が流れている。森口川の周りは平野となり、田畑が広がる。森口山は冬、北から吹く冷たい風を防ぎ、そのため、桜町は冬でも暖かい。この暖かい気候を利用して、ミカン、スイカ、トマトが一年中作られている。

面する *to face on*
沖 *the open sea near a coast*
漁業 *commercial fishing*
さかん(な) *prevalent, abundant*
かつお *bonito (a kind of fish)*
まぐろ *tuna*
ハマチ *yellowtail (a kind of fish)*
アサリ *clam*
真珠の人工養殖 *artificial culturing of pearls*
行う *to carry out*
標高 *height above sea level*
田畑 *rice paddies and dry fields*
防ぐ *ward off*
スイカ *watermelon*

Now Read It!

What do you think are advantages and disadvantages that a golf course on Mt. Moriguchi would present to the residents? Discuss in class.

桜町は自然資源に恵まれた、住みやすい町である。しかし、この町が変わろうとしている。

　最近、桜町の北にある森口山をけずり、ゴルフ場を建設する計画が、南日本観光開発 会社により発表された。県内各地にヨットハーバー、リゾートランド、マリンランド、キャンプ場、ハンググライダー場などを作り、日本のリゾートの中心にしようとする県もこの計画に賛成のようである。しかし、このゴルフ場建設計画が桜町の自然と環境にどのような影響を与えるか、御存じだろうか。

　先ず、町の北にあって、北風を防いでくれている森口山がなくなると、冬でも暖かい桜町の気候は変わってしまうだろう。また、森口山の樹木は土中深く根を張り、大雨の時も、洪水を防いでくれている。そして、雨の降らない時でも、土中の水が川に流れ、森口川の水量を一定に保ってくれる。桜町が洪水や干ばつの被害にあわないのも、森口山のおかげである。

　ゴルフ場が作られると、芝に農薬がまかれ、森口川に流れるおそれがある。農薬で汚れた水は山の麓のミカン、スイカ、トマトの畑や田んぼに流れこむだろう。さらに、この水は海に流れ、桜町沖のハマチ、アサリ、真珠の養殖にも影響を与えるだろう。

　森口山は先祖代々伝わる桜町の宝である。私たちは森口山の春の新緑、秋の紅葉を見て、四季の変化を知ってきた。そして、花見、遠足の場所として、私たちの生活の一部となってきた。この森口山がゴルフ場に変わろうとしている。

恵まれる *to be endowed*
しかし *however*
けずる *to whittle away at, to grade (a hill or mountain)*
建設 *construction*
計画 *plan*
観光開発会社 *company for the development of tourism*
県内各地 *in every part of the prefecture*
中心 *center*
賛成 *agreement*
影響を与える *to have an influence*
深い *deep*
根を張る *to extend roots*
洪水 *flood*
一定 *uniform, consistent*
保つ *to maintain*
干ばつ *drought*
被害にあう *to sustain damage*
…のおかげで *thanks to . . .*
芝 *turf, sod*
農薬をまく *to spread fertilizer*
おそれ *fear*
汚れる *to get dirty*
田んぼ *rice paddy*
さらに *moreover*
先祖代々伝わる *to be passed down from generations of ancestors*
宝 *treasure*
新緑 *spring greenery*
紅葉 *autumn leaves*
変化 *change*
遠足 *excursion, outing*
もたらす *to bring about*
断固 *firm, decisive*
反対 *opposition*
講堂 *auditorium*
反対集会 *protest rally*
参加 *participation*

自然破壊、農薬汚染をもたらすゴルフ場の建設に断固反対しよう。6月4日 6時から、桜町小学校講堂で反対集会がある。皆さんの参加をお待ちしている。

「桜町の自然と環境を守り、ゴルフ場建設に反対する会」

会長
吉本太一

After You Finish Reading

1. The above letter consists of six paragraphs. Summarize the main points of each paragraph in English, following the example.

[例] Paragraph 1: Introduction to the letter. Sakura-machi with all its natural beauty is about to change.

2. According to the letter, what would or could happen to each of the following features of Sakura-machi after the construction of the golf course? Answer in English.

The climate
Moriguchi River
Agricultural fields
Fisheries

3. Explain what function each of the following words plays in the structure of Mr. Yoshimoto's argument.

Paragraph 2 しかし

Paragraph 3 先ず

Paragraph 3 また

Paragraph 4 さらに

Paragraph 5 そして

Writing 1

1. Write a letter to support or argue against Mr. Yoshimoto's letter. Include supporting arguments for your position.
2. Write a letter to express your opinion on a current issue that you feel strongly about.

Writing

You can develop a more mature writing style in Japanese by using transitional words to link shorter sentences. Here are some suggestions.

1. Write a first draft of your composition, trying to express your ideas in short, simple sentences.
2. Determine which sentences have a logical relationship and can be linked together. Choose transitional words that show these relationships.
3. Rewrite the composition, adding the transitional words and making other changes to reduce choppiness, if necessary.

Remember to use words that you are already familiar with. If you need to use unfamiliar words or expressions, check with your instructor or someone else who speaks Japanese well. Beware of 英語の直訳 (えいごのちょくやく), direct translation from English, because it almost never works.

Reading 2　書評
しょひょう

The following is a brief review of a book on Japanese culture.

Before You Read

What stereotypical ideas do people in your country have about Japanese people and their culture? What stereotypical ideas do you think Japanese people have about your country and culture(s)? Discuss in class.

Useful vocabulary

日本人論 *discussions about the nature of the Japanese people (a popular topic for books in Japan)*, 自ら *self*, 気にする *to give a lot of attention or thought to*, 民族 *ethnic group*, 氏 *a title similar in meaning to* -さん *but used mostly in formal, written contexts*, タテ社会の人間関係 *lit., Human Relations in a Vertical Society (English title:* Japanese Society*)*, 特に *especially*, 概念 *general concept*, 甘えの構造 *lit., The Structure of Presuming on the Kindness of Superiors (English title:* The Anatomy of Dependence*)*, 主張する *to assert*, 両氏 *both of the people mentioned (This is a very formal expression, rarely used in conversation.)*, 共通する *to have traits in common*, 独特の *unique*, これに対して *over and against this*, 縮み志向の日本人 *The Japanese, Who Aim to Shrink Things*, 著者 *author*, 欧米人 *Europeans and North Americans*, 比較する *to compare*, 独自の *original, peculiar to*, 特性 *unique characteristic*, 事物を縮小すること *scaling things down*, 扇子 *folding fan*,

機能 *function*, つめこむ *to pack in*, 表れ *expression*, 文字 *written symbol*, 宇宙 *universe*, 歌いこむ *to put all one's poetic expression into something*, 枯山水 *a Japanese-style dry garden*, おしこめる *to push into*, 常に *ordinarily*, 向く *to face toward something*, 西欧 *Western Europe*, 偏重 *over-valuation*, するどい *sharp*, 警告 *warning*, 是非 *by all means*, すすめる *to suggest, to urge*

Now Read It!

本屋の日本人論のコーナーには、多くの本が並べられている。これは日本人が自らに興味があり、自らのことをとても気にする民族であるからだろう。

日本人、日本社会の特性について書かれた本の中では、中根千枝氏の「タテ社会の人間関係」や土居健郎氏の「甘えの構造」が特に有名である。中根氏は「タテ社会」の概念により、日本文化のメカニズムを説明しようとしている。土居氏は日本社会が「タテ社会」なのも、日本人が義理人情を大切にするのも、「甘え」によると主張している。両氏に共通していることは「タテ社会」も「甘え」も日本独特の概念であり、外国には見られないということである。

これに対して、「縮み志向の日本人」の著者李御寧氏は、これまでの日本人論は日本人を欧米人と比較して書かれたものが多く、「タテ社会」も「甘え」も日本独自のものではなく、韓国にも見られると主張している。

李氏は日本人の特性は「事物を縮小すること」であると言う。トランジスタを使った日本の小さいラジオもウォークマンも、この特性によるものであると李氏は考える。扇子にいろいろな機能をつめこむのも、弁当にいろいろなものをつめこむのも、この「縮み」の表われであるし、17文字の俳句に四季と宇宙を歌いこむのも、盆栽、いけ花、枯山水に自然と宇宙をおしこめるのも、「縮み」の特性によると言う。

「縮み」の概念で日本人の特性を説明しようというのも面白いが、常に文化の中心を欧米と考え、アジアを忘れ、欧米を向いてきた日本人の西欧文化偏重に対するするどい警告でもある。ぜひ、読むことをすすめたい本である。

After You Finish Reading

The above review consists of five paragraphs. State in English the gist of each paragraph.

Writing 2

Write a review of a book you have read. Before writing, think about what information you would like to include. Some suggestions:

    a. information about the author
    b. chapter organization (in the case of nonfiction books)
    c. short description of the plot (in the case of fiction books)
    d. good points about the book
    e. points of disagreement with the author
    f. whether or not you recommend that others read this book

Language Functions and Situations

Presenting One's Opinion Clearly and Logically

Here are some expressions you can use during discussions.

Clarifying the topic you would like to deal with in your speech

今日は日本の庭園についてお話ししたいと思います。
Today I want to speak <u>about</u> Japanese gardens.

Starting to state your first point

<u>まず</u>（最初に）、環境破壊の問題について述べたいと思います。
<u>First</u> I want to discuss the problem of environmental damage.

Moving to the next point

<u>次</u>に、自然保護についてお話ししたいと思います。
<u>Next</u>, I want to speak about protecting nature.

Explaining in other words

大気汚染、<u>簡単に言えば</u>、空気がきたなくなることですが…
Air pollution, or, <u>to put it simply</u>, the air becoming dirty . . .

ゴルフ場の建設は中止になりました。**というのは**、住民が反対したからです。

The construction of the golf course was halted. That is to say, it's because residents were opposed.

Comparing

兵庫県はゴルフ場の数が多い。**それに比べて**、高知県は少ない。

Hyogo prefecture has a large number of golf courses. Compared with that, Kochi prefecture has a small number.

Citing an example

いろいろな公害病がおこりました。**例えば**、富山ではイタイイタイ病が問題となりました。

Various sorts of pollution-caused illnesses arose. For example, in Toyama itai itai disease became a problem.

Itai itai disease, the result of exposure to toxic wastes containing cadmium, causes bone degeneration. The name comes from the fact that it is extremely painful.

Citing someone's statement or book

東京大学の大野先生**によると**、この問題を無視 (ignore) するわけにはいかないそうです。

According to Professor Oono of the University of Tokyo, it won't do to ignore this problem.

Adding a point

ゴルフ場建設により山がけずられました。**さらに**、農薬の使用により川も汚染されました。

The mountain was shaved down through the construction of the golf course. Moreover, the river was polluted through the use of fertilizers.

Transition to the next topic

さて、次の問題に移りたいと思います。

Well then, I think I want to move on to the next problem.

Summarizing

まとめると、次のようになります。

If we bring everything together, we end up with what follows.

Finishing your speech

最後に、御清聴感謝申し上げます。

Finally, I thank you for listening to me attentively.

Activity

Make a short presentation on Japan and Japanese culture in class based on research done outside class. Try to use graphs and other visual aids to help clarify your points.

Having a Discussion

Asking for someone's opinion

どうお考えですか。
What do you think?
御意見お聞かせください。
Tell me your opinion.

Agreeing

はい、私もそう思います。
Yes, I think so, too.
はい、賛成 (同感) です。
Yes, I agree.

Asking someone if he or she agrees

その意見に賛成ですか。
Do you agree with this opinion?

Confirming one's position

では、賛成と考えていいわけですね。
So, it's all right to think of ourselves as being in agreement, right?

Expressing Disagreement

As mentioned in コミュニケーション・ノート on p. 289, Book 1, Japanese are reluctant to refuse a request or express their disagreement directly. This is because いいえ carries a strong connotation of *you are wrong,* and is therefore potentially offensive. Maintaining silence, refusing to answer the question, and answering vaguely are the most common means of indirect refusal.

A: 新しいコンピュータを買うことにしましょうよ。
B: 今は何とも言えませんね。
A: *Let's buy a new computer.*
B: *I can't say anything right now.*

A: 新しいコンピュータを買うことにしましょうよ。
B: ええ、まあそうできるといいですけど、…
B: *Yes, it would be good if we could do this, but . . .*
(Note that this sounds like a *yes* to an English speaker.)

Other common ways include changing the subject and avoiding the responsibility for answering.

A: 新しいコンピュータを買うことにしましょうよ。

B: ところで、昼御飯はもう食べましたか。

B: *By the way, have you eaten lunch yet?*

A: 新しいコンピュータを買うことにしましょうよ。

B: 田中さんに聞いてみてください。

B: *Try asking Mr. Tanaka.*

Agreeing first and then giving a negative qualification is another common strategy for refusing.

A: 新しいコンピュータを買うことにしましょうよ。

B: ええ、でも、もう少し待ったほうがいいんじゃありませんか。

B: *Yes, but wouldn't it be better to wait a bit?*

Finally, apologizing is another common way to avoid saying *no*.

A: 新しいコンピュータを買うことにしましょうよ。

B: すみませんが、コンピュータのことはよくわからないんです。

B: *I'm sorry, but I don't know much about computers.*

Activity

Have a discussion in Japanese about some current issues pertinent to you. One of you will play the role of discussion leader or chairman.

Listening Comprehension

1. The following people are talking about their hometowns. Listen to their conversation, and write down the most important facts about each person's hometown.

NAME	HOMETOWN
Kuriyama	
Sasaki	
Komada	
Matsuno	
Hosokawa	

2. The following people are discussing their experiences with foreign cultures. Listen to their discussion and fill in the following table.

NAME	WHERE DID HE OR SHE GO?	EXPERIENCE
Ichikawa		
Mano		
Tokuyasu		
Yoshikura		

Review
Chapter 2

今日は七五三です。

Culture Reading: Japanese Traditional Observances

If you continue to study Japanese and if you ever live in Japan, you will have occasion to read materials containing a lot of unfamiliar vocabulary. The following passage contains a large number of words that you don't know. Read it through once quickly to get a general idea of what it is about, and then reread it in detail, consulting the marginal notes as necessary.

日本の年中行事

　正月は、日本人にとって一番大切な行事と言っていいだろう。昔は、新しい年の初めに当たり、祖先の霊を迎えて、その年の家内安全、繁栄を祈る目的があったが、現在は新しい年が来たことを祝うことが目的となってきている。正月の間は会社、官庁、学校も休みとなり、地方出身の人は故郷に帰って家族と一緒にお正月を祝う人が多い。

　正月の準備は、前の年の12月に始まる。家の中や外の掃除をしたり、正月のためのもちやおせち料理を用意したりする。1月1日の元旦から3日までは正月三か日と言われ、多くの人が神社やお寺に参拝して、その年の無事と繁栄を祈る。これを「初詣で」と言う。また、いつもお世話になっている会社の上司、親戚、知人などに新年の挨拶をして歩く。これを「年始回り」と言う。「年賀状」を交換するのも正月の一般的な習慣となっている。また、子供に「お年玉」というお小遣いをあげる習慣もある。

　二月になると節分の行事がある。これは立春の前の日の晩に豆をまいて、家の中の鬼を追い出し、福の神を家に招く行事である。

　三月三日は雛祭りで、女の子の節句だ。「桃の節句」とも言われる。この日には女の子のいる家では雛人形を飾り、女の子の成長を祈る。

　一方、五月五日は「端午の節句」と言い、男の子の節句である。男の子のいる家では五月人形を飾り、家の外に鯉のぼりを立てて、男の子の成長を祈る。この日は「子供の日」として祝日にもなっている。

　七月七日は「七夕」と言われる星の祭である。これは天の川によって隔てられている牽牛星と織女星が、1年に一度七月七日に会うという中国の伝説に基づいたもので、奈良時代に日本に伝わった。この日は短冊に自分の願い事を書き、竹につるしておく。

　お盆はおそらく正月に次いで、重要な年中行事であろう。関東では7月の13日から三日間、関西や地方の一部では1ヶ月遅れて8月に、仏壇に供え物をしたり、火をともして先祖の魂を迎える。この時期には各地で盆踊りが行われる。お盆の期間に夏休みを取り、故郷に帰る人が多く、お盆の前後は正月の前後と同様、交通期間が混雑する。

　11月15日は「七五三」で、三歳と五歳の男の子、三歳と七歳の女の子が晴れ着を着て、神社に参拝する。これは江戸時代から続く、子供の成長を祈る行事である。

年中行事 *annual event, annual observance*
...にあたり *in connection with*,
祖先 *ancestors*, 霊 *spirit of a dead person*, 迎える *to greet, go out to meet*,
家内安全 *safety of the household*,
繁栄 *prosperity*, 祈る *to pray for*,
目的 *purpose, goal*, 祝う *to celebrate*,
官庁 *government offices*,
地方出身 *coming from areas outside the major cities*, 故郷 *hometown*,
準備 *preparations*
もち *cakes made from pounded rice. When grilled or immersed in hot soup, they take on a gummy texture.*,
おせち料理 *foods traditionally served at New Year, the most well known being* **mochi** *and o-zooni*, お雑煮, *a kind of soup.*, 用意する *to prepare, to have ready*, 元旦 *the first day of the year*,
参拝する *to visit a shrine for religious purposes*, 無事 *freedom from harm*,
初詣で *first visit to a shrine in the New Year, usually shortly after midnight*,
お世話になる *to have favors done*,
親戚 *relatives*, 知人 *acquaintance*,
挨拶 *greeting*, 年賀状 *New Year's cards*, 交換する *to exchange*,
一般的 *general, widespread*,
お小遣い *spending money*, 節分 *an unofficial festival observed on February 3*, 立春 *the traditional beginning of spring*, 豆をまく *to scatter beans*,
鬼 *demon, evil spirit*, 福の神 *gods of good luck*, 招く *to beckon, invite*,
雛祭り *the Doll Festival*, 節句 *seasonal festival*, 桃 *peach*, 人形 *doll*, 飾る *to set up as a decoration*, 成長 *growth*,
一方 *on the other hand*, 端午の節句 *Boys' Day*, 鯉のぼり *a wind sock in the shape of a carp*, 祝日 *holiday*, 星 *star*,
天の川 *the Milky Way*, ...によって *by*,
隔てる *to separate*, 牽牛星 *the Herdsman Star*, 織女星 *the Weaver Woman Star*, 伝説 *legend*, 基づく *to be based on*, 奈良時代 *the Nara Period (710–796)*, 短冊 *small, vertical strip for writing on*, つるす *to hang something from a string*, ...に次いで *[next in ranking] after...*, 重要(な) *important*,
仏壇 *Buddhist altar in a home*,
供え物 *offerings*, ともす *to light*,
魂 *soul*, ...と同様 *in the same way as...*, 混雑する *to be crowded*,
晴れ着 *fancy clothes*, 江戸時代 *the Edo Period (1615-1868)*

Oral Activities

京都の<ruby>祭<rt>まつ</rt></ruby>り

アクティビティー　1

<ruby>祝日<rt>しゅくじつ</rt></ruby> (*Festive occasions*)

A. What holiday is being described by each of the following sentences? Refer to the Culture Reading at the beginning of the chapter if you don't remember.

1. イエス・キリストの<ruby>誕生<rt>たんじょう</rt></ruby>を<ruby>祝<rt>いわ</rt></ruby>う (*to celebrate*) 日
2. <ruby>一年<rt>いちねん</rt></ruby>の<ruby>始<rt>はじ</rt></ruby>まりを<ruby>祝<rt>いわ</rt></ruby>う日
3. 日本で<ruby>先祖<rt>せんぞ</rt></ruby>の<ruby>魂<rt>たましい</rt></ruby>　(*spirit*) を<ruby>迎<rt>むか</rt></ruby>える<ruby>行事<rt>ぎょうじ</rt></ruby>
4. 好きな人にチョコレートをあげる日
5. 日本で男の子の<ruby>成長<rt>せいちょう</rt></ruby>を<ruby>祈<rt>いの</rt></ruby>る (*to pray for*) 日
6. アメリカの<ruby>独立<rt>どくりつ</rt></ruby> (*independence*) を<ruby>祝<rt>いわ</rt></ruby>う日
7. 日本の女の子の<ruby>成長<rt>せいちょう</rt></ruby>を<ruby>祈<rt>いの</rt></ruby>る日
8. 人が<ruby>短冊<rt>たんざく</rt></ruby>に<ruby>願<rt>ねが</rt></ruby>い<ruby>事<rt>ごと</rt></ruby>を書く日

B. Explain in Japanese to your classmates which holiday is the most important to you and why.

C. What does the graph at the right tell you about attitudes prevalent among Japanese people? Discuss in Japanese in class.

結婚記念日 *wedding anniversary*

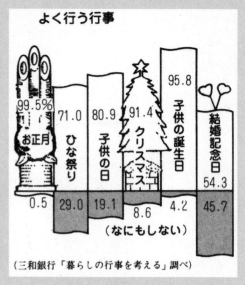

よく行う行事

99.5%	71.0	80.9	91.4	95.8	54.3
お正月	ひな祭り	子供の日	クリスマス	子供の誕生日	結婚記念日
0.5	29.0	19.1	8.6	4.2	45.7

（なにもしない）

（三和銀行「暮らしの行事を考える」調べ）

文化ノート

Japanese Religion

Unlike the religions that North Americans are most familiar with, neither Buddhism nor Shinto expects its followers to attend weekly services. Instead, people go to temples or shrines on certain holidays, when they want to have ceremonies performed, or when they have private spiritual needs. Most Japanese people consider themselves Buddhists and call on Buddhist priests to officiate at funerals, but most weddings are performed by Shinto priests, and new business ventures typically start with a Shinto blessing.

The religious holidays observed in Japan come from both traditions. For example, the New Year's celebrations feature both a visit to a Shinto shrine and the ringing of the Buddhist temple bells.

In addition, many Japanese are also adherents of the so-called "new religions" (新興宗教 [しんこうしゅうきょう]). Most of these have arisen out of the Buddhist or Shinto tradition, with elements of other religions mixed in. Usually they allow their followers to practice the new religion in addition to, not instead of, Buddhism and Shinto.

Christian missionaries have been active in Japan since the 1870s, but the percentage of Christians in the population has held steady at less than 1 percent down to the present day.

アクティビティー 2

職探し (*Job search*)

Work in pairs. The following is a help-wanted advertisement from a company that is looking for office clerks. See how much information you and your partner can retrieve from this ad. Then discuss with your partner what questions you would ask if you interviewed applicants and what questions you would like to ask the interviewer during a job interview if you were applying for a job.

After finishing your discussion, change partners. Now act out a job interview with your new partner by using the two lists of questions you prepared.

アクティビティー 3

職業紹介所 (*Employment agency*)

You are working for an employment agency. What job would you recommend for each of the people who have made the following statements? Before recommending a job, what questions would you ask these people?

1. 旅行が大好きで、これまでにもいろいろな国に行ったことがあります。フランス語とドイツ語が話せるので、ヨーロッパへ行くことが多いです。面白い場所やショッピングにいい場所を探すのが大好きです。

2. 朝早く起きるのが苦手です。長く机に座っているのも苦手です。人と話すのも苦手だし...得意なこと？踊ったり、歌ったりすることですね。

3. 子供の時から、いろいろなことを習うのが好きでしたし、大人になってからは、人にものを教えるのが好きです。特に子供に音楽を教えたり、子供とゲームをしたりしていると、時間がたつのを忘れますね。

4. 小さい時から、人の先頭に立って、いろいろなことをするのが好きでした。人のためなら、どんなにつらい (hard to take) ことでも、大変なことでもします。

5. 今までいろいろなことをしてきましたが、すぐ飽きて (get tired of) しまいます。何か面白い仕事を探しています。自分で何かを考えたり、作ったりするのが好きです。

6. 前に働いていた会社はつぶれてしまいまいた。(went bankrupt) 今度は安定性 (stability) のある仕事がいいですね。給料はそんなに高くなくてもいいです。

7. 家族ともっと一緒に過ごしたいので、土曜日、日曜日もきちんと休めて、出張があまりなくて、残業 (overtime) のない仕事がいいですね。夏休みもたくさん取れる仕事はありませんかね。

アクティビティー　4

健康に注意していますか。(Do you pay attention to your health?)

Work in pairs. Discuss the following statements with your partner in Japanese. Do they reflect your own attitudes?

1. となりの人が咳をしたら、席を変える。
2. ルームメート (ご主人、奥さん) が風邪をひいている時は、別の部屋で寝る。
3. 病気になっても、薬は飲まない。
4. 医者にいくのは嫌いだ。
5. 朝は早く起きて、夜は早く寝る。
6. タバコは吸わない。お酒も飲まない。
7. 十分、休みをとって、ストレスもためない。(accumulate stress)
8. コレステロールや血圧には気をつけている。

アクティビティー　5

人生 (A person's life)

A. These are the photographs of four Japanese people who have become internationally famous in four different fields. Do you recognize any of their faces? Can you figure out which of the four statements in each category pertains to each person? You may need to consult with your classmates or your instructor or use reference books to figure out who these people are and what they are famous for.

1. 大阪で生まれました。
   名古屋で生まれました。
   東京で生まれました。
   中国の満州 (*Manchuria*) で生まれました。
2. 小さい時に、両親に死なれました。
   若い時は、画家になる勉強をしました。
   東朋学園で音楽を勉強しました。
   高校の時から、スポーツ界で有名でした。
3. オーケストラの指揮者 (*conductor*)
   スケートの選手 (オリンピックで銀メダルを取りました。)
   作家 (日本人で初めてノーベル文学賞 [*Nobel Prize*] を受けました)。
   映画監督 (*director*) (日本の映画を世界で有名にした人です。)
4. 1972年に自殺 (*suicide*) しました。
   ボストンに住んでいます。
   現在 (*at present*) は、テレビのコメンテーターです。
   「乱」がその人の有名な映画の一つです。

B. Work in pairs. One student thinks of a famous person and gives a short biographical sketch, describing at least two of the person's positive traits and, if possible, one negative trait. The second student tries to guess the identity of the famous person.

アクティビティー　6

賛成ですか。反対ですか。(*Do you agree or not?*)

Work in pairs. Exchange opinions about television and the news media while talking about whether you agree with the following statements. After expressing your agreement or disagreement, give an example to support your opinion.

1. テレビのニュース・レポーターは公平 (*fair*) で客観的に (*objectively*) ニュースを伝えている。
2. 最近のテレビ番組は暴力 (*violence*) やセックス・シーンが多すぎる。
3. 犯罪率 (*crime rate*) が高いのは、最近のテレビ番組の影響 (*influence*) だ。
4. テレビのニュースは新聞ほど詳しく (*detailed*) ないから、見る必要はない。
5. テレビのファミリードラマは現実 (*reality*) の生活を反映 (*reflect*) している。
6. テレビのコマーシャルは生活の役に立つ。

アクティビティー　7

都会がいいですか。田舎がいいですか。(*Do you prefer the city or the countryside?*)

Work in pairs. Compare the city and the countryside with regard to the following questions.

1. 空気がきれいか
2. 自然が多いか
3. 買物に便利か
4. 生活のペースが速いか
5. 仕事があるか
6. 人が親切か
7. 交通機関が (*transportation*) 発達 (*development*) しているか
8. 犯罪率 (*crime rate*) が高いか
9. 様々 (*a variety of*) な人がいるか
10. 寂しい (*lonesome*) か

Discuss what kind of place you would prefer to live in, based on the above comparisons.

賛成<ruby>賛成<rt>さんせい</rt></ruby>ですか、反対<ruby><rt>はんたい</rt></ruby>ですか。(*Do you agree or not?*)

Do you agree with the following statements? Defend your opinions.

1. エネルギーを節約<ruby><rt>せつやく</rt></ruby>するために、夏はエアコンをできるだけ (*as much as possible*) 使わない方がいい。
2. エネルギーを節約<ruby><rt>せつやく</rt></ruby>するために、冬は厚着<ruby><rt>あつぎ</rt></ruby>をして、できるだけ暖房<ruby><rt>だんぼう</rt></ruby> (*heating*) を使わない方がいい。
3. 石油<ruby><rt>せきゆ</rt></ruby>を使うのをやめて、核燃料<ruby><rt>かくねんりょう</rt></ruby> (*nuclear power*) を使った方がいい。
4. ゴルフコースは公園<ruby><rt>こうえん</rt></ruby>に変<ruby><rt>か</rt></ruby>えた方がいい。
5. 車で会社や学校へ通<ruby><rt>かよ</rt></ruby>うのをやめて、公共交通機関<ruby><rt>こうきょうこうつうきかん</rt></ruby> (*public transportation*) を使うべきだ。
6. 公害<ruby><rt>こうがい</rt></ruby>を引<ruby><rt>ひ</rt></ruby>き起<ruby><rt>お</rt></ruby>こした (*bring about*) 会社や人は、厳<ruby><rt>きび</rt></ruby>しく (*strictly*) 罰<ruby><rt>ばっ</rt></ruby>する (*punish*) べきだ。
7. エネルギーを節約<ruby><rt>せつやく</rt></ruby>するために、もっとシンプルな生活<ruby><rt>せいかつ</rt></ruby>をした方がいい。
8. 環境<ruby><rt>かんきょう</rt></ruby>の問題<ruby><rt>もんだい</rt></ruby>も大切<ruby><rt>たいせつ</rt></ruby>だが、経済<ruby><rt>けいざい</rt></ruby>の発展<ruby><rt>はってん</rt></ruby> (*growth*) はもっと大切<ruby><rt>たいせつ</rt></ruby>な問題<ruby><rt>もんだい</rt></ruby>だ。
9. 現在<ruby><rt>げんざい</rt></ruby>の世界<ruby><rt>せかい</rt></ruby>の人口<ruby><rt>じんこう</rt></ruby>は多過<ruby><rt>おおす</rt></ruby>ぎる。人口<ruby><rt>じんこう</rt></ruby>を増<ruby><rt>ふ</rt></ruby>やさないようにするべきだ。
10. 科学<ruby><rt>かがく</rt></ruby>の発達<ruby><rt>はったつ</rt></ruby>により、環境問題<ruby><rt>かんきょうもんだい</rt></ruby>は解決<ruby><rt>かいけつ</rt></ruby> (*solve*) できるから、心配<ruby><rt>しんぱい</rt></ruby>する必要<ruby><rt>ひつよう</rt></ruby>はない。

ペットか子供<ruby><rt>こども</rt></ruby>か (*A pet or a child?*)

Minoru and Megumi Morioka have been married for a year. Megumi thinks that it's time for them to have a baby, while Minoru doesn't want a child and would rather buy a pet. Help them decide which is better for them by listing the advantages and disadvantages of having a pet or a child.

ペット		子供<ruby><rt>こども</rt></ruby>	
いい点<ruby><rt>てん</rt></ruby>	悪<ruby><rt>わる</rt></ruby>い点<ruby><rt>てん</rt></ruby>	いい点<ruby><rt>てん</rt></ruby>	悪<ruby><rt>わる</rt></ruby>い点<ruby><rt>てん</rt></ruby>

敬語 (Honorifics)

In Book 2, Chapter 5 of *Yookoso!* you learned a lot about Japanese honorifics. The following brief article appeared in a Japanese magazine. It mentions eight points to be aware of when using honorifics. Guess what each point is about, based on your reading skills and knowledge of honorifics.

ビジネスマンのための 敬語入門講座

① 敬語には次の3種類があります。

A。尊敬語
B。謙譲語
C。ていねい語

② 尊敬語は、相手や話題に上がった人を尊敬して表現する言葉です。

「鈴木さんが言った」という会話も、尊敬語にすると、「鈴木さんがおっしゃいました」になります。

③ 謙譲語は、へりくだった表現をすることで、相手を高める言葉です。

「わたしは課長に言った」は「わたしは課長に申し上げた」という表現になります。

④ ていねい語は、ていねいに表現することで、相手に敬意を表する言葉です。

「電話だ」は「電話です」、あるいは「電話でございます」

⑤ 動作の主体が自分であるとき尊敬語にするのはおかしい！

「わたしがおっしゃった」という言葉をあてはめてみて下さい。

また、動作の主体が相手なのに謙譲語をつけるのは誤り。

「あなたが申し上げた」は、変だと思いませんか。

⑥ 尊敬語、謙譲語、ていねい語それぞれに専用の言葉があります。

尊敬語▼いらっしゃる、なさる、

⑦ 尊敬語だと、「書かれる」「お書きになる」

例えば「書く」という言葉が、

謙譲語だと、「お書きする」「お書きいたします」。

召しあがる、おっしゃる、くださるなど。

謙譲語▼あげる、差し上げる、いただく、いたす、参る、伺(うかが)う、申し上げる、拝見する、拝聴する、弊社など。

ていねい語▼存じます、ございますなど。

【尊敬語】
「…れる」「お（ご）…になる」「お（ご）…くださる」

【謙譲語】
「お（ご）…する」「お（ご）…いたす」「お（ご）…申す」
※これだけではわかりにくいかもしれませんが

⑧ ちょっとした公式があります。それを覚えておくと便利。

アクティビティー 11

健康について話しましょう。(*Let's talk about your health*.)

What do the following words remind you of? Think of all the related words you can, and then talk about your experiences connected with these words.

1. アスピリン
2. ビタミン
3. 風邪
4. 食欲
5. リラックス

6. 健康
7. 病院
8. 感情
9. レントゲン
10. シロップ

Interview

In the last three chapters of *Yookoso!* you have gained the ability to talk about health, careers, jobs, telecommunications, media, nature, cultural matters, and the environment. This activity will give you a chance to explore the topics you have been talking about by speaking to an unfamiliar person.

Your instructor will invite a Japanese-speaking person to your class: another faculty member or teaching assistant in the Japanese language program, a professor from another department, or an individual from the local Japanese community. Working in groups, make up questions to ask the person about his or her background, training and profession, and opinions about current topics of interest. Try to invent questions that will motivate the person to talk about his or her life.

Situations

Listen to your instructor role play the following situations. You may not understand everything you hear, but make some educated guesses about what your instructor is saying while acting out the roles. As you listen, think about whether you would say or do the same thing.

After your instructor finishes role playing, act out the situations with your instructor or one of your classmates. Try to use as much of the vocabulary that you know as possible.

1. A reporter from Japan is interviewing you about holiday customs in your country. Tell the journalist in detail what you and your family normally do to celebrate a holiday of your choice, emphasizing activities unique to your family but including an account of how most people celebrate this holiday.

2. A journalist from Japan is interviewing a young professional who also has a spouse and two young children. Play the role of the professional, answering the journalist's questions about how you and your spouse handle the responsibilities of your personal and professional lives.

3. You are the personnel manager of a large office. Today you are interviewing a candidate for a secretarial position. Find out all you can about the applicant's education, experience, ambitions, interests, family, and so on.

4. You notice that a friend of yours has red eyes and can barely talk. Since you are very worried, you ask this person what the problem is. Your friend then gives you more details about the illness, including how long it has been going on, what the symptoms are, and what the doctor has recommended.

This Is My Life!: 池島信一(定年退職者)

6年前、62歳で、40年間勤めた時計会社を定年退職しました。最後は本社の部長でした。小さなコンピュータ・ソフトの会社を経営する友人が再就職しないかと誘ってくれました。まだ体も大丈夫だったので、働こうと思えば、まだ働けたのですが、少しゆっくりしたかったし、家内ともう少し一緒の時間を過ごしたかったので、せっかくの誘いでしたが、断りました。定年後は悠々自適の生活を送っています。うちの裏にある小さな庭で野菜を作ったり、本を読んだり、音楽を聞いたりの毎日です。5年前から家内とテニスを始めました。一週間に二度、近所のテニス・コートで家内とテニスをします。家内も私もクラッシック音楽が大好きなので、時々コンサートへ行ったりもします。一年に二回は家内と旅行に出かけます。今年の夏はオーストラリアへ行きました。結婚以来、家内には苦労をさせたので、楽をさせてやりたいと思います。

　子供は娘一人と息子一人です。二人とも結婚して、子供がいます。娘の家族は近所に住んでいるので、娘夫婦が週末、孫を連れてよく遊びに来ます。息子は今、家族を連れて、ニューヨークに滞在しています。一年に一回日本に帰ってきますが、孫の顔を見るのが楽しみです。

　日本は平均寿命が世界でも一番長く、中高年者が人口の中に占める割合が高い、いわゆる高齢化社会になってきています。中高年者の再就職や社会保障などの問題がクローズアップされてきています。私も家内も将来病気で倒れたらどうしようか、などと話し合うことがあります。娘が面倒を見てくれるといいますが、娘には娘の家庭があるので、迷惑はかけたくありません。やはり将来のことは少し心配です。

定年退職 *compulsory retirement*
本社 *company headquarters*
再就職 *reemployment*
誘う *to invite*
断る *to refuse*
悠々自適 *leisurely retirement*
…以来 *ever since …*
苦労 *difficulty, hardship*
滞在する *to stay, to live temporarily*
平均寿命 *average life expectancy*
中高年者 *middle-aged and elderly people*
占める *to occupy, to comprise*
割合 *percentage, proportion*
高齢化社会 *aging society*
保障 *security, guarantee*
病気で倒れる *to become incapacitated by illness*
面倒を見る *to take care of someone's needs*
家庭 *household*
迷惑 *trouble, inconvenience*

ていねんご　か　ない　いっしょ
定年後は家内と一緒に
た　ご　　　　　　　　ふ
過す時間が増えました。

Answer these questions in English.

1. What company did Mr. Ikejima work for?
2. When did he retire?
3. Why didn't he go to work for another company after retirement?
4. What activities does he do now?
5. What activities does he do with his wife?
6. How many children does he have?
7. Where does his daughter live?
8. What are the problems of Japan's aging society?
9. What concerns do he and his wife have?
10. What does his daughter say about this?

Appendices

APPENDIX 1: Verb Conjugation

	CLASS 1						
Dictionary Form	^あ会う	^か書く	^{はな}話す	^た立つ	^し死ぬ*	^よ読む	^の乗る
Root	会(わ)	書	話	立	死	読	乗
Plain, Nonpast, Negative	会わない	書かない	話さない	立たない	死なない	読まない	乗らない
Polite, Nonpast, Affirmative	会います	書きます	話します	立ちます	死にます	読みます	
ましょう Form (Polite Volitional)	会いましょう	書きましょう	話しましょう	立ちましょう	死にましょう	読みましょう	乗りましょう
たい Form	会いたい	書きたい	話したい	立ちたい	死にたい	読みたい	乗りたい
Command	会いなさい	書きなさい	話しなさい	立ちなさい	死になさい	読みなさい	乗りなさい

Note: Don't forget! Horizontal bold lines in this chart set off verb forms whose endings contain the same sound from the **hiragana** syllabary.

	CLASS 1		CLASS 2		CLASS 3	
Dictionary Form	泳ぐ	呼ぶ	How to create forms	食べる	する	来る
Root	泳	呼	Drop る ending	食べ	Irregular	Irregular
Plain, Nonpast, Negative	泳がない	呼ばない	Root + ない	食べない	しない	来ない
Polite, Nonpast, Affirmative	泳ぎます	呼びます	Root + ます	食べます	します	来ます
ましょう Form (Polite Volitional)	泳ぎましょう	呼びましょう	Root + ましょう	食べましょう	しましょう	来ましょう
たい Form	泳ぎたい	呼びたい	Root + たい	食べたい	したい	来たい
Command	泳ぎなさい	呼びなさい	Root + なさい	食べなさい	しなさい	来なさい

	CLASS 1						
Dictionary Form	会う	書く	話す	立つ	死ぬ	読む	乗る
Potential	会える	書ける	話せる	立てる	死ねる	読める	乗れる
Imperative	会え	書け	話せ	立て	死ね	読め	乗れ
ば Conditional	会えば	書けば	話せば	立てば	死ねば	読めば	乗れば
Volitional	会おう	書こう	話そう	立とう	死のう	読もう	乗ろう
Ta-Form	会った	書いた	話した	立った	死んだ	読んだ	乗った
Te-Form	会って	書いて	話して	立って	死んで	読んで	乗って
たら Conditional	会ったら	書いたら	話したら	立ったら	死んだら	読んだら	乗ったら
Passive	会われる	書かれる	話される	立たれる	死なれる**	読まれる	乗られる
Causative	会わせる	書かせる	話させる	立たせる	死なせる	読ませる	乗らせる
Passive-Causative	会わせられる	書かせられる	話させられる	立たせられる	死なせられる	読ませられる	乗らせられる
Other Verbs	洗う 使う 歌う 買う 手伝う 笑う 言う 習う	聞く 行く† 磨く 働く はく 歩く	探す 直す	持つ 勝つ 待つ		飲む 休む 住む 楽しむ	帰る 入る 知る 降る 走る 泊まる 止まる 取る 切る 終わる 始まる

---

*死ぬ is the only verb whose dictionary form ends in ぬ.

†The ta-form and te-form of 行く are 行った and 行って, respectively.

**Used in adversative passive constructions.

	CLASS 1		CLASS 2		CLASS 3	
Dictionary Form	泳ぐ	呼ぶ		食べる	する	来る
Potential	泳げる	呼べる	Root + られる	食べられる	できる	来られる
Imperative	泳げ	呼べ	Root + ろ	食べろ	しろ	来い
ば Conditional	泳げば	呼べば	Root + れば	食べれば	すれば	来れば
Volitional	泳ごう	呼ぼう	Root + よう	食べよう	しよう	来よう
Ta-Form	泳いだ	呼んだ	Root + た	食べた	した	来た
Te-Form	泳いで	呼んで	Root + て	食べて	して	来て
たら Conditional	泳いだら	呼んだら	Root + たら	食べたら	したら	来たら
Passive	泳がれる	呼ばれる	Root + られる	食べられる	される	来られる
Causative	泳がせる	呼ばせる	Root + させる	食べさせる	させる	来させる
Passive-Causative	泳がせられる	呼ばせられる	Root + させられる	たべさせられる	させられる	来させられる
Other Verbs	脱ぐ 急ぐ	飛ぶ 遊ぶ		見る 起きる 寝る 出かける 出る 着る 教える All potential verb forms	Nominal verbs (勉強する、 洗濯する)	連れてくる 持ってくる

APPENDIX 2: Adjective and Copula Conjugation

Adjectives

	DICTIONARY FORM	PRENOMIAL	PREDICATE			
			Plain			
			Nonpast		Past	
			Affirmative	**Negative**	**Affirmative**	**Negative**
I-Adjectives	赤い	赤い	赤い	赤くない	赤かった	赤くなかった
	いい	いい	いい	よくない	よかった	よくなかった
Na-Adjectives	静か	静かな	静かだ	静かではない／静かじゃない	静かだった	静かではなかった／静かじゃなかった

Copula

DICTIONARY FORM	PRENOMIAL	PREDICATE			
		Plain			
		Nonpast		Past	
		Affirmative	**Negative**	**Affirmative**	**Negative**
だ	の／である	だ／である	ではない／じゃない	だった	ではなかった／じゃなかった

	PREDICATE			ADVERBIAL
	Te-Form	ば **Conditional**	たら **Conditional**	
I-Adjectives	赤くて	赤ければ	赤かったら	赤く
	よくて	よければ	よかったら	よく
Na-Adjectives	静かで	静かならば／ 静かであれば	静かだったら	静かに

PREDICATE						
Polite				**Te-Form**	ば **Conditional**	たら **Conditional**
Nonpast		**Past**				
Affirmative	**Negative**	**Affirmative**	**Negative**			
です	ではありません／ じゃありません	でした	ではありません でした／ じゃありません でした	で	なら（ば）／ であれば	だったら

APPENDIX 3: Kanji List

Kanji	Total Number of Strokes	Radical	Name of Radical	Number of Strokes Beyond the Radical
CHAPTER 1				
京	8	亠	（なべぶた）	6
都	10	都	（おおざと）	8
社	7	示	（しめすへん）	3
内	4	入	（いりがしら）	2
目	5	目	（め）	0
所	8	戸	（と）	4
約	9	糸	（いと）	3
予	4	亅	（はねぼう）	3
車	7	車	（くるま）	0
早	6	日	（にち）	2
歩	8	止	（とめる）	4
館	16	食	（しょく）	8
乗	9	ノ	（の）	8
待	9	彳	（ぎょうにんべん）	6
駅	14	馬	（うま）	4
止	4	止	（とめる）	0
旅	10	方	（ほう）	6
客	9	宀	（うかんむり）	6
寺	6	寸	（すん）	3
神	9	示	（しめす）	5
地	6	土	（つち）	3
図	7	囗	（くにがまえ）	4
海	9	水	（みず）	6
曲	6	日	（いわく）	2
私	7	禾	（のぎへん）	2
CHAPTER 2				
新	13	斤	（きん）	9
開	12	門	（もん）	8
公	4	八	（はち）	2
園	13	囗	（くにがまえ）	10
住	7	人	（にんべん）	5
階	11	阜	（こざと）	9
広	5	广	（まだれ）	2
直	8	十	（じゅう）	6
戸	4	戸	（と）	0
古	5	十	（じゅう）	3
門	8	門	（もん）	0
室	9	宀	（うかんむり）	6

Kanji	Total Number of Strokes	Radical	Name of Radical	Number of Strokes Beyond the Radical
伝		人	（にんべん）	4
洗	9	水	（みず）	6
建	9	又	（えんにょう）	6
友	4	又	（また）	2
貸	11	貝	（かい）	4
借	10	人	（にんべん）	8
置	13	网	（あみがしら）	8
静	14	青	（あおい）	6
庭	10	广	（まだれ）	7
不	4	一	（いち）	3
便	9	人	（にんべん）	7
利	7	刀	（かたな）	5

CHAPTER 3

Kanji	Total Number of Strokes	Radical	Name of Radical	Number of Strokes Beyond the Radical
自	6	自	（みずから）	0
路	13	足	（あし）	6
交	6	亠	（なべぶた）	4
通	9	辶	（しんにゅう）	7
転	11	車	（くるま）	4
駐	15	馬	（うま）	5
教	11	攴	（とまた）	7
窓	11	穴	（あな）	6
閉		門	（もん）	3
消	10	水	（みず）	7
変	9	夂	（なつあし）	6
故	9	攴	（とまた）	5
横	15	木	（き）	11
働	13	人	（にんべん）	11
工	3	工	（たくみ）	0
速	9	辶	（しんにゅう）	7
違	11	辶	（しんにゅう）	9
反	4	厂	（がんだれ）	2
差	10	工	（たくみ）	7
点	9	火	（ひ）	5
信	9	人	（にんべん）	7
号	5	口	（くち）	2
走	7	走	（はしる）	0
帰	10	巾	（はば）	7
注	8	水	（みず）	5
意	13	心	（こころ）	9

CHAPTER 4

Kanji	Total Number of Strokes	Radical	Name of Radical	Number of Strokes Beyond the Radical
体	7	人	（にんべん）	5
頭	16	頁	（おおがい）	7

Kanji	Total Number of Strokes	Radical	Name of Radical	Number of Strokes Beyond the Radical
鼻	14	鼻	(はな)	0
式	6	弋	(しきがまえ)	3
耳	6	耳	(みみ)	0
歯	12	歯	(は)	0
御	12	彳	(ぎょうにんべん)	9
首	9	首	(くび)	0
指	9	手	(てへん)	6
足	7	足	(あし)	0
毛	4	毛	(け)	0
形	7	彡	(かみかざり)	4
丸	3	、	(てん)	2
角	7	角	(つの)	0
持	9	手	(て)	6
立	5	立	(たつ)	0
心	4	心	(こころ)	0
配	10	酉	(さけづくり)	3
苦	8	艸	(くさかんむり)	5
死	6	歹	(いちた)	2
元	4	儿	(ひとあし)	2
病	10	病	(やまいだれ)	5
院	9	阜	(こざと)	7
痛	10	病	(やまいだれ)	7
熱	15	火	(ひ)	11
薬	16	艸	(くさかんむり)	13
局	7	尸	(しかばね)	3
顔	18	頁	(おおがい)	9

CHAPTER 5

Kanji	Total Number of Strokes	Radical	Name of Radical	Number of Strokes Beyond the Radical
校	10	木	(き)	6
卒	8	十	(じゅう)	6
業	13	木	(き)	9
仕	5	人	(にんべん)	3
就	13	尤	(むにょう)	9
職	18	耳	(みみ)	12
退	8	辶	(しんにゅう)	6
育	8	肉	(にくづき)	4
若	8	艸	(くさかんむり)	5
老	6	老	(ろう)	0
愛	13	心	(こころ)	9
恋	10	心	(こころ)	6
初	7	刀	(かたな)	5
結	12	糸	(いと)	6
婚	11	女	(おんな)	8
召	5	口	(くち)	2
様	14	木	(き)	10

Kanji	Total Number of Strokes	Radical	Name of Radical	Number of Strokes Beyond the Radical
研	9	石	(いし)	4
究	7	穴	(あなかんむり)	2
医	7	匚	(はこがまえ)	5
者	8	老	(ろう)	4
師	10	巾	(はば)	7
銀	14	金	(かね)	6
亡	3	亠	(なべぶた)	1
忙		心	(こころ)	3
知	8	矢	(や)	3
存	6	子	(こ)	3
申	5	田	(た)	0
式	6	弋	(しきがまえ)	3

CHAPTER 6

Kanji	Total Number of Strokes	Radical	Name of Radical	Number of Strokes Beyond the Radical
換	12	手	(て)	9
際	12	阜	(こざと)	10
留	10	田	(た)	5
守	6	宀	(うかんむり)	3
受	8	爪	(つめ)	4
取	8	又	(また)	6
器	15	口	(くち)	12
報	12	土	(つち)	9
文	4	文	(ぶん)	0
打	5	手	(て)	2
調	15	言	(ことば)	8
英	8	艸	(くさかんむり)	5
映	9	日	(にち)	5
画	8	凵	(うけばこ)	6
郵	10	邑	(おおざと)	8
紙	10	糸	(いと)	4
送	8	辶	(しんにゅう)	6
達	11	辶	(しんにゅう)	9
宅	6	宀	(うかんむり)	3
重	9	里	(さと)	2
刊	5	刀	(かたな)	3
雑	14	隹	(ふるとり)	6
誌	14	言	(ごんべん)	7
記	10	言	(ごんべん)	3
放	8	攴	(とまた)	4
組	11	糸	(いと)	5
試	13	言	(ことば)	6
験	18	馬	(うま)	8
困	7	囗	(くにがまえ)	4
忘	7	心	(こころ)	3

CHAPTER 7

Kanji	Total Number of Strokes	Radical	Name of Radical	Number of Strokes Beyond the Radical
然	12	火	（ひ／かれつ）	8
化	4	匕	（さじ）	2
島	10	山	（やま）	7
村	7	木	（き）	3
湖	12	水	（みず）	9
川	3	川	（かわ）	0
州	6	川	（かわ）	3
石	5	石	（いし）	0
岩	8	山	（やま）	5
林	8	木	（き）	6
森	12	木	（き）	3
世	5	一	（いち）	4
界	9	田	（た）	4
球	11	玉	（たま）	7
昔	8	日	（にち）	4
害	10	宀	（うかんむり）	7
例	8	人	（にんべん）	6
他	5	人	（にんべん）	3
最	12	日	（いわく）	8
犬	4	犬	（いぬ）	0
馬	10	馬	（うま）	0
虫	6	虫	（むし）	0
頼	16	頁	（おおがい）	7
植		木	（き）	8
咲	9	口	（くち）	6
必	5	心	（こころ）	1
要	9	西	（にし）	3
習	11	羽	（はね）	5
練	8	糸	（いと）	8
慣	14	心	（こころ）	10

Japanese-English Glossary

This glossary is not intended to be used as a dictionary. Instead, it lists all Japanese words and phrases that are introduced for the first time in Book 2, with the exception of well-known place names, some proper nouns, conjugated forms, compound words, foreign loanwords that are very similar to the source language, and words and phrases that appeared in the glossary for Book 1. If you try to look up a word appearing in Book 2 and can't find it in this glossary, try the Book 1 glossary.

Entries are arranged in a-i-u-e-o Japanese alphabetical order. As in Japanese dictionaries, each word is presented in hiragana or katakana, followed by the kanji transcription, if appropriate. Compound nouns are grouped together with the parts that are identical indicated by 〜. For example,

ほん（本）book; 〜や（屋）bookstore

Phrases containing the same key word are also grouped together, with the identical portions indicated by "…". For example,

でんわ（電話）telephone; …をきる（切る）to hang up.

Verbs and adjectives are cited in their dictionary form except when appearing as part of a set phrase.

Nominal verbs are followed by [する]. I-adjectives are unmarked, but na-adjectives are followed by（な）.

English translations for nouns are given in the singular, and the plural is an option in most cases.

Finally, remember that these translations are not exact equivalents, but only reminders of the meanings you have learned in class. Only real-life contexts and native usage can be relied on to provide the full range of meanings for each word.

JAL（ジャル）　Japan Airlines
JR（ジェーアル）　Japan Rail, the privatized national passenger rail system
NHK（エヌエチケー）　Japan's public broadcasting system (*abbreviation for* 日本放送協会［にほんほうそうきょうかい］)
OA（オーエー）　office automation
OL（オーエル）　female clerical worker (from オフィス・レディー *office lady*)

あ

あいて（相手）　partner, opponent
あかちゃん（赤ちゃん）　baby
あがる（上がる）　to raise, go up
あきかん（空き缶）　empty can
あく（開く）　to open, to be opened
アクセル　accelerator
あける（開ける）　to open [something]
あげる　to give (*to a second or third person*)
あげる（上げる）　to raise
アサリ　clam
あし（脚、足）　leg, foot
あしくび（足首）　ankle
あしのゆび（足の指）　toe
あたえる（与える）　to give (*abstract*)
あつかう（扱う）　to deal with
あつぎ（厚着）　warm clothes
あつまる（集まる）　to gather, congregate
あてな（宛名）　addressee
あと（後）　after; あとで　afterwards
アニメ　animation, animated cartoons
アパート　apartment
あひる　duck
あぶない（危ない）　dangerous
あやまる（謝る）　to apologize
あらたまる　to become formal
あらわれ（現れ）　expression, indication
アルバイト　part-time job
あんき（暗記）［する］　memorization; (to memorize)
あんさつ（暗殺）［する］　assassination; (to assassinate)
あんしん（安心）［する］　peace of mind; (to feel relieved)
あんない（案内）［する］　guidance, information; (to guide, to lead)

い

いいまちがい（言い間違い）　misstatement, slip of the tongue
いけ（池）　pond
いけん（意見）　opinion
いし（石）　stone
いじ（維持）［する］　maintenance; (to maintain)
いし（医師）／いしゃ（医者）　medical doctor
いじょうきしょう（異常気象）　abnormal weather
イスラムきょう（イスラム教）　Islam
いそいで（急いで）　quickly, hurriedly

いたい（痛い）　painful
いたずらでんわ（いたずら電話）　crank phone call
いただく　to receive (*from a superior*); to eat, to receive (*humble form*)
いち（位置）　position
いちじてき（一時的）（な）　temporary
いってい（一定）　uniformity, consistency
いっぱい　full
いっぱくにしょくつき（1泊2食付き）　one night's lodging including two meals
いっぽうつうこう（一方通行）　one-way traffic
いぬ（犬）　dog
いはん（違反）［する］　violation of rules; (to violate rules)
いま（居間）　living room
いや（な）　disagreable
イライラする　to be irritated
いらっしゃる　to be, come, go (*honorific form*)
いれる（入れる）　to turn on (a switch), to insert, put in, include
いわ（岩）　rock outcropping
いわう（祝う）　to celebrate
インコ　parakeet
いんさつ（印刷）［する］　printing; (to print)
インターフォン　intercom
インドかい（インド海）　the Indian Ocean

う

ウインカー　turn signal
うえき（植木）　potted plant
うえる（植える）　to plant
うけとる（受け取る）　to receive, to accept
うける（受ける）　to undergo (*surgery, X-rays, a test, etc.*)
うごかす（動かす）　to move [something]
うごく（動く）　to move, to be in motion
うさぎ（兎）　rabbit
うし（牛）　cow, cattle
うちゅう（宇宙）　outer space, the universe
うつる（移る）　to move from one place to another
うで（腕）　arm
うま（馬）　horse
うむ（生む）　to give birth
うめ（梅）　plum tree
うれしい（嬉しい）　happy, delighted
うんが（運河）　canal
うんちん（運賃）　fare
うんてんしゅ（運転手）　driver
うんてんせき（運転席）　driver's seat
うんてんめんきょ（しょう）（運転免許［証］）　driver's license

え

え（絵）　[drawn or painted] picture
エアコン　air conditioner
えいきょう（影響）　influence; …をあたえる（与える）　to have an influence

えいじしんぶん（英字新聞）　English-language newspaper
えきいん（駅員）　station employee
えきたい（液体）　liquid
えきべん（駅弁）　box lunch sold in train stations
えさ（餌）　animal food, bait
エチケット　etiquette
える（得る）　to obtain
えんか（演歌）　(*a type of popular song*)
エンスト　engine stall
えんそく（遠足）　excursion, outing
えんとつ（煙突）　chimney

お

おいかける（追いかける）　to chase
おいこす（追い越す）　to pass, to overtake
おいでになる　to come (*honorific form*)
おうせつま（応接間）　guest reception room, parlor
おうだんほうどう（横断歩道）　crosswalk;　～きょう（～橋）
　　pedestrian bridge
おうふく（往復）　round trip;　～きっぷ（～切符）　round trip
　　ticket;　～はがき（～葉書）　a postcard with a prepaid return
　　portion for the recipient's reply
おうべい（欧米）　Europe and North America, Western countries
おうぼ（応募）［する］　to apply for something
おうぼようし（応募用紙）　application form
おえる（終える）　to end something
おおやさん（大家さん）　property owner, landlord, landlady
　　(*informal*)
オートバイ　motorcycle
おか（丘）　hill
おかげ（お陰）　favor, kind intentions;　…のおかげで　thanks to . . .
おき（沖）　the open sea near a coast
おく（置く）　to place, to put;　～ておく　to do something ahead
　　of time
おくりもの（贈り物）　gift, present
おこなう（行う）　carry out, perform (*a procedure*)
おこる（怒る）　to get angry
おこる（起る）　to occur, to happen
おしいれ（押入）　**futon** closet
おじぎ（お辞儀）［する］　(to) bow
おしこめる（押し込める）　to push into
おじゃま（お邪魔）［する］　to visit someone's house (*humble*)
おす（押す）　to push
おせちりょうり（お節料理）　a type of cuisine served at New Year
おせん（汚染）［する］　pollution; (to pollute)
おそれ（恐れ）　fear
おつかい　errand
おっしゃる　to say (*honorific form*)
おてあらい（お手洗い）　restroom, toilet
おとなしい　proper, well-behaved, quiet
おどる（踊る）　to dance
おどろく（驚く）　to be surprised
おなか　stomache, belly;　～がすく　to get hungry (*lit., the
　　stomach empties out*)

～がすいている　is hungry
おふろ（お風呂）　bath (*especially Japanese-style*);　…にはいる
　　（入る）　to take a bath
おぼん（お盆）　O-Bon (*summer festival honoring the spirits of
　　the dead*)
おみこし（お御輿）　**o-mikoshi** (*a portable shrine carried during
　　festivals*)
おみまい（お見舞い）　paying a condolence call, visiting a sick
　　person
おみやげ（お土産）　souvenir
おめしになる（お召しになる）　to wear (*honorific form*)
おも（主）（な）　principal, main;　おもに　mainly
おり（檻）　cage
おる　to be (*humble equivalent of* いる)
おわび（お詫び）　apology
おんがくか（音楽家）　musician
おんせん（温泉）　hot spring

か

か（蚊）　mosquito
カーブ　curve
かいがい（海外）　overseas
かいがん（海岸）　beach, shore
かいきょう（海峡）　channel, straits
かいけいし（会計士）　accountant
かいけつ（解決）［する］　solution; (to solve)
がいこうかん（外交官）　diplomat
かいすうけん（回数券）　coupon ticket, strip of tickets
かいそう（海藻）　seaweed
かいだん（階段）　stairway, steps
がいねん（概念）　general concept
かいはつ（開発）　development
かう（飼う）　to raise or keep an animal
がか（画家）　painter
かがくしゃ（科学者）　scientist
かかと（踵）　heel
かがみ（鏡）　mirror
かかりちょう（係長）　subsection chief (*in a company*)
かぎ（鍵）　key, lock;　…をかける　to lock
かきとめ（書留）　registered mail
かぐ（家具）　furniture
がくれき（学歴）　educational history, school records
かける　to hang something up;　エンジンをかける　to start an
　　engine;　でんわ（電話）をかける　to make a phone call;　おめ（目）
　　にかける　to show (*humble*)　かぎ（鍵）をかける　to lock;
　　かけ直す（かけなおす）　to call back (on the phone)
かこむ（囲む）　to surround
かざん（火山）　volcano
かじ（火事）　fire (*a building burning, etc.*)
かじつ（果実）　fruit
かしべっそう（貸し別荘）　vacation rental
かしゅ（歌手）　singer
かず（数）　number (*amount*)
ガスレンジ　gas stove

かぜ (風邪) a cold or the flu; …をひく to catch a cold or the flu

かせいふ (家政婦) housekeeper

かた (肩) shoulder

かた (+ *name of body part*) (片〜) one [of something that comes in pairs]; かたて (片手) one hand

かたち (形) shape

かたづける (片付ける) to straighten up, to clean off, to put away

かたみちきっぷ (片道切符) one-way ticket

かだん (花壇) flower bed

かちょう (課長) section chief (of a company)

かつお bonito (*a kind of fish*)

がっかりする to be disappointed

かってぐち (勝手口) back (or side) door

かつやく (活躍) [する] (to play an) active role

かなしい (悲しい) sad

かなしむ (悲しむ) to be sad

かのうせい (可能性) possibility

かぶしきがいしゃ (株式会社) corporation that issues stock

かふん (花粉) pollen

かまう to be bothered, to mind something; かまいません it doesn't matter

がまん (我慢) [する] patience, endurance; (to put up with something unpleasant)

かむ to bite

かゆい itchy

かようきょく (歌謡曲) popular song

カルテ patient's chart

ガレージ garage

かれさんすい (枯山水) a Japanese-style dry garden

かれる (枯れる) to wither, die (*plants and trees only*)

かわ (川) river

かわいがる to treat with affection, to make a pet of

かわかす (乾かす) to dry something

かわり (代わり) exchange, replacement; お金の代わりに instead of money

かわる (変わる) to undergo change, to change

かんする (関する) to be connected with; X に関する regarding X

かんがえる (考える) to think, to ponder

かんきょう (環境) circumstances, environment; 〜はかい (〜破壊) environmental damage; 〜ほご (〜保護) environmental protection

かんけつ (簡潔) (な) brief, concise

かんこう (観光) [する] sightseeing; (to sightsee); 〜あんないじょ (〜案内所) tourist information center; 〜きゃく (〜客) tourist, sightseer

かんごふ (看護婦) nurse

かんじゃ (患者) patient (*in a hospital or clinic*)

かんじる (感じる) to feel an emotion or sensation

かんぜい (関税) tariff

かんそうき (乾燥機) clothes drier

かんちょう (官庁) government office

かんづめ (缶詰) canned food

かんとく (監督) superintendent, [film] director

かんぬし (神主) Shinto priest

かんばつ (旱魃) drought

がんばる (頑張る) to do one's best, to hang in there, to come through a difficult situation all right

かんめい (感銘) [する] (to be struck with) admiration

き

きえる (消える) to go off, go out (*lights, fire, etc.*), disappear

きがるに (気軽に) feeling free, without hesitation

きかん (期間) period, length of time

ききちがい (聞き間違い) mistake in hearing

きぎょう (企業) enterprise, business

きく (菊) chrysanthemum

きげん (起源) origin

ぎこちない awkward, clumsy

きじ (記事) article (*in a newspaper or magazine*)

ぎし (技師) engineer

きしゃ (記者) reporter

ぎせい (犠牲) [にする] (to) sacrifice

きつえんせき (喫煙席) smoking seat

きづく (気づく) to notice

きつね (狐) fox

きっぷ (切符) ticket

き (気) spirit, mind; 〜にする to give a lot of attention or thought to; 〜になる to cause worry or concern

きにゅう (記入) [する] writing in; (to fill out a form)

きのう (機能) function

きぼう (希望) [する] (to) hope, aspiration (to aspire)

きほんてき (基本的) (な) basic

きまる (決まる) to be decided

きめる (決める) to decide

きもち (気持ち) feeling, mood, atmosphere

きゃくしつ (客室) guest room

ぎゃくたい (虐待) [する] cruel treatment; (to treat cruelly)

きゃくま (客間) sitting room for entertaining guests, parlor

きゃっかんてき (客観的) (な) objective, impartial

きゅうきゅうしゃ (救急車) ambulance

きゅうこう (急行) express train

きゅうりょう (給料) salary

きょういく (教育) education

きょうし (教師) schoolteacher (*non-honorific form*)

きょうじゅ (教授) college or university professor

きょうつう (共通) [する] (to have) traits in common

きょうみ (興味) interest; X に興味がある to be interested in X

きょうりょく (協力) [する] cooperation; (to cooperate)

ぎょぎょう (漁業) commercial fishing

きょく (曲) tune, melody

キリストきょう (キリスト教) Christianity

きる (切る) to cut; スイッチを… to turn off a switch

きれる (切れる) to be cut

きんえんせき (禁煙席) non-smoking seat

きんにく (筋肉) muscle

く

くうき（空気）　air
くうこう（空港）　airport
くうしつ（空室）　vacant room
クーペ　coupe
クーラー　air conditioner
くさ（草）　grass
くじら（鯨）　whale
くずいれ（屑入れ）　trash basket
くずす　to break into smaller pieces, to make change (*money*)
くすり（薬）　medicine; …を飲む　to take medicine
くださる　to give to me, give to us, give to my group (*honorific*)
くだり（下り）　train moving away from Tokyo
くち（口）　mouth
くちひげ（口髭）　moustache
くちびる（唇）　lip
くつばこ（靴箱）　shoe cabinet
くつみがき（靴みがき）　polishing shoes, a person who shines shoes
くび（首）　neck; …にする　to fire someone from a job; …になる　to be fired
くま（熊）　bear
くみあい（組合）　union
クラクション　automobile horn
グリーンしゃ（グリーン車）　first class car (*on a train, lit.* "green car")
くるしい（苦しい）　oppressively painful
くれる　to give to me, give to us, give to my group
ぐんじん（軍人）　military personnel

け

け（毛）　hair, strand of hair
けいえい（経営）［する］　management; (to manage)
けいけん（経験）［する］　(to) experience
けいこうとう（蛍光灯）　fluorescent light
けいこく（警告）　warning
けいざい（経済）　economics; 〜てき（〜的）　economical
けいさつ（警察）　the police; 〜かん（〜官）　police officer; …につかまれる　to be caught by the police
けいしき（形式）　form
げいじゅつか（芸術家）　visual artist
けいたいでんわ（携帯電話）　cellular phone
けが（怪我）　injury; 〜をする　to be injured
けす（消す）　to turn [something] off, extinguish, to erase
けずる　to whittle away at, to grade (a hill or mountain)
げた（下駄）　**geta** (*Japanese-style wooden clogs*)
けつえきがた（血液型）　blood type
けっこん（結婚）［する］　marriage; (to get married); 〜きねんび（〜記念日）　wedding anniversary; 〜しき（〜式）　wedding ceremony
けっちゅう（血中）　in the blood
げり（下痢）　diarrhea; …をする　to have diarrhea
ける（蹴る）　to kick

けわしい（険しい）　steep
〜けん（軒）　counter for buildings
げんいん（原因）　cause
げんかん（玄関）　entry hall, foyer
けんきゅうしつ（研究室）　a professor's office
げんきんかきとめ（現金書留）　cash registered mail
けんこう（健康）（な）　health; (healthy)
けんさ（検査）　(medical) test
けんじ（検事）　prosecutor (*similar to a district attorney in the U.S. legal system*)
げんじつ（現実）　reality
げんしりょく（原子力）　nuclear power
けんせつ（建設）［する］　construction; (to construct)
げんだいじん（現代人）　people of the modern age
けんちくか（建築家）　architect
けんばいき（券売機）　ticket vending machine
けんぶつ（見物）［する］　sightseeing; (to sightsee)

こ

こい（濃い）　thick, dense, strong (*coffee, tea, etc.*)
こういん（工員）　factory worker
こうがい（郊外）　the suburbs
こうがい（公害）　pollution
こうかんしゅ（交換手）　telephone operator
こうぎ（講義）　lecture
こうくうびん（航空便）　air mail
ごうけい（合計）　total
こうげん（高原）　plateau
こうこう（高校）　high school
こうこく（広告）　written advertisement; …を出す　to place an advertisement; きゅうじん〜（求人〜）　help wanted advertisement
こうさてん（交差点）　intersection
こうじちゅう（工事中）　under construction
こうしゅうでんわ（公衆電話）　public phone
こうしょう（交渉）　negotiation
こうじょう（工場）　factory
こうそくどうろ（高速道路）　freeway
こうつう（交通）　traffic; 〜きかん（〜機関）　means of transportation; 〜じゅうたい（〜渋滞）　traffic jam
こうどう（講堂）　auditorium
こうどく（購読）［する］　subscription; (to subscribe)
こうひょう（好評）　popularity, favorable comment
こうぶざせき（後部座席）　rear seat
こうへい（公平）（な）　fair, equitable
こうむいん（公務員）　government employee
こうよう（紅葉）　autumn leaves
こえる（超える）　to exceed
こおる（凍る）　to freeze up
ごかい（誤解）［する］　misunderstanding; (to misunderstand)
こきょう（故郷）　home town
こくさい（国際）　international
こくない（国内）　domestic, within the country
こころ（心）　mind, feelings, "heart"; …をこめて　with feeling

こし（腰）　waist, hips; 〜かける　to sit down
ごじ（誤字）　misspelling, wrong letter
こしょう（故障）［する］　(to have a) mechanical breakdown; (to become) out of order
ごぞんじ（御存じ）だ　to know (*honorific form*)
こたつ　table with built-in heater
コック　professional cook
こづつみ（小包）　package
こと　[abstract] thing, matter, concept; …ことにする　to decide on…; …ことになる　to be decided that…; することがある　There are occasions when I do it; したことがある　I have had the experience of doing it.
ことわる（断る）　to reject, refuse
ごふくや（呉服屋）　Japanese **kimono** store
こまる（困る）　to have difficulty, to be troubled, to be a problem; しては困る　It will cause trouble if you do that; 困った　What a hassle! 困っている　is upset
ごみ（塵）　garbage; 〜や（〜屋）　garbage collector
ごらん（御覧）になる　*honorific form of* 見る
こる　to become stiff
ころす（殺す）　to kill
こわい（怖い）　frightening, afraid
こわがる（怖がる）　to be frightened
こわす（壊す）　to break [something]
こんやく（婚約）［する］　engagement; (to become engaged); 〜しゃ（〜者）　fiance(e)

さ

サービスりょう（料）　service charge
さいこう（最高）　the highest, the best, the greatest
さいごに（最後に）　lastly
ざいさん（財産）　property (*including money and possessions*)
さいてい（最低）　lowest, worst, "the pits"
サイドブレーキ　parking brake
さいばんかん（裁判官）　judge
さがる（下がる）　to come/go down, to dangle
さかん（な）　prevalent, abundant
さきゅう（砂丘）　sand dune
さくいん（索引）　index
さげる（下げる）　to lower [something]
さしあげる　to give (*to a superior or outsider*)
さしだしにん（差出人）　sender
〜さつ（〜冊）　(*counter for books, magazines, and other bound and printed materials*)
さっか（作家）　author
ざぶとん（座布団）　floor cushion
さらに（更に）　furthermore, moreover
さる（猿）　monkey
さわやか（な）　fresh, refreshing
さわる（触る）　to touch; Xに触る　to touch X
さんか（参加）［する］　participation, (to participate)
さんかく（三角）（の）　triangle (triangular)
さんぎょう（産業）　industry; 〜こうがい（〜公害）　industrial pollution

ざんぎょう（残業）　overtime work
さんこうしょ（参考書）　reference book
さんせい（賛成）　agreement
さんぱい（参拝）［する］　(to) worship at a shrine or temple

し

し（死）　death
し（氏）　(*a title similar in meaning to* - さん *but used mostly in formal, written contexts*)
しあわせ（幸せ）（な）　contented happiness; (happy)
しおれる　to wither, fade, droop
しか（鹿）　deer
しかく（四角）　rectangle, square; しかくい（四角い）　rectangular, square-shaped
しかる（叱る）　to scold
じぎょう（事業）　enterprise, business
しげん（資源）　resources
じけん（事件）　event, incident
じこくひょう（時刻表）　timetable (*for trains, buses, etc.*)
じこ（事故）　accident; …にあう　to be involved in an accident; …をおこす（起す）　to cause an accident
しぜん（自然）　nature, the natural world; 〜はかい（〜破壊）　destroying nature
じそく（時速）　speed per hour
した（舌）　tongue
じだい（時代）　era, period of history; 〜げき（〜劇）　**samurai** drama
しちめんちょう（七面町）　turkey (*the bird, not the meat*)
しっかり　firmly
しつぎょう（失業）［する］　unemployment; (to become unemployed)
じつげん（実現）［する］　realization; (to be realized, to materialize)
じつは（実は）　actually, in fact
しっぱい（失敗）［する］　failure; (to fail)
していせき（指定席）　reserved seat
してつ（私鉄）　privately owned railroad
してん（支店）　branch store, bank branch office
じてん（事典）　encyclopedia
じどうしゃ（自動車）　automobile, car
しな（品）　item, goods, product
じなん（次男）　second son
しば（芝）　turf, sod
しばい（芝居）　theatrical play
しばふ（芝生）　lawn
じぶつ（事物）　things, matters, affairs (*formal*)
しほうしけん（司法試験）　bar examination
しまる（閉まる）　to close; ドアがしまる（閉まる）　the door closes
じむいん（事務員）　office clerk
じむしょ（事務所）　business or administrative office
しめる（閉める）　to close [something]; ドアをしめる（閉める）　to close the door

しゃかい（社会）　society；〜じん（〜人）　a person who has finished school and entered the workforce；〜ほしょう（〜保障）　social guarantees
しゃくやにん（借家人）　tenant
しゃこ（車庫）　garage, carport
しゃしょう（車掌）　train conductor
しゃしんか（写真家）　photographer
しゃちょう（社長）　president (of a company)
しゃどう（車道）　road, highway
じゆう（自由）（に）　freedom (freely)
じゆうせき（自由席）　non-reserved seat
しゅう（州）　state, province
しゅうかん（習慣）　habit, custom
しゅうかんし（週刊誌）　weekly magazine
しゅうきょう（宗教）　religion
じゅうしょ（住所）　address
しゅうしょく（就職）［する］　getting a job；(to get a job)
じゅうたく（住宅）　residence, housing；〜ち（〜地）　residential area
しゅうちょうりょく（集中力）　power of concentration
じゅうぶん（充分）　sufficient
じゅうよう（重要）（な）　important
しゅうり（修理）［する］　(to) repair；〜こう（〜工）　mechanic
じゅうりょく（重力）　gravity
じゅきょう（儒教）　Confucianism
じゅく（塾）　cram school
しゅくしょう（縮小）［する］　reduction；(to scale down)
しゅくはく（宿泊）［する］　lodging；(to stay, to lodge)
じゅけん（受験）　preparing for and taking school and university entrance examinations
しゅじゅつ（手術）　surgery；…をする　to perform surgery；…をうける（受ける）　to undergo surgery
しゅだん（手段）　means of doing something
しゅちょう（主張）［する］　assertion；(to assert)
しゅつえん（出演）［する］　appearance as a performer；(to appear as a performer)
しゅっきん（出勤）［する］　coming to work；(to show up at work)
しゅっせき（出席）［する］　attendance；(to attend)
しゅっちょう（出張）［する］　(to go on a) business trip
しゅっぱん（出版）［する］　publication；(to publish)
しゅふ（主婦）　housewife
じゅみょう（寿命）　lifespan
じゅもく（樹木）　trees and shrubs
しょうがつ（正月）　the New Year's holiday
しょうがっこう（小学校）　elementary school
じょうきゃく（乗客）　passenger
じょうざい（錠剤）　pill
しょうじ（障子）　**shooji** (*screen made of transclucent paper*)
じょうし（上司）　superior, supervisor (*at work*)
しょうしゃ（商社）　trading company
しょうしん（昇進）［する］　promotion；(to be promoted at work)
しょうせつ（小説）　novel
しょうとつ（衝突）［する］　collision；(to collide)
じょうほう（情報）　information

しょうぼうし（消防士）　fire fighter
しょうぼうしゃ（消防車）　fire engine
しょうらい（将来）　future
しょくぎょう（職業）　occupation
しょくご（食後）　after meals
しょくせいかつ（食生活）　customary diet
しょくぜん（食前）　before meals
しょくどうしゃ（食堂車）　dining car (*on a train*)
しょくば（職場）　workplace
しょくぶつ（植物）　plant
しょくれき（職歴）　employment history
しょさい（書斎）　study, home office
じょゆう（女優）　actress
しょるい（書類）　document, papers
しらせる（知らせる）　to notify
しり（尻）　buttocks
しんごう（信号）　traffic light
じんこうようしょく（人工養殖）　artificial culturing (*of pearls*)
しんこく（深刻）（な）　serious
しんこんりょこう（新婚旅行）　honeymoon
しんさつ（診察）［する］　(to perform a) medical examination
しんしつ（寝室）　bedroom
じんじぶ（人事部）　personnel department
しんじゅ（真珠）　pearl
しんじる（信じる）　to believe
じんせい（人生）　life
しんせき（親戚）　relatives
しんせん（新鮮）（な）　fresh
しんだいしゃ（寝台車）　sleeping car (*on a train*)
しんちく（新築）（の）　newly built
しんちょう（身長）　height (*of a person*)
しんとう（神道）　Shintoism
しんぱい（心配）［する］　worry；(be worried)
しんぷ（神父）　Catholic priest
しんぽ（進歩）　progress
しんりん（森林）　forest
スイカ　watermelon
スイッチ　switch (*machine or appliance*)；…を入れる　to turn on a switch；…をきる（切る）　to turn off a switch

す

すいはんき（炊飯器）　rice cooker
すいへいせん（水平線）　horizon
すぎ（杉）　Japanese cedar
すすめる　to recommend
スタジオ　studio
スタンド　floor lamp, desk lamp
…ずつ　… each, per …
ずつう（頭痛）　headache；…がする　to have a headache
スッキリする　to feel refreshed
スト（ライキ）　strike (*by workers*)
すなお（素直）（な）　gentle, mild
ズバリ　boldly, decisively

スピード speed; …をだす (出す) to increase speed; …をおとす (落とす) to decrease speed

すべて (全て) all

スポーツせんしゅ (スポーツ選手) athlete

すませる to get by with doing, to manage

するどい sharp

せ

せいおう (西欧) Western European

せいかつ (生活) [する] life, lifestyle; (to lead a life)

せいき (世紀) century

せいけいしゅじゅつ (整形手術) cosmetic surgery

せいげんそくど (制限速度) speed limit

せいざ (正座) [する] sitting on the floor in formal Japanese style; (to sit Japanese-style)

せいさん (生産) [する] production; (to produce)

せいじか (政治家) politician

せおう (背負う) to carry on one's back

せかい (世界) world; 〜てき (〜的) (な) worldwide

せき (席) seat; …をゆずる (譲る) to give up one's seat to someone else

せき (咳) a cough; …をする to cough; …がでる (出る) to have an ongoing cough

せきてい (石庭) rock garden

せきどう (赤道) equator

せきにん (責任) responsibility

せっかく having gone to all the trouble; …の long-awaited

せっけん (石鹸) soap

せつめい (説明) [する] explanation; (to explain)

せつやく (節約) [する] saving, economizing; (to save, to economize)

せなか (背中) back (of the body)

ぜひ by all means

セロテープ cellophane tape

せわ (世話) personal care, favors; …をする to take care of someone; お…になる to receive favors

せんご (戦後) after the war (usually refers to World War II)

ぜんこく (全国) all over the country

せんす (扇子) folding fan

せんそう (戦争) war

せんたく (洗濯) [する] laundry; (to do laundry); 〜き (〜機) washing machine; 〜もの (〜物) things to be laundered

せんとう (先頭) forefront, leading position

せんとう (銭湯) public bath

せんぷうき (扇風機) electric fan

ぜんぶざせき (前部座席) front seat

せんめんじょ (洗面所) washstand (area with sink for washing hands and face)

そ

ぞう (像) statue

ぞう (象) elephant

そうじ (掃除) [する] housecleaning; (to clean house); 〜き (〜機) vacuum cleaner

そうしき (葬式) funeral

そうだん (相談) [する] consulation; (to consult); 〜しつ (〜室) conference room

そうりょ (僧侶) Buddhist priest or monk

そくたつ (速達) express mail

そくど (速度) speed

そせん (祖先) ancestor

そだつ (育つ) to grow up

そのかわり in its place

そろばん abacus

ぞんじる (存じる) to think, to know; ぞんじている (存じている) know (humble form); ぞんじない (存じない) not know (humble form)

た

たいいん (退院) [する] getting out of the hospital; (to get out of the hospital)

たいおん (体温) body temperature; 〜けい (〜計) clinical thermometer

だいがくいん (大学院) graduate school

たいきおせん (大気汚染) smog

だいく (大工) carpenter

たいじゅう (体重) body weight

だいじょうぶ (大丈夫) (な) all right, without problems

たいしょく (退職) [する] retirement; (to retire)

たいせいよう (大西洋) the Atlantic Ocean

たいせつ (大切) (な) important

たいど (態度) attitude

だいなし (台無し) totally ruined

タイプをうつ (打つ) to type

たいへいよう (太平洋) the Pacific Ocean

たいよう (太陽) sun

たいりく (大陸) continent

たいりょうせいさん (大量生産) mass production

たおす (倒す) to knock over, to set back

たかさ (高さ) height

たから (宝) treasure

たき (滝) waterfall

たけ (竹) bamboo

たしかめる (確かめる) to make sure

たしょう (多少) more or less

たずねる (尋ねる) to ask, to inquire

ただいま (只今) right now

たたく (叩く) to hit with the hand, to knock

ただしく (正しく) correctly

たたみ (畳) **tatami** (woven reed floor matting)

たつ (発つ) to leave; 東京を… to leave from Tokyo

たつ (立つ／建つ) to stand up, to be built

だつじ (脱字) missing letter or character in a piece of writing

たてる (建てる) to build

たとえば (例えば) for example

たな (棚) shelf

たに（谷）　valley
たね（種）　seed
たのしい（楽しい）　enjoyable, fun
たのしみ（楽しみ）　pleasure, looking forward to something;
　　パーティーを...にする　to look forward to the party
たはた（田畑）　rice paddies and dry fields
ためる（貯める）　to save (money, etc.)
たもつ（保つ）　to maintain as is
タレント　television personality
だんこ（断固）（な）　firm, decisive
たんす（箪笥）　chest of drawers, wardrobe
だんたいりょこう（団体旅行）　group travel
だんち（団地）　subsidized housing development
ダンプカー　dump truck
たんぼ（田んぼ）　rice paddy

ち

ちい（地位）　position, status
チェンジレバー　gear shift lever
つかむ　to catch, grab, hold
ちかみち（近道）　shortcut
ちきゅう（地球）　earth
ちこく（遅刻）［する］　to be late for something
ちじん（知人）　known person
ちゃくりく（着陸）［する］　landing; (to land [airplanes])
ちゅうい（注意）［する］　attention; (to watch out for, to pay
　　attention to); ～りょく（～力）　power of concentration
ちゅうがっこう（中学校）　middle school, junior high school
ちゅうけい（中継）［する］　(to do a) live broadcast
ちゅうこ（中古）　second-hand, used
ちゅうこく（忠告）［する］　advice, warning; (to advise, to warn)
ちゅうしゃ（注射）　an injection, a shot; ...をする　to give an
　　injection; ...をうける（受ける）　to receive an injection
ちゅうしゃ（駐車）［する］　parking; (to park); ～じょう（～場）
　　parking lot; ～きんし（禁止）　no parking
ちゅうしん（中心）　center
ちゅうねん（中年）　middle age
ちょう（蝶）　butterfly
ちょうきょりでんわ（長距離電話）　long distance phone call
ちょうさ（調査）［する］　investigation, survey; (to investigate)
ちょくせつ（直接）　direct
ちょしゃ（著者）　author
ちょっとした　simple, easy, effortless
ちり（地理）　geography

つ

ついとつ（追突）［する］　rear end collision; (to rear-end)
つうやく（通訳）　interpreter
つうわ（通話）　telephone call
つき（月）　moon
つく（着く）　to arrive
つく（付く）　to become attached, to go on (appliances, lights, etc.)
つけね（付け根）　base, root

つち（土）　soil
つねに（常に）　ordinarily
つばさ（翼）　wing
つぶれる　to go under, to fail
ツボ　**tsubo**, pressure point (*shiatsu*)
つぼ（坪）　**tsubo**, (*measurement of land area equal to 3.3 m²*)
つめ（爪）　fingernail, toenail
つめこむ　to pack in
つめる　to pack; 服をスーツケースにつめる　to pack clothes into
　　a suitcase
つれてくる（連れてくる）　to bring [people]

て

て（手）　hand
ていきけん（定期券）　monthly commuter pass
ていきけんしん（定期検診）　regular health check-up
ていきてき（定期的）（な）　periodic, regular
ていりゅうじょ（停留所）　bus or tram stop
てくび（手首）　wrist
てっぺん　top of the head
てん（点）　point
でんきせいひん（電気製品）　electrical appliance
でんきゅう（電球）　light bulb
てんきん（転勤）［する］　changing jobs, (to change jobs)
でんごん（伝言）　message
てんじょう（天井）　ceiling
でんしレンジ（電子レンジ）　microwave oven
でんせつ（伝説）　traditional legend
でんたく（電卓）　electric calculator
でんぽう（電報）　telegram; ...をうつ（打つ）　to send a telegram
でんわ（電話）　telephone; ...がなる（鳴る）　the telephone
　　rings; ～こうかんしゅ（～交換手）　telephone operator;
　　～ちょう（～帳）　telephone book; ～ボックス　telephone
　　booth; ...をかける　to make a phone call; ...をきる
　　（切る）　to hang up

と

と（戸）　door
といあわせる（問い合わせる）　to inquire
...といえば（...と言えば）　speaking of . . . , Now that you
　　mention it.
とうげ（峠）　mountain pass
どうせい（同棲）　living together
どうぶつ（動物）　animal; ～えん（～園）　zoo
どうよう（同様）　in the same way
どうりょう（同僚）　colleague
どうろ（道路）　street, road; ～ちず（～地図）　road map
とおす（通す）　to send through
とおる（通る）　to go through, to go along [a street]
どくじの（独自の）　original, peculiar to
とくしゅう（特集）　special collection, special feature (*in a
　　newspaper or magazine*)
とくせい（特性）　unique characteristic

どくとくの（独特の）　unique
とくべつ（特別）（な）　special
どくりつ（独立）［する］　independence; (to become independent, to start one's own business)
とこのま（床の間）　alcove
ところ　place, point in time
とち（土地）　land
とちゅう（途中）　on the way, in the midst of
とっきゅう（特急）　super express train
とっておきの　best, treasured, valuable
とっておく　to keep, maintain
とどける（届ける）　to deliver
となり（隣）　neighboring, next door to; （お）となり（お隣）next door neighbor
とぶ（跳ぶ）　to jump
とまる（止まる）　to come to a stop
とまる（泊まる）　to stay overnight
とめる（止める）　stop [something]
とら（虎）　tiger
とり（鳥）　bird
とりい（鳥居）　gate of a Shinto shrine
どりょく（努力）　effort
とんや（問屋）　wholesale store

な

ないせん（内線）　[telephone] extension
ないよう（内容）　contents
なおす（直す）　to repair, to mend
なおる（直る）　to be repaired, to get better
なおる（治る）　to recover from illness
ながし（流し）　sink (kitchen, bathroom, etc.)
ながめ（眺め）　view, vista
ながもち（長持ち）［する］　durability; (to be durable)
ながれる（流れる）　to flow
なくす　to lose
なくなる　to get lost, to disappear
なくなる（亡くなる）　to die (polite)
など　and so on, etc.
なやみごと（悩みごと）　worries, personal problems
なやむ（悩む）　to fret, to brood
ならす（鳴らす）　to sound (a horn, a bell, etc.)
ならぶ（並ぶ）　to get in line
ならべる（並べる）　to line [something] up
なる（鳴る）　to ring
なわとび　jumping rope
なんきょく（南極）　South Pole
ナンバープレート　license plate

に

にぎる（握る）　to grip
にちじょうせいかつ（日常生活）　daily life
にっか（日課）　daily schedule
にっき（日記）　diary

にぶる　to decline, to become weakened
にほんま（日本間）　Japanese-style room
にもつ（荷物）　luggage
にゅういん（入院）［する］　hospitalization; (to be hospitalized)
にゅうがく（入学）［する］　matriculation; (to enter a school)
にゅうしゃ（入社）［する］　entering a company; (to start work at a company)
にわ（庭）　garden, yard
ニワトリ　chicken
にわいじり（庭いじり）　gardening (as a hobby)
にんぎょう（人形）　doll
にんしん（妊娠）［する］　pregnancy; (to get pregnant)

ぬ

ぬいもの（縫い物）　sewing
ぬま（沼）　marsh

ね

ね（根）　root; …をはる（張る）　to extend roots
ねがう（願う）　to request
ねかす（寝かす）　to put to bed
ねずみ（鼠）　mouse, rat
ねつ（熱）　fever; …がある　to have a fever
ねむい（眠い）　sleepy
ねんがじょう（年賀状）　New Year's card
ねんじゅうぎょうじ（年中行事）　annual event

の

のうみん（農民）　farmer
のうやく（農薬）　fertilizer; …をまく　to spread fertilizer
のこす（残す）　to leave behind
のこる（残る）　to be left over, remain
のど（喉）　throat
のばす（伸ばす）　to extend or stretch [something]
のぼり（上り）　train going toward Tokyo
のりかえる（乗り換える）　to transfer (from one vehicle to another)
のりもの（乗り物）　vehicle
のる（載る）　to be covered, to appear (in a newspaper or magazine)
ノロノロうんてん（ノロノロ運転）　sluggish traffic

は

は（葉）　leaf
は（歯）　tooth; 〜いしゃ（〜医者）　dentist
はいく（俳句）　**haiku** poetry
はいけん（拝見）［する］　to see, to look at (humble form)
はいしゃく（拝借）［する］　to borrow (humble form)
はいたつ（配達）［する］　delivery; (to deliver)
はいゆう（俳優）　actor, actress
はえ（蠅）　housefly

はえる（生える）　to grow, flourish (*refers to plants and trees*)
はか（墓）　tomb, grave
はがき（葉書）　postcard; え〜（絵〜）　picture postcard
ばかり　only, just
はかる（量る）　to measure (*weight*); （計る）　to measure (*size, length, etc.*)
はきけ（吐き気）　nausea; …がする　to be nauseated
はく（吐く）　to vomit
はく（掃く）　to sweep (*with a broom*)
はこぶ（運ぶ）　to move or transport a large object
はし（橋）　bridge
はしら（柱）　pillar
はずかしい（恥ずかしい）　shameful, embarrassed
はたらきざかり（働き盛り）　the prime of life
はち（蜂）　wasp
はっきり（と）　clearly
バック・ミラー　rearview mirror
ばっする（罰する）　to punish
はったつ（発達）［する］　development, unfolding; (to develop)
はってん（発展）［する］　expansion, development; (to expand)
はっぱ　leaf
はつばい（発売）［する］　sales; (to put on the market); 〜ちゅう（〜中）　now on sale
はっぴょう（発表）［する］　announcement; (to announce)
はつめい（発明）［する］　invention; (to invent)
はと（鳩）　pigeon, dove
パトカー　patrol car, police car
はな（鼻）　nose
はなやか（華やか）（な）　splendid, showy
はなれる（離れる）　to be separated
はば（幅）　width
ハマチ　yellowtail (*a kind of fish*)
はやい（早い）　early
はやい（速い）　fast
はやし（林）　woods
はらう（払う）　to pay
はる（貼る）　to paste
はんえい（反映）［する］　reflection; (to reflect)
はんが（版画）　woodblock print
パンク（する）　(to get a) flat tire
はんざい（犯罪）　crime
はんたい（反対）［する］　opposition; (to be opposed)
ハンドブレーキ　parking brake
ハンドル　steering wheel; …をきる（切る）　to turn the wheel; …をにぎる（握る）　to take the wheel

ひ

ひかく（比較）［する］　comparison; (to compare)
ひきだし（引き出し）　drawer
ひこうき（飛行機）　airplane
ひごろ（日頃）（の）　daily
ひざ（膝）　knee
ひじ（肘）　elbow
ひしがた（菱形）　diamond shaped

ひしょ（秘書）　secretary
ひだりがわ（左側）　left side; 〜つうこう（〜通行）　driving on the left
ひだりきき（左利き）　left-handed
びっくりする　to be surprised
ひっこす（引っ越す）　to move (*from one address to another*)
ひつじ（羊）　sheep
ひつよう（必要）（な）　necessary
ひとりたび（一人旅）　traveling alone, solo travel
ひふ（皮膚）　skin, skin surface
ひょうが（氷河）　glacier
ひょうこう（標高）　height above sea level
ひょうさつ（表札）　nameplate
びようし（美容師）　hair stylist
ひょうろんか（評論家）　critic
びんせん（便箋）　stationery

ふ

〜ぶ（〜部）　(*counter for newspapers, sets of documents, etc.*)
ふうとう（封筒）　envelope
ぶか（部下）　subordinate (*on the job*)
ふかさ（深さ）　depth
ふく（拭く）　to wipe
ふくさよう（副作用）　side effect
ふくつう（腹痛）　stomach ache
ふしぎ（不思議）（な）　weird
ふじゆう（不自由）（な）　inconvenience, deprivation
ふすま（襖）　**fusuma** (*sliding door of opaque material*)
ふせぐ（防ぐ）　to ward off
ぶた（豚）　pig
ふだん（普段）　usually
ぶちょう（部長）　department head (*at a company*)
ふつうしゃ（普通車）　second-class car (*on a train*)
ふつうれっしゃ（普通列車）　local train
ぶつかる　to run into, collide with, be hit
ぶっきょう（仏教）　Buddhism
ぶつける　to hit something, to throw forcefully
プッシュフォン　push-button telephone
ぶつぞう（仏像）　statue of the Buddha
ふどうさんや（不動産屋）　real estate agency or agent
ふとりすぎ（太り過ぎ）　overweight
ふとん　**futon** bedding; …を上げる　to put a **futon** away; …をしく（敷く）　to lay out a **futon**
ふなびん（船便）　surface mail
ふね（船）　ship, boat
ぶひん（部品）　part (*of a mechanical object*)
ふむ（踏む）　to step on, to pedal
ふやす（増やす）　to increase [something]
プランをたてる　to make a plan
ふる（振る）　to shake [something]
フロント　front desk of a hotel
フロントガラス　windshield
ふんかす（噴火）［する］　eruption; (to erupt)
ぶんこぼん（文庫本）　paperback book

ぶんしょ（文書）　document, paper
ぶんや（分野）　field (of study)

へ

へい（塀）　outside wall
へいや（平野）　plains
へそ（臍）　navel
べっそう（別荘）　vacation home
へび（蛇）　snake
へらす（減らす）　to decrease [something]
ベル　doorbell
へんか（変化）［する］　change; (to undergo change)
べんごし（弁護士）　lawyer
へんじ（返事）［する］　reply; (to reply)
へんちょう（偏重）　over-valuation

ほ

ほいくえん（保育園）　daycare center
ほうげん（方言）　dialect
ほうそう（放送）［する］　television or radio broadcasting; (to broadcast)
ほうっておく（放っておく）　to leave as it is
ぼうりょく（暴力）　violence
ほお（頬）　cheek
ホーム　railroad station platform
ほか（他）（の）　other; ...の他に　in addition to . . .
ポケベル　beeper
ほけん（保険）　insurance; ...に入る　to enroll in insurance
ほこうしゃ（歩行者）　pedestrian
ほご（保護）［する］　protection; (to protect)
ぼさつ（菩薩）　bodhisattva (Buddhist supernatural being)
ほし（星）　star
ぼしゅう（募集）［する］　to advertise for applicants
ほす（干す）　to air-dry [something], to air [something] out
ほっきょく（北極）　North Pole
ホッチキス　stapler
ほっぺた　cheek
ほどう（歩道）　sidewalk
ほね（骨）　bone
ほぼ（保母）　childcare attendant
ほめる　to praise
ぼんさい（盆栽）　**bonsai** (artificially dwarfed trees grown in containers)
ほんしゃ（本社）　company headquarters
ほんだな（本棚）　bookshelf
ほんてん（本店）　main store, bank headquarters
ボンネット　hood (of a car)
ほんやく（翻訳）［する］　translation; (to translate); ～しゃ（～者）　translator

ま

まいる（参る）　to come, to go (humble form)
まがる（曲がる）　to turn (in a direction)
まげる（曲げる）　to bend [something]
マスコミ　mass communication
まちあいしつ（待ち合い室）　waiting room
まちがえる（間違える）　to make a mistake about something
まつ（松）　pine tree
まっすぐ　straight
まとめる　to summarize, compile
まねく（招く）　to invite
まねる（真似る）　to imitate
まもる（守る）　to obey [a rule], to follow [a custom], to protect
まよう（迷う）　to wander; 道に...　to be lost
まる（丸）　circle
まるで　just like, just as if
まわす（回す）　to turn [something], to send around
まわりみち（回り道）　detour
まわる（回る）　to turn [in place], to go around from place to place
まんかい（満開）　full bloom
マンション　apartment building, condominium

み

みがく（磨く）　to polish, to wipe clean; 歯を...　to brush one's teeth
みぎがわ（右側）　right side
みぎきき（右利き）　right-handed
ミキサー　blender
ミシン　sewing machine
みずうみ（湖）　lake
みずから（自ら）　self
みせいねん（未成年）　minor, under-age person
みぞ（溝）　[tire] tread
みだし（見出し）　headline
みつ（蜜）　honey, nectar; ～ばち（～蜂）　honey bee
みつかる（見つかる）　to be found
みっともない　unseemly, improper, disreputable
みなと（港）　harbor, port
みならい（見習い）　apprentice
みまい（見舞い）［に行く］　(to pay) a visit to a sick person
みみ（耳）　ear; ～たぶ　earlobe
みんしゅく（民宿）　Japanese-style bed and breakfast
みんぞく（民族）　ethnic group
みんよう（民謡）　traditional Japanese folksong

む

むかえる（迎える）　to greet [someone who is arriving]
むかし（昔）　long ago, in the old days
むく（向く）　to face toward, to be suited for
むくち（無口）（な）　taciturn, untalkative
むし（虫）　insect

むし（無視）［する］　disregard; (to ignore)
むね（胸）　chest

め

〜め（〜目）　〜th (*cardinal numbers*); よんさつめ (4冊目)　the fourth volume
め（目）　eye
めいしょ（名所）　tourist sights
めいよ（名誉）　prestige, honor
めぐまれる（恵まれる）　to be blessed with
めざましどけい（目覚し時計）　alarm clock
めしあがる（召し上がる）　to eat, drink (*honorific form*)
めん（面）［する］　(to) face (on)
めんせき（面積）　land area
めんせつ（面接）［する］　(to give a) job interview

も

もうしあげる（申し上げる）　to say (*very humble form*)
もうす（申す）　to say (*humble form*)
もくじ（目次）　table of contents
もくてき（目的）　purpose, objective
もじ（文字）　written symbol
もたらす　to bring about
もち（餅）　**mochi** (*rice cakes made from pounded rice*)
もったいない　wasteful
もつ（持つ）　to have, to hold in the hand; もっていく（持っていく）　to take (*inanimate objects*); 持ってくる（持ってくる）　to bring (*inanimate objects*)
もどす（戻す）　to return something to its previous place
もどす　to vomit
もどる（戻る）　to return to a previous position, to back up
もの　[concrete] thing; …ものだ　It used to be that . . .
ものおき（物置）　storeroom
ものぐさ（な）　lazy
もよう（模様）　appearance, pattern
もらう　to receive (*from an equal or inferior*)
もり（森）　forest
もんく（文句）　complaint; …を言う　to complain

や

やく（役）　role; …にたつ（立つ）　to be useful
やくしょ（役所）　municipal office
やちん（家賃）　rent
やっきょく（薬局）　pharmacy
やとう（雇う）　to hire
やぬし（家主）　property or apartment owner (*formal*)
やね（屋根）　roof
やまのぼり（山登り）　mountain climbing
やる　to give (*to a social inferior*)

ゆ

ゆうびん（郵便）　mail; 〜ちょきん（〜貯金）　postal savings; 〜ばんごう（番号）　postal zone code; 〜ポスト　mailbox (*for sending mail*); …をだす（出す）　to mail
ユース・ホステル　youth hostel
ゆしゅつ（輸出）［する］　(to) export
ユダヤきょう（ユダヤ教）　Judaism
ゆび（指）　finger
ゆめ（夢）　dream; …を見る　to dream

よ

ようい（用意）［する］　preparation in advance; (to prepare in advance)
ようしつ（洋室）　Western-style room
ようちえん（幼稚園）　kindergarten
ようぼう（要望）　request
ようま（洋間）　Western-style room
よくしつ（浴室）　bathing room (*room with a bathtub or shower*)
よごれる（汚れる）　to get dirty
よっぱらいうんてん（酔っ払い運転）　drunk driving
よぶ（呼ぶ）　to summon, to call for
よぶん（余分）（な）　excessive, extra
よやく（予約）［する］　(to make a) reservation
よろこぶ（喜ぶ）　to be delighted

ら

らくてんてき（楽天的）（な）　optimistic
らん（欄）　newspaper section; スポーツ欄　sports section

り

りかい（理解）［する］　understanding; (to understand)
りこん（離婚）［する］　(to get a) divorce
りゆう（理由）　reason
りょう（量）　amount
りょう〜（両〜）　both . . .; 〜手　both hands
りょうきん（料金）　fee, charge
りようし（理容師）　barber
りよう（利用）［する］　use; (to make use of)
りょかん（旅館）　Japanese-style inn
りりく（離陸）［する］　(to) take off (*airplanes*)
りれきしょ（履歴書）　resume

る

るすばんでんわ（留守番電話）　answering machine

れ

レジ　cash register
れんあい（恋愛）　romantic love
れんぞくドラマ（連続ドラマ）　miniseries
レントゲン　X-rays; ...をとる（撮る）　to take X-rays
れんらく（連絡）［する］　contact; (to get in touch with)

ろ

ろうか（廊下）　hallway
ろうじん（老人）　elderly person
ろくおん（録音）［する］　sound recording; (to record)
ろくが（録画）［する］　videotaping; (to videotape)

わ

わか（和歌）　**waka** poetry
わけ　reason, circumstances; ...わけだ　So it's the case that ...
わしつ（和室）　Japanese-style room
わたす（渡す）　to hand over
わたる（渡る）　to cross
わりあい（割合）　comparatively
わる（割る）　to break [something]
われる（割れる）　break, become broken, shatter
わん（湾）　bay
ワンマンバス　bus without a conductor

Index

About the Author

Yasu-Hiko Tohsaku is Associate Professor at the University of California, San Diego, where he is the Director of the Language Program at the Graduate School of International Relations and Pacific Studies and the Coordinator of the Undergraduate Japanese Language Program. He received his Ph.D. in Linguistics from the University of California, San Diego, in 1983. He is the author of numerous articles on second language acquisition and Japanese language pedagogy. In addition, he has been involved with the development of Japanese language teaching videos and computer-assisted language learning programs.

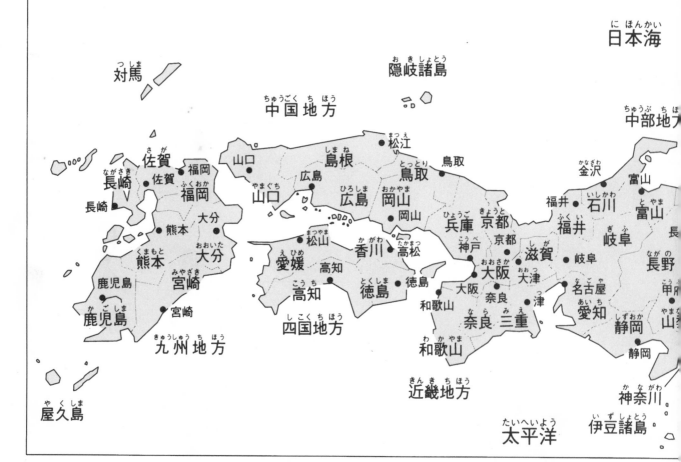

0 100 200 km

対馬

隠岐諸島

中国地方

日本海

中部地方

松江

島根

鳥取

鳥取

金沢

佐賀

福岡

山口

広島

岡山

富山

石川

福井

長崎

佐賀

福岡

山口

広島

岡山

岡山

兵庫

京都

福井

石川

富山

岐阜

長崎

大分

熊本

愛媛

松山

香川

高松

京都

神戸

大阪

滋賀

岐阜

長野

熊本

大分

高知

徳島

大津

名古屋

鹿児島

宮崎

愛媛

高知

徳島

大阪

奈良

津

愛知

静岡

鹿児島

宮崎

四国地方

和歌山

奈良

三重

静岡

九州地方

和歌山

近畿地方

神奈川

屋久島

太平洋

伊豆諸島